The Politics of Strategic Adjustment

NEW DIRECTIONS IN WORLD POLITICS
John Gerard Ruggie, General Editor

Sponsored by the Committee on
International Peace and Security
of the Social Science Research Council

The Politics of Strategic Adjustment

Ideas, Institutions, and Interests

Peter Trubowitz, Emily O. Goldman,
and Edward Rhodes, Editors

COLUMBIA UNIVERSITY PRESS   NEW YORK

Columbia University Press
Publishers Since 1893
New York Chichester, West Sussex
Copyright © 1999 Columbia University Press

Library of Congress Cataloging-in-Publication Data

The politics of strategic adjustment : ideas, institutions, and
    interests / Peter Trubowitz, Emily O. Goldman, and Edward Rhodes,
    editors.
        p.   cm. — (New directions in world politics)
    Includes bibliographical references and index.
    ISBN 0-231-11074-X (cloth). — ISBN 0-231-11075-8 (pbk.)
    1. United States—Foreign relations—20th century.   2. United
States—Politics and government—20th century.   3. National
security—United States—History—20th century.   4. United States—
Military policy—History—20th century.   5. Strategy—History—20th
century.   I. Trubowitz, Peter.   II. Goldman, Emily O., 1961–
III. Rhodes, Edward Joseph.   IV. Series.
E744.P62   1998
327.73—dc21   98-17371
                                                                          CIP

Casebound editions of Columbia University Press books are printed on permanent and
durable acid-free paper.
Printed in the United States of America
c 10 9 8 7 6 5 4 3 2 1
p 10 9 8 7 6 5 4 3 2 1

NEW DIRECTIONS IN WORLD POLITICS

John Gerard Ruggie, General Editor

Contents

Part IV. The Institutional Dimension

Part V. Theory and Practice

Acknowledgments

This volume grew out of a workshop sponsored by the Social Science Research Council. The idea behind the workshop was to bring together scholars who were actively engaged in research on American security policy and who represented a wide spectrum of approaches to the study of strategic adjustment. The purpose of the volume is to present this diversity in the hopes of broadening and sharpening debates about the future course of American grand strategy and the forces that will determine it. The contributors met at the University of Texas at Austin in April 1994 to present papers. At that meeting we benefited from the comments and criticisms of a larger group of scholars, including Lynn Eden and Michael Desch. Encouraged by the enthusiasm for the project, we commissioned additional papers for a larger conference at Monterey, California, in February 1995, sponsored by the Joint Center for International and Security Studies at the University of California, Davis and the Naval Postgraduate School.

A number of people have helped make this volume possible. Steven Heydemann, then the Director of the Program on International Peace & Security at the SSRC, offered valuable assistance. Kate Wittenberg of Columbia University Press has been an engaged and supportive editor. Leslie Bialler, our production editor at Columbia, did not lose his good humor during the process of preparing the manuscript for publication.

List of Contributors

John Arquilla is associate professor of defense analysis at the U.S. Naval Postgraduate School

Jan S. Breemer is associate professor of defense analysis at the U.S. Naval Postgraduate School

Emily O. Goldman is associate professor of political science at the University of California at Davis

Gerard Gorski is a Ph.D candidate in political science at the University of California at Davis

Miroslav Nincic is professor of political science at the University of California at Davis

Edward Rhodes is associate professor of political science at Rutgers University

Roger Rose is assistant professor of political science at Benedictine University

Mark Shulman is a law student and an adjunct associate professor of international affairs at Columbia University.

Edward A. Smith, Jr., Capt. Navy Ret., served on the staff of the U.S. Chief of Naval Operations and is senior principal technical specialist in the Boeing Corporation's Washington Studies and Analysis Group.

Bartholomew H. Sparrow is assistant professor of government at the University of Texas at Austin

Peter Trubowitz is associate professor of government at the University of Texas at Austin

The Politics of Strategic Adjustment

Part 1

Introduction

1   Explaining American Strategic Adjustment

Peter Trubowitz and Edward Rhodes

> The interval between the decay of the old and the formation and establishment of the new constitutes a period of transition, which must always necessarily be one of uncertainty, confusion, error, and wild and fierce fanaticism.
>
> —John Calhoun, *A Disquisition on Government*

There is widespread agreement that America's strategic interests are changing. The breakup of the Soviet Union, the political transformation of Central Europe, renewed concern about regional conflict around the globe, and reborn hope for a stable, progressive international order have pressured American leaders to rethink the nation's strategic objectives and reconsider America's security needs. In recent years, plans for reducing the nation's costly foreign commitments, "downsizing" the national security establishment, and converting to a peacetime economy have been placed on the table, as have been proposals for increasing the government's role in promoting America's overseas economic competitiveness and commercial expansion and for sustained or increased American action to promote democracy and capitalism abroad.[1] Ideas virtually unthinkable only a decade ago are now not only on Americans' minds but also part of the political agenda. A process of strategic adjustment is underway.

This process, however, is both uncertain and contentious. The post-Cold War international environment has not yet crystallized, making it difficult to assess foreign opportunities and threats and inviting dissension regarding appropriate security preparations. Equally bedeviling, alternative approaches to strategic adjustment engage different domestic interests, empower or imperil different domestic institutions, and invoke different images of security. Defenders of laissez-faire liberalism clash with those who caution against the dangers of military demobilization not simply over projections of future global conditions but also over the goals and objectives of policy and over the evaluation of inevitable tradeoffs. While the choices the nation makes will be shaped by judgments about the country's strategic imperatives in the new setting, in the final analysis these choices will also necessarily be influenced by political, social, economic, cultural, and intellectual forces within America itself.

The striking lesson that emerges from an examination of other turning points in American history is that strategic choice does not occur in a domestic political vacuum. In the 1890s, the 1920s, and the 1940s, the United States engaged in a process of strategic adjustment, dramatically changing its approach to providing security. Like the 1990s, these periods were marked by great uncertainty over the meaning of international developments for the nation's security and well-being, as well as by protracted and divisive debate over how the nation's interests could be most effectively promoted and secured. The key issues then, as now, were questions of grand strategy: What types and levels of military capacity would the nation require? What foreign commitments should be made? What military doctrines and strategies would best preserve national values?

This volume examines a century of American experience to draw lessons about how the United States chooses its security policies. The authors are frankly critical of our understanding of this process. For the last half century in America, analysis of international security has been dominated by "Realists" who explain state behavior from the "outside in," that is, in terms of international pressures, constraints, and opportunities. In its strongest variant, structural Realism, the competitive nature of international politics defines the objective and policies of all states, even those as powerful as the United States.[2] The anarchic character of the international environment dictates that the fundamental goal of every state is to ensure its security from external threats; this implies all states will seek to pursue opportunities for increasing power and wealth. Thus, the interests and motives of states are fixed; what varies are external constraints.[3] For Realists, therefore, explaining how states choose security policies involves identifying features of the international environment that threaten a state's security and welfare and the opportunities available for negating these threats.

The Realist approach has strengths and weaknesses. One of its great virtues is that it reminds us of the importance of international constraints and pressures in explaining state behavior. Big changes in a nation's strategic environment can lead to big changes in its security policies. A major weakness of this approach, however, is that it is profoundly underdetermining. The international situation facing a country may well create incentives for action. But rarely are external imperatives clear and unambiguous; rarely is there no range of alternative responses.[4] Moreover, international pressures or opportunities are not the only sources of innovation in state policy. America has often adopted security policies that cannot be adequately explained by its international position alone. In the late nineteenth century, for example, the United States rapidly expanded its military capabilities despite the absence of a "clear and present danger" to its physical security. Conversely, in the aftermath of World War I, when America was in a position to impose its will on other nations, it declined to act. Instead of offering bold leadership, America retrenched and turned inward. Explanations of such paradoxes cannot be found in the international system itself.

The following chapters show how domestic pressures both drive and direct the process of strategic innovation. While international constraints may limit the range of choice open to statesmen, in the final analysis their decisions about grand strategy are critically shaped by domestic politics and the factors that influence it—political ideologies, state structure, and societal interests. What emerges is a view of how states choose their security policies that is more politically motivated, institutionally constrained, socially constructed, and, ultimately, historically contingent than most Realists would permit. The authors analyze this process from three distinct angles: one stresses the role that ideas, culture, and myth play in shaping how nations deal with their external security environment; a second focuses on the domestic political and socioeconomic setting within which decisions about the national interest are made; and the third centers on the impact of government officials, political institutions, and bureaucratic politics in adjustment decisions. In each case, the authors are primarily concerned with the domestic determinants of policy choice. Accounts differ in terms of which domestic "variables" are privileged in the analysis, and how much weight they assign to external pressures and constraints.

Four interrelated themes run through this volume, and the authors develop and explore variations on these themes in their contributions. The first theme concerns the Janus-faced nature of grand strategy and the dual purposes served by strategic adjustment. A second is the fundamentally political character of the strategic adjustment process. The third is the enabling and constraining impact of domestic institutions in this political process. The fourth and final theme is the role of ideas and beliefs in shaping political discourse and institutions—and, ultimately, in shaping foreign policy choices.

Two Faces of Strategy

In most Realist accounts, the term strategy refers to a state's response to specific, identifiable foreign threats to its security. Barry Posen, for example, has defined grand strategy as "a state's theory of how it can best 'cause' security for itself" within an anarchic and competitive world.[5] Statesmen are assumed to be primarily attentive to the international environment in defining the nation's vital interests and in choosing means to secure these goals. To the extent that domestic considerations enter into their thinking, they do so only because political leaders recognize that their ability to succeed abroad depends in part on their ability to control the home front and to mobilize national resources.[6] Elite support must be cultivated, mass opinion must be shaped, and the nation's industrial potential must be harnessed. This is especially true in nations like the United States, where the power and authority to make important national decisions is fragmented and dispersed. Thus while Realists recognize that the character of a nation's institutions can affect its ability to act strategically—that weaknesses or peculiarities in domestic institutions may limit the capacity of particular states to translate resources into usable power[7]—Realists still tend to view a nation's grand strategy from the outside-in, as an instrument for preserving and enhancing the state's international position. Realist accounts therefore tend to be preoccupied with the first, or outward-looking, face of strategy.

As the authors of this volume note, however, there is also a second, inward-directed face of strategy, which, they argue, goes far in determining the actual character and content of a nation's grand strategy.[8] When considering how issues are framed and policies are formed, a focus on the second face of strategy directs attention to the domestic realm and the ways grand strategies help manage and solve domestic problems—political, economic, and social. Illuminating the domestic meaning and consequences of grand strategy, an examination of the second face suggests that state policies must be understood as a response to internal imperatives and demands, rather than to purely external ones.

Critiques of Realism's simplistic *primat der aussenpolitik* are of course not new: Revisionist historians of the Cold War, for example, have explored the internal pressures and tensions shaping American attitudes and behavior toward the Soviet Union.[9] The contributors to this volume, however, suggest a more complex and nuanced account of this second face. Moving beyond class-centered accounts that focus on national economic contradictions and imperatives, they explore a range of internal conflicts "solved" by strategic change and trace a range of political and cultural mechanisms involved in this process.

This "second-face" theme is most strongly developed in the three chapters on American navalism by Peter Trubowitz, Edward Rhodes, and Mark Shulman. From their examinations of the history of American strategic adjustment in the late nineteenth century each author concludes that the nation's decision to become a great naval power was shaped more by domestic imperatives than strategic necessity. For Trubowitz these imperatives are largely political in origin. Reversing the Rankean dictum on the primacy of foreign policy, Trubowitz argues that politicians think about foreign policies the same way they think about domestic policies: as instruments or tools for party-building and state-building. For Rhodes and Shulman, by contrast, the second face of strategy reflects the struggle to construct national identity and the search for individual and cultural meaning. What all three accounts share is a societal-centered view of strategic change that brings domestic conflicts and imperatives more directly into the explanation of policy.

In developing this view, Trubowitz stresses the broader political context in which choices about grand strategy are made. His chapter focuses on the connection between navalism, commercial expansion, and party-building during the Populist-Progressive era. He argues that Republican party leaders, who dominated the industrial Northeast, viewed naval expansion as part of a larger political strategy that was designed to stimulate growth in hard-pressed urban-industrial centers and check the spread of agrarian discontent in the trans-Mississippi West. Drawing on strategic arguments popularized by Captain Alfred Thayer Mahan, the Republicans coupled the promise of foreign markets with the lure of federal largesse to divide the Populist movement and consolidate their control over the machinery of the national government. What distinguishes Trubowitz's account of strategic change and innovation from traditional Realist views is the emphasis on coalition-building, party competition, and log-rolling. His account suggests that a nation's willingness to to initiate programmatic strategic change depends on the ability of its politicians to forge a coalition of sectional interests that is large

enough to sustain them in office and inclined to regard the policy innovations as something that is in their interest. The likelihood that such a coalition will emerge depends on the ingenuity of politicans and the constellation of preferences expressed by the relevant sectional interests.

The late nineteenth century was not only an era of economic and political
upheaval, however. Except for the Civil War, no crisis of the nineteenth
century challenged America's social order—and the cultural myths that
helped preserve it—so profoundly as that of the 1890s. For Rhodes the crisis
of the late nineteenth century was one of national identity brought on by
rapid industrialization and urbanization, immigration, the closing of the
national frontier, and the post-Reconstruction integration of the South into
the body-politic. These challenges demanded new definitions of "American-
ness" and new institutions to bridge class, ethnic, religious, economic, and
regional fissures in American society.[10] Creation of a new, socially unifying
image of America, however, necessitated a new account of America's relationship to the world, the role of the state, and the nature of war. Thus
Rhodes sees the rise of American navalism as the strategic consequence of
cultural change and as part of what Robert Wiebe has called "the search for
order"—a search for new organizing principles around which a viable domestic social order could be constructed.[11] Where Realists interpret strategic
change as a rational adjustment to shifting international realities, Rhodes
suggests it is an unplanned corollary of cultural adaptation to mitigate domestic social tensions.[12]

Shulman's account of American navalism in the late nineteenth century
also privileges ideas and culture in explaining strategic change. He draws
attention to the role that intellectual entrepreneurs play in this process and
argues that these "agents" of change used navalism as a tool for reforming
American political culture along Hamiltonian lines. They did this for reasons that were only indirectly connected to the nation's position in the international system. As members of what was essentially a Progressive, anti-
commercial cultural movement aimed at reinvigorating American society,
navalists like Theodore Roosevelt, Henry Cabot Lodge, and Alfred Thayer
Mahan were motivated by visions of national greatness and destiny, not class
or sectional interest. For them, the prevailing "world view," Jeffersonianism,
was ill-suited to a nation of America's stature and inappropriate in a world
where power, not principle, was the coin of the realm. The success of navalists in transforming American political culture led to the strategic innovations of the 1880s and 1890s and the emergence of the United States as
a great power.[13] Shulman emphasizes the interplay of ideas and domestic

politics, exploring the role of political "entrepreneurship" in the propagation of new ideas and the political process involved in institutionalizing new ideas at the elite and mass levels. Ultimately, however, he shares with Rhodes the view that strategic change is, to large degree, a consequence of domestic cultural transformation.

Politics and Choice

This first theme—that strategic choice is not simply a matter of interstate interaction but has a domestic face—logically suggests the second: that strategic choice is a product of a political process. In Realist accounts, the process by which states select their grand strategies is remarkably bloodless, unencumbered by the political divisions, frictions, and cleavages that plague policymaking on the domestic front. Such a view is too stylized, mechanical, and apolitical.[14] It ignores the real differences of interest that exist within the nation-state, even on foreign policy matters, and the impossibility of deciding strategic questions purely "on their merits" without an appeal to the political power and authority of the domestic interests engaged. As Lynn Eden suggests, Realism "flattens the sense of choice" that characterizes statecraft.[15] In each of the periods examined in this book, the process of strategic adjustment was far more acrimonious and protracted than Realist models would have predicted. Each of these periods was marked by intense domestic struggle over policy.

For example, the decision in the late nineteenth century to build the military forces necessary to compete with the world's imperial powers was a bitterly contested one, as both Shulman and Trubowitz demonstrate. Shulman's account analyzes the bitter political struggle for ideological hegemony, between proponents of traditional Jeffersonian notions of defense and the Progressive forces who derided traditionalists as "mollycoddlers and flapdoodle pacifists." This battle, fought at both the elite and mass level, involved a broad array of "political" tactics—including, inter alia, rewriting American history, reeducating the nation's youth, popularizing particular images of masculinity, appealing to the cult of technology and technical efficiency, reforming naval institutions to be consistent with new images, and providing public spectacle and entertainment—and ended with the victory of the neo-Hamiltonian ideologues who seized control of the American foreign policy agenda.

As Trubowitz notes, however, the struggle over American policy was not solely an ideological one. Powerful political and economic interests were involved and competing visions of how the nation should define its interests carried with them different prescriptions for using the taxing, spending, and investment powers of the federal government. The decision to build a world-class navy, he observes, served the interests of America's industrial core; adoption of the new policy was the outcome of political coalition-building between the industrial Northeast and agrarian West, effected at the expense of Southern commercial and agricultural interests. Far from being an obvious or inevitable choice, as Realists presume, America's entry onto the world's politico-military stage was, Shulman and Trubowitz demonstrate, the result of a hard-fought political victory by the Progressive elite and Northeastern industrial interests over traditional social groups and the raw-material producing periphery.

To acknowledge the political character of strategic choice in a democratic setting, however, is to recognize the importance of both public opinion and of the institutions that influence, mobilize, and transmit it. Contrary to Realism's presumption that the "national interest" is self-evident or can be defined by the state in isolation, and that the state will have a free hand in making tradeoffs, the authors stress the susceptibility of the state and its leaders to societal pressure. Arguing that social forces shape national priorities, determine the availability of resources, and establish behavioral norms, Miroslav Nincic, Roger Rose, and Gerard Gorski turn to the 1990s and explore American public opinion and the kinds of constraints it imposes on American strategic adjustment. Their analysis suggests that the freedom of American policymakers to pursue new strategic directions may be limited by the difficulty they will face in predicting public support, by public unwillingness to shoulder significant costs, and by the lack of a clear public consensus on national goals, at least in a form that would yield an overarching grand strategy.

The contributors also highlight the importance of domestic institutions in mobilizing public opinion and translating it into effective political pressure for particular policies. These institutions include both explicitly political ones, such as political parties, and more general social ones, such as literary and journalistic media. The dominance of the Republican party at the national level, Trubowitz notes, facilitated the inter-regional horse-trading that yielded a Northeast-West coalition in favor of navalism in the late nineteenth century; alternative party structures might have yielded different regional coalitions and different policies. In the same time period, as Shulman observes, elite and popular journals played a critical role in facilitating strategic change by both inculcating a pro-military mentality and stimulating explicit support for navalism.

Bartholomew Sparrow, in his study of the press in the 1890s and 1990s, addresses this issue most directly, exploring the impact of the meteoric rise of "yellow journalism" as a new institution in American society. Able to play a critical independent role, undercutting and transforming traditional patterns of political authority and communication and wielding resources not yet available to political parties or the state, the press was able dominate the political agenda and bend the will of other institutions. This account also underscores the contingency of strategic adjustment: in the case Sparrow considers, the emergence of a critical new political institution reflected a congruence of technical, economic, and social factors unrelated to international events. Other political institutions adapted and evolved in response, but at a slower pace, creating an unusual window of political possibility.

What emerges from this analysis is a much richer, more exciting—less dessicated and lifeless—conception of strategic choice than Realism would allow. By reintroducing politics into strategic behavior, the authors transform the flat, dry, mono-institutional, state-centric world of Realism into a textured, fluid reality, in which authority and power are not only constantly contested but also constantly reconstructed as new social institutions and capacities emerge. Choice ceases to be regarded as something that states "do": it becomes an evanescent reflection of ever-shifting social forces employing a changing variety of institutions to impose demands on political leadership.

Institutions and Strategic Adjustment

This recognition that strategic choice grows out of an inherently political process thus suggests the third theme of this book: the critical impact of institutional structure on strategic adjustment. Obviously, the notion that weak political institutions may pose an obstacle to the state's rational pursuit of national interest is hardly a novel one. Realist analyses of international politics have long recognized that nation-states differ from each other not only in terms of national resources such as population and economic output but in terms of the ability of the state to impose its will on its domestic society.[16] Sophisticated Realist accounts of balance of power thus routinely take into account the fact that "weak" states are limited in their ability to mobilize and direct individual efforts to collective purpose and that, ceteris paribus, weak states can generate relatively less state power—for example, relatively smaller armed forces—from a given resource base.[17]

More problematic from a Realist perspective, however, is that weak states have relatively less freedom in defining the national interest than strong ones. In the case of the United States, constitutional arrangements dictate a fragmentation of authority, separation of powers, and regular elections that guarantee both constituents and special interests access to the policymaking process.[18] In the foreign policy sphere, these constitutional limits mean that a variety of political and parapolitical institutions—among them political parties, the press (the "fourth branch" of government), and economic and ethnic interest groups—possess the capacity to challenge the state's authority to define national goals and objectives. The inability of the state to isolate itself from societal pressures results in a blurring between state institutions and nonstate ones, as the latter enter into the policy arena and seek to exploit the former's constitutional weaknesses to accomplish parochial objectives. As suggested above, the weakness of the American state and its vulnerability to societal pressures thus inevitably means that policy can not be divorced from politics. To the extent that their costs and benefits are unequally distributed, national security decisions become a matter of domestic politics.[19]

But it is not simply the *weakness* of the state vis-àa-vis the society it rules that prevents a consistent definition of "the national interest" and a rational pursuit of it. The *nonunitary* and *bureaucratic* character of state institutions also limits and shapes the state's ability to react to changing and ambiguous external threats.[20] The nonunitary structure of the state means that its behavior will reflect regularized political competition between parochially self-interested actors within the government: the state is not simply penetrated by societal pressures but is also divided internally among competing fiefdoms with conflicting interests and world-views. Security politics and strategic adjustment reflect, in most instances, compromises among political officials and agencies with distinctive and different agendas and preferences.

At the same time, the bureaucratic character of the modern state means that national security decisionmaking will be highly routinized and that policy change will tend to be incremental and sluggish. The tendency of bureaucratic organizations to factor problems into discrete tasks and these organizations' reliance on standard operating procedures—the routine procedures they follow to collect information, prepare options, and make decisions—make it difficult for states to respond flexibly and creatively to changes in the external world.[21] The bureaucratic nature of the state thus

suggests that strategic adjustment will occur only when organizational pre-
dispositions toward stasis can be overcome. The inference is that "in bureaucracies the absence of innovation is the rule, the natural state,"[22] and that

> military organizations will seldom innovate autonomously, particularly
> in matters of doctrine. This should be true because organizations ab-
> hor uncertainty, and changes in traditional patterns always involve
> uncertainty. It should also be true because military organizations are
> very hierarchical, restricting the flow of ideas from the lower levels to
> the higher levels. Additionally, those at the top of the hierarchy, who
> have achieved their rank and position by mastering the old doctrine,
> have no interest in encouraging their own obsolescence by bringing
> in a new doctrine.[23]

Given this organizational bias toward stability, it has been suggested that
innovation like that involved in strategic adjustment is most likely to occur
in the wake of a disaster or when individuals outside the organization inter-
vene/COP[24] or, alternatively, when the culture of the organization is transformed through a generational change in leadership.[25]

The principal institutional characteristics of the American state—its vulnerability to societal pressures and its nonunitary, bureaucratic organizational structure—thus appear critical to any understanding of strategic adjustment. The contributors to this volume focus on three aspects of the
institutional dimension of strategic adjustment.

First, this book offers a critical appraisal of simplistic accounts of institutional behavior that presume bureaucratic organizations face insurmount-
able obstacles to undertaking self-conscious, intelligent, nonincremental adjustment in response to changed threats. What emerges is a nuanced
understanding, recognizing that neither the external determinism of Realism
nor the internal determinism of classical bureaucratic politics fully catches
the complex nature of institutions and their influence on outcomes.

Emily Goldman's examination of innovation by the American military
services during the interwar years suggests that bureaucratic organizations
are indeed able to react to changing or ambiguous external circumstances
and can do so without intervention from actors outside the organization.
Her study also suggests, however, that the ability of organizations to adjust
nonmyopically and nonincrementally to changing threats is limited. First,
the ability to learn to behave differently demands some sort of experiential

base from which the organization can draw lessons. Second, perceptions of the desirability, possibility, and urgency of learning will be tied not simply to institutional characteristics but to geopolitical circumstances as well.

Edward Smith provides a detailed and historically important case study of the Navy's institutional response to the end of the Cold War, the decline of the Soviet/Russian threat, and the emergence of a new, ambiguous threat environment. This investigation suggests that, far from being an obstacle to forward-looking strategic adjustment, military organizations may be an active proponent. The transformation of the U.S. Navy in the 1990s was neither the inevitable consequence of changes in international circumstances nor dictated by individuals or groups outside of the naval service. The new ideas that were to shape the Navy were developed within the Navy itself, and the "re-creation" of the Navy reflected the institutionalization of these ideas. The institutional capacity of the Navy to carry out this transformation is thus of note.

In the second place, the volume explores the complex relationship between institutions and technological change. Obviously, in the post-Cold War and post-Desert Storm world, this subject has acquired a heightened salience: as the United States has downsized its forces and tried to learn lessons from its stunning victory in the Gulf, defense planners have wrestled with questions of how best to harness the power of new communications and computer technology, and of whether these new technologies will result in a "revolution in military affairs." Plainly there is an interaction between technological change and institutional change. On the one hand, new technological possibilities challenge existing institutions and create pressure for new institutional structures that are better designed to exploit the potential inherent in these technologies. On the other hand, institutions shape the realm of the technologically possible, determining which technologies will be tested, if not which technologies will be developed. Ultimately, of course, revolutionary improvements in military capabilities, and the strategic adjustment those improvements permit, require a symbiotic evolutionary development of technology and institutions.

Jan Breemer investigates this relationship between technological change and military institutions. His study of the nineteenth-century revolution in naval technology underscores the power of new technological developments to transform the logic of security and to compel institutions both to engage in strategic adjustment and to adapt themselves to the new realities. As he demonstrates, the application of the fruits of the industrial revolution to naval architecture in the second half of the 1880s resulted in a situation of offense dominance. Warships became "offensive ship killers." This new technological potential meant that the concentration of firepower in large battleships and the pursuit of decisive, offensive victories made operational and economic sense. Indeed, Breemer argues, this new technological reality was sufficiently powerful that it overrode not only considerations of international amity and enmity but domestic political pressures and cultural traditions as well.

Both Goldman's work and Smith's work also shed revealing light on the relationship between institutions and technology. The cases they examine suggest that not all technological imperatives are perfectly clear, and that the capacity of institutions to understand the technological opportunities and threats confronting them, and to engage in appropriate strategic adjustment, is real but limited. The institutional shaping of "revolutions in military affairs" thus moves to center stage.

Third, this volume also explores the relationship between nonstate institutions and state institutions in a weak-state setting like the United States. The studies by Trubowitz, Sparrow, and Nincic, Rose, and Gorski each explore the ability of domestic actors to dominate state institutions, effectively redefining the national interest to suit parochial purposes.

Examining the construction of the modern American Navy in the early 1890s, Trubowitz shows how powerful industrial, commercial, and financial interests worked through the Republican party to win support for a massive federal program that redistributed wealth from the South to the Northeast. Looking at the redefinition of America's international objectives in the late 1890s, Sparrow demonstrates the inability of state institutions to control this process and the dominant—and self-interested—role played by the press. Turning to the 1990s, Nincic and his colleagues look both at the role of public opinion in shaping state choices and at the power of state institutions to shape public opinion and the freedom of action available to the state despite the pressures of public opinion.

These general insights about the American state's political institutions— that they are dynamic and institutionally capable, if constrained, participants in the struggle to define visions of war and foreign policy, that they both drive and are driven by technological change, and that they compete with extra-state institutions to control the political agenda—imply the inseparability of ideas, institutions, and interests in an explanation of strategic adjustment.

The Power of Ideas

This, of course, suggests the fourth and final theme of this volume: that, like interests and institutions, ideas matter. At first blush, there is perhaps nothing novel in this observation. In a recent, widely cited volume, for example, Judith Goldstein and Robert Keohane credit Max Weber for the key insight that "Ideas help to order the world. By ordering the world, ideas may shape agendas, which can profoundly shape outcomes. Insofar as ideas put blinders on people, reducing the number of conceivable alternatives, they serve as invisible switchmen, not only by turning action onto certain tracks rather than others, as in Weber's metaphor, but also by obscuring other tracks from the agent's view."[26]

Nor is there anything novel in the observation that ideas shape states' foreign policy choices. The incorporation of insights derived from cognitive psychology into the study of international relations has resulted in widespread appreciation of the impact of beliefs on foreign-policy decisionmaking. Because of the tendency to maintain cognitive consistency, the human mind distorts perception, interpretation, and analysis; scholars of international relations have carefully observed the impact of cognitive structures and processes on state behavior, noting, for example, the existence of idiosyncratic national and cultural patterns in decisionmaking and the occurrence of spirals of hostility based on unmotivated biases in mutual perceptions.[27] Both state behavior and patterns of interaction between states are, then, influenced by the particular ideas embedded in decisionmakers' belief systems. As Michael Shafer has put it, paraphrasing the old bureaucratic-politics adage, in foreign-policymaking "where you stand depends on what you think."[28]

Empirical support for this proposition has come from a wide range of studies examining a wide range of policy areas, from international trade and monetary policy to counterinsurgency policy and high strategy.[29] How states react to changes in their environment—the kind of "strategic adjustment" they undertake in their foreign economic and security policies—appears to depend in important respects on the ideas and beliefs that decisionmakers share. This, in itself, is an important observation. It suggests not only that external events are underdetermining but also that state responses to external stimuli can not be predicted simply on the basis of the societal interests that are engaged, or on the basis of institutional constraints on state action. Belief structures affect reaction to stimuli in at least four respects.

First, whether or not changes in the external environment are recognized and characterized as requiring response will depend on the cognitive blinders being worn. Threats and opportunities must be interpreted as such before they will impact decisionmaking, and this process of interpretation is subject to unmotivated bias.

Second, the types of responses that are conceivable are determined by the dominant ideas of the day. To return to the Weberian metaphor, only a small subset of the real range of possible policy tracks will be apparent to an individual or society. What can be imagined is limited by the intellectual and cultural tools that are available. Policies, choices, and modes of behavior that are obvious to one society in one age will be simply inconceivable in another; as John Ruggie has mused, "fundamental modernist concepts such as market rationality, sovereignty, and personal privacy would not have been comprehensible before the development of appropriate terms of social discourse."[30]

Third, by providing the logical and philosophical structure used by decisionmakers to order and arrange options, the dominant ideas of the day do more than determine which "tracks" are visible and which are concealed: in the event that there are multiple equally attractive tracks, dominant ideas may make certain tracks appear particularly salient and reduce the salience of others. As Geoffrey Garrett and Barry Weingast have argued, "shared beliefs may act as 'focal points' around which the behavior of actors converges."[31] Shared ideas thus have the capacity to facilitate the emergence of cooperation within or between decisionmaking institutions and to dictate the character of the cooperation that emerges: in the absence of a single efficient, Pareto optimal solution to a problem facing a group of decisionmakers, dominant belief structures may permit these decisionmakers to overcome the ambiguity inherent in the situation and to agree on a single policy. In other words, "ideas, social norms, institutions, and shared expectations may influence both the way actors choose to cooperate and the stability of these arrangements over time."[32]

Fourth and possibly most importantly, decisionmakers' beliefs can shape how they define and appraise "interest"—how they evaluate ends and means, and costs and benefits. What outcomes are desired, what measures are regarded as acceptable, and how the tradeoff between various goals and various costs is evaluated are all a function of decisionmakers' normative assumptions, embedded in their cognitive framework. Thus the state's perceived need for strategic adjustment, the options it considers, the options around which expectations converge, and its evaluation of the utility of various options all hinge on the identity of the ideas around which decisionmakers organize their cognitive processes.

From this existing explanation of how ideas impact strategic choice, however, the authors of this volume offer four important theoretical departures. In the first place, this volume suggests that the intellectual construction of reality can not only shape how states respond to changes in their external environment but also yield programmatic changes in state behavior in the absence of external change. That is, this volume explores the independent power of ideas. Second, where the principal focus of most recent work has been on the effects of ideas—that is, on the impact of particular ideas on policy choice[33]—the research in this book is explicitly interested in the cultural and institutional sources of ideas and cognitive change. Regarding ideas as contestable and contested, this volume probes the process by which ideas gain currency and the timing and content of cognitive change. Third, starting from the observation that ideas may become embodied in institutions and consequently influence behavior long after the social forces associated with those ideas have ebbed,[34] this volume explores the active dynamic between ideas and institutions, investigating the real but bounded capacity of government organizations actively to seek out, or to create, new ideas and to institutionalize them. By doing so, this volume steps away from the assumption that institutions are simply the passive embodiment of ideas, recognizes that organizations are sentient entities continuously and purposefully revising their understanding of their environment, and suggests a connection between the burgeoning literature on institutional learning and the existing literature on the role of ideas.[35] Fourth, this volume demonstrates that ideas not only serve as focal points in elite bargaining, but also play a similarly critical role in domestic politics, helping to determine what domestic political coalitions will or will not form.

The strongest claims about the role played by ideas in the process of strategic adjustment are advanced by Rhodes and Shulman. As noted above, from their examinations of the history of American strategic adjustment in the late nineteenth century, Rhodes and Shulman conclude that strategic adjustment was the logical and inevitable corollary of the transformation that took place in the ideas and images that dominated American political culture. Thus in their analyses ideas play the role not only of "invisible switchmen," influencing the destination of new policy initiatives being propelled by external forces, but also of locomotives, capable of moving policy even in the absence of new or altered international threats.

Rather than viewing ideas as a static lens, distorting a state's behavior in an idiosyncratic but essentially constant fashion, Rhodes and Shulman each underscore not only the contestability and changeability of ideas but also the deep-cultural quality of the process by which idea structures are transformed. Beliefs about the nature of the world and about appropriate behavior in that world are neither fixed nor an immediate reflection of material forces. These beliefs serve a critical role in identity formation. The emergence of new threats to identity—like those triggered by industrialization in the 1890s or by the collapse of an ideological adversary and the move to a multicultural post-industrial society in the 1990s—calls into question existing accounts of the nature of war and foreign policy.

While both Rhodes's and Shulman's analyses focus on the late nineteenth century, their findings clearly raise intriguing questions about the dynamics underlying post-Cold War strategic adjustment. The strongly idea-centric perspective advanced by Rhodes and Shulman implies that the evolution of American foreign and security policy currently underway may be best understood not as a response to shifting international conditions but as a reflection of a struggle to redefine American political culture. The challenge of constructing a "multicultural" American society at home, for example, has important implications for how external enemies, and hence war and required military capacity, are conceptualized.

Breemer's analysis of the naval technology revolution of the late 1800s, Goldman's study of the 1920s, and Smith's account of the U.S. Navy's strategic redirection in the 1990s share Rhodes's and Shulman's concern with the process by which ideas change. Breemer, Goldman, and Smith, though, shift the spotlight from the cultural and ideational realm to the institutional one. Their research examines the ongoing struggle of state institutions to deal with a dangerous and uncertain world. New understandings of the external environment and new appreciations of possible responses to that environment are, for Breemer, Goldman, and Smith, the product of organizational learning. Breemer's study shows how compelling the logic of particular technologies can be, at least at times—how technological change can force intellectual change despite political and cultural obstacles and can result in the development of key new intellectual constructs, such as deterrence and crisis instability. Smith's work documents the ability of state institutions to self-consciously and deliberately generate new ideas about how best to protect vital interests and project power. Goldman's study investigates the conditions that permit or facilitate intelligent adaptation of belief systems by organizations facing changed or ambiguous environments.

As the studies in this volume suggest, when the field of vision is widened beyond the state itself, it becomes apparent that ideas also play a critical role in constraining options and facilitating compromise in the larger domestic political struggle over foreign policy and strategic adjustment. Perhaps most obviously, as Nincic, Rose, and Gorski observe in their study of changing post-Cold War attitudes toward strategic adjustment, public and elite conceptions of America's role in the world and of American priorities will shape and bound the highly political choices involved in strategic adjustment. Less obviously but equally interestingly, Trubowitz's analysis of the regional struggle associated with strategic adjustment in the 1890s reveals the importance of ideas as focal points in facilitating particular transregional political coalitions: the emergence of new politico-economic beliefs and the existence of shared terms of discourse permitted Western farmers and Eastern industrialists to identify common interests in an expansionist foreign policy.

Taken together, then, the contributors to this volume suggest that an awareness of dominant beliefs and intellectual currents is a central element in understanding the process of strategic adjustment. Ideas matter, and not simply because they shape threat perceptions, limit the range of conceivable options, focus attention on particular options, and determine how costs and benefits will be evaluated. Some authors argue that given the central place of external relations and conflict in identity formation, the character of the security policies that are imaginable and imagined is linked to the resolution of basic cultural issues, and strategic adjustment is a reflection of deep cultural conflicts. At the same time, however, state institutions can not be regarded as a blank slate: they are capable of actively participating in the struggle to define and control the intellectual terrain of national strategic choice. By shaping public pressures and by creating particular focal points around which political compromises can emerge, dominant belief structures also influence the domestic political debate over the national interest.

Strategic Adjustment Beyond Realism: Understanding the 1990s

What emerges from this examination is thus a very different conception of strategic adjustment than that suggested in classical Realist accounts. Where Realist analyses have been preoccupied with the external face of strategy—that is, with national security and foreign policy choices as a means of dealing with external threats—the authors of this volume underscore the dual nature of strategy. Strategic choice, they observe, is also a means of addressing internal divisions and contradictions within the body-politic and an opportunity for redistributing the burdens and benefits of national governance. As a consequence, strategic adjustment is a necessarily and deeply political process: it grows out of the polity's understanding of itself, shapes and is shaped by the character of political interaction and political institutions, and is an effective political tool for allocating costs and rewards, rewarding allies in domestic coalitions, and punishing adversaries. Particular choices must be regarded not as some sort of rational, automatic response to external threats to "the national interest," but as the outcome of elite debates and mass mobilization in which the external threat and "the national interest" are both ambiguous icons and only a single face of "the problem."

In this political process, institutions play a key role in determining the possible and the probable: the governmental and societal institutions that happen by historic circumstance to exist at a particular juncture will critically influence the elite alliances that will form or emerge triumphant, the levers that will exist for shaping mass attitudes and the identity of the individuals or organizations that will control those levers, and the channels that will be available for translating public opinion and particularistic interests into political pressure. These institutions are in a constant evolution, driven not only by particular interest groups that seek to modify institutional structures to enhance their political power and by organizations that seek to preserve their own survival and effectiveness, but by changing technological, economic, social, and cultural realities as well. This fluidity, and the historical contingency and contextuality inherent in it, is drained out of Realist accounts.

This recognition that strategic choice represents the outcome of a political process rather than an autonomous, automatic response to external stimuli also focuses our attention on the "constructed" and contested nature of the intellectual terrain on which the strategic adjustment process takes place. The meaning of events, both domestic and external, and the nature of political realities, entities, and processes are not self-evident. What we make of them depends on the presumptions we start with, and these are influenced by a variety of motivated and unmotivated biases. To understand—or to predict—choices, it is necessary to understand not simply their political nature and the existing institutions but also the terms in which decisionmakers understand their predicament and the pressures on them to think in these terms. Again, this is absent from Realist accounts, which presume that all decisionmakers view the world in the same framework that Realist authors do.

Thus where Realists interpret American strategic adjustment in the 1990s in terms of the logic of a unipolar moment, or as a struggle to deal with emerging multipolarity, the authors of this volume offer a strikingly different assessment. It is, they argue, a response to an ambiguous international environment, a response that emerges from profound domestic political struggles over the allocation of resources, that is shaped by particular institutional endowments and by the real but constrained adaptive capacity of those institutions, and that reflects a struggle over ideas and meaning that mirrors political tensions within American society. This is, perhaps, a less simple and parsimonious understanding than one that appeals to hegemonic stability, imperial overstretch, or balance of power. As the following analyses suggest, however, it is an understanding that is more consistent with how America has chosen its security policies in the past.

Notes

1. For a review and discussion of some of these options see Barry R. Posen and Andrew L. Ross, "Competing Visions for U.S. Grand Strategy," *International Security* 21 (Winter 1996/97), 5–53.

2. For a good summary of this perspective see Gordon A. Craig and Felix Gilbert, "Reflections on Strategy in the Present and Future," in *Makers of Modern Strategy from Machiavelli to the Nuclear Age*, ed. Peter Paret (Princeton: Princeton University Press, 1986), 863–71. On Realism more generally see Hans J. Morgenthau, *Politics Among Nations*, 5th ed., rev. (New York: Knopf, 1978); on structural Realism see Kenneth Waltz, *Theory of International Politics* (New York: Random House, 1979), 80–111.

3. Kenneth Waltz, for instance, writes that Realist balance-of-power theory "is a theory about the results produced by the uncoordinated actions of states. The theory makes assumptions about the interests and motives of states, rather than explaining them. What it does explain are the constraints that confine all nations." *Theory of International Politics*, 122.

4. For a fuller discussion of this point see Peter Trubowitz, *Defining the National Interest: Conflict and Change in American Foreign Policy* (Chicago: University of Chicago Press, 1998). See also Peter Gourevitch, *Politics in Hard Times: Comparative Responses to International Economic Crises* (Ithaca: Cornell University Press, 1986), especially 63–66.

5. Barry R. Posen, *The Sources of Military Doctrine: France, Britain, and Ger-*

many Between the World Wars (Ithaca: Cornell University Press, 1984), 13.

6. See John Lewis Gaddis, *Strategies of Containment: A Critical Appraisal of Postwar National Security Policy* (New York: Oxford University Press, 1982) or, more recently, Henry Kissinger, *Diplomacy* (New York: Simon and Schuster, 1994). For an application of this view to the issue of arms control, see Steven E. Miller, "Politics over Promise: Domestic Impediments to Arms Control," *International Security* 8 (Spring 1984), 67–90.

7. See, for example, Stephen D. Krasner, *Defending the National Interest: Raw Materials Investments and U.S. Foreign Policy* (Princeton: Princeton University Press, 1978), 55–90 and Aaron Friedberg, "Is the United States Capable of Acting Strategically?" *Washington Quarterly* 14 (Winter 1991), 5–23.

8. For a more extensive discussion of this dimension of grand strategy see Trubowitz, *The Second Face of Strategy: Presidential Politics and Foreign Policy* (manuscript in preparation).

9. See, for example, Walter Lippmann, *The Cold War* (New York: Harper, 1947), William Appleman Williams, *The Tragedy of American Diplomacy*, 2d ed. (New York: Dell, 1972), or Lloyd Gardner, *Architects of Illusion* (Chicago: Quadrangle, 1970). For an excellent illustration of the second face of grand strategy—in this case, German naval strategy—see Volker Berghahn, "Navies and Domestic Factors," in *Doing Naval History: Essays Toward Improvement,* ed., John B. Hattendorf (Newport, R.I.: Naval War College Press, 1995), 53–66.

10. See, for example, Henry Steele Commager, *The American Mind* (New Haven: Yale University Press, 1950) for an account of the American cultural transformation of the 1890s.

11. Robert H. Wiebe, *The Search for Order, 1877–1920* (New York: Hill and Wang, 1967).

12. See also Rhodes, "Constructing Peace and War," *Millennium* 24 (Spring 1995), 53–85 and Rhodes, "Do Bureaucratic Politics Matter? Some Disconfirming Findings from the Case of the U.S. Navy," *World Politics* 47 (October 1994), 1–41.

13. See also Shulman, *Navalism and the Emergence of American Sea Power, 1882–1893* (Annapolis, Md.: Naval Institute Press, 1995).

14. This argument is developed more thoroughly in Trubowitz, *Defining the National Interest.*

15. Lynn Eden, "The End of U.S. Cold War History?" *International Security* 18 (Summer 1993), 195.

16. See, for example, Krasner, *Defending the National Interest*; David A. Lake, *Power, Protection, and Free Trade: International Sources of U.S. Commercial Strategy, 1887–1939* (Ithaca: Cornell University Press, 1988); and Jack Sny-

der, *Myths of Empire: Domestic Politics and International Ambition* (Ithaca: Cornell University Press, 1991).

17. See, for example, Klaus Knorr, *The Power of Nations* (New York: Basic Books, 1975), 64–65.

18. Robert A. Dahl, *Pluralist Democracy in the United States* (Chicago: Rand McNally, 1967); Edwin Corwin, *The President's Control of Foreign Relations* (Princeton: Princeton University Press, 1917); Samuel P. Huntington, *Political Order in Changing Societies* (New Haven: Yale University Press, 1968); Nelson W. Polsby, *Congress and the Presidency* (Englewood Cliffs: Prentice-Hall, 1971); David B. Truman, *The Governmental Process* (New York: Knopf, 1971).

19. Trubowitz, *Defining the National Interest*, 15–17.

20. The political science and international relations literature of the 1970s explored these implications extensively. The most widely cited treatments of the causes and consequences of "bureaucratic politics" in American foreign and security policy are Graham T. Allison, *Essence of Decision* (Boston: Little, Brown, 1971), 144–84 and Morton H. Halperin, *Bureaucratic Politics and Foreign Policy* (Washington: Brookings, 1974). For critical appraisals of this approach see Robert J. Art, "Bureaucratic Politics and American Foreign Policy: A Critique," *Policy Sciences* 4 (December 1974), 467–90; Jonathan Bendor and Thomas H. Hammond, "Rethinking Allison's Models," *American Political Science Review* 86 (June 1992), 301–22; Stephen D. Krasner, "Are Bureaucracies Important? (Or Allison Wonderland)," *Foreign Policy* 7 (Summer 1972), 159–79; Rhodes, "Do Bureaucratic Politics Matter?"; and David A. Welch, "The Organizational Process and Bureaucratic Politics Paradigms: Retrospect and Prospect," *International Security* 17 (Fall 1992), 112–46.

21. Key works on organizational decisionmaking include Allison, *Essence of Decision*, 67–100 and John Steinbruner, *The Cybernetic Theory of Decision* (Princeton: Princeton University Press, 1974). Though its intellectual roots are to be found in Weber, this understanding of organizational behavior grows more immediately out of the literature on the organizational theory of the firm produced beginning in the 1930s. See, for example, Richard Cyert and James G. March, *A Behavioral Theory of the Firm* (Englewood Cliffs, NJ: Prentice-Hall, 1963) and James G. March and Herbert A. Simon, *Organizations* (New York: Wiley, 1958).

22. Stephen Peter Rosen, *Winning the Next War* (Ithaca: Cornell University Press, 1991), 5.

23. Posen, *Sources of Military Doctrine*, 224.

24. Ibid., 47.

25. Rosen, *Winning the Next War*, 105.

26. Judith Goldstein and Robert O. Keohane, "Ideas and Foreign Policy: An An-

alytical Framework," in *Ideas and Foreign Policy: Beliefs, Institutions, and Political Change*, eds. Judith Goldstein and Robert O. Keohane (Ithaca: Cornell University Press, 1993), 12.

27. See, for example, Alexander L. George, "The 'Operational Code': A Neglected Approach to the Study of Political Leaders and Decision-Making," *International Studies Quarterly* 13 (June 1969), 190–222; Ole R. Holsti, "The Belief System and National Images: A Case Study," *Journal of Conflict Resolution* 6 (September 1962); Robert Jervis, *Perception and Misperception in International Politics* (Princeton: Princeton University Press, 1976); and Nathan Leites, *A Study of Bolshevism* (Glencoe, Ill.: Free Press, 1953).

28. D. Michael Shafer, *Deadly Paradigms* (Princeton: Princeton University Press, 1988), 32. Graham Allison attributes the aphorism "Where you stand depends on where you sit" to Don K. Price. Allison, *Essence of Decision*, 316.

29. A very partial list of this research would include Judith Goldstein, "The Impact of Ideas on Trade Policy," *International Organization* 43 (Winter 1989); Peter Hall, ed., *The Political Power of Economic Ideas* (Princeton: Princeton University Press, 1989); Deborah Welch Larson, *Origins of Containment* (Princeton: Princeton University Pres, 1985); John Odell, *U.S. International Monetary Policy* (Princeton: Princeton University Press, 1982); and D. Michael Shafer, *Deadly Paradigms*.

30. John G. Ruggie, as cited by Goldstein and Keohane, "Ideas and Foreign Policy," 8.

31. Geoffrey Garrett and Barry R. Weingast, "Ideas, Interests, and Institutions: Constructing the European Community's Internal Market," in *Ideas and Foreign Policy*, eds. Goldstein and Keohane, 176.

32. Ibid.

33. See, for example, Goldstein and Keohane, "Ideas and Foreign Policy," 7.

34. See, for example, ibid., "Ideas and Foreign Policy," 20–24.

35. See, for example, Jack S. Levy, "Learning and Foreign Policy: Sweeping a Conceptual Minefield," *International Organization* 48 (Spring 1994), 279–312; Rosen, *Winning the Next War*; or George Breslauer, "Ideology and Learning in Soviet Third World Policy," *World Politics* 39 (April 1987), 429–48.

Part II

The Role of Ideas and Culture

2 Constructing Power: Cultural Transformation and Strategic Adjustment in the 1890s

Edward Rhodes [1]

A little over a century ago, the American republic abandoned its traditional, defensive military posture and set out to acquire the naval tools that would permit it to intervene politically and militarily on the world stage. This remarkable historical case of strategic adjustment poses a considerable theoretical challenge for students of international relations and American politics. It is, as this chapter demonstrates, extraordinarily difficult to identify changes in American interests—national, bureaucratic, or domestic—or in threats to them that would account for this dramatic change in policy.

But if the empirical analysis presented in the following pages is correct—if Realist, bureaucratic politics, and domestic politics explanations of strategic adjustment are simply inconsistent with the facts of the 1890s—how then can we explain the radical transformation we observe and, more generally, how are we to understand the phenomenon of strategic adjustment? The critical lesson of the 1890s, this chapter concludes, is that strategic adjustment reflects a reconstruction of the cultural and cognitive landscape, not necessarily a response to change in the physical or political one. Strategic adjustment occurs not because of shifts in the pattern of interests and power or in the structure of political institutions, but because of changes in how individuals in society visualize their world, their society's mission in that world, and the relationship between military power and political ends.

This chapter argues that the American decision in 1890 to compete militarily with the imperial European powers proves explicable only in terms of a revolution in American culture and cognitive structure. This intellectual revolution was stimulated by the failure of traditional American beliefs about the nature of the American state and about war to fulfill key cultural and cognitive functions in the face of the extraordinary social challenges of the late 1880s. The construction of a new navy in the 1890s reflected the construction of new beliefs that could serve these fundamental cultural and cognitive roles. Only by viewing strategic choice as a manifestation of core political beliefs, and by recognizing the dramatic reconstruction of the cognitive and cultural landscape necessitated by the disintegrative pressures at work in traditional American society in the late nineteenth century, can the departure from historical "republican" security policy be explained.

This understanding of strategic choice and change has two critical implications for how we think about the adjustment process currently underway. In the first place, a careful historical examination of the 1890s raises serious doubts about the predictive power of the theoretical explanations which have generally been employed to inform discussions of anticipated American post-Cold War behavior. Examinations of international power distributions, of bureaucratic interests, and of domestic political alignments are unlikely to cast much useful light on how the American state will choose to pursue security in the new century. At the same time, and perhaps more helpfully, this chapter's analysis suggests the utility of understanding strategic choice as a reflection of belief structures whose content functions to provide socially unifying and individually empowering cultural myths and institutions. Viewed from this perspective, it becomes possible to see America's current strategic adjustment process as a logical reflection of the reconstruction of American political culture occurring in response to today's social and economic dislocative pressures. As in the 1890s, how the American state chooses to deal with its external environment will depend on the interlocking images of the citizen, state, outside world, and war that come to dominate the American imagination, and these in turn will reflect the challenge of finding meaning and creating order in a "multicultural," postindustrial society.

The Case

There is relatively little dispute about the basic facts of U.S. strategic adjustment in the 1890s. Prior to 1890, despite its long Atlantic coastline and the acquisition of territory along the Gulf of Mexico and Pacific, the American republic had never sought a major blue-water fleet like those of the great European powers. Indeed, between 1865 and 1883, the United States allowed its naval forces to slip into technological and materiel obsolescence. Between 1883 and 1890, the United States undertook a modest modernization program. The aim and consequence of this program was more cost-effective use of existing levels of funding to produce modern warships designed to fulfill the traditionally limited strategic role assigned to the U.S. Navy.

Historically, the American republic's Navy had been charged with three missions. First, in peacetime the U.S. Navy would represent American commercial interests abroad. U.S. warships would patrol overseas "stations," cruising waters frequented by U.S. flag commerce to provide protection from piracy, to discourage insult to American citizens, and, where necessary, to open ports to American vessels and trade. Second, in wartime the republic's Navy would attempt to protect American ports and commercial centers from bombardment or seizure. If successful, this "first line of defense" against invasion—really a seaward extension of coastal fortifications—would guarantee a military stalemate by preventing an imperial power from doing serious harm to the American people. Third, in wartime the U.S. Navy, possibly assisted by privateers, would harry the adversary's commerce and raid his coasts. Such actions were not expected to be decisive, but they would impose costs on the enemy, making continuation of the stalemate obtained by coastal defense unacceptable and thereby coercing the adversary to seek peace. Against weaker neighbors—like Mexico or the Confederacy—this wartime strategy of coastal protection and commerce raiding would be applied in reverse: the Navy would transport an army of invasion which would achieve a decisive political victory by seizing the adversary's sovereign territory and destroying the opposing society's will or ability to fight on. While these decisive terrestrial operations were underway, the Navy would protect American commerce and attempt to impose pressure on the adversary's society by denying it economic intercourse with the world.

This was, in its logic, the naval policy of a continental republic: without sea-going capital ships, the state could not hope to dominate distant waters, nor could it ensure that its overseas trade would not be cut off, as indeed happened during the Revolution and War of 1812. Such a policy assumed that the republic could afford to be denied the use of the oceanic commons.[2] It reasoned that security was essentially a terrestrial matter: so long as American homes, industry, and domestic commerce were protected from enemy assault, the state was effectively performing its security function. Denying the adversary—presumably an imperial power, and therefore dependent

upon the oceans—unhindered use of the oceanic commons through commerce raiding was a continental republic's means of retaliating and thus
compelling negotiation.

The forces required for this naval strategy were modest. Coastal warships
of limited range and seaworthiness—like Jefferson's fleet of in-shore gunboats or the monitors and heavily armored rams of the Civil War—would,
in conjunction with land-based fortifications and harbor obstacles, protect
American ports and littoral waters. Frigates or cruisers—warships able to
operate independently on the high seas over relatively great ranges and for
relatively long periods of time—would patrol overseas stations in peacetime
and prey on foreign commerce during war. In this republican strategy there
was no need for capital ships—"ships-of-the-line" or battleships—designed
to operate in a fleet and to concentrate as much firepower as possible, presumably against a similar fleet, in a decisive naval battle such as Trafalgar.
These were the tools of imperial powers, which needed to control the seas
so that their access to colonial possessions, whose wealth was the empire's
lifeblood, would be secure and so that they could wage wars of aggression
against each other.

In 1890, however, American naval policy abruptly reversed. "That year
marked the onset of a revolution in doctrine which transformed the United
States Navy from a loosely organized array of small coast defenders and light
cruisers into a unified battle fleet of offensive capability."[3] The first suggestion of this revolution came in November 1889, when Benjamin Harrison's
newly appointed Secretary of the Navy, Benjamin Tracy, submitted his first
annual report to the President. In it, he challenged the entire logic of traditional American naval policy. The United States required a battleship fleet,
Tracy asserted, able to destroy an adversary's battle fleet on the oceans. Passive defense of the coasts and raiding against the adversary's commerce did
not constitute an acceptable strategy. Tracy's justification for this shift was
that

> We must have the force to raise blockades. . . . We must have a fleet
> of battleships that will beat off the enemy's fleet on its approach, for
> it is not to be tolerated that the United States . . . is to submit to an
> attack on the threshold of its harbors. Finally, we must be able to divert
> an enemy's force from our coast by threatening his own, for a war,
> though defensive in principle, may be conducted most effectively by
> being offensive in its operations.[4]

In sum, Tracy argued that the American republic required an offensive fleet of capital ships, able to wrest control of large reaches of the oceanic commons away from the imperial powers.

To reach this end, Tracy called for a 15-year construction program to yield a twelve-battleship Atlantic fleet and an eight-battleship Pacific one. Although, in deference to traditional policy, Tracy's annual report also called for the construction of twenty coastal defense monitors and twenty-nine more cruisers, the battleships were to receive priority in construction and Tracy's lack of interest in the monitors and cruisers was apparent. In December 1889, in the wake of Tracy's report, legislation was introduced to construct eight battleships (and, incidentally two monitors and three cruisers).[5]

In 1889 Tracy also authorized a naval advisory board, the McCann Board, and its findings, issued in January 1890, went much farther than Tracy's annual report—or, as it developed, Congressional sentiment. The McCann Board recommended not twenty battleships, but thirty-five. If implemented and if foreign states did not respond, this program would catapult the U.S. Navy from twelfth largest in the world (directly behind such naval giants as Turkey, China, Norway-Sweden, and Austria-Hungary) to second place, behind only Great Britain.[6] The board's report dismayed Congress with its excessive requirements and imperialist tone, for a time jeopardizing hopes for any battleships at all. In the end, however, Congress made the jump, voting in its 1890 appropriations money for three "seagoing coastline" battleships, a direct departure from existing American policy.

The significance of the events of 1889 and 1890 should thus be clear. For the first time in its history, the American republic seriously turned its attention to the possibility of controlling large expanses of the sea and to the task of attacking an imperial adversary's naval forces. Abandoning a security strategy based on coastal defense and commerce raiding, the United States chose to become a blue-water naval power and undertook a large and expensive naval expansion centered on a capital-ship fleet built to rival, seek out, and destroy those of the European powers. The three *Indiana*-class battleships Congress authorized in the summer of 1890 were designed neither to protect American ports, like the old monitors still in service, nor to range the oceans individually, representing American commercial interests during peacetime and disrupting an adversary's commerce in time of war. Rather, these warships were designed to dominate wide ocean areas by operating together as a fleet, able to meet an adversary's fleet in line-to-line combat. In sum, "any resemblance between the *Indiana*-class battleships and

earlier American warships was purely deceptive. . . . The United States Navy
. . . had discarded its earlier confidence in a ship peculiarly fitted to the
American geopolitical position, the frigate, in favor of one conceived to meet
the exigencies of great-power naval rivalry in European waters."[7] This embrace of a battleship navy and transformation in American naval strategy was
essentially total. As Robert Albion observed, "For the next thirty years, new
battleships dominated the annual discussions of naval appropriations. In fact,
the 1890 conversion was so complete that, thereafter, it was difficult to get
enough of the lesser types of ships to form a well-balanced Fleet."[8]

The 1890 strategic adjustment was not reversed when the Republicans
were voted out in 1892. Rather than returning to the traditional security
policy it had pursued in its first term, the second Cleveland administration,
and its new Secretary of the Navy Hilary Herbert, continued with the battleship program of the Harrison administration, adding five battleships to
the four begun by the Republicans.

Subsequent administrations continued this battleship program and new
naval policy. Throughout the period from 1890 to 1919, this shift from
commerce raiders and coastal defenders to battleships was coupled with an
enormous expansion of the resources devoted to naval construction. America
rose from the ranks of minor naval powers in 1890 to second place among
the world's navies a quarter of a century later.[9] By the close of World War I,
this newfound navalism had transformed the United States and its Navy: at
the time of the Washington Naval Treaties in 1922, the United States had
a navy second to none, and the building programs of 1916 and 1919 promised to go even further. Had the United States completed these plans — an
undertaking clearly within America's economic capacity — only a major
building program would have saved the Royal Navy from distinct
inferiority.[10]

Four Alternative Explanations

A transformation of this magnitude, and of such sweeping historical importance, deserves an explanation. In an effort to develop some plausible
understanding of this strategic adjustment, this chapter examines four con-
trasting accounts of state behavior.

Possibly the most obvious explanation of state behavior and strategic adjustment is the one offered by the Realist school: states are driven by their
interests vis-à-vis other actors in the international system. They react more

or less intelligently to external threats to national values—they acquire the types and levels of military power that will cost-effectively protect state sovereignty, national economic well-being, and social and political ways of life. Decisions regarding types and levels of military power follow directly from each state's interests and objectives in the international system and its vulnerability or sensitivity to the actions of other states. Strategic adjustment reflects change in national interest or in international threat.

A second, perhaps more cynical, explanation is the bureaucratic one: while states are indeed driven by "their" interests, these interests are not national ones and states are not unitary actors. In this view, the key interests driving behavior are *intra*state ones: state decisions regarding military power reflect the competing parochial interests of the various bureaucracies and intragovernmental players that compose the state. To predict the military capabilities a particular state will acquire it is necessary to examine the internal structure of state decisionmaking—who controls information, decision, and implementation; how, according the rules of the game, problems are factored and what action-channels have been established; what each participant's interests are; and what standard operating procedures have been developed to protect and serve those interests. Strategic adjustment reflects changing bureaucratic interests or power relationships.

A third alternative is the domestic-political account: states are driven not by their own autonomous interests but by the interests of dominant or competing societal groups. In this view, states are the tool of domestic interests, not the master; they are agents, not principals. Strategic adjustment is dictated by changes in interest or relative power of various social actors.[11]

What these three answers have in common is their emphasis upon *interests* as the motivator of behavior. Where they differ is in their level of analysis: *whose* interest is the state serving? Are the rational and self-interested players in this game states, bureaucratic actors, or domestic groups? Is strategic adjustment a logical reflection of the structure of the international system, of the state, or of the domestic society?

By contrast, the fourth explanation considered in this chapter approaches the puzzle of choice from an entirely different perspective. It abandons the presumption that political behavior is based in any clear or deterministic fashion on interests, at any level of analysis. Rather, this fourth, cultural-cognitive explanation starts from the recognition that state policies have not only international, bureaucratic, and domestic roots but *intellectual* ones as well.

Beliefs, as distinct from interests, critically influence the shape of state decisions. Political behavior, in this account, is rooted not in interests but in ideas: it is the expression of core political beliefs—beliefs that serve critical cultural and cognitive functions. Like religious beliefs, political beliefs provide individuals with an intellectual framework that permits them to maintain cognitive consistency, acquire and structure information parsimoniously, and engage in effective ego defense; at the same time, again like religious beliefs, these political beliefs permit societies to develop stable institutions, assign property rights (including those to be retained by the collectivity), resolve disputes authoritatively, and overcome dilemmas of collective action. Substantial shifts in state behavior, like the one witnessed in 1890, are a consequence of the failure of core political beliefs to serve these functions effectively and the construction of alternative beliefs that logically imply a different mode of behavior. As Michael Shafer has argued, in treating foreign policy it is necessary to recognize that "where you stand depends on what you *think.*"[12] Nonevolutionary strategic adjustment in this view is a product of ferment not in the material world but in the cultural and cognitive ones: changes in the world of ideas, unrelated to changes in the world of objective interests, result in major shifts in the types and levels of military forces states maintain.

Cultural-cognitive explanations of state behavior are thus rooted in the observation that, because of the cognitive operation of the human mind and because of the impact of cultural norms and institutions, beliefs exert a major impact on behavior. Beliefs represent typically unchallenged organizing presumptions about positive or normative matters—that is, relatively fixed presumptions individuals make about others, about values, and about causal relationships in the world in which they operate. These presumptions not only dictate what kinds of information about the environment the individual will regard as relevant and therefore seek but also imply appropriate responses to environmental stimuli. As Alexander George has observed,

> in order to function, every individual acquires during the course of his development a set of beliefs and personal constructs about the physical and social environment. These beliefs provide him with a relatively coherent way of organizing and making sense of what would otherwise be a confusing and overwhelming array of signals and cues picked up from the environment by his senses. . . . These beliefs and constructs necessarily simplify and structure the external world. . . .

Much of an individual's behavior is shaped by the particular ways in which he perceives, evaluates, and interprets incoming information about events in his environment.[13]

Three further observations are, however, necessary. First, as noted, a cultural-cognitive account of behavior presumes that changes in the way decisionmakers perceive, evaluate, and interpret incoming information may result in sharply changed behavior, without—or despite—changes in the actual environment. Thus, while behavior is a reaction to environmental stimuli, changes in behavior do not necessarily imply that a change in environment has occurred. Although, given the nature of cognitive processes and cultural institutions, political belief structures will tend to remain unchallenged and will be examined, discarded, and replaced only in response to unusual circumstances, in a long-run context both beliefs and the environment must be regarded as variable.

Second, beliefs cannot be regarded—or disregarded—as pure superstructure.[14] Beliefs cannot simply be reduced to interest. Because of the cognitive character of the human mind, they cannot be treated as the intellectual manifestation of material relationships or interests. Just as religions have an internal logic of their own that transcends the immediate instrumental interest of any of their adherents, so too do political beliefs. And, rather than reflecting the power of various interest groups, the influence of beliefs—political or religious—reflects their ability to permit individuals to overcome key cultural and cognitive problems and to impose an acceptable order on social relationships and intellectual processes.[15]

Third, as this implies, individuals' political beliefs are not constructed in a vacuum but within a larger cultural framework. In this context, they represent a *shared* understanding of normative and positive issues, an understanding that serves as the foundational intellectual basis for social and political institutions and interaction. Thus, while no two individuals will ever share precisely the same set of beliefs or personal intellectual constructs, within any given society or body-politic at any given time we would expect to find either a hegemonic set of core political beliefs or a struggle for hegemony taking place.[16] Around these beliefs institutions form and on the basis of these beliefs and institutions interaction occurs.

The implications of this cultural-cognitive account are simple: to understand the choices states make in the acquisition of tools of violence and means of providing security it is necessary to understand dominant political images of the state and of war. These images do not exist in isolation: they are deeply grounded in political culture and serve important cultural and cognitive needs. They are constructed by societies at times of crisis in a functional process aimed at overcoming fissiparous tendencies inherent in social groups. They are closely tied to the historical myths that are employed to facilitate self-identification and self-definition and are important in binding the nation together, in creating in-group/out-group distinctions, and in legitimizing social relationships. These images play a key role in defining the central rules of societal interaction, such as the appropriate boundaries or extent of state activity, and may be important in justifying specific state institutions or defining the essence of particular state organs. Given these functions, these core political images are likely to be reexamined only when the continued viability of the political society has been called into question.

While this cultural-cognitive theory suggests that the external environment is indeterminant in its impact on behavior—that reactions to the external environment depend on how that environment is conceived or "constructed" in a given cognitive and cultural framework—it does not exclude the possibility that existing economic or political realities may establish physically binding constraints on choices and action. Japan in the 1940s, for example, could not outbuild the United States militarily regardless of the beliefs of its leadership about the desirability of doing so.

More fundamentally, this cultural-cognitive theory recognizes that political beliefs are *socially* constructed—that is, are constructed in the context of the day's social problems and struggles. Obviously, beliefs tend to be deeply held, to be resistant to information that would tend to discredit them, and to be chosen for their simplicity, elegance, familiarity, and cognitive and cultural utility, not on the basis of scientific or rational tests of accuracy. But the social context within which political beliefs are constructed and exist necessarily implies that significant changes in material realities that yield social crisis may stimulate a reappraisal of beliefs and that, when core beliefs have been challenged, these realities may lend strength to one competing set of beliefs over another. In other words, material-world traumas that destroy the perceived legitimacy of the society's implicit political contract generate a demand for new cultural institutions and influence the attractiveness of alternatives. Thus, for example, massive economic change (such as industrialization or the urbanization of economic activity) that threatens existing familial and social patterns, the incorporation or reincorporation of dissimilar populations into a society, and war (even successful war, if it demands unusual sacrifice on the part of particular members of society) are all likely to threaten a political society and to generate a need for new cultural myths and and other institutions. Associated with such social dislocations, we would expect to see an intellectual competition among various new ideas and images, continuing until opinion coalesces around a set of beliefs that provides a cognitively consistent and parsimonious structure meeting the cultural needs of the society.

Each of these four theoretical approaches—Realist, bureaucratic, domestic politics, and cultural-cognitive thus offers quite distinct explanations of strategic choice and yields quite distinct predictions about when, and what type of, strategic change will occur. Realism suggests that strategic change is a response to changes in international threat; bureaucratic models suggest it is a response to organizational imperatives or changes in the balance of bureaucratic interests and power; domestic politics accounts point to shifting patterns of domestic interests; and cultural-cognitive explanations draw our attention to changed constructions of beliefs. Which if any of these, though, is consistent with the actual events of 1890?

Realist Explanations

Realist accounts of strategic adjustment focus on shifts in national interests and international threats. At least four superficially plausible Realist explanations for the 1890 revolution in naval policy can be identified. The first two posit that strategic adjustment was made necessary by changing military realities that either endangered American territory directly or generated an increased threat to the hemisphere. The second two point to the economic rather than military realm, positing changing American economic interests or changing threats to those interests.

1. Strategic adjustment was made necessary by a growing or changing military threat to the territory of the United States

Perhaps the most obvious potential explanation for why the American republic suddenly altered its naval policy is that it faced a heightened security risk. In such an account, expanding the Navy and altering it to mirror those of the European imperial powers represented an effort to ensure the security of the American people from foreign invasion or depredations.

Unfortunately, such an explanation simply cannot be squared with the facts of the situation. As Russell Weigley bluntly concludes: "An invasion of the United States by a European power was out of the question."[17] The security of American territory from military assault was rendered virtually total by geography and the day's technology, regardless of the weakness of American naval forces or the choice of American naval policy. Indeed, the combination of geography and technology meant that even American ability to conduct coastal commerce was probably reasonably safe. "There was . . . no threat to American security from overseas, and none was rationally conceivable. . . . Steam power and dependence upon coal so limited the range of warships that no great power, not even Britain with her Canadian bases, could have maintained a close blockade of the War of 1812 type or risked a large-scale invasion of America."[18] And if the problem of operating a fleet so far from home were not enough, potential aggressors faced a political obstacle as well: "the tensions within the European state system accompanying the transformation of the Prussian Kingdom into the German Empire precluded the diversion of any large European force to the Western Hemisphere anyway."[19]

Indeed, if we assume that naval policy was shaped by the need to protect the American nation from European imperialism, a dispassionate examination of the changing military realities of the late nineteenth century might well lead us to expect the atrophy rather than offensive expansion of American naval power. The American state's need to compete with European states in naval armament in order to secure American territory was declining for at least four reasons.

First, somewhat ironically, the European naval arms competition had the effect of rapidly reducing the scale of any potential foreign threat to the United States. European navies were becoming specialized to compete with each other, with the consequence that their ability to threaten American interests was greatly diminished. As noted, the move from wind to coal limited the range and endurance of enemy warships. At the same time, increasing cost and sophistication limited European navies' numbers, while the quickening pace of technological change further reduced the size of any aggressor's force by reducing the lifespan of warships. The danger of attack or close blockade was not simply remote: it was vanishing.

Second, demographic trends further reduced the danger of an imperial assault on the American republic. Population growth and westward territorial expansion of the United States reduced the republic's vulnerability to coastal forays and increased the required size of an invading army. The days of the early nineteenth century, when small British armies, operating from the sea or from Canadian bases, could hold the American people hostage, were becoming increasingly distant.

Third, changes in military technology reduced an invader's ability simply to live off the land. In 1774, 1812, 1848, or even 1864, armies could cut loose from their logistics and operate deep in enemy territory: by the 1890s this was simply not a plausible alternative. The rise of mass armies, coupled with increased ammunition requirements, meant that an imperial power could not even threaten to campaign away from supply bases. Given the size of the American continent and the difficulty of trans-Atlantic supply, logistical problems made the notion of invasion increasingly ludicrous.

Finally, U.S. economic development ensured increasing military self-sufficiency: while the United States would indeed pay an economic price if it were denied access to the world, unlike the Confederacy in 1861 it would still be able to forge and support the instruments of war. As the nineteenth century (and America's industrial revolution) progressed, military action short of invasion posed less and less of a challenge to the American republic's long-run security.

In sum, the old double-barreled wartime policy—coastal defense to guard against a naval *coup de main* and raiding to impose costs on an imperial adversary—made eminent sense in the 1890s; indeed, it made even better sense than in earlier periods. More to the point, given the state's responsibility to plan for the future, these trends clearly seemed likely to continue. Each passing year promised to leave the territory and people of the republic more secure from imperial aggression. Even the threat that inflamed the public's imagination in the 1890s—the danger that a powerful enemy warship might descend suddenly on the American coast and bombard, or threaten to bombard, a great American city—did not demand a change in policy: construction of newer, more heavily armed and armored coastal monitors, dispersed along the coast so as to be always on guard, would meet this imaginary threat.

2. Strategic adjustment was made necessary by increased military threat to regional security interests

Even if the republic's territory were safe, though, perhaps strategic adjustment was required because of heightened imperial involvement in the Caribbean that threatened America's long-standing commitment to the

Monroe Doctrine. Again, however, it is difficult to square such a hypothesis with the facts. To be sure, plans for an isthmian canal did indeed generate popular concerns about the Caribbean and Pacific approaches to such a canal and worries about great-power meddling close to U.S. shores. And in the late 1890s, in the worsening of German-American relations in the wake of the Spanish-American War, German war-plans were briefly expanded to include an option for attacking Puerto Rico or Cuba as a means of pressuring the United States.[20]

No serious threat to American security interests in the Caribbean basin ever developed, however. Contrary to Mahan's warnings, construction of an isthmian canal offered no real danger of substantially increased European interest in the region: given the width of the Pacific, the direct route from Liverpool (or Hamburg or Cherbourg) to India and China still passed through Suez, not Panama. Nor, given the European balance, was there ever a significant risk that a serious threat to the Monroe Doctrine would develop, despite occasional imperial shows of force. The notion that any of the European great powers, with the exception of Great Britain, would have stationed a major fraction of its navy in the Caribbean was patently absurd, particularly given the declining economic importance of the region.[21] Put simply, Britain was not going to allow European imperialism in Latin America, a region in which she had established major markets—and Britain had the wherewithal to prevent such imperialism.

Further, if the naval revolution of 1890s were a rational response to concerns, however implausible, about imperial meddling in the Caribbean and Latin America, we would expect to see two developments that we do not, in fact, observe. First, we would expect to find the acquisition of Caribbean bases receiving a priority similar to that of naval construction. But though Harrison and his Secretary of the Navy, Tracy, did engage in clumsy attempts to acquire a base at the Mole St. Nicolas in Haiti in 1889–91 and at Samana Bay in Santo Domingo in 1891–92, these efforts divided the administration and (unlike in the construction of the battleship fleet) lacked substantial public and Congressional support; the one base site that was easily available in 1890, the Danish Virgin Islands, was not pursued. The second Cleveland administration, even while continuing the Harrison administration's construction program, made no effort to acquire a Caribbean base.[22] Second, if fleet construction were a response to perceived imperial threats to the Americas, we would expect to see serious planning for war, specifically against Germany, which was typically identified as the most probable violator of the

Monroe Doctrine. This, however, was not the case: there was no linkage between construction and plans and, as Herwig and Trask note, "the United States of America did not draw up an official war plan against Germany until 1913."[23]

Of course, even while European imperialism in the Americas was improbable, the danger of British meddling remained. As the 1895 Venezualan crisis illustrated, U.S. and British interests, though for the most part congruent, were not always identical, and the possibility of a clash existed. But if fear of British threats to U.S. security interests were the motivation for strategic adjustment, then the naval revolution of 1890 was distinctly and self-evidently counterproductive. Of all potential adversaries, Britain was by far the most sensitive to a policy of commerce raiding and (given the size of her own battle fleet and the implications of losing command of the seas) the least likely to be intimidated by the construction of capital ships.[24] In the short- or medium-run, the British could quickly and easily neutralize the American investment in battleships by stationing a superior force in Jamaica or Bermuda (or even by "Copenhagening" the American fleet—destroying it preventatively); should the European situation preclude the diversion of naval forces away from home waters, a temporary loss of control over the American reaches of the North and South Atlantic would in no way compromise fundamental British security requirements. In the long run, of course, a major American build-up might compel a British reaction, as the German construction program did. But given the dependence of the American economy on British markets, a strategy of deliberately challenging Britain to an open-ended arms race not only offered little immediate leverage but also risked substantial costs if Britain retaliated commercially. Constructing a battleship fleet thus might well provoke Britain even though it was unlikely to intimidate her.

By contrast, possession of a significant force of commerce raiders offered a realistic hope of imposing naval pressure on Britain. To the degree, therefore, that conflict with Britain was regarded as a real possibility, we would expect to see construction of a specialized force of raiders. Indeed, historically this is exactly what we *do* see: war-scares with Britain prompted raider construction. In the 1860s, when Anglo-American tensions were high, the United States responded by developing the remarkable high-speed commerce-raider *Wampanoag*—and when Anglo-American relations improved with the resolution of the *Alabama* claims, the *Wampanoag* was first modified for peacetime station-keeping and then discarded.[25]

Further, had fear of British activity in the Americas been the motivation for strategic adjustment, however misguided, in 1890, we would expect that as Anglo-American entente developed the new naval policy would be reexamined or abandoned. Yet this was not the case. In the wake of the Spanish-American War, Anglo-American relations improved dramatically and, with the conclusion of the Hay-Pauncefote Treaty and the rise of the Anglo-German arms race, British presence in the Caribbean declined. But rather than slackening, work on the U.S. battle fleet not only continued but accelerated.

3. Strategic adjustment was made necessary by increasing overseas economic interests which demanded overseas political expansion

This third Realist explanation for the strategic adjustment of the 1890s argues that American national economic interests were driving the United States to acquire an overseas empire and that it therefore needed to acquire an imperial-type navy, like those of the European powers, which would enable it to control key stretches of the ocean between metropole and colony.

This explanation fails on two grounds. In the first place, there was no burst of export activity or interest in exports in the 1880s. Overall, America prospered in the 1880s—GNP and per capita GNP rose impressively—but this prosperity was not being driven by foreign trade.

In the second place, America's overseas economic interests did not require and indeed were likely to be threatened by efforts at overseas political expansion and by increases in U.S. politico-military power created by the naval revolution of 1890. Half of America's exports went to Britain: these could only be jeopardized by an American naval program that Britain would naturally assume was directed at it. Equally to the point, American exports to the third world were protected by British free trade policy: America was positioned to play the opportunist under British hegemony—a hegemony that the United States had no interest in undermining or threatening. Nor did the United States have an interest in acquiring colonies of its own: as the second most efficient economy in the system, U.S. industry was sufficiently competitive that it could operate successfully in the free-trade environment created by Britain. Finally, to the extent that American trade was expanding in the late nineteenth century, the focus of interest was Latin America, where Britain had already opened markets.[26]

These realities were recognized at the time. The American business community had little interest in expanding foreign markets: it was the government, notably under Harrison and his Secretary of State, James G. Blaine, that had to take the lead in stimulating interest.[27] Business interests were consistently anti-imperialist until the Spanish-American War created a fait accompli. Economic prosperity in the 1880s and 1890s was seen as demanding peace, not overseas expansion. Though controversial, there is much to support Julius Pratt's thesis that "the rise of an expansionist philosophy in the United States owed little to economic influences."[28] Indeed, it is instructive to note that after acquiring Cuba and the Philippines, America's only significant colonies, the United States very quickly began trying to figure out how to dispose of them rather than how to turn them to economic profit. Whatever popular sentiments for overseas expansion may have existed, these sentiments were not reflections of material interests, nor did they result in an appetite for colonies that would have explained a decision to build an imperial-style fleet.[29]

4. Strategic adjustment was made necessary by increasing threats to U.S. overseas economic interests

Perhaps, though, the root of strategic adjustment was not an economically based interest in colonies but a changing international climate that was undermining an acceptable status quo, closing overseas markets, threatening existing American overseas economic interests, and forcing the United States to construct a navy to defend these interests.

Unfortunately for this hypothesis, the politico-military threat to America's principal overseas markets was *not* expanding. British commitment to free trade remained strong during this period, effectively guaranteeing access to key markets, and the American state fully recognized this security and indeed exploited it. As Lake concludes,

> As long as Britain remained committed to free trade and abstained from protection, the United States could protect its increasing returns industries, exploit its market power through an optimal tariff, and expand its trade with traditional English markets in Latin America while continuing to ship nearly half of its exports to the United Kingdom. As Britain's interests evolved in later phases, American trade strategy

would shift in response. But in the period between 1887 and 1897, the United States faced an era of opportunity in which its preferred policies could be easily obtained. The United States responded to this opportunity by free riding on free trade.[30]

But what if the strategic adjustment was aimed not at protecting access to the all-important European markets and to British-dominated Latin American ones, but to the relatively minor East Asian ones? Given European imperialism in China, might not the United States need to expand its naval forces in order to preserve access there? After all, even though the East Asian market was small, it might eventually grow, and failure to protect American access to the region might have long run costs.

Regrettably, continued European imperialism in East Asia fails to provide a logically coherent explanation for the strategic adjustment that actually occurred. At least three problems must be noted. First, had representing American commercial interests in a developing competition for Far Eastern markets been the motivation for U.S. naval expansion, we would expect to see aggressive expansion of the U.S. cruiser force, not a shift to battleships. Construction of a fleet of battleships would hardly be a cost-effective means of ensuring U.S. access to East Asian markets. Such a fleet was unlikely to spend much time in that region, nor could it be maintained there. And since European capital fleets were effectively restricted to home waters by the balance of power and were hardly likely to be sent halfway around the world on some colonial errand (and since, in 1890, Japan had yet to emerge as a major naval power), the need for a fleet of vessels specifically designed to battle the other side's capital force was slight. The general point should be clear: capital ships were designed to destroy an adversary's fleet or (if geography permitted, as in the British case vis-à-vis Germany) to deny it access to the high seas. They were not cost-effective tools for maintaining a political presence in distant Asian waters or for blocking imperial aggrandizement. Actual U.S. behavior in the region underscored the applicability of traditional U.S. naval policy: East Asian waters were the one place after 1890 where the United States continued to cling to the traditional policy of peacetime "overseas station," maintaining a small squadron of cruisers to show the American flag, exert political leverage, and protect American citizens from insult.

More specifically, it is impossible to square an East Asian motivation for strategic adjustment with the range limitation deliberately imposed on the first three U.S. battleships. The "seagoing coastline" battleship, while quite capable of venturing far out into the oceanic commons and contesting that common with an adversary, was hardly designed for operations on the far side of the broad Pacific. Had the aim of strategic adjustment been protection of East Asian markets, why explicitly and deliberately build capital ships that would have difficulty operating there? It was only after the acquisition of the Philippines created a regional obligation that American battleships were designed for trans-Pacific range.[31]

Second, if the point of strategic adjustment was to permit the United States to prevent American exclusion from East Asian markets, it is difficult to understand Congressional and, under Cleveland, presidential reluctance to acquire key bases, most notably Hawaii. If the motivation for strategic adjustment lay in the western Pacific, then fleet expansion and Pacific bases should have been inextricably linked—but in fact they were not. Acquisition of Hawaii was an adjunct to the seizure of the Philippines, which itself was a somewhat inadvertent outcome of Caribbean conflict; as Grenville has observed, "incredible as it may seem, the attack on the Philippines was a secondary consideration, a by-product of the war with Spain. . . . [an] almost incidental operation, to be undertaken merely to humiliate and embarrass Spain."[32] Pacific expansion thus seems to have been a *result* of strategic adjustment, not a stimulus for it.

Finally and most obviously, if the reason for U.S. naval expansion was the protection, through imperialist or anti-imperialist measures, of U.S. trade opportunities in China, why do we fail to see it used for this purpose? Why does the United States neither acquire Chinese colonies nor employ its naval power as a stick in its anti-imperial diplomacy?

In sum, a Realist examination of changing American security and economic interests, and of the changing threats to those interests, fails to provide a plausible explanation of the strategic adjustment of the 1890s. Traditional naval policy continued to offer effective defense of the American republic from external adversaries, to allow the republic to defend its commitment to the Monroe Doctrine, and to ensure access to the overseas markets that might enhance American economic well-being.

Bureaucratic Explanations

Bureaucratic explanations interpret state behavior as the logical consequence of competition among self-serving organizations that comprise the state. This focus on the nonunitary nature of the state and the peculiarly bureaucratic character of its components gives rise to two sets of hypotheses about strategic adjustment.

1. Strategic adjustment was a consequence of organizational behavior

Allison's Model II emphasizes the routinized, organizational character of state decisionmaking. Policy choices in this view reflect the essence and logic of bureaucracies: to survive and prosper, bureaucratic actors have an interest in controlling uncertainty. This means narrowing the range of variance in their environment and developing routinized standard operating procedures for dealing with assigned tasks. As a consequence, behavior at any time typically resembles that in the preceding period. The dominant inference of this theory, Allison notes, is that "the best explanation of an organization's behavior at t is t− 1; the best predictor of what will happen at t + 1 is t."[33]

The organizational quality of state behavior may help us to understand the stasis we observe in naval policy in the 1880s when the Navy incorporated new technologies into its existing strategy and force structure. Similarly, it may help us to understand continued fixation on the battleship in the years between Jutland and Pearl Harbor when, despite the inconclusiveness of engagements between battleships, despite the remarkable successes of German U-Boat operations, despite the technological development of naval aviation, and despite promising experiments with amphibious warfare, U.S. standard operating procedure continued to assume that the essence of naval war was the clash of battleship-dominated war-fleets.[34] But Allison's Model II offers little explanatory power for the dramatic shift of 1890. Three problems must be noted.

First, if behavior reflected standard operating procedures, we would expect the 1890s to mirror the 1880s. The organization and procedures that resulted in cruisers and coastal defense vessels for nearly 100 years were still in place. Indeed by most obvious measures the Navy's existing standard operating procedures were at least minimally satisfactory: the United States had not lost any wars recently, and thanks to the new cruisers built in the 1880s the U.S. Navy was no longer an international laughing stock. But, contra Model II's dominant inference, 1889 is a bad predictor of 1890.

Second, if stasis were for some reason not possible in 1890, Model II, with its emphasis on "quasi-resolution of conflict" and "problemistic search"[35] would lead us to expect marginal rather than revolutionary change: if battleships were constructed at all, we would expect to see them phased in as an addition to the existing program, as indeed was implied by the Navy's in-house McCann Board, not substituted as a wholesale replacement for it. But this is not at all what we observe. Even a historian as favorably disposed toward capital ships as Albion concedes that the post-1890 building program was surprisingly lopsided in favor of battleships.[36]

Third, the revolution of 1890 not only is inconsistent with the dominant inference of Model II but also cannot be reconciled with Model II's foundational premise of institutional uncertainty minimization. The revolutionary changes of 1890 were guaranteed to render the Navy's environment vastly more unpredictable and uncontrollable. Most obviously, building battleships was a risky business, fraught with potential for technological or fiscal embarrassment. Second, as Congressional response to the McCann report illustrated, a change in naval policy threatened long-standing Navy-Congressional relations, running a danger of provoking a budgetary backlash from isolationists. Third, because of the cost of the battleships and the rapid rate at which they, unlike cruisers, would obsolesce, the Navy would become increasingly dependent on Congress and vulnerable to its pressure and whim, reducing the Navy's ability to manage its environment. Fourth, the Navy's ability to control its environment would be further eroded because, with a battleship fleet, definitions of military sufficiency would no longer be highly predictable or controllable by the Navy. With a battleship fleet, sufficiency would depend on other states' building programs and on potentially revolutionary developments in armor and ordnance, neither of which was under the control of Navy planners. By contrast, the Navy's need for cruisers and the technical requirements of those cruisers were dictated by relatively unchanging factors such as the number of overseas stations to be patrolled in peacetime and the size and composition of potential adversaries' merchant marine. In total, rather than being an outgrowth of existing standard operating procedures or an effort to better isolate the Navy from dangerous shocks, the decision to pursue a large battleship navy was a revolutionary departure that sharply reduced the ability of the Navy to plan for its future or to prepare to perform its assigned functions.

Interestingly, the revolution of 1890 also posed a stark challenge to the essence of the institution as it was understood by naval officers. Independent command was the core institutional value in the traditional navy: captains patrolling "on station" had a free hand in running their ships and considerable discretion to protect American interests within the general guidelines provided by political authorities. By replacing independent cruising with fleet action, a capital-ship navy eliminated this independence. The naval revolution of 1890 thus not only promised to leave the Navy less able to control its environment and plan its future but also threatened to remake the very nature of the institution in ways foreign to its members.[37]

All this said, it is still of course notoriously difficult to disconfirm "organizational process" explanations because of their predictive indeterminacy: given the range of goals an organization might conceivably be pursuing, given the variety of ways it could define its essence, and given the acknowledged but unspecified ability of organizations to learn and of governments to intervene in organizational processes, an ad hoc account can be formulated to explain nearly any outcome. As Allison candidly observed about his Model II, "these loosely formulated propositions amount simply to *tendencies*. Each must be hedged by modifiers like 'other things being equal' and 'under certain conditions.' . . . Additional information about a given organization is required for further specification of the tendency statements."[38] Even allowing for the theory's striking flexibility in predicting outcomes, however, there is a striking disjuncture between the revolutionary change of 1890 and the proposition that "the behavior of these organizations—and consequently of the government—relevant to an issue in any particular instance is, therefore, determined primarily by routines established in these organizations prior to that instance. Explanation of a government action starts from this base line, noting incremental deviations."[39] Perhaps more telling, the *process* described by Allison's model is wildly inconsistent with the one involved in building a new navy in 1890: Allison posits that

> the decisions of government leaders trigger organizational routines. Government leaders can trim the edges of this output and can exercise some choice in combining outputs. But most of the behavior is determined by previously established procedures. . . . Existing organizational routines for employing present physical capabilities constitute the range of effective choice open to government leaders confronted with any problem.[40]

By contrast, in 1890 political leaders dictated the establishment of a fundamentally new navy.

2. Strategic adjustment was the product of competition among governmental actors

By contrast to his Model II, Allison's Model III emphasizes the parochial, competitive character of state decisionmaking: "players-in-positions" occupying offices in the government and representing various bureaucracies compete to advance their parochial interests. Outcomes are political resultants—the reflection of bargaining along regular action channels and according to the existing rules of the game. Changes in behavior reflect changes in relative power or changes in the interest of relevant actors.[41]

Given that change occurred in the 1890s, this model would lead us to infer that there must have been a shift either in the interest of key bureaucratic actors or in the structure or rules of decisionmaking, resulting in changes in relative power among bureaucratic actors. In fact, however, we find neither.

The critical bureaucracy engaged was obviously the Navy itself. In 1890 did key players in the Navy come to see strategic adjustment as in the institution's interest and push their representative, the Secretary, to shift policy? The answer is no. Though Secretary Tracy was indeed a leading proponent of strategic adjustment, there is no evidence that he was pressed or even encouraged by the Navy's top officers. To be sure, we do witness, as the 1880s progress, the rise of an insurgent group within the Navy, interested in strategic adjustment and willing to define the Navy's and nation's interest in terms of development of a battleship fleet. This group, however, had a diverse agenda and was not united in support of battleships until after 1890. And it certainly did not bureaucratically dominate the Navy in the 1880s or 1890s: it was, bureaucratically, nearly powerless until *after* the revolution transformed the Navy.[42] Indeed, in 1890 the top brass in the Navy viewed this reform effort as irrelevant or inappropriate: the center and institutional home of the insurgents, the Naval War College, was nearly disestablished and in 1893 the uniformed Navy's foremost proponent of battleships, Alfred Thayer Mahan, was banished to sea duty.

In sum, there is no evidence that Tracy's advocacy of strategic adjustment was the consequence of pressure from his bureaucratic constituency. The Navy threw its bureaucratic weight behind battleship construction only *after* strategic adjustment was undertaken. In the years leading up to 1890, the Navy's top officers denied not only the need for battleships to protect American interests but also the likelihood of fleet-fights and the decisiveness of fleet engagements. In the view of the admirals, traditional commerce-raiding policies represented an appropriate strategy.[43]

We encounter a similar timing problem if we attempt to explain the revolution as a product of a change in action channels, rules of the game, or relative power of actors within the Navy. To be sure, we do see important changes in bureaucratic structure. But these come *after*, not before, strategic adjustment. Organizational reform, reducing the independent power of the bureaus and centralizing power in the hands of potential policy-reformers, comes a decade or more after the decision to abandon cruisers and monitors. It is not until 1900 that we see the creation of the General Board—and not until 1915 that we see the establishment of an Office of the Chief of Naval Operations and the definite relaxation of the strangling grip of the competing bureau chiefs. The long-standing competition between line and engineering officers in the Navy also remained unresolved and unchanged in the 1890s.

Neither was there any shift in bureaucratic power outside the uniformed Navy that would account for the reform of 1890. To be sure, Secretary Tracy was a forceful individual who, because of personal tragedy, became close to President Harrison. But his power was not unchecked: within the cabinet, Blaine served as a counterweight until 1892, well after strategic adjustment was underway. Nor was Tracy's power qualitatively different from that of his immediate predecessors, Hunt, Chandler, and Whitney, all three of whom (successfully) advocated a very different naval program. Even if Tracy's close ties to Harrison help to explain his ability to push the battleship bill through in 1890, despite Congressional opposition and concerns raised by publication of the McCann Board report, it does not explain why Tracy wanted to construct a navy very different from the one Hunt, Chandler, and Whitney wanted. Nor can it be argued that Tracy's predecessors would have wanted battleships if they could have gotten them: Chandler actively opposed Tracy's battleships in 1890.[44]

Domestic Explanations

Perhaps, though, we can successfully explain the strategic adjustment of the 1890s in terms of the changing interest or power of particular domestic groups. In such an account "politics is viewed as a competition among organized interests. Government policy is understood to be the 'resultant of effective access by various interests.' "[45] This sort of explanation leads us to focus our attention on the four interest groups that might plausibly have been interested in strategic adjustment: the shipbuilding industry, the steel industry, American exporters broadly conceived, and the Northeast region. We would hypothesize that strategic adjustment correlated with the interests or growing power of at least one of these groups.

1. Strategic adjustment reflected the interest of the shipbuilding industry

This explanation fails on three grounds. First, there is no evidence that shipbuilders lobbied for an increase in navy building, either individually or as a group. Second, far from pressing the state to create navy work, private shipbuilders do not seem to have been particularly interested in taking such work on. In 1883, when the Navy began its construction program, for example, only eight shipbuilders even bothered to bid for any of the new cruisers.[46] Third, in 1889–90, at the time of the revolution in policy, the government understood shipbuilders to want "unarmored vessels which could be produced quicker and more profitably"[47]—that is, the economic interests of shipbuilders were seen as running *counter* to the strategic adjustment.

2. Strategic adjustment reflected the interest of the steel industry

At least on first blush, the case here seems more plausible. The shift from lightly armored and armed cruisers to battleships meant an enormous increase in the Navy's demand for steel. Given economies of scale, only a few firms were likely to become involved in forging the required weapons and armor, and these firms were quite able to collude to garner monopoly profits. Further, the steel industry was clearly able to exert considerable pressure on the government.

Closer analysis, however, yields substantial reason for skepticism. How much profit the colluding oligopolists were able to make on arms and armor contracts was then, and remains now, a matter of debate. What is clear, however, is that the arms and armor business remained a relatively minor sideline for the steel corporations, and (thanks to the Navy's insistence on high quality and bothersome inspections) an irritating one. How literally one should take Andrew Carnegie's obviously strategic and self-interested assessment is unclear, but nonetheless there is something to his lament that "We make about 150,000 tons of finished steel per month and the two or three hundred tons of Armor we make per month demand greater attention and give more trouble than all the 150,000 tons. We shall be delighted if the Government will let us out of the Armor business. We can use the Capital in several lines of our business to better advantage."[48] In fact, Carnegie was quite willing to get out of the armor business—though the price was regarded as too steep by the Navy—and in the mid- and late 1890s it was not unusual for government armor contracts to elicit no bids from the steelmakers.[49]

More to the point, it is quite clear who was the supplicant in the arms and armor business—and it was not the steel companies. Far from pressing the government to create work, the steel companies repeatedly had to be cajoled or bribed into producing the products required for the battleships and armored cruisers of the post-1890 Navy. This uninterest was manifestly clear to government officials even before the strategic adjustment was undertaken: even in 1884 Secretary of the Navy Chandler was writing that "patience, forbearance, and liberal treatment of the manufacturers are necessary in order to encourage them to undertake the development of the production in this country of steel plate and armor for naval vessels and ingots for heavy cannon."[50] In 1886, only one firm could be induced to bid on steel for coastal fortifications. Historian B. F. Cooling's account of the Navy's efforts to get steelmakers interested in the idea of forging armor is replete with references to "actively wooing the elusive steelmen" and the Secretary's writing "imploringly" to steel concerns.[51] In response to the first major request for bids on armor and ordnance in 1887, for the armored cruisers *Maine*, *Texas*, and *New York*, only three firms bid on the ordnance contract and only two on the armor. Despite substantial pressure, Carnegie refused to bid, "claiming excessive costs, little rewards, and too many headaches";[52] It was only in 1890 that Carnegie could be convinced to become a second supplier of armor to the Navy, and his obvious willingness to forego this opportunity meant that he was able to extract excellent terms.[53]

Explaining the dramatic policy reversal of 1890 as a response to pressure from steelmakers thus encounters substantial evidential difficulties; beyond these, however, it also encounters a significant logical one. Even if a desire to support the steel industry had been a major factor in the calculus of decisionmakers, it still does not follow that decisionmakers would turn to the construction of battleships: increasing the state's consumption of iron and steel, and the revenues of steelmakers, did not require a major departure in American defense policy. As Jan Breemer notes, heavily armored coastal defense monitors were at least as metal-intensive as oceangoing battleships: "as long as warships were 'ironclads,' it made little profit-making difference whether they were coastal or high sea battleships. Ton-for-ton, the two types cost about the same."[54]

In sum, there is no evidence to suggest that the steel industry pressed for armor and ordnance contracts. But even if Bethlehem and Carnegie had, their demands could have been accommodated without strategic adjustment: increased construction of coastal defense warships, or even completion of the nation's languishing Endicott-Board harbor-defense program, would have provided the same business without demanding a revolution in naval policy.

3. Strategic adjustment reflected the interest of exporters

The principal problem with this hypothesis is that, as noted above, in general American business quite correctly saw peace and free trade as the keys to the export market and concluded that British naval hegemony ensured both. Given the competitiveness of U.S. industry and the size of the U.S. domestic market, the development of a U.S. empire overseas, particularly if it involved conflict with European imperial powers, was unnecessarily expensive and potentially counterproductive.[55]

As a consequence, exporters tended to plead for restraint, not expansion, in U.S. foreign policy. Pratt's analysis of business sentiment leads him to conclude that the business community's belief in the efficacy of free trade led it to oppose political expansion:

> Confidence in the continued expansion of the export trade was based upon faith in the working of natural forces in a world given over largely to a system of free trade. American industry had reached a point where it could meet the world on more than even terms in both the price and the quality of its products. Given a fair chance, these products would make their own way. Government could aid them, not by acquiring colonial markets but by removing or lowering the barriers that restricted imports of raw materials and exchange commodities.[56]

Rather than coming from the business community or reflecting objective material interests of the American nation, Pratt argues, the pressure for expansion came from Social Darwinists such as John Fiske, from advocates of a militant Anglo-Saxon Christianity such as Josiah Strong, from popularizers of the white man's burden such as John Burgess, and from naval intellectuals such as Alfred Thayer Mahan. Far from a commercial movement, the campaign for strategic adjustment was, Shulman observes, "part of a larger movement in late nineteenth century American political culture—an elite rebellion against the long-standing commercial and agrarian national ethos."[57] Indeed, it appears that American firms were relatively uninterested in pursuing new markets. As Lake notes, Harrison and Blaine were not pushed toward their imperialist policies by business interests; to the contrary, they pushed business interests to pursue exports more aggressively.[58]

Given the diversity of American exports, it is potentially dangerous to treat exporters as a homogeneous group. But even if we disaggregate exporters, it is difficult to discover significant groups who would be interested in strategic adjustment. Producers of raw materials—cotton and tobacco in the south, grain and meat in the west—and the eastern banking and commercial interests associated with the export of these commodities would hardly be served by measures that antagonized European (principally British) markets.[59] Producers of finished goods for Latin American markets similarly would be unlikely to see the benefit of challenging the British navy. And it was doubtful that even those few exporters who traded in East Asia would gain from the construction of a battle fleet likely to be concentrated in Atlantic waters: cruisers, not battleships, would represent U.S. commercial interests in China and the Far East.[60] As Breemer notes, "that America's exporters *might* be shut out from foreign markets [was] hardly a convincing reason for a fleet of expensive *battleships*. If naval 'presence' was believed necessary to capture and hold onto foreign markets, a few cruisers would have sufficed. The same type of ship was also the weapon-of-choice to protect shipping (and attack the enemy's)."[61]

4. Strategic adjustment reflected the interests of the east coast

Perhaps, though, as Peter Trubowitz has argued, the special interest involved was not a particular economic group but a geographic one.[62] The steel industry was heavily concentrated in Pennsylvania; shipbuilding was concentrated in the Middle Atlantic and New England; manufacturing was concentrated in the Northeast and the upper Midwest; increased naval spending would provide a justification for the tariff, which protected Northeastern manufactures and penalized the South. Perhaps the Northeast region — the nation's industrial core — effecting a logroll with agricultural Midwestern interests also represented by the Republican party, managed to exploit the national government, shifting funds to its own economy.

Superficially, this explanation seems plausible enough. Support for naval expansion and the battleship fleet was indeed significantly stronger among Republicans and Northeasterners. Further, the timing of the beginning of strategic adjustment fits the thesis well: strategic adjustment began when the Republicans acquired control of the White House and both houses of Congress in 1889. But if the policy shift of 1890 reflected the rise to power of Republicans who sought to exploit the South for the benefit of the Northeast, we are left with four problems.

First, how do we explain the widespread opposition of Northeastern Republicans to a large blue-water battleship fleet prior to 1890? As Paullin notes, until 1890

The opinion was common that the United States should not adopt the policy of building seagoing war vessels after the manner of the European nations, but should confine its construction to coastwise vessels of defense, to monitors, torpedoes and marine rams. This view was well expressed by Senator George S. Boutwell, of Massachusetts, the most seafaring state in the union. In February 1877 he said in the Senate that he believed that the "time passed several years ago when it was for the interest of this country to make the least preparation for an open sea fight. Anybody who looks at the character and extent of this country, the number of its people, and the magnitude of our influence as a nation, must see that an open sea fight would settle nothing in any controversy that we might have with any power upon the face of the globe; and to be expending money year after year, whether one million a year or ten millions a year, or twenty millions a year, with the idea that something is to be gained in a naval contest, has no foundation in any generous conception of public policy." He thought that it was not for the "interest of this country to expend a dollar for naval appropriations directly, except such as are necessary for coast defenses."[63]

Northeastern commercial interests in the 1870s and 1880s counted on peace, the competitiveness of American industry, and the British Navy to ensure prosperity: any navy was probably a waste, and a departure from the coastal-defense-and-raider policy was downright dangerous. In 1889, Maine Senator Eugene Hale led the fight for a relatively inexpensive monitor-and-cruiser navy, one that would contain "none of those vast, unwieldy, and monstrous structures which have consumed millions upon millions of the money of other powers."[64] If the United States were to construct seagoing vessels, as far as Maine Senator Lot Morill were concerned the U.S. aim should not be "to build up a fighting force to rival those of France and Great Britain, but simply . . . to provide . . . a naval police force to guard the country's peacetime commerce."[65]

Second, how do we explain the continuation of the strategic adjustment program when the Democrats regained the political upper hand? Democrats regained control of the House in 1891 and of the White House in 1893, yet the program continued unabated. Surely if naval expansion and the construction of a battleship fleet reflected Republican pork barrel, paid for by Democratic regions of the country, the Democratic party in office should be expected to have reversed the expansion policy, not to have vigorously advanced it. In 1892, as in 1884 and 1888, every Southern and border state gave its support to Cleveland, while steelmaking Pennsylvania and most of New England remained Republican: if regional spoilsmanship were the name of the game, certainly Cleveland's supporters should have expected relief from the onerous burden of the new navy.

Third, how do we explain the growing support of Southerners after 1890? To be sure, Southerners (and Midwesterners) were less enthusiastic than Northeasterners about strategic adjustment, but key figures in the strategic adjustment story were from the South. Most notable was Hilary Herbert—an Alabama Democrat—chair of the House Naval Affairs committee from 1885 to 1889 and from 1891 to 1893 and Secretary of the Navy from 1893 to 1897, who stands with Tracy and Mahan as one of the fathers of the battleship navy.

Fourth, how do we explain the vigorous opposition of key partisan Northeastern Republicans after 1890? Senior Northeastern Republican figures, individuals who surely were in a position to understand whatever regional advantages of strategic adjustment that existed—men such as former Secretary of the Navy Chandler from New Hampshire—were active in the fight against the new, large, battleship navy.[66]

It is, further, ironic to note the Northeast's actual reaction to war in 1898. In the event, Northeasterners hardly seem to have felt that their interests had been served by abandoning coastal defense. The clamor to use ocean-going warships for harbor defense was sufficient to force the Navy to ignore Mahanian teaching and divide the fleet. That the material interests of Northeasterners were served by building a navy that could steam away to conquer Cuba was certainly not evident at the time, nor is it self-evident in retrospect.

Finally, it should be apparent that, to the extent that differences existed in how average Southern Democrats and average Northeastern Republicans viewed the construction of a large battleship navy, it is far from obvious that this was a product of regional spoilsmanship. A quarter of a century after the Civil War, there remained significant ideological and cultural differences between the two groups—differences, for example, in how they viewed the essence of the American nation and what they assumed was the appropriate relationship between state and nation. The industrialization of the 1880s, too, had a different impact upon Southern and Northeastern societies. The failure of pre-industrial cultural institutions to provide a satisfactory basis for daily activity, personal individuation, and national cohesion was surely most apparent in the large cities of the industrial North. It is hardly surprising that Southerners, less pressed than Northeasterners by the social turmoil of the 1880s and more skeptical about giving the central government greater power, were slower in adopting a new cultural understanding of war that glorified the state, or that the initial, and strongest, support for a new navy should be associated with progressive Republicans, concerned with the social collapse they witnessed.

Cultural-Cognitive Explanations

A fourth approach to explaining the 1890s is to focus not on changing national, bureaucratic, or special interests, but on the fall and rise of beliefs. Does the assumption that policy change occurs because of changes in the world of ideas—changes reflecting the functional reconstruction of core cultural images in response to social traumas that threaten the survival of political institutions—permit us to explain the shift in 1890 from a small navy designed for protecting coasts and interfering with imperial commerce to a large navy designed for controlling large expanses of ocean and meeting opposing imperial fleets in battle?

If our cultural-cognitive explanation is correct, we should expect to see at least three substantial changes in core political beliefs to account for this complete transformation of naval policy. First, to account for the sudden acquisition of forces capable not merely of protecting America against imperial predators but also of defeating foreign adversaries and forcing them to acquiesce to American demands, we would need to see a change in images of the state and its role—that is, we would assume there must have been a rejection of the early republican conception of the state as a hopefully weak but potentially tyrannical institution existing in parallel to other organic manifestations of a national civil society and functioning principally to shield a stable, peaceful domestic order from imperial aggression. In place of this traditional vision, to account for the development of an offensive fleet we would need to see the construction of a new conception of the state, one that identified the state as the political embodiment of the nation and that defined the success of the state by its ability to represent and advance the national interest on a world stage. In other words, to explain 1890 we would need to see a cultural upheaval that resulted in a fundamentally new, *internationalist* image of the state replacing a traditional, *isolationist* image of the state.[67]

Second, to account for the abandonment of commerce raiding in 1890 and the new focus on fleet encounters, we would need to see a reconstruction of the culture's image of war. Obviously, images of war—like images of the state—lie near the center of any political culture or cognitive structure. War may possess a variety of cultural and symbolic meanings and serve a number of cultural and social purposes; as one of the central institutions of society, it is potentially critical in establishing membership and core values.[68] Changes in how nations understand themselves, define their membership, and conceive their purpose are thus likely to demand changes in images of war. Prior to 1890 war generally figured in American thinking as a *countersocietal* exercise—a struggle between two peoples or ways of life, won when one or the other was destroyed or when the pain imposed on one society was sufficient to force its political representatives to sue for peace. Our cultural-cognitive model would lead us to predict that this conceptualization ceased to serve effectively basic cultural and cognitive functions in the late 1880s and that after 1890, in response to the social challenges of the day, a *countermilitary* image of war was constructed—that of a highly structured struggle between opposing military establishments, won when one side's military forces were decisively defeated.

Third, to account for the new national willingness to spend on the Navy, we would expect to find that a transformation in dominant images of the military objective of war had taken place. Underlying early republican policies was the presumption that political victory in war required achieving control over the "private" territorial property of the other state. To explain the new force posture of 1890 in cultural-cognitive terms we would need to see this traditional image of victory discarded and the construction of a new belief that political victory could be achieved by seizing control over the international common—the ocean—and thereby dominating the international system. In other words, observing the military revolution of 1890, we would expect to find an underlying intellectual revolution, from a *cisoceanic* image of victory, in which naval power served a supportive and instrumental role in assisting land forces in the vital terrestrial theater, to an *oceanic* image of victory, in which naval power was perceived as independent and decisive.

But do we actually find these changes in how Americans conceived of the state, of war, and of the military requirements for political victory? And, to the extent that we do find them, can we demonstrate that these changes in the world of ideas are not mere epiphenomenon—mere reflection of changes in material circumstance? Finally, did the new beliefs about the state and war that emerged in the 1880s and 1890s represent a functional response to social challenges that threatened the survival of the political community?

1. Strategic adjustment reflected changes in dominant beliefs about the nature of the state and the state's relationship to the outside world

The 1880s and 1890s were a period of profound cultural transformation in America: long-dominant images of the American republic's nature and its relationship to the world failed to provide the cultural tools necessary to overcome the new fissiparous pressures tearing American society.[69] Political culture faced two critical functional challenges at this juncture. First, with the end of militarily imposed Southern political reconstruction, reintegration of the South into the national polity necessitated an image of the American state and its mission that would establish a common identity and national purpose. Simultaneously, the nation faced a series of interconnected economic and social problems associated with industrialization, including the social dislocation associated with the replacement of small-scale agricultural and commercial capitalism by larger-scale industrial capitalism; the closure of the frontier, with all that implied about the relative price of factors of production; the rise of new class fissures within American society; and the arrival of substantial numbers of linguistically, religiously, and ethnically distinct immigrants from Central and Southern Europe. Just as Southern reintegration required the development of new cultural myths and institutions to bind the two edges of the regional wound together, the trauma of industrialization demanded new myths and institutions to overcome the alienation of the new urban proletariat, to stem the nativism and angry populism of the increasingly economically and politically disenfranchised members of the old economy, and to harness and rein in the vital yet destructive power of the new industrial capitalism.

Industrialization in particular generated two problems, one cognitive and the other cultural. Cognitively, the daily experience of life was increasingly inconsistent with traditional images of American national essence, creating problems not only of cognitive consistency but also of ego defense in the face of social and economic alienation. Culturally, the old republican intellectual touchstone of an American nation composed of independent yeomen, a nation unbowed by the tyranny of state power that enslaved Europe, a nation whose contribution to world progress was to be the demonstration of the glory of human liberty and of the benefits of a polity based on individual independence and consent, provided a less and less plausible account of a "good" society, how it was to be achieved, and of the role of the state. It offered no explanation of why an urban proletariat should join in common society with an industrial capitalist class, or of why Protestants of English, German, and Dutch descent should work in common cause with Catholics and Jews from Southern and Eastern Europe. The traditional construction of "America"—a light on the hill, whose unique essence could best be protected and preserved by the republic remaining untainted by involvement in world politics—and the image of a weak, isolationist American state that flowed logically from this vision of American political society thus no longer served the critical cultural function of binding the nation together into a single civil society.

But if not this vision, what gave the American nation purpose and destiny? What made the nation a nation? The new national myth, and the new account of the state implicit in it, was both state-centric and explicitly outward-looking. In the absence of other common institutions—religion, language, freehold agriculture—citizenship became the essential element in social membership. The state thus became central to social identity. What made Americans American was their common participation in and fealty to the American state. At the same time, however, the state remained a culturally problematic symbol and institution: the republic's heritage and rhetoric denied the legitimacy of a domestically strong state, while a construction of the state that legitimated its control over domestic society was plainly anathmatic in the South. A strong state must, therefore, be outward-looking: the state must be an institution embodying the American nation, but at the same time its essence must be defined not in terms of its authority to reorder domestic life but in terms of its ability to represent the American people against an external "them."

The new construction thus neatly squared the circle: the American nation—and its political manifestation, the American state—had been called into being to transform the world, not simply advancing civilization to a new plane but also spreading that civilization. This vision of American destiny, however, implied a new relationship between America and the world and a new, internationalist image of the state and its duties. Ensuring that the American nation was left alone was no longer sufficient: America must be empowered to perform its ordained mission of transforming the world. Christian duty and Social Darwinist necessity both legitimated this doctrine of societal justification through external action.

As we have already noted, it is difficult to model this new external drive, this new concern with the world beyond the American state's borders, as a function of new security threats or of economic interests. This change is not epiphenomenal, except perhaps to the enormous social and political dislocation taking place within the American nation—and even in this regard it is difficult to understand the intellectual ferment of the period as consciously manipulated by any identifiable interests. It is, in fact, relevant to note where the new image takes root first. As O'Connell observes, this image's key proponents were

> a small circle of political reformers, publicists, and intellectuals who collectively were about to become a dynamic force behind American self-assertion. Anglo-Saxons of upper-class origins and anticommercial leanings, the most important other members of the clique were John Hay, Henry Cabot Lodge, Albert J. Beveridge, Brooks Adams, and editors Whitelaw Reid and Albert Shaw. In one way or another, each

had been led to embrace foreign policy as an outlet for excess energy. One and all they dreamed of the day when the United States would play a role on the world stage commensurate with its size and prosperity. As a consequence, they gloried in military power and the prestige it represented.[70]

Thus, what we witness during the 1880s and 1890s is that while America's place and interests in the world remained unchanged, its *understanding* of its place and interests changed substantially. The widespread attraction of Social Darwinism and the appeal of "Anglo-Saxon Christian" imperialism bear witness to the weakening of the old liberal-republican national myth and the rise of a new one: as Herrick notes, "American imperialists, though few in number [in the 1880s], were winning recruits by linking their ideology to democracy and humanitarianism and by stretching Darwinism to support the thesis that national survival depended wholly on armed might."[71]

While the rise of internationalist visions of the American state and its duty logically said nothing about whether the United States needed to acquire cruisers or battleships, it implied the necessity of a modern, oceangoing force. The face the American republic presented to the world—its legitimacy as a transformative agent—was important. What followed logically was the rejection of the technologically laggard "Dark Ages" fleet of the post-Civil War years: the construction of a new fleet of steel cruisers began in 1883, roughly the time when internationalist images were making inroads into policymaking circles. The new cruisers of the 1880s were warships that could honorably represent America in distant waters and that could compete with European cruisers in the task of civilizing the world.

Indeed grasping the fact that dominant images of the state's place in the world changed over the course of the 1880s is necessary to make sense of both the 1890s and the "Dark Ages" of the 1870s, when the American fleet sank into obsolescence. The "Dark Ages" have baffled historians who assume that the American state's manifest destiny to transform the world was as self-evident to leaders of the period as it was to those of later years and who have therefore been forced to assume that policymakers of the period were peculiarly stupid or venal.[72] As Stephen Howarth observes, though, the behavior of "Dark Ages" policymakers (like the very different behavior of their successors) makes perfect sense, given their image of the American state.

To lay the blame for the dark years entirely on ignorant naval secretaries and reactionary naval officers is . . . a mistake, although some
of the secretaries of the period were incredibly ignorant and some
officers abnormally reactionary. . . . This (which might be called the
imperial interpretation) viewed the dark years as an incomprehensible
error, a blind alley in the United States' journey to world power. But
that hundred-year-old view from other countries (particularly Great
Britain and France) was based on the assumption that everyone wanted
world power. To see a nation capable of the challenge rejecting it
voluntarily was mystifying. Guardians of empire saw empire as the
thing most to be desired. The only explanation for not wanting an
empire and its essential partner, a great navy, had to be folly, ignorance,
or reaction. . . . That interpretation assumes that in the twenty-five
years from 1865 to 1890, Americans thought the same and had the
same values as British and French people then and Americans today.
On the whole, though, they did not, which is why their twentieth-
century descendants (and nineteenth-century Europeans) called the
dark ages dark.[73]

2. Strategic adjustment reflected changes in American beliefs about the nature of war

On examination, it is easy to find considerable support for the contention
that America's understanding of the nature of war was reconstructed in a
subtle yet fundamental fashion in the 1880s. Historically, the frontier experience and the weakness of the state had figured prominently in American
constructions of war. While elements of European thinking can certainly be
found (for example, in the creation and employment of a continental army),
the peculiarly American character of American images of war prior to the
industrial revolution is abundantly evident: the most obvious example is the
continued survival, and indeed glorification, of the essentially pre-state notion of a militia. For Americans, war was conceived of as both a total undertaking and, frequently, a matter of self-help. War, in the American imagination, was inherently countersocietal and only secondarily countermilitary.
It was a struggle of people against people, not military against military. Defensively, war was viewed as involving the protection, principally by locally
organized and controlled forces, of farms and commercial centers; offen-

sively, the American image of war focused on the destruction of the adversary's economic or political base in order to eliminate his will or ability to fight on. In the Indian Wars, this meant destroying villages at times of maximum vulnerability; in the Mexican War it involved the shelling of Veracruz and the seizure of Mexico City; in the American Civil War it translated into the Federal fixation on protecting Washington and capturing Richmond, into Sherman's March to the Sea, into Lee's two northern invasions, and into Confederate investment in commerce raiders. None of these operations was directed against the adversary's military forces: each sought to deny the legitimacy of the opposing state (or political institution) as a representative or protector of the opposing nation, or to destroy the national capacity upon which that opposing state relied. As the most famous exemplar of this American tradition of war, William Tecumseh Sherman, explained in 1864, "war is cruelty, and you can't refine it."[74]

In the 1890s, however, this countersocietal construction of war was abandoned. Rather than a struggle between nations, it was reconceived in American culture as a stylized clash between military units, testing the discipline and valor of the men on either side. This duel between the organized representatives—the "champions"—of competing states would decide the fate of the nations represented; further struggle was at most anticlimactic. Alfred Thayer Mahan was one of the great exponents of this new—for America— vision of war, attributing it to Jomini: "Jomini's dictum that the organized forces of the enemy are the chief objective, pierces like a two-edged sword to the joints and marrow of many specious propositions."[75]

What should be clear is that the old countersocietal image of war did not simply fail to offer a cultural solution to the social challenges facing the American people in the 1880s and 1890s; it actually painfully exacerbated them. If war were a struggle between disparate societies—between good and evil ways of life—then how could the South be peacefully rejoined and reincorporated into the Union without either denying the outcome of the war or demanding massive social change in the South? Only by redefining the meaning of war—by reconstructing it as a chivalric encounter between military units, in which victor and vanquished alike demonstrated their worthiness to be part of the nation—could the Civil War be used as a positive, healing symbol rather than a divisive one.

But, of course, it was not only the challenge of postwar reconstruction but also that of creating a multiethnic industrial society, and creating bonds of communal loyalty that transcended ethnicity and class, that demanded a new construction of of war. The problem here was twofold. On the one hand, the absence of other common institutions—language, Protestantism, or Anglo-German-Dutch political culture—meant that the state and loyalty to the state were a critical glue holding society together. But how was loyalty to the state to be demonstrated or proved? How was citizenship to be bought? The traditional countersocietal image of war, in which the state occupied a minor place, offered no help: war and the state were not intimately linked. War was a personal and local matter, not the exclusive competence of the state. A countermilitary construction of war, by contrast, made military service a proof of citizenship and hence membership in civil society. Importantly, it also made military service a proof of manhood, thus offering an attractive solution to the second problem posed by industrialization, that of personal individuation.[76] American society in the 1880s and 1890s required a culture of military heroism—a bond of patriotic self-sacrifice and national dedication that promised to give meaning to individual lives and, simultaneously, to bind a fissiparous nation together.

This profound individual and cultural need to employ war—or the concept of war—as a personal touchstone and cultural cement is evident in naval historian James Barnes's argument in the 1890s that "the country that has not national heroes whose deeds should be found emblazoned on her annals, that can boast no men whose lives and conduct can be held up as examples of what loyalty, valor, and courage should be, that country has not patriotism, no heart, no soul."[77] As Shulman concludes, for Progressives of the 1880s and 1890s, for individuals such as Barnes and (popular naval historian as well later president) Theodore Roosevelt, "war gave the nation its soul, and tested the mettle of its leaders."[78] This cultural imperative led to reinforcing prospective and retrospective revision: future war was envisioned as a countermilitary clash, while past American wars, particularly the War of 1812, were reinterpreted, reappraised, and popularized in these terms.[79]

The argument here is that the new social realities and fissures of the 1880s and 1890s rendered the countersocietal image of war cognitively and culturally dysfunctional, leaving that image vulnerable to challenge. That challenge came most notably in the form of Alfred Thayer Mahan's writings, the most influential of which, *The Influence of Sea Power upon History, 1600–1783*, was published in 1890.[80] Mahan presented a countermilitary image of war that possessed a number of positive attributes: it was intellectually simple, it met cultural and societal needs created by industrialization, and it served well both the intellectual and emotional needs of the emerging "professionalized" military officers and the cultural needs of political figures like Roosevelt concerned about the implications of industrialization for American society. Although these Mahanian ideas ran contrary to the interests of dominant elements in the Navy and were relatively unappealing to major business interests, they caught on. Progressive Northeasterners were perhaps most susceptible to them: Mahan's teachings fit best with their other beliefs about the role of the state and with their concerns about the decay of society and the body politic. But once initially established, Mahan's ideas spread like a virus until by the mid-1890s they had infected most of the policymaking community. In 1890, although Secretary Tracy was fully conversant with Mahan's ideas, Congress was familiar with them only secondhand, largely through Tracy.[81] By 1892, the uniformed Navy had been thoroughly infected with Mahanism and had adopted in its studies the premise that raiding was not an effective strategy.[82] By 1895, Mahan's ideas were broadly known and fully endorsed by Congress.[83]

The implications of this changing image of war for the U.S. Navy were dramatic. If war were a heroic contest between warriors and between highly organized military institutions representing the best capabilities of the state, rather than an effort to exterminate or render abject an opposing population, then the United States needed to abandon its historic collection of cruisers — warships that could impose pain on the adversary's nation by destroying its unprotected commerce or raiding its unguarded shores, but which, like lowly jackals of the sea, were fit only to flee from any armed opponent — and turn its effort to constructing a fleet of battleships. Only these could manfully duel, proving in mortal conflict which state deserved to live. Where America had previously assumed that the protection of American economic resources and the destruction of the adversary's were of primary importance, in the 1890s the dominant assumption quickly shifted. "The destruction of the enemy fleet is the first task of a navy in war. Everything else is a sideshow. Once the enemy fleet is destroyed, the victorious navy can exploit its resulting control of the sea for any further purpose that is desirable."[84] Violence at sea, as on land, must be concentrated and directed against the enemy's principal military forces, not dissipated in blows against commerce or industry.[85] This need for concentration logically implied construction of a capital-ship fleet, and later the construction of the all-big-gun capital ship (and still later the construction of supercarriers); it further implied that naval sufficiency needed to be measured in comparative terms, gauged against the size of potential adversaries' forces.

3. Strategic adjustment reflected changes in dominant beliefs about the military requirements for political victory

At the same time this shift from a countersocietal to a countermilitary image of war was taking place, we also witness the triumph of an oceanic, rather than cisoceanic or transoceanic, image of victory in conflict. The oceanic commons, not the sovereign territories it washed, came to be regarded as the key to success. As a consequence, sea power came to be perceived as critical in and of itself, rather than as simply an adjunct to terrestrial power. This was a revolutionary notion: the contrast between this view and America's historical experience could not be more striking. Deployed offensively, naval power had historically provided the Army with artillery and mobility; defensively, it had shielded the American coasts. However valuable, these duties hardly suggested the independent decisiveness of naval power or the importance of the ocean in itself.

This shift in images served both cognitive and cultural functions. Cognitively, it provided a powerful parsimonious thesis—in this case, again Mahan's—that rendered a complex reality easily understandable and manageable. Control of the oceans, Mahan argued, ultimately translated into national victory. Mahan was thus able to render a complicated world simple: international greatness (a matter of increasing concern to an American people whose isolationist self-image had proven unacceptable) depended on a single factor, sea power. What a relief for straining minds! Equally to its credit, this simple answer also had the convenient attribute of being consistent with existing American prejudices against large professional armies. It squared a difficult cultural circle for Americans. If international greatness was a measure of national success but a large peacetime standing army was un-American (and would make the state too powerful domestically), then international dominance must be possible through naval power alone, and therefore naval power must be independently decisive.[86]

Taking together these two changes in the vision of warfare—from a countersocietal and cisoceanic one to a countermilitary and oceanic one—we would expect to see increased attention given to the accumulation of naval power and the development of a naval force able to engage the military forces of adversary states directly, rather than by hurting their people. In a nutshell, this is what we observe in 1890.

One last point seems worth reemphasizing. These three changes in how Americans envisioned foreign policy and warfare—the new images of America as internationalist and of war as countermilitary in character and oceanic in focus—did not simply reflect changed material realities. The changes in beliefs that drove the naval revolution of 1890 were unsupported by changes in circumstance: indeed, to a significant degree they flew in the face of the technological and political shifts taking place. Even as the old isolationist image of America was abandoned, the feasibility of an isolationist policy was growing: the evolution of technology, the expansion of American power, and the increased preoccupation of Britain with the European balance of power all decreased the already minimal security concerns facing America, making isolation a more, not less, attractive policy. Even as the countersocietal image of the nature of war was set aside, technological and social developments were dramatically increasing the ability of states to wage strategic war and decreasing the probable utility of destroying an adversary's military forces: the evolution of submarines, mines, and torpedoes and the rise of nationalism combined to make the new countermilitary image of war increasingly unreal. As for the Mahanian image of the oceanic commons as key to world power, his writings appeared at the same time that the rise of the railroad and telegraph dramatically reduced the importance of the technological-economic forces on which his logic had been based.

Conclusions

This examination of the strategic adjustment undertaken by the United States in 1890 thus leads us to two general conclusions. On the one hand, it proves quite difficult to make sense of the adjustment in terms of shifting interests or the power of particular actors—at *any* of the three levels of analysis we examined. Even with perfect historical hindsight, it is hard to construct plausible interest-based explanations for what we observe. On the other hand, the strategic adjustment does follow upon an upheaval in how Americans conceptualized their state and war. These intellectual shifts represented cultural responses to social upheavals that undermined the effectiveness of existing images in binding society together and providing meaning in daily life.

Realist explanations of the 1890s would direct our attention to the evolving foreign threats to American national interests. There was, however, nothing in the international environment to justify constructing an imperial-style navy: the sovereign territory of the republic was increasingly secure; the threat to the hemisphere from European powers other than Britain was minimal and the construction of a battleship fleet was not accompanied by the acquisition of bases or development of plans for hemispheric defense; the American economy did not demand the acquisition of an empire, nor was the construction of the fleet associated with other policies designed for imperial aggrandizement; and the protection of existing American overseas markets was not well-served by the shift from cruisers to battleships. In sum, given the external environment of 1890, Realism would have led us to predict a continuation of traditional naval policy.

Similarly, bureaucratic politics models of 1890 would have led us to expect stasis rather than change. The naval revolution flatly contradicted the dominant inference of Allison's Model II, rendered the Navy's external environment much more difficult to manage, and threatened the Navy's traditional essence. Nor can we identify any changes in the distribution of power within the government that would account for the developments of 1890 in the terms suggested by Allison's Model III.

As for domestic politics accounts, it is difficult to identify specific interest groups served by the naval revolution of 1890. Shipbuilders were not interested in battleships, steelmakers had to be coaxed into armor and ordnance contracts, and exporters generally saw their interests served by peace and cruisers, not by a naval competition with imperial powers. To be sure, a case can be made that, broadly speaking, the Northeast benefited from the new navy: this, however, leaves us with the problem of explaining why the program was continued after Northeast Republicans lost power, why Northeast Republicans were uninterested in naval expansion prior to 1890, why key Southerners came to support the program after 1890, and why old-line Northeast Republicans continued to oppose the new navy after 1890.

While it is difficult to find a connection between interests and the new navy, it is easy to find one between the social upheaval of the late nineteenth century and the construction of new cultural images of the state and war, and between these new images and the construction of the fleet. Reintegration of the South, the rise of an urban-industrial society, and the incorporation of a new wave of immigrants all demanded a reconstruction of cultural institutions. An internationalist image of the state and a countermilitary oceanic image of war logically implied the construction of a large, modern, imperial-style battleship fleet.

A careful reading of the 1890s and of America's decision to compete with the imperial powers for naval mastery thus offers interesting, if surely only tentative, insights into the forces that shape American security policy. To focus on national, bureaucratic, or special interests, and to assume that changes in these will somehow translate into changes in behavior, may be to miss the real story and to lead to substantial misexpectations about American strategic choices in the post-Cold War world.

If the 1890s are a guide, it is today's cultural and cognitive upheaval — today's struggle to find images of the polity and of conflict that provide a foundation for resolving emerging social tensions and for imposing coherence, parsimony, and order on individual mental processes — that has the potential to transform America's politico-military choices. Americans' search to find meaning in their daily postindustrial lives, and their efforts to develop and justify political institutions that provide order and stability and facilitate collective action in a multicultural society, will have critical impact on the images of the state, its external role, and war that dominate American thinking. These in turn will logically imply the strategic adjustment the state undertakes.

Notes

1. An earlier version of this chapter appeared as "Sea Change: Interest-Based vs. Cultural-Cognitive Accounts of Strategic Choice in the 1890s" in *Security Studies* 5 (Summer 1996). I am grateful to *Security Studies* for permission to publish this revised and expanded version of that article. I wish gratefully to acknowledge the financial support of the Rutgers University Research Council, the Social Science Research Council and MacArthur Foundation, and the Joint Center for International and Security Studies; the critical review of the other contributors to this volume; and the valuable comments of John Duffield, Emily Goldman, Ted Hopf, Chaim Kaufmann, Jack Levy, Roy Licklider, Doug Macdonald, Jim Richter, Michael Shafer, Mark Shulman, Peter Swartz, Peter Trubowitz, and Jim Wirtz. All remaining errors of fact and interpretation are my responsibility alone.

2. Perhaps the most striking expression of this republican view of international commerce, and of the assumption of one-sided imperial dependence on it, can be found in the Jeffersonian embargo of 1807: Jeffersonian democrats viewed a severing of foreign trade not as a threat to the well-being of the American republic but as a stick to be used by it.

3. Walter R. Herrick, Jr., *The American Naval Revolution* (Baton Rouge: Louisiana State University Press, 1966), 3.

4. As cited in Herrick, *Revolution*, 55.

5. Ibid., 56, 61.

6. Interestingly, the McCann Board proposal was in important respects more traditional and less revolutionary than Tracy's annual report: naval officers were more hesitant about embracing and advocating innovative strategic adjustment than were their civilian masters. While the McCann Board demanded more ships than provided for by Tracy's annual report, it also envisioned a more balanced fleet that would exhibit some continuity with past American practices of coastal defense and commerce raiding. See Mark Russell Shulman, *Navalism and the Emergence of American Sea Power* (Annapolis, Md.: Naval Institute Press, 1995), 128.

7. Kenneth J. Hagan, *This People's Navy* (New York: Free Press, 1991), 197.

8. Robert Greenhalgh Albion, *Makers of Modern Naval Policy, 1798–1947* (Annapolis, Md.: Naval Institute Press, 1980), 211.

9. See, for example, Harold Sprout and Margaret Sprout, *The Rise of American Naval Power, 1776–1918* (Princeton: Princeton University Press, 1939), 202–346 and Albion, *Makers*, 209–36.

10. See, for example, Herrick, *Revolution*; Hagan, *People's Navy*, 185–265; Robert G. Kaufman, *Arms Control During the Pre-Nuclear Era* (New York: Columbia University Press, 1990), 7–8, 24–30; Sprout and Sprout, *Rise*, 202–36; Harold Sprout and Margaret Sprout, *Toward a New Order of Sea Power* (Princeton: Princeton University Press, 1940), 3–44; Albion, *Makers*, 205–36.

11. In his contribution to this volume, Peter Trubowitz offers a powerful (though, I argue below, ultimately problematic) version of this argument to explain American strategic adjustment in the 1890s. He points to the economic interests of the northeastern portion of the United States and the ability in the 1890s of representatives of those interests to effect a political logroll through the mechanism of the Republican Party.

12. D. Michael Shafer, *Deadly Paradigms* (Princeton: Princeton University Press, 1988), 32.

13. Alexander L. George, *Presidential Decisionmaking in Foreign Policy: The Effective Use of Information and Advice* (Boulder, Colo.: Westview, 1980), 57.

14. This view is clearly at odds with some popular Gramscian notions. See, for example, Robert W. Cox, "Labor and Hegemony," *International Organization* 37 (Summer 1977), 387.

15. For a more extended discussion on the disjuncture between ideas and interests, see Edward Rhodes, "Constructing Peace and War," *Millennium* 24 (Spring 1995), 55–56.

16. For a fuller account, see Edward Rhodes, *The Pursuit of Hegemony* (New York: Columbia University Press, forthcoming).

17. Russell Weigley, *The American Way of War* (Bloomington: Indiana University Press, 1973), 169.

18. Ibid., 168–69.

19. Ibid., 168–69.

20. Richard W. Turk, "Defending the New Empire, 1900–1914," in *In Peace and War: Interpretations of American Naval History, 1775–1978*, ed. Kenneth J. Hagan, (Westport, Conn.: Greenwood, 1978), 188. For a detailed account of the evolution of German war plans see H. H. Herwig and D. F. Trask, "Naval Operations Plans between Germany and the USA, 1898–1913: A Study of Strategic Planning in the Age of Imperialism," in *The War Plans of the Great Powers*, ed. Paul M. Kennedy (Boston: Allen & Unwin, 1979), 39–74. Herwig and Trask note that the 1889 German contingency plan, at the time of the Samoan Crisis, called for cruiser raids on American coastal shipping and that it was only in 1897–98, nearly a decade after the American battleship buildup began, that the German Navy began to study seriously the problem of German-American war: in other words, German war plans were a reaction to American competition with the imperial powers, not an initial stimulus for it. By 1903, German planners had recognized the obvious military difficulties and dubious politico-military effectiveness of an amphibious assault on the American seaboard and turned their attention to the Caribbean as a point of political leverage; by 1906, German planners acknowledged that European conditions made any American war, even an indirect one in the Caribbean, essentially unthinkable.

21. See, for example, Philip A. Crowl, "Alfred Thayer Mahan: The Naval Historian," in *Makers of Modern Strategy from Machiavelli to the Nuclear Age*, ed. Peter Paret (Princeton: Princeton University Press, 1986), 463–65.

22. Herrick, *Revolution*, 86–107.

23. Herwig and Trask, "Plans," 61.

24. On this score it is worth noting the impact of Germany's construction of a battle fleet on British behavior: far from forcing British concessions, the German "risk fleet" ensured British hostility and drew Germany into a naval arms race it had no reasonable hope of winning. See, for example, Paul Kennedy, *Strategy and Diplomacy, 1870–1945* (London: Fontana, 1984), 129–60. Of course, until the advent of the U-boat, because of its geographic position Germany had no real naval alternative to a battleship fleet. For the United States, with its two long oceanic coasts, however, commerce raiding would remain a real alternative for creating naval leverage.

25. With hindsight admittedly unavailable to decisionmakers at the time, it should be quite clear that the World War I experience suggests that the tra-

ditional strategy would have been enormously effective in dealing with a British threat. A handful of German cruisers, operating under an enormous geographic disadvantage that America, with its long Atlantic and Pacific coastlines, would not face, demonstrated that surface raiders had enormous potential to harass an oceanic empire. And German submarine raiders demonstrated convincingly that Britain's economy could be brought to a standstill even while British battleships controlled the oceans.

26. David A. Lake, *Power, Protection, and Free Trade* (Ithaca: Cornell University Press, 1988), 91ff.
27. Ibid., 111–12.
28. Julius Pratt, *Expansionists of 1898* (Baltimore: Johns Hopkins University Press, 1936), 22.
29. See, for example, Robert Dallek, *The American Style of Foreign Policy* (New York: Oxford University Press, 1983), 3–61.
30. Lake, *Power*, 117.
31. Robert L. O'Connell, *Sacred Vessels: The Cult of the Battleship and the Rise of the U.S. Navy* (New York: Oxford University Press, 1991), 323.
32. J.A.S. Grenville, "Diplomacy and War Plans in the United States, 1890–1917," in *War Plans*, 25.
33. Graham T. Allison, *Essence of Decision* (Boston: Little, Brown, 1971), 87–88.
34. On the cult of the battleship, see O'Connell, *Sacred Vessels*.
35. Allison, *Essence*, 76, 77.
36. Albion, *Makers*, 211.
37. See Shulman, *Navalism*, 44.
38. Allison, *Essence*, 68.
39. Ibid., 68.
40. Ibid., 78–79.
41. Ibid., 173.
42. For an excellent discussion of the rise of the young Turks in the Navy, see Peter Karsten, "Armed Progressives," in *The Military in America*, revised ed., ed. Peter Karsten (New York: Free Press, 1986), 240–58.
43. Sprout and Sprout, *Rise*, 173–74.
44. Herrick, *Revolution*, 71; Benjamin Franklin Cooling, *Gray Steel and Blue Water Navy* (Hamden, Conn.: Archon Books, 1979), 89.
45. Stephen D. Krasner, *Defending the National Interest* (Princeton: Princeton University Press, 1978), 26. Krasner is citing David Truman.
46. Cooling, *Gray Steel*, 36–38.
47. Ibid., 89.
48. As cited in ibid., 127.
49. Ibid., 133, 140.

50. Chandler, *1884 Annual Report of the Secretary of the Navy*, as quoted in Cooling, *Gray Steel*, 51–52.

51. Cooling, *Gray Steel*, 72.

52. Ibid., 73.

53. Ibid., 59, 76, 94–96.

54. Jan Breemer, "Technological Change and the New Calculus of War: The United States Builds a New Navy" (manuscript presented at SSRC-MacArthur Workshop on "The Politics of Strategic Adjustment," Austin, Texas, April 1994), 5.

55. Lake, *Power*, 91–97.

56. Pratt, *Expansionists*, 257.

57. Shulman, *Navalism*, 2.

58. Lake, *Power*, 111–12.

59. Throughout the period from 1870 to 1900, U.S. exports were principally raw materials and foodstuffs, not manufactures. Semi-manufactured and manufactured products, excluding food, amounted to only 20 percent of U.S. exports in the decades of the 1870s and of the 1880s; they climbed only to 25 percent in the decade of the 1890s. In 1880, unmanufactured cotton alone represented 26 percent of U.S. exports. In 1890, this percentage had actually risen to 30 percent of U.S. exports; and wheat, meat and animal products, and tobacco represented another 30 percent. See *Historical Statistics of the United States: Colonial Times to 1970*, 2 vols. (Washington, D.C.: GPO, 1975), Series U213–224, U274–294.

60. A word on the Asian export market seems in order, since this seems the most plausible commercial explanation for building an "imperial" navy. Never in the period between 1870 and 1900 was the Asian market a significant proportion of the U.S. export business. In the 1870s, all of Asia took only 1.2 percent of U.S. exports; in the 1880s, this rose only to 2.4 percent; in the 1890s, it still represented only 2.9 percent. Even in the 1890s, more than three-quarters of all U.S. exports went to Europe. Ibid., Series U317–334.

61. Breemer, "Technological Change," 3.

62. See Peter Trubowitz, *Defining the National Interest* (Chicago: University of Chicago Press, 1998).

63. Charles Oscar Paullin, *Paullin's History of Naval Administration, 1775–1911* (Annapolis, Md.: Naval Institute Press, 1968), 337–38.

64. Hale, as quoted by George T. Davis, *A Navy Second to None* (New York: Harcourt and Brace, 1940), 53.

65. Sprout and Sprout, *Rise*, 171.

66. Herrick, *Revolution*, 71; Cooling, *Gray Steel*, 89.

67. Shulman argues—correctly, I believe—the usefulness of understanding the debate over the construction of the new navy in terms of a struggle between

Jeffersonian and Hamiltonian constructions of republican democracy. The Hamiltonian vision of a strong, outward-looking republican state was central to the thinking of progressive forces in the 1880s and 1890s and logically implied an internationalist image of the state; by contrast, the Jeffersonian vision of an essentially agrarian-commercial democratic state logically implied the isolationist construction of the state that dominated discussion in the hundred years prior to 1890. Shulman, *Navalism*, 2.

68. For an extraordinary exposition of this point, see John Keegan, *A History of Warfare* (New York: Vintage, 1993), 3–60.

69. For a classic account of America's cultural upheaval and transformation, see Henry Steele Commager, *The American Mind* (New Haven: Yale University Press, 1950).

70. O'Connell, *Sacred Vessels*, 69.

71. Herrick, *Revolution*, 24. For an excellent history and analysis of "the imperialism of righteousness," see Pratt, *Expansionists*, 279–316. On the psychological basis for the rise of Social Darwinist and Anglo-Saxon Christian imperialism, see also, for example, Dallek, *American Style*, 3–31.

72. Sprout and Sprout, for example, account for the "material decline and intellectual stagnation" of the the late 1860s and 1870s by pointing to "an ultra-conservative professional group within the Service," "a virulent attack of politics, graft, and corruption," a lack of "intelligent executive leadership," and a Congress "preoccupied with internal problems, and torn by partisan strife." *Rise*, 175, 177, 180, 181, 182.

73. Stephen Howarth, *To Shining Sea: A History of the United States Navy, 1775–1991* (New York: Random House, 1991), 225.

74. William Tecumseh Sherman, letter to James M. Calhoun. Sherman—appropriately named for a famous American Indian chief—represents an important transitional figure. Raised in the traditional countersocietal conception of war, Sherman lived to see the evolving, stylized countermilitary construction take hold. In 1880, in a famous remark in Columbus, Ohio, Sherman was to observe "There's many a boy here today who looks on war as all glory; but boys it is all hell." As military historian J. F. C. Fuller observed, "Sherman must rank as the first of the modern totalitarian generals. He made war universal, waged it on his enemy's people and not only on armed men, and made terror the linchpin of his strategy." Fuller, as cited in Justin Wintle, *Dictionary of War Quotations* (New York: Free Press, 1989), 458. Sherman, of course, was merely adapting the traditional American style of war—a style both the original Tecumseh and his white adversaries would have understood—to take advantage of the resources provided by industrialization. Sherman's image of war, however, had by the 1890s become anachronistic: in the new culture of

the 1890s, the dominant image of war had indeed been refined of cruelty
and glorified.

75.   Alfred Thayer Mahan as cited by Weigley, *American Way*, 175. On Mahan's
      views on the primacy of the adversary's military forces as the target of any
      campaign see also William E. Livezey, *Mahan on Sea Power* (Norman: Uni-
      versity of Oklahoma Press, 1981); Margaret Sprout, "Mahan: Evangelist of
      Sea Power," in *Makers of Modern Strategy*, ed. Edward Meade Earle (Prince-
      ton: Princeton University Press, 1943), 415–45; and Crowl, "Alfred Thayer
      Mahan."

76.   For an introduction to the role played by war in individuation see, for ex-
      ample, Anthony Stevens, *The Roots of War* (New York: Paragon, 1989), 1–5.
      Dallek, *American Style*, 19, cites a telling passage from Stephen Crane on
      how ordinary American soldiers viewed military conflict in the Spanish-Amer-
      ican War: " 'I got mine,' one trooper told another after killing a Spaniard.
      'Now you go an' git yours.' " It is hard to imagine attacks on civilian targets
      as serving the same psychological function as attacks on military opponents
      in proving manhood.

77.   James Barnes, *Naval Actions of the War of 1812* (New York: Harper and Broth-
      ers, 1896), preface, 1, as cited in Shulman, *Navalism*, 16.

78.   Shulman, *Navalism*, 16.

79.   For my interpretation I am heavily indebted to Shulman, ibid., especially 9–
      25.

80.   Shulman makes the case that, far from being a prophet alone in the wilder-
      ness, Mahan must be understood as part of a broad movement including other
      progressive navalists, such as Theodore Roosevelt, James Russell Soley, and
      Henry Cabot Lodge. Ibid., 2.

81.   Sprout and Sprout, *Rise*, 220; Robert W. Love, Jr., *History of the U.S. Navy*,
      Volume 1 (Harrisburg, Penn.: Stackpole, 1992), 362; Herrick, *Revolution*, 78.

82.   Love, *History, Volume 1*, 375.

83.   Sprout and Sprout, *Rise*, 221–22.

84.   Weigley, *American Way*, 175. Weigley is characterizing Mahan's thesis.

85.   On Mahan's views on the primacy of the adversary's military forces as the
      target of any campaign see also Livezey, *Mahan*; Margaret Sprout, "Mahan";
      and Crowl, "Alfred Thayer Mahan."

86.   On Mahan's impact see also, for example, Margaret Sprout, "Mahan"; Live-
      zey, *Mahan*; O'Connell, *Sacred Vessels*, 69; and Crowl, "Alfred Thayer
      Mahan."

3 Institutionalizing A Political Idea: Navalism and the Emergence of American Sea Power

Mark Shulman

Despite the absence of major changes in threats to its external security, the U.S. naval policy changed radically between 1882 and 1893. The policy change was propelled by local economic interests, internal institutional reforms, and technological change. Foremost, however, the new strategic posture emerged as a result of the political institutionalization of an idea: navalism. This idea offered a popular amalgam of nationalism and progressivism that linked order and efficiency to a sense of shared national destiny. As Edward Rhodes noted in chapter 2, navalism succeeded because the political culture was ripe for this adjustment. Essential to this achievement, however, were the marketing and reforms of the navalists.

The new navalist strategy reflected a melding of international and domestic political agendas and efforts by the U.S. federal government to provide structure and stability at home and in the non-European world. As such, it reflected a "realist" perspective of politics, one descended directly from the ideas of Thomas Hobbes. The new naval strategy embodied this drive for ordering and hierarchy and called for a navy composed of a battle fleet of battleships and battle-cruisers that would engage and defeat great power contenders at sea — in blue water. Eventually the revolution in military affairs spawned by the navalists fundamentally altered the critical power nexus and shifted the fulcrum of global power from Europe to the United States.

The Old System and the New

The first American peacetime buildup (1882–1893) created a new navy that inevitably and irreversibly reshaped the nation's strategic posture and its role in world affairs.[1] In the seven decades following the 1815 Peace of Ghent, the United States had relied mostly upon Pax Britannica and the land's natural defenses for protection of national sovereignty. In peace, most of the small regular army was scattered along the western frontier while the militia remained on the books if needed to protect local order or to mobilize for a major war. War broke out twice, against Mexico (1846–1847) and between the states (1861–1865). In each instance, the Navy expanded as needed. By 1865, in fact, the U.S. Navy was the largest such force in the world, with more than seven hundred vessels capable not only of the cruiser operations that dominated its activities but also of amphibious assaults, of riverine operations, and even major battles of the line.

In the decade following Appomattox, the Navy fell into considerable disrepair through inattention, intentional reductions, and a widespread consensus that such vast capabilities were no longer required. Instead it provided a traditionally balanced defense. On one side of the equation were commerce raiding cruisers for a deterrent or an "offensive-defense." On the other, small boats, coastal batteries, and the local militia provided a "defensive-defense." The major ships were propelled by mixed steam and sail systems, outdated by most measures of technological sophistication. They were manned by thousands of foreign-born illiterates with few developed skills and even less allegiance to the stars and stripes. The officers, with some notable exceptions, generally lacked talent, ambition, and vision. The annual budget was $15 million, much of it poured into corrupt and inefficient yards that serviced the decrepit fleet. Despite these limitations, the Navy of 1882 served the nation adequately. In times of peace, the cruisers would police American trade and perform diplomatic functions while the defense systems would stand by, costing little and threatening no one.[2] The militia had additional advantages of enhancing regime stability not only as an ancillary police force but also as an institution for the education and experience of civic virtue. Overall, this system accurately reflected the lack of strategic threats that remained constant throughout the post-Civil War era.

A dozen years changed everything with astounding rapidity. By 1893, an emergent internationalist agenda evoked a new strategy, with the United States independent of Britain's defensive umbrella and capable of undertaking its own offensive operations against the navies of other nations. The budget had been doubled to $30 million. These changes reflect neither a split with the British agenda nor a change in the importance of the natural land defenses. Nor were they driven primarily by "interests." The navalist revolution had succeeded by 1893, before "interests" were seriously engaged, except for a couple of impoverished shipbuilding concerns and pacifistic steelmakers. Rather, the new strategic posture resulted from the actualization or institutionalization of the ideas of navalism by politically savvy navalists.[3] Samuel Huntington calls this process "political institutionalization." He notes,

> Political community in a complex society thus depends upon the strength of the political organizations and procedures in the society. That strength, in turn, depends upon the *scope of support* for the organizations and procedures and their *level of institutionalization*. Scope refers simply to the extent to which the political organizations and procedures encompass activity in the society. If only a small upperclass group belongs to political organizations and behaves in terms of a set of procedures, the scope is limited. If, on the other hand, a large segment of the population is politically organized and follows the political procedures, the scope is broad. Institutions are stable, valued, recurring patterns of behavior. . . . Institutionalization is the process by which organizations and procedures acquire value and stability. The level of institutionalization of any political system can be defined by the adaptability, complexity, autonomy, and coherence of its organizations and procedures.[4]

Huntington's illumination of this process explains how the United States came to adopt the new blue-water naval doctrine that eventually allowed the nation to become a great and then a superpower.

Ideas and their Proponents

The navalists were part of a larger movement in late-nineteenth-century American political culture—an elite rebellion against the long-standing commercial and agrarian national ethos. Taking up a century-old debate, they intended to replace the Jeffersonian democracy with a more Hamiltonian republic. Like Alexander Hamilton, they believed that the state could and should play a significant role in creating the circumstances by which the people of the nation could improve their lot and that of the nation through industry and commerce. Followers of Thomas Jefferson had long opposed these notions; they perceived the strength and moral integrity of the nation as derived from close ties to its agrarian, rural roots; they supported a minimalist government—one that would police and protect people and property while allowing for the greatest possible release of creative energy.

Neo-Hamiltonian navalists such as Theodore Roosevelt, James Russell Soley, and Alfred Thayer Mahan saw America as the world's great hope, but only if they could bring its people to understand the importance of its mission. They believed that the Civil War and Reconstruction had distracted the nation. Secession had been a misguided effort to return the South to a Jeffersonian system. The Republican Reconstruction's implicit goals were to strengthen (as well as to restore) the Union. Only then could Americans fulfill this mission to provide order and justice to an anarchical and menacing world.[5] The same drive, turned inward, fed the progressive movement. Navalists called for a navy to fulfill the nation's expansionist destiny, and by 1890 agreed that it required a blue water navy—a battle-oriented fleet of fighting ships. Taking advantage of a service aggressively rebuilding at every level—officers and men, ships and guns, public relations, and even the nation's intellectual culture—navalists catalyzed America's emergence as a great power.

Only in retrospect are navalists recognizable as a group. And yet, they made up a cohesive political unit throughout much of the late nineteenth and early twentieth centuries. Their backgrounds were diverse. Their numbers included officers and civilians, Republicans and Democrats, and individuals from the various quarters of the nation. Most famous, Theodore Roosevelt was a leading intellectual and political light in the movement from his 1882 publication of *The Naval War of 1812* until his death in 1919. The scion of an Old Dutch-American family, and a 1880 graduate of Harvard, Roosevelt's only nongovernment job was a brief stint as a cowpuncher while mourning the early death of his first wife. His meteoric rise from Assistant Secretary of Navy (1897–1898) to Vice President and then President (1901) was interrupted only by his Spanish War service in the 1st U.S. Volunteer Cavalry, the Rough Riders, and a brief postwar stint as Governor of New York. Throughout his long public life, Roosevelt remained devoted to building and improving the Navy as a tool for and measure of national greatness.

Alfred Thayer Mahan was born at West Point where his father served as the longtime professor of geography and tactics. An Annapolis graduate and career officer, the younger Mahan only took up writing history when assigned to lecture on strategy at the new Naval War College in 1885. The resulting books and articles on sea power expressed theories on the relationship between war and empire that became more true the more they were read.[6] Mahan died soon after the guns of August opened the Great War, which should have disproved some of the value of his ideas about sea power. It is testimony to the political effectiveness of Mahan and his navalist allies that their ideas lived considerably after material circumstances had shown their limitations.

Finally, among the pantheon of lesser-known navalists can be found James Russell Soley. Like Roosevelt, the Marylander was Harvard-trained, as a historian and lawyer. For many years he taught at Annapolis and then at the Naval War College. Throughout the 1880s and 1890s Soley wrote on naval history and legal topics. A Democrat, he preceded Roosevelt as Assistant Secretary of Navy during the second Cleveland administration. Soley shared with Mahan and Roosevelt a vision of American greatness through sea power. Each of these men knew the others well, cooperating over decades to institutionalize that idea.[7]

Never a cabal nor even a society, navalists were united only by the belief that a larger navy could not fail to benefit the nation. It was not until after the 1890 publication of Captain Mahan's *The Influence of Sea Power Upon History, 1660–1783* that they even agreed as to the shape of such an expansion. Until then, their ranks included those, like Rear Admiral Stephen Luce, who would have built cruisers and those, like Secretary Benjamin Franklin Tracy, who favored battleships. They encompassed Professor Soley, who was interested in the education of sailors and officers, and former Harvard Professor Henry Cabot Lodge who had a much larger audience in mind. A navalist society could even have counted among its brothers former Lieutenant Colonel Hilary A. Herbert, who had led the Eighth Alabama Regiment during the Wilderness Campaign against a Union army that included Colonel B. F. Tracy's 109th New York Volunteers. Yet such a society never existed.

One might wonder if the navalists constituted a movement motivated by class interests. This might be the case, but this line of reasoning only pushes the investigation back one step. How would they determine their class and what its interests were? (1) Was increased mercantile exchange in their favor? If so, then why would Mahan and many of his messmates write so meanly of commerce in their private letters? Given their generally limited access to capital, what made them think that expanding commerce was going to benefit them? (2) Was it the preservation of old class virtues—such as deference to a natural aristocracy? If so, then why were they so Darwinian in their perception of what made nations strong? (3) Was it simply anti-agrarian? If so, then why are most of the navalists silent on such burning agricultural issues as Populism, the Grange movement, immigration, and even the tariff?

In one form or another, navalism had existed since the earliest days of the republic. Craig Symonds noted of the early nineteenth century that:

> Navalists were men for whom the practical problems directly concerned with national defense were not the sole or even a primary consideration. Navalists were generally concerned with image, honor, prestige, and diplomatic clout. . . . Navalists yearned for empire, not only for purposes of economic exploitation, but also from a unique vision of what constituted national greatness. To them a naval fleet was physical evidence of national adulthood.[8]

Nevertheless, the navalists of the early nineteenth century focused their efforts too narrowly and, on the whole, were out of step with the increasingly democratic ways of the Jacksonian republic. Finally they died off, and the drive to empire was subsumed in the conquest of North America. It awaited the consolidation of the continental empire at the conclusion of the crises of Civil War and Reconstruction. Not surprisingly, it reemerged only a few short years later. When it did so, the new navalists set about to institutionalize their strategic ideas through a variety of intellectual, institutional, and political means. They revised history to reflect some newly discovered principles about the alleged relationship between sea power and the rise and fall of great nations. They also changed popular perceptions of the Navy through the written and graphic media. They wrote essays and sponsored parades. They fed articles to newspapers and constructed impressive exhibits at the world's fair. They changed the Navy itself, by cleaning up its procurement, construction, and repair systems, and by improving the quality of training and education of officers and sailors. And they worked assiduously and effectively within the political arenas to ensure greater financial and institutional support for the construction programs required by a blue-water navy.

As the revolution began in 1882, navalists limned out its intellectual guidelines. Navalist historians—from within the service and without—paved the way for the buildup, generating new historical treatments of the War of

1812. The revised history lessons, drawn from the reexamination of the second Anglo-American conflict, emphasized the dangers of inadequate preparations for war, the inefficacy of land war, and the need to control the seas. Much like the siren call "Pearl Harbor" two generations later, these historiographical changes directly supported the authors' contemporary political agendas, which advocated the creation of a large battle fleet to defend the nation's interests and to support increasing expansionism across the seas. Recasting a single historical interpretation, navalists reformulated the predominant intellectual rationale for the nation's geostrategic perspective.[9]

They believed that the American Revolution had not secured the nation's full birthright, including freedom of the seas. Only the War of 1812, feebly fought a generation too late, eventually clinched this freedom. To push the nation into a more aggressive nationalist position, the navalist historians wrote with a more expansive notion of freedom — now including an inalienable right to trade, even with belligerents. The notion of "Free Bottoms, Free Goods," however, contradicted the Union position taken during the time of the Civil War's leaky blockade. This in part explains why the small-scale War of 1812 better served the purposes of the navalists than did the cataclysmic war of 1861–1865. Furthermore, the personal wounds of the earlier war had generally healed, leaving the issues relatively open to dispassionate discussion, North and South.

The War of 1812, then, provided fertile ground for debate of America's foreign policy. To support their new interpretation of prerogatives, the navalist historians emphasized first the mistakes of the leaders and second the costs of neglecting national rights. The chief culprit was Thomas Jefferson for his notorious failure to prepare the nation adequately for war and in particular for war at sea. The eminent historian and political economist Francis A. Walker, for one, adopted this interpretation for his standard text. He wrote sarcastically of Jefferson's embargo: "The customs of oriental nations were not so well known as at the present; and Mr. Jefferson was not able to strengthen his convictions by reference to the usage in certain provinces in India, by which a person who has been wronged sits down before the door of the evildoer and there rips open his abdomen to bring a curse down on his enemy. Had Mr. Jefferson known this, it might have been of a great comfort to him" [and given him the strength to maintain his embargo].[10]

Despite Jefferson's shortcomings, the valor and extreme efforts of the officers and men of the Navy bestowed upon the United States its de facto freedom in 1815. Such revisionist interpretations quickly came to dominate navalist history, and soon popular discourse as well. In this paradigm, Jef-

ferson's "embargo" became a watchword, the 1880s version of "Munich" —
a craven and dangerous occasion of appeasement. The navalist historians
used their new-formed historical lessons to rail against similarly treacherous
cowardice in the late nineteenth century. Instead, they called on the nation
to build a strong navy capable of preserving American integrity and rights,
as it should have done in the era of the early national republic. These lessons
quickly spread to the works of more general authors, into popular histories,
and even primers and schoolbooks. In this way they soon generally introduced the reading public to the importance of sea power to American
freedom.

While historians were laying an intellectual framework for the New Navy,
they and other navalists were doing everything they could to popularize the
service, employing a remarkable array of media. As well as histories, navalists
wrote pro-Navy pieces for fictional, journalistic, and even technical media.
In the mid-eighties and especially the nineties, the entire spectrum of American publications allowed a growing group of navalist authors to describe
and discuss the merits of the Navy for the reading public. While the elite
magazines offered space to navalist writers, the more popular publications
were even more enthusiastic.[11] The newly powerful yellow press, always on
the verge of demagoguery, picked up the cause of the Navy with at least as
much fervor as had such self-consciously elite journals as the *North American
Review*. Pulitzer's editors, for instance, swelled with pride, noting, "the success of our guns must be flattering to Americans."[12] Editors across the spectrum increasingly offered space to Navy secretaries and officers or amateur
enthusiasts, space to explain the necessity of naval preparedness and the
virtues of its heroism. Boys' magazines, for instance, used navy stories to
portray the paradigm of the modern boy—brash, adventurous, and honorable. For the literate adult public, officers produced discourse on *machtpolitik*
as well as stories of brave deeds and gallant officers. Beyond their highly
successful literary efforts, the navalists succeeded in marketing the idea via
parades, exhibitions, and expositions.

These grand events appealed to the public fascination for heroes and the
gee-whiz technology of great machines. For example, the full-scale battleship
constructed in Lake Michigan, for 1893's Columbian Exposition, allowed
hundreds of thousands of Americans to step on board and experience the
wonders of the electric lights, massive engines, and great guns. Even the
cosmopolitan Henry Adams was awed by the power on display at Chicago.
At the same time, the Navy treated its visitors to the staged heroics of mock

sea rescues regularly performed by the crew of the *U.S.S. Illinois*. As a fighting vessel, however, the ship was a sham, constructed of plywood laid over concrete pylons. Still, it was the most useful battleship in the navalists' fleet. Such demonstrations, as well as reenactments, parades, and commissionings, encouraged the public to participate in the excitement of the New Navy. Also in this era, the music of John Philip Sousa and his United States Marine Corps Band entertained millions, encouraging their support for the brightwork of the Navy. His "Semper Fidelis," for instance, contributed to the Corps' image as a smart elite while his "Washington Post" did the service no harm to relations with the influential namesake newspaper.[13] Through many trials and few errors, the Navy sold the nation a fleet of *Illinois*—ships barely more useful than the one resting on stilts in Lake Michigan.

Making a New Navy

As well as giving the Navy a new intellectual rationale and stirring cultural support, navalists had to provide it with an improved image based upon a more efficient service. In many ways the Navy Department modernized its organization and facilities. Its administration abandoned obsolete management techniques to become competent and more cost-effective. The acquisition process temporarily turned away from wholesale "pork barrel" politics, and the service was able to purchase 30 cents more for each dollar spent. The new secretaries also reformed or reduced the administration at antiquated and corrupt Eastern and Southern yards, while opening new coaling stations and drydocks on the blossoming Pacific. Recruiting and educational practices also took advantage of the period's penchant for rationalization and specialization. These changes typify the efforts to reorganize naval administration along the lines of efficiency and economy and explain how the growth of the surface fleet could so far outstrip that of naval expenditures.

The navalists "polished up that handle so carefully" to ensure support for the advancement of their political agenda. This work brought great changes to the actual condition of the Navy as well. Men and officers were taught to think professionally about how to organize their efforts in the management of violence. In the late 1870s and early 1880s, Rear Admiral Stephen Luce, the preeminent leader in the reorganization of the naval education system, provided training programs for youths, for sailors, and, most notably, for officers. Opening in 1884, his Naval War College gave to the service an academic veneer, a professional military direction and the notion of a professional military education for senior officers. It provided as well a coherent new strategy that grew out the efforts to validate strategy with historically "proven" tradition. From the start, the war college embraced and inculcated the political need for a forward-oriented military strategy and for an engaged domestic political strategy as well.

The most visible precipitate of Luce's Naval War College—the battleship philosophy—not only established the discourse for America's naval strategy but also reflected the new American way of doing business. The concentration of battleships into fleets appeared just when the concentration of industrial and commercial might was beginning to become the standard American business practice. For many industries, bigger *was* better.[14] It is not surprising that the trusts developed in the 1880s were followed by analogous concentrations of force in the military. Since before the Civil War, as Alfred D. Chandler points out, the military had been cooperating with big business, sharing production techniques and logistical skills. The two most influential secretaries of the New Navy, William C. Whitney (served 1885–1889) and Benjamin F. Tracy (1889–1893), had previously worked as corporate lawyers. In fact, all of the secretaries of the emerging New Navy had been trained as lawyers—a profession devoted to actualizing ideas or theories.[15] Luce's reforms, then, were not *sui generis* but arose and succeeded in part because they reflected current organizational practices. Reorganizing inefficient yards, halting excessive repairs, retiring alcoholic or incompetent officers, and opening up the bidding-contracting system were among the secretaries' most important contributions to creating efficient land and personnel establishments.

Much like the early national navalists described by Symonds, the leaders of this new movement used emergent technologies to support an imperial agenda. In fact, their emphasis upon gee-whiz machinery often undermined support for more practical tools of war. Martin van Creveld has labeled these diverse pursuits "Make-Believe War" and "Real War."[16] In general, contemporary naval construction plans in less-democratic powers tackled "Real War" with greater enthusiasm: witness Britain's battle cruisers and Germany's U-boats.[17] But for American navalists, technology foremost supported a public appeal, frequently at the expense of military effectiveness.[18] It also suited the changing world view of the officers who designed it.

The New Navy of the 1890s spawned not only from a new strategic rationale but also from new attitudes among naval officers regarding the Pacific

Ocean. In many ways, I agree with Edward Rhodes who argues that for these
navalist ideas to succeed, they must be in sympathy with the cultural climate
of the day. Navalism did fit nicely within the imperialist notions that naval
officers were developing on the Pacific in the late nineteenth century. Their
personal recollections in diaries, letters, memoirs, and autobiographies reflect a mentality ripe for empire.[19] They reflect a dramatic shift from those
of the Civil War-era navy. For instance, Midshipman David Dixon Porter
had joined his father's ship during the War of 1812 and eventually rose to
succeed David G. Farragut as Admiral of the Navy, serving in that post from
1868 until 1890. Through the 1880s, Porter's leadership provided a visible
symbol of nostalgic and traditional service. Officers of Porter's Navy viewed
the Pacific as a place of physical challenge, where natives controlled their
own destinies and where commerce was best based upon exporting fine
goods to the United States. By the 1890s, the officers of the New Navy had
reversed these notions. The Pacific no longer represented a challenge to
modern ships and men, while its peoples came to be seen as less individu-
alistic and more like shadows. Naval officers valued the region more for its
strategic position, as a field upon which the great powers would express a
counter-force sea power in place of the counter-value warfare of the Old
Navy. Mahan the officer represented this cultural shift, while Mahan the
writer embodied and popularized it. And the newly conceptualized Pacific
was the slate upon which the U.S. battleship-dominated fleet was going to
fulfill the nation's destiny. By the time of the scramble for the Pacific at the
end of the 1880s, the officers of the New Navy had adopted stances that
justified or even catalyzed American participation in it, with great
enthusiasm.

The biggest challenge in the creation of a new naval strategy was to
procure authorizations for the required hardware—a challenge to navalists'
political and institutional ability more than to their technological capacity.
While Peter Trubowitz makes a good argument for representatives voting to
benefit their specific constituents, my analysis of the Congressional and public debates over naval construction and strategy emphasizes different conclusions.[20] It details the traditional wartime strategy generally favored by most
of the defense establishment, including many senior officers, Congressional
Naval Affairs Committee members, strategic writers in the press, and armaments manufacturers. Through the early 1880s, this traditionally balanced strategy called for a coastal defense bolstered now by the deterrent of
all-steel, fast, steam cruisers that would engage in *guerre de course* or com-

merce raiding. Through the mid-eighties, the Navy altered its strategy, succumbing to pressures from navalists and a Congress that authorized only large ships. By 1886 a forward maritime strategy, in which the Navy abandoned coastal defense, had replaced the old one. To a great extent the efforts of Secretary Tracy and the Congressional navalists explicitly authorized construction for this forward strategy, which by the early nineties had discontinued even commerce-destroying for complete dependence upon battle fleets or *guerre d'escadre*—the expressions of sea power popularized by Captain Mahan.

In the end, navalists within Congress provided the critical component of the revolution in military affairs. To succeed, they had to move unprecedentedly expensive weapons systems through the authorization process, all the while disarming opponents who claimed that they were merely unneeded and unwelcome manifestations of porkbarrel politics. One might wonder how the navalists could turn away from pork (inefficient consensus building) and logrolling (relatively efficient coalition building) and still have succeeded. First, one must note that the type of success they achieved was somewhat limited in that the nation did not receive a balanced fleet. The navalists could build a battleship-dominated fleet largely because they were willing to sacrifice many other elements that would have gone into the creation of a balanced fleet.

Secondly, it must be said that this minority movement included a few consummate politicians capable of remarkable maneuvers. After a decade of increasing naval authorizations, the Republicans lost control of the House in 1890. Consider the events of 1892 and the Congress that sat after the dramatic reversals of GOP fortune in 1890. Although the House had a large Democratic majority, the Senate and the Executive branch remained in the control of the GOP, which was able to enforce its pro-big navy position. Undoubtedly expecting opposition, the House Naval Affairs Committee introduced a bill calling for the authorization of only one ship, a *New York*-class armored cruiser and providing only $23,726,823.71 for the service, nearly $9 million less than the provisions for fiscal year 1892. The House debate in early spring reflects the range of opinions, from the emerging Mahanian orthodoxy to an idealistic pacifistic position, with all positions in between. An interesting "triangular debate" opened on the House floor, among those in favor of the bill (most of the Democrats), those opposed to it for being too small (GOP), and those disputing it for its excessive largesse (Populists and left-leaning, Midwestern Democrats). The navalists, led in the House by Maine Republican Charles Boutelle, pointed to the crises in which the United States had involved itself in the early nineties (especially in Chile and the Bering Sea). Boutelle went into the by-then standard discourse on the lessons of 1812, as did the young Massachusetts Republican, Henry Cabot Lodge, while proposing the substitution of two battleships and ten torpedo boats for the armored cruiser.

On another side of the triangle, an embryonic "peace" party called for no new authorizations, employing a variety of arguments. Owen Scott (D-IL), picking up on the Navy's favorite historical debate, claimed that the United States had suffered no genuine invasion threat since 1814 and postulated, "The time has come when nations should cease warfare. The progress of civilization, Christianity, humanity, demands that swords shall be sheathed." Tom Watson, agrarian rebel and a Democrat from Georgia, contributed his views on the folly of war in 1812 and opposed any new construction that might foster another pointless war. However cogent their arguments, the anti-navalists struggled against the current.

On the last face of the debate triangle, the one with the broadest base of support, was the new, mostly Democratic, majority position favoring the Naval Affairs Committee's *New York*-type armored cruiser and the money to continue the ongoing construction. Once again the debate focused on the question of the nation's strategic needs as informed predominately by interpretations of early national history. After Chairman Hilary A. Herbert's introduction, John O. Pendleton (D-WV) submitted one rendition, "The Navy has been extremely popular with our people since the war of 1812" and concluded that the present bill provided sustenance for the moderate navy fitting the national requirements.[21] In the end, split opposition and arguments such as this enabled the majority to pass the bill on to the Senate.

The Republican-dominated Senate fought the meager appropriations, acceding to the House's requests only after many debates and intercameral conferences. Debate within the upper chamber was only two-sided: for and against increases. As in the House, the anti-navalist sentiment came mostly from the Midwest. William F. Vilas (D-WI), typically, opposed further construction, claiming that the Navy had already proved adequate for the nation's nonaggressive needs. Francis Cockrell (D-MO) concurred, contributing a new reinterpretation of 1812 as a case of a suitable *ad hoc* response to the threat of an invasion. Sounding "1812," however, only brought more debates on the lessons of history. John T. Morgan (D-AL) retorted, "the mere fact that we were considered to be very weak upon the sea, [provoked the] war of 1812." Most of the Senate agreed on the need to protect against another invasion. Creating a consensus on naval construction, most Southern Democrats joined with the Republicans only as far as agreeing to support the creation of a coastal defense force. Significantly, the Senate did not request authorizations for any more battleships, but only for defense vessels: a coastal monitor, four river gunboats, and six harbor-based torpedo boats. The Senate, attempting to take the initiative in reformulating the national defense strategy, thus sought to reintroduce the capability for a defensive-defense.

The House majority had already abandoned any pretense of a defensive-defense, and it took three intercameral conferences finally to force the Senate to acquiesce to a solely offensive-defense formula. The conferees, navalists appointed by each house, readily agreed among themselves. In the critical second conference, the House had explicitly charged its representatives with securing funding just for one armored cruiser. The Senate, meanwhile, had instructed its conferees to authorize a monitor, four gunboats and six torpedo boats. The navalist-dominated conference, in turn, reported in favor of one 9,000-ton battleship (*Iowa*) and the armored cruiser (*Brooklyn*). On a smaller scale, this foreshadows Winston Churchill's statement about British dreadnought authorizations some years later: the admiralty "demanded six ships: the economists offered four: and we finally compromised on eight."

Herbert had slid the *Iowa* into the legislation calling merely for its authorization with virtually no concomitant appropriation. This ruse allowed a cost-conscious House to authorize a $6 million battleship as a less expensive defense option than the million dollars required for the ten small boats (at approximately $100,000 apiece). With the sly addition of the largest battleship to date, the bill was reported again. The Senate approved the report essentially intact and intransigently fought the House for its approval. Finally after a third conference, Congress authorized the construction of the *Iowa* and the *Brooklyn* on July 16, 1892. Only the battleship and its half-sibling, the armored cruiser, passed through the perilous shoals of the appropriations process. The hardware of naval strategy moved increasingly and irreversibly toward the offensive-defense.

Where Ideas Failed

The 1892 debates tell not only about the success of navalism but also about the failure to oppose it. Opposition to navalism was weak, fragmented, and politically crippled. Theodore Roosevelt derided the opponents of na-valism and empire as "Flapdoodle Pacifists and Mollycoddlers." Like the American anti-anti-communists of the Cold War, anti-navalists were some-times branded traitors. Actually they were merely expressing their different visions of America's destiny. Some were pacifists from the cash-poor Midwest or South who held economic or religious perspectives that opposed war. Some were politicians who wanted to save, or at least to appear to save, money. Others, like journalist Carl Schurz, wanted to avoid foreign entan-glements precisely because they diffused efforts to improve the domestic situation. Schurz, a "forty-eighter," had watched as his native Germany's rulers used the strains of an aggressive foreign policy as a pretense to stifle domestic reform and progress. Perhaps the most confusing anti-navalists were men working both sides of the issue, such as Francis A. Walker, whose historical writing helped popularize the Navy, and steel monger Andrew Carnegie, who personally negotiated large contracts for armor plate. Both men were dedicated anti-imperialists by the late 1890s. Overall, anti-naval-ism was a fragmented movement, unable to coalesce until the imperial crises of 1898 and successive wars with the Spanish and then the Filipinos.

The failure of the anti-navalists to gain support is also, in part, explained by falling prices and increased efficiency that diminished the short-term costs. During the dozen years examined by this work, the purchasing power of naval expenditures increased extremely rapidly. The naval expenditure price index decreased between 1882 and 1893, from 106 to 76—showing a drop in real costs of close to 30 percent.[22] The big new navy, as a conse-quence of this and the elimination of waste, cost only $15 million per year more than had the old. In the days of great trusts, no income tax, and, for part of the time, even a considerable treasury surplus, few voters begrudged these paltry sums. Surprisingly little literature, American or other, docu-ments the anti-imperialist efforts during the era of new imperialism.[23] This dearth accurately reflects the comparatively small size and fragmented na-ture of the anti-navalist movement and its diversity. By contrast, the cam-paign to build a great American navy can be documented through sources in fictional and nonfictional literature, exhibitions, monuments, and even music, as well as in an understanding of the changing economic and political situations. Investigating those opposed to the buildup, however, points more often to what they were not, and to resources or arguments they failed to use.

The opposition failed not only because of the effective popularization of the service, but also because the opponents of the New Navy came from diverse backgrounds with often contradictory agendas; they could not agree what they did want. At various times, opponents included mugwumps, religious pacifists, and populists from the old Northwest and the deep South: groups unlikely to coalesce into a strong political force. In the end, Roosevelt had little to fear from the mollycoddlers.

The Navalists' Triumph

Politics created strategy in the late nineteenth century; navalists could alter the political discourse sufficiently to create an offensive navy, the embodiment of their assertive agenda. Historically, two schools have vied to shape and to explain America's increasingly aggressive role in world affairs. Internalists, who tend to come from the political left with an overt anti-interventionist agenda, generally find the roots of "American empire" in the selfish search for economic gain. Realists, on the other hand, coming from the center or the right, explain "liberal internationalism" as derived in reaction to foreign threats.[24] In this case, at least, the truth lies somewhere in between. There will always be opportunities for intervention: a Cuban Revolution to aid (1873–1898) or thwart (1959-present), a Chilean Civil War to encourage (1891) or subvert (1973), and an oppressive and apparently fragmenting China in which to intervene (1900) or not (1994). Still, this theory of institutionalization of ideas provides a bridge between the two schools, showing how ideas (whether domestic or of foreign origin) shaped foreign relations. It argues that the navalists were the effective agents of this dramatic shift.

The navalists understood the contingency of America's relations with the world and confidently believed that America's proper role was to take part in foreign affairs by using sea power to influence other nations and thereby to help the people of the United States and the world. They had no dreams of creating a formal empire, but still they set out to write their self-confident vision on their home and foreign lands. In their sincere efforts to encourage America to take the lead among nations, the navalists conceived of an agenda that allowed the best and brightest to lead the new nation. The self-assuredness of navalism was based on a belief in the ideas of rationalization and professionalization as well as the intellectual consensus then emerging that battleships represented the apex of naval construction.

American navalism emerged during a historical moment in the 1880s when the nation seemed destined for greatness with sea power the standard by which it would be judged as well as the tool with which it would be effected. An examination of navalism's first dozen years affords insights into the dynamics of militarism, the remarkable degree to which politics, pork, policy, and strategy are inextricably linked, and the interrelatedness of various social discourses in the early progressive era. It also places the extraordinary fame and impact of Mahan and his writings into a context from which his successors too quickly removed him. The cost of placing him upon a pedestal has been paid many times over by the Navy and by the nation. Over the past century, the Mahanian navy is the single most expensive organization ever, a status toward which it had been launched by 1893.[25]

In the end, navalism triumphed for three reasons. First, foreign crises granted reprieves from domestic travails. For as Paul Kennedy writes, "The emperors, kings, prime ministers and presidents of great powers have always preferred the heady world of diplomacy, war and international affairs to the less than glamorous realm of fiscal reform, educational change, and renewal."[26] In the battleship revolution, presidents could focus on great affairs of state and on the inevitable naval crises. Secondly, it succeeded quickly because it faced immature and fragmented opposition. But finally and critically, the comprehensiveness and cohesiveness of navalist efforts made for an overwhelming movement. As noted, they fought for a large navy by creating historical and strategic justifications, by reorganizing and professionalizing the service, and by marketing it based on the widespread appeal of the big and heroic. They institutionalized a political notion—a strategic idea—through a multi-front, creative political campaign of a mere dozen years.

By 1893 the United States had become a naval power. Certainly the impetus was provided by elites, but at each stage domestic politics and social constructs molded the shape and direction of American expansion. The complex negotiations between the leaders and the followers explain in part how a self-absorbed inward-looking nation became an imperial power.

Notes

1. Much of this material is derived from my book, *Navalism and the Emergence of American Sea Power, 1882–1893* (Annapolis, Md.: Naval Institute Press, 1995). For the larger geopolitical context, see first Paul M. Kennedy, *The Rise and Fall of the Great Powers* (New York: Random House, 1987). The standard military history of the United States (especially for the nineteenth century) is Allan R. Millett and Peter Maslowski, *For the Common Defense: A Military*

History of the United States of America (New York: Free Press, 1984, 1991); also see Russell F. Weigley, *The American Way of War* (Bloomington: Indiana University Press, 1973) and James Chace and Caleb Carr, *America Invulnerable: The Quest for Absolute Security from 1812 to Star Wars* (New York: Summit, 1989).

This work has profited from the University of Texas, Austin/SSRC workshop on strategic readjustment in 1994 and a follow-on 1995 conference at the Naval Post-graduate School in Monterey, and particularly from discussions with Emily Goldman, Peter Trubowitz, and especially Edward Rhodes.

2. For the "Old Navy," see in particular Kenneth J. Hagan, ed., *This People's Navy: The Making of American Sea Power* (New York: Free Press, 1991); Lance Buhl, "Maintaining 'An American Navy,'" *In Peace and War*, ed. Kenneth J. Hagan (Westport, Conn.: Greenwood, 1984); David Long, *Gold Braid and Foreign Relations: Diplomatic Activities of U.S. Naval Officers, 1798–1883* (Annapolis: Naval Institute Press, 1988). For the "Old Army," see Walter Millis, *Arms and Men: A Study in American Military History* (New York: Putnam, 1956).

3. For comparison of navalism in other nations, see: William R. Langer, *The Diplomacy of Imperialism* (New York: Alfred Knopf, 1935); Jonathan Steinberg, *Yesterday's Deterrent: Tirpitz and the Birth of the German Battle Fleet* (London: MacDonald, 1965); Arthur J. Marder, *Anatomy of British Sea Power* (Hamden, Conn.: Archon Books, 1964); Volker Berghahn, *Der Tirpitz-Plan* (Dusseldorf: Droste Verlag, 1971); Theodore Ropp, *The Development of a Modern Navy: French Naval Policy, 1871–1904*, ed. Stephen S. Roberts (Annapolis, Md.: Naval Institute Press, 1987); Paul M. Kennedy, *The Rise and Fall of British Naval Mastery* (London: Macmillan, 1976); and Janet Robb, *The Primrose League, 1883–1906* (New York: Columbia University Press, 1942).

4. Huntington's italics in original. *Political Order in Changing Societies* (New Haven: Yale University Press, 1968), 12.

5. In another society, at a slightly later time, this type of impulse could well lead to more menacing philosophies. See Paul M. Kennedy, "Levels of Approach and Contexts in Naval History: Admiral Tirpitz and the Origins of Fascism," in *Doing Naval History: Essays Towards Improvement*, ed. John B. Hattendorf (Newport, R.I.: Naval War College Press, 1995). For the softer domestic analogue in the U.S., see Richard Abrams, *Conservatism in the Progressive Era* (New York: Columbia University Press, 1964).

6. Mahan's seminal works include: *The Influence of Sea Power Upon History, 1660–1783* (Boston: Little, Brown, 1890) published in nearly 30 English-language editions as well as in Russian, German, French, Spanish, Japanese and Swedish; *The Influence of Sea Power Upon the French Revolution and*

Empire, 1793–1812 (Boston: Little, Brown, 1892); *The Interest of America in Sea Power, Present and Future* (Boston: Little, Brown, 1897).

The literature for Mahan is exhaustive. To start, see: John B. Hattendorf, ed., *The Influence of History Upon Mahan* (Newport, R.I.: Naval War College Press, 1991) and John B. Hattendorf and Lynn C. Hattendorf, comps., *A Bibliography of the Works of Alfred Thayer Mahan* (Newport: Naval War College Press, 1986). And see Shulman, "The Influence of Mahan Upon Sea Power." *Reviews in American History* (December 1991), 522–27.

7. My book, *Navalism*, provides more biographical details of these and other navalists, as does Peter Karsten's remarkable study, *The Naval Aristocracy* (New York: Free Press, 1972). For works chronicling these men specifically, see Edmund Morris, *The Rise of Theodore Roosevelt* (New York: Ballantine, 1979); Robert Seager II, *Alfred Thayer Mahan, The Man and His Letters* (Annapolis, Md.: Naval Institute Press, 1977); and Richard Turk, *The Ambiguous Relationship: Theodore Roosevelt and Alfred Thayer Mahan* (Westport, Conn.: Greenwood Press, 1987) *inter alia*. There is no comprehensive study of Soley. John Hattendorf's forthcoming biography of Luce will no doubt fill an important gap in the literature.

8. Craig Symonds, *The Navalists and Anti-Navalists* (Newark: University of Delaware Press, 1981), introduction.

9. Shulman, "The Influence of History Upon Sea Power: The Navalist Interpretations of the War of 1812," *Journal of Military History* (April 1992). For original sources see Theodore Roosevelt, *Naval War of 1812* (New York: G. P. Putnam, 1st ed., 1882 and 4th ed., 1894); James Barnes, *Naval Actions of the War of 1812*, (New York: Harper and Brothers, 1896); James R. Soley, *The Boys of 1812 and Other Naval Heroes* (Boston: Little, Brown, 1887); and Alfred Thayer Mahan, *Sea Power in its Relations to the War of 1812* (Boston: Little, Brown, 1905). For more historiography, see Kenneth J. Hagan and Mark Shulman, "Mahan Plus One Hundred: The Current State of Naval History in the United States," in *Ubi Sumus? The State of Naval and Maritime History*, ed., John B. Hattendorf (Newport, R.I.: Naval War College Press, 1994).

10. Francis A. Walker, *The Making of the Nation* (New York: Charles Scribner's Sons, 1895), 202–7, 293–97. In an effort to avoid becoming entangled in the Napoleonic wars, President Jefferson had declared an embargo on traffic with countries at war. Mostly because the costs of adherence were so high and the ability to enforce the embargo so low, the effort failed. Merchants did trade. Their ships were captured and their men impressed into the desperate Royal Navy, and the U.S. did enter the European war following precisely the course Jefferson had sought to avoid. A century later, Woodrow Wilson's analogous efforts were also similarly scorned and undermined by navalists.

11. For a partial list of journals, magazines, and newspapers that support these claims, see: *Army and Navy Journal*; *Atlantic Monthly*; *Century*; Chicago *Daily Tribune*; *Comfort*; Dawson (GA) *News*; *Frank Leslie's Illustrated Newspaper*; *Harper's Weekly* and *Monthly*; *Ladies Home Journal*; Laramie (WY) *Boomerang*; New Orleans *Daily Picayune*; New Haven *Evening Register*; New York *Herald*; New York *Times*; New York *World*; *North American Review*; *Peacemaker and Court of Arbitration*; *Public Service Review*; Puck; San Francisco *Chronicle*; *Scientific American*; *United Service Review*; Virginia City (NV) *Territorial Enterprise*; *World Affairs*; *Youth's Companion*.

12. New York *World Almanac* (New York: World Publishing, 1892), 251. For more on the importance of the yellow press, see Bartholomew Sparrow's chapter below.

13. For the Marine Corps in this period, see Allan R. Millett, *Semper Fidelis* (New York: Macmillan, 1980, 1991) and Jack Shulimson, *The Marine Corps' Search for A Mission, 1880–1898* (Lawrence: University Press of Kansas, 1993) which does not mention Sousa. For the band leader, see W. C. White, *A History of Military Music in America* (New York: Exposition Press, 1944). Or see Shulman, "From the Sea," *Reviews in American History* 23 (1995) 277–83.

14. Of trusts, Alfred D. Chandler, Jr. notes "By the 1880s these federations had become part of the normal way of doing business in most American industries," *The Visible Hand: The Managerial Revolution in American Business* (Cambridge: Harvard University Press, 1977), 316. Companies generally maintained this belief in economies of scale for at least a century. Edward Bellamy's 1888 futurist novel *Looking Backward* so strongly embraces the notion of economies of scale that Bellamy apparently believed they would eventually allow men and women to support themselves on a few hours of work each week. Only recently has American industry started intentionally to de-massify production, taking advantages of technological changes in information processing and hardware configuration to tailor production to specific needs while maintaining a high level of efficiency.

15. For the classical literature on professionalization, first see Samuel Huntington, *The Soldier and the State: The Theory and Politics of Civil-Military Relations* (Cambridge: Harvard University Press, 1957), particularly chapter 9 and Robert Wiebe, *The Search For Order* (New York: Hill and Wang, 1967).

16. Martin van Creveld, *Technology and War: From 2000 B.C. to the Present* (New York: Free Press, 1991), especially 285–310; see also van Creveld, *The Transformation of War* (New York: Free Press, 1989, 1991).

17. See Jon T. Sumida, *In Defence of Naval Supremacy: Finance, Technology, and British Naval Policy, 1889–1914* (Boston: Unwin Hyman, 1989) and *Inventing Grand Strategy and Teaching Command* (Baltimore: Johns Hopkins

University Press, 1997) and Nicholas A. Lambert, "The Influence of the Submarine Upon Naval Strategy, 1898–1914," Ph.D. dissertation, University of Cambridge, 1992 (to be published by the University of South Carolina Press). Also see Andrew Krepenevich, "From Cavalry to Computer: The Pattern of Military Revolutions," *The National Interest*, 37 (Fall 1994), 30–42, for an interesting summary and interpretation of revolutions in military affairs. See also Andrew J. Bacevich, "Preserving the Well-Bred Horse," *The National Interest*, 37 (Fall 1994), 43–49.

18. This case makes evident the problem with military-technical revolutions. Without proper understanding of the political and cultural context within which their technical solution is derived, enthusiasts assume that they have solved the strategic situation they face. In reality they have made a limited assessment of the problem and applied a technological system imperfectly. The shortcomings of this imperfect solution become evident only when the next war breaks out.

19. For memoirs see Daniel Ammen, *Old Navy and New* (Philadelphia: J. B. Lippincott, 1891); Charles E. Clark, *My Fifty Years in the Navy* (Boston: Little, Brown, 1917); George Dewey with Frederick Palmer, *Autobiography of George Dewey* (New York: Charles Scribner's Sons, 1913); A. M. Dewey, *The Life and Letters of Admiral Dewey* (New York: Woodfall Co., 1899); Robley D. Evans, *Sailor's Log* (New York: Appleton, 1901); Evans, *Admiral's Log* (New York: Appleton, 1908); Bradley A. Fiske, *From Midshipman to Rear Admiral* (New York: Century Co., 1919); Samuel R. Franklin, *Memories of a Rear Admiral* (New York: Harper and Brothers, 1898); Albert Gleaves, *Life and Letters of Stephen B. Luce* (New York: Putnam, 1925); Gleaves, *The Life of an American Sailor: Rear Admiral William Hemsley, United States Navy, from his Letters and Memoirs* (New York: George H. Doran, 1923); William Goode, *With Sampson through the War* (New York: Doubleday and McClure Company, 1899); John D. Hayes and John B. Hattendorf, eds., *The Writings of Stephen B. Luce* (Newport: Naval War College Press, 1975); Harris Laning, *An Admiral's Yarn: The Autobiography of Harris Laning*, edited and introduced by Mark Shulman (Newport, R.I.: Naval War College Press, forthcoming); John A. Lejeune, *Reminiscences of a Marine* (Philadelphia: Dorrance, 1930); Daniel P. Mannix, *The Old Navy* (New York: Macmillan, 1983); Alfred Thayer Mahan, *From Sail to Steam* (New York: Harper & Brothers, 1907); Hugh Rodman, *Yarns of a Kentucky Admiral* (Indianapolis: Bobbs-Merrill, 1928); Winfield Scott Schley, *The Greely Relief Expedition* (Washington, D.C.: Government Printing Office, 1887); Schley, *Forty-five Years Under the Flag* (New York: D. Appleton & Co., 1904); Seaton Schroeder, *My Half Century of Naval Service* (New York: D. Appleton & Co., 1922); Robert Seager II and D. Maguire Seager, *Letters and Papers of Alfred Thayer Mahan*

(Annapolis, Md.: Naval Institute Press, 1975); Thomas Selfridge, *Memoirs of Thomas O. Selfridge Jr.*, edited by Dudley Knox (New York: Putnam, 1924); Charles Steedman, *Memoir and Correspondence of Charles Steedman, Rear Admiral, United States Navy, with his Autobiography and Private Journals, 1811–1890*, edited by Amos Lawrence Mason (Cambridge: Riverside Press, 1912).

20. See Peter Trubowitz, "Building America's Blue-Water Navy: Putting Interests in their Place," a paper presented before the International Studies Association Annual Meeting, Acapulco, Mexico, March 1993; and Shulman, *Navalism*, chapters 6 and 7. Previous accounts of this transformation are included in: Benjamin Franklin Cooling III, *Benjamin Franklin Tracy: Father of the Modern American Fighting Navy* (Hamden, Conn.: Archon, 1973) and *War, Business, and American Society: Historical Perspectives on the Military-Industrial Complex* (New York: Kennikat Press, 1977); Walter Herrick, *American Naval Revolution* (Baton Rouge: Louisiana State University Press, 1966); Harold Sprout and Margaret Sprout, *The Rise of American Naval Power, 1776–1918* (Princeton: Princeton University Press, 1939, 1966); and for a dissenting opinion, George T. Davis, *A Navy Second to None: The Development of Modern American Naval Policy* (New York: Harcourt, Brace, 1940). And see Ronald Spector, "Triumph of Professional Ideology: The U.S. Navy in the 1890s," *In Peace and War: Interpretations of American Naval History, 1775–1984*, ed. Kenneth J. Hagan (Westport, Conn.: Greenwood, 1984) and *Professors of War: The Naval War College and the Development of the Naval Profession* (Newport, R.I.: Naval War College Press, 1977). For a more complete discussion of the historiography, see Hagan and Shulman, *Mahan Plus One Hundred*.

21. Herbert, a Democrat representing Mobile, AL was probably the leading navalist in his party. He served as Secretary of Navy in the second Cleveland administration, 1893–1897.

22. The Naval Expenditure Purchasing Index was created by George Modelski and William Thompson to compare relative growth and decline of the naval powers. It represents the average purchasing power of the year's appropriations. For a more detailed analysis of this materials see Shulman, *Navalism*, 139 *ff.* For methodology and comparative data, see Modelski and Thompson, *Sea Power and Global Politics, 1494–1993* (Seattle: University of Washington Press, 1988).

23. Some of the better works on the American peace movements include: Merle Curti, *The American Peace Crusade, 1815–1860* (New York: Octagon Books, 1929); *Peace or War: The American Struggle, 1636–1936* (New York: Norton, 1936); Roland Marchand, *The American Peace Movement* (Princeton: Princeton University Press, 1972); and David Sands Patterson, *Toward a Warless*

World: The Travail of the American Peace Movement 1887–1914 (Blooming-ton: University of Indiana Press, 1976).

24. Gaddis Smith, *Morality, Reason and Power: American Diplomacy in the Carter Years* (New York: Hill and Wang, 1986), 12–15; and see Bruce Cum-ings, "Revising Postrevisionism," *Diplomatic History* 17 (Fall 1993) 539–60. When considering the historical writing of the period of approximately 1963 to 1993, one could generally categorize the authors as "revisionist" or "realist." These terms are falling away quickly with post-Cold War evaluations.

25. Recent years have brought a bounty of surveys of the century that followed. See Baer's *One Hundred Years of Sea Power* (Stanford: Stanford University Press, 1994); Kenneth Hagan, *This People's Navy: The Making of American Sea Power* (New York: Free Press, 1991); Robert W. Love, Jr., *History of the United States Navy* (Harrisburg, Penn.: Stackpole, 1992); Stephen Howarth, *To Shining Sea: A History of the United State Navy, 1775–1991* (New York: Random House, 1991); Nathan Miller, *The U.S. Navy: An Illustrated History* (Annapolis, Md.: Naval Institute Press, 1977); and Robert O'Connell, *Sacred Vessels: The Cult of the Battleship and the Rise of the U.S. Navy* (Boulder, Colo.: Westview, 1991).

26. Quoted in *New York Times*, September 24, 1990.

Part III

Politics and the Electoral Connection

4 Geography and Strategy: The Politics of American Naval Expansion

Peter Trubowitz

Why does the United States find it so difficult to respond to international change? Why is the making of American security policy so conflict-prone? These old questions have been asked in one form or another since Alexis de Tocqueville wrote *Democracy in America*. From Tocqueville to Lippmann to Kennan, observers have argued that the policymaking process in the United States is poorly suited to the needs of a great power.[1] In contrast to other industrialized nations, where leaders often enjoy considerable latitude in setting strategic priorities and committing national resources, the American policymaking process is highly politicized and notoriously inefficient, making it extremely difficult for the nation's leaders to articulate a vision of the national interest that commands broad domestic support.[2] Questions of national security often assume a prominent role in national politics and provoke intense and bitter debate. One consequence is that the nation's ability to act strategically or purposefully in international affairs is compromised.

Scholars explain this shortcoming in two general ways. Some locate the source of the problem in America's political culture. They argue that, since the country's founding, Americans have held deeply divergent images of their nation is, or what it should be, and that these differences invariably give rise to profound disagreements over the purposes of American power and the authority to exercise it.[3] Scholars have described this tension in Americans' understandings of their place in the world in various ways: as

Hamiltonian versus Jeffersonian philosophies, realism versus idealism, power versus liberty, or pragmatism versus principle. From the view that emphasizes political culture, conflicts over security policy are essentially conflicts over America's identity. They surface during periods of international instability and crisis. It is then that the conflict between the imperatives of security (centralization, secrecy, and dispatch) and democracy (liberty, openness, and accountability) is most conspicuous.

A second explanation is institutional. It focuses on the structure of the American state and identifies the nation's fragmented political system as an obstacle to coherent and purposeful statecraft.[4] The "weakness" of the American state, manifest in the sharing of foreign policymaking powers between the White House and Congress, is considered to be, in Edwin Corwin's famous phrase, "an invitation to struggle" for control over the authority to make policy. The fact that presidents and members of Congress face different electorates—one national, the other local—compounds the problem by providing additional incentives to disagree.[5] Presidents are held accountable for the broad effect of policy choices. Individual congressmen generally are not. As a result, presidents must make decisions based on a national interest while members of Congress can respond to the needs of narrower, more particularistic interests. In short, the American Constitution invites conflict by dividing the authority to make security policy between the branches of government and by giving self-interested politicians who occupy different positions in the national government reason to compete for control over foreign policy.

This chapter offers an alternative way of thinking about American security policy and the difficulties leaders face when responding to international change. In contrast to accounts that grant primacy to national ideologies or institutions, the interpretation put forward here identifies America's *regional* diversity as the most important source of tension and conflict over security policy. I show that conflicts over the purposes of American power, as well as the constitutional authority to exercise it, are fundamentally conflicts over the distribution of wealth and power in American society among coalitions with divergent interests and claims on the central state's resources. They are regional in nature, and they grow out of the uneven nature of the nation's economic development and integration into the international economy. Different parts of the country have different stakes in how the national government responds to international challenges and opportunities because of differences in what they produce, where they look for markets, their level of technological development, and more generally, their position in the world economy. Domestic conflict over how to define America's "national interest" is the result.

The argument is developed by analyzing the debate over American naval expansionism in the 1890s. Sometimes viewed as an inevitable byproduct of America's rise as an economic power, the rise of the modern navy was actually a more protracted process marked by intense and bitter disputes and lasting well over a decade. Like so many of the debates over American security policy before and since, this fight broke down along regional lines.[6] At one end of the spectrum were politicians who represented areas—mostly in the industrial Northeast—that had the most to gain from a strategy of imperial expansion at the turn of the century. At the other end were political leaders from the agrarian South, a region that for its own economic and political reasons favored the status quo—a small coastal navy. These two regions clashed over the need for a battleship navy, and over the strategy of overseas expansion that naval development implied. This is because they occupied significantly different positions in the international and national economies. Debates that were expressed in terms of conflicting values, and that were played out at the national level, sprang from underlying conflicts of regional interest. In the 1890s, when America debated its place in the world, the geographic dimension of conflicts over the national interest was revealed in stark form.

One would not necessarily expect this to be the case. The late nineteenth century was the highwater mark of party politics in the United States. Parties were stronger and more cohesive than they are today, and thus one might expect national considerations to outweigh local ones in the minds of politicians, especially in dealing with issues of national defense. Indeed, most of the literature on the politics of national defense claims that elected officials' views on defense policy have never had much to do with whether (or how much) their districts or states benefit from military spending.[7] Whatever impact local interests have on politicians' views of domestic policy, ideological and partisan considerations are believed to determine their stance on national security. The 1890s provide a hard test not only for this argument but also for any argument that gives America's position in the world economy pride of place in the analysis. The national economy was then far less integrated into the international economy than it is today. If my argument holds for that era, then it should hold as well for America today—a time when one would expect political representatives to be more, not less, sensitive to the domestic consequences of the nation's foreign policies than they were in the past.

Regions, Politicians, and Strategy

Regionally based political competition and conflict is one of the most distinctive features of American politics. Frederick Jackson Turner first identified the significance of regionalism in the United States, and since then a large literature has developed on the sources of regional strife over national political decisions. A common theme in this literature is that regional political competition is rooted in the geographically uneven nature of economic growth and development.[8] In other industrialized countries, where political systems are also based on spatial representation, regional economic differentiation is often coterminus with ethnic or religious difference. While ethnic and religious difference is also an important feature of American politics, it is most conspicuous at the neighborhood and city level. At the regional level the absence of the kinds of cultural cleavages present in other nations has meant that regionalism is usually grounded in conflicts of economic interest.

Geographers identify a number of factors to explain the uneven nature of regional growth. Some emphasize geographic differences in resources, markets, or the costs of factors of production.[9] Others focus on regional variation in technological innovation or the organization of labor and production. In addition to analyzing factors internal to regions, geographers have also studied how interaction between intraregional factors and larger national and international processes shapes regional economic trajectories. There is also an important literature on the role that the federal government plays in shaping patterns of private investment and spending in the national economy and thus the possibilities for regional growth and development. Employing these approaches, geographers working on the United States have documented and analyzed sharp differences in regional economic structure.

These differences give rise to divergent interests which, in turn, can produce regional conflict. The spatially decentralized structure of political representation in the United States ensures that these regional differences find political expression at the national level, where the dispersal of decision-making power and competition between the national parties for regional electoral advantage magnifies the role of regional interests, economic needs, and political imperatives in shaping the national agenda. Institutional decentralization provides various channels for elected officials to levy claims on the federal government's resources, initiate or obstruct policy change, and build policy coalitions with political elites from other parts of the country through logrolling, vote-trading, ideological appeals, and the like. Regional political competition is the result. This is well understood by analysts who study the regional bases of political conflict over domestic policy matters. I argue that this is also true in the foreign policy domain.

Three main factors appear to be particularly relevant in shaping regional preferences about security policy.[10] The first is export dependence.[11] Regions that specialize in sectors that are export dependent are likely to favor policies that promote liberal, open, or free trade, and to be more willing to permit the market to control their trade flows.[12] Regions that are heavily dependent on the home market (or less well placed in global competition) are more likely to support active government intervention to shelter or protect their markets from foreign competitors. This is most obvious in the area of trade policy but, as I will show, the same considerations can influence regional preferences toward security policy. A second consideration has to do with effects of military spending on regional economies. Various locational factors (availability of skilled labor, industrial specialization, local tax structures, real estate prices, etc.) give some regions advantages as "sites" for military production, as well as for military bases and military fortifications.[13] Regions that stand to reap the largest rewards (i.e., jobs, profits, growth) from military spending are more likely to favor such federal outlays than those which are less "ideal" as defense-production locations.[14] Parts of the country that pay the "overhead costs" of an expensive national defense while receiving a disproportionately small share of the rewards are likely to see costly foreign policies in "guns-versus-butter" terms. A third consideration has to do with the terms of trade between regions. The goods produced by one region may provide the inputs into the production of commodities in other regions, either in the form of raw materials, capital goods, or labor costs. This sets the stage for conflict over terms of trade and the various institutional arrangements that serve to subsidize growth in one region at the expense of another. The classic example is the struggle between North and South over the protective tariff in the nineteenth century.

The concept of regional economic differentiation is a structural one. Regional economic differences give rise to divergent interests which shape, constrain, and influence the behavior of politicians. Yet to explain political struggles at the national level, structural features of the American economy must be linked to the decisions of politicians. I establish this link by making a simple assumption about political behavior: politicians are political entrepreneurs who for electoral reasons seek to secure benefits for "constituents" (voters, producers, and investors) in the form of jobs, markets, and revenue. Their responses to international challenges are shaped by their interests in promoting the fortunes of geographically defined constituencies.[15] Those who promote and support programmatic agendas for strategic adjustment do so for three broad reasons. First is their belief that policy reform will promote (or simply sustain) growth in the districts and states they represent. Second is their interest in generating and distributing (or maintaining) federal pork and patronage, thereby shoring up and expanding their political base of support. Third, politicians back programmatic agendas because they see broad policy platforms as ways of building political coalitions that enhance their power at the national level. The discussion that follows traces these dynamics as they were manifest in the struggle over strategic adjustment at the end of the nineteenth century.

The Struggle Over Naval Expansion

Few eras in American history have had a more profound impact on the nation's foreign policy, or enjoyed more attention by American diplomatic historians, than the 1890s. Having created a continental empire in the nineteenth century, Americans set their sights on more distant frontiers. As every textbook on American diplomatic history declares, in the 1890s the United States became a great power, breaking with its long-standing tradition of self-isolation and adopting a more assertive and vigorous role in world affairs. The American state began to actively promote economic activity overseas for the first time.[16] New government bureaus were created to encourage foreign trade and investment, and new policy tools were devised to give leaders more military and diplomatic leverage in their dealings with foreign states. America built a modern battleship navy, transformed the tariff from a passive instrument of protection into a bargaining tool for opening foreign markets, and seized foreign lands to extend the nation's strategic reach.

These policy initiatives were supplemented by others: the decision to rebuild the merchant marines, efforts to reform the spoils-based diplomatic corps, and the creation of a larger, more professional army.

The development of the modern Navy was arguably the most important strategic change initiated by American leaders in the 1890s. In a way that few actions could, the decision to begin building a battleship navy in 1890 signalled the nation's willingness to assume a more vigorous role in world affairs. In the quarter century that followed the Civil War, the Navy had distintegrated into what historian Walter LaFeber described as a "flotilla of deathtraps and defenseless antiques."[17] Most politicans in the 1870s had been preoccupied with other matters and had seen little need for anything other than light-draft gunboats and seagoing raiders. Even in the 1880s, when attitudes toward the Navy began to change and when Congress started to replace the nation's obsolete ironclad and wooden-ship fleet with new steel-hulled, steam-powered cruisers, there was little change in the Navy's primary missions: defending the coastline and protecting American commerce. The result was that at the end of the 1880s, the American Navy was still a third-rate power, slow in speed and short on firepower. It lagged far behind the great navies of Europe.

America did not begin to produce a world-class navy until 1890.[18] In that year, Congress broke new ground by authorizing the construction of the first three in a new fleet of battleships, equal in size and power to the best in the world, at the unprecedented cost of more than $3 million apiece. Secretary of the Navy Benjamin Franklin Tracy had set the stage for this departure in naval policy the year before. He deplored the nation's long-standing tradition of relying on light cruisers as the first line of defense, and insisted that only a fleet of heavily armored battleships capable of interdicting and destroying an enemy fleet of capital ships at sea could safeguard the nation's wealthy port cities and expanding overseas trade.[19] Echoing the views of a growing number of naval strategists, Secretary Tracy argued that the Navy's traditional missions were no longer sufficient to guarantee the nation's security. In the future, the best defense would be a good offense. What was needed were two new battleship fleets—one stationed in the Atlantic, the other based in the Pacific.

A vigorous proponent of expansion, Secretary Tracy set the Navy on a new course. The program to rebuild the Navy gained tremendous momentum during the 1890s. Over the course of the decade the Navy's share of the federal budget more than doubled, rising from $22 million in 1890 to

$56 million, with Congress authorizing on average at least one battleship per year. By 1905, it had doubled again. The shift toward a battleship navy was reflected in the Department of the Navy's budget: a growing share went for investment and capitalization, spurring demand for the output of America's shipyards and steel mills.[20] The results were dramatic. In 1890, the American Navy ranked twelfth among the navies of the world, behind Turkey and China. By the turn of the century, the United States had become a major naval power. It was now fourth in battleship strength and sixth in overall fleet size. America had developed a navy worthy of Secretary Tracy's ambitions: "The sea will be the future seat of empire. And we shall rule it as certainly as the sun doth rise."[21]

Strategic Adjustment: Necessity or Choice?

America had never pursued a military program of this magnitude in peacetime. Such a break with the nation's long-standing opposition to European-style military establishments would not have been possible without the active support of many naval enthusiasts in Congress. While successive Republican and Democratic administrations both favored developing a battleship navy, the program repeatedly encountered resistance. In the face of untiring opposition, those in favor of naval buildup found it necessary to compromise to win sufficient backing for naval appropriations. They pushed their radical agenda under the banner of "reform." At first, this meant presenting their case in ways that resonated with the Navy's traditional mission of coastal defense.[22] Naval expansionists stressed the danger of colonial encirclement and even the possibility of a British attack. Such arguments for strategic adjustment were dismissed by opponents who claimed that the country's geopolitical position made a large battleship navy superfluous. A small navy consisting of light cruisers and backed up by coastal fortifications, they insisted, would be more than adequate to guarantee American security for the foreseeable future.

The scope of the debate over naval expansion was soon broadened. Arguments about the threat facing America's seaports were subsumed by a more fundamental and pressing issue: commercial expansion. Drawing on the writings of Captain Alfred Thayer Mahan, whose influential book *The Influence of Sea Power upon History* pointed to a future marked by increasing rivalry among the Great Powers for overseas markets and colonies, naval expansionists linked sea power and commercial promotion.[23] Successful competition in the struggle for commercial supremacy would require a strong merchant marine which, in turn, would require adequate protection from foreign predators. Only a fleet of capital ships, they argued, could provide such protection for American ports and shipping. The key to all was, in Mahan's words, "command of the seas." Without control of the sea lanes in broad areas contiguous to the United States, American shipping would be at the mercy of the great powers. One member of Congress captured the essence of the argument: "Our future growth lies in the success of our commerce, and no great commerce has ever been built up without the assistance of a navy to protect the merchant marine and enforce the rights of merchants and traders."[24]

Those who believed that the American government should play an active role in opening foreign markets found the case for strategic adjustment irrefutable. Hard economic times in the 1870s and 1880s contributed to the perception that foreign markets were essential to American well-being. Overproduction was seen as the cause of these crises, and each one sent more and more farmers and manufacturers in search of new markets to sell their surplus goods.[25] The discontent and turmoil engendered by these economic downturns had no less an impact on America's lawmakers. They eyed foreign markets the way an earlier generation of politicians had looked to the national frontier: as a "safety valve" for economic and social problems. There was a growing conviction in the 1890s that continental expansion had reached an end, and this only underscored the sense of urgency that many felt about the "export solution." Many on Capitol Hill concluded that unless surplus manufactures and foodstuffs could be sold abroad, it would be impossible to break the cycle of "boom and bust" that had already produced so much economic hardship and social unrest.

Not everyone agreed that naval supremacy was the key to American commercial expansion. Many claimed that the relationship was a spurious one: Commercial advantage flowed to those who produced goods that were in demand. Why, opponents charged, should the United States rely on a navy to accomplish what could be achieved at much less expense to the taxpayer by a strategy of free and open trade? Foreign nations, they argued, were so dependent on trade with the United States that they had little incentive to harass American commerce or blockade the nation's ports. In a fiery speech on the House floor, the populist "Sockless" Jerry Simpson of Kansas mocked the navalists' arguments about a British blockade: "Every interest of Great

Britain," Simpson declared, "puts her under bonds to keep the peace with us. Why, sir, if Great Britain should throw her shells into any of our great cities—Boston, New York, or Philadelphia—she would in all human possibility destroy more property belonging to British subjects than to American subjects."[26] The real threat facing America was not foreign aggression but rather misguided government policies. A large and expensive steel-hulled navy might feather the nests of shipbuilders and steel producers, but it would do little to address the nation's most pressing economic and social problems: idleness, poverty, and hunger. Worse yet, a big naval establishment raised the spectre of European despotism.

Navalists invariably dismissed such arguments as misleading, and worse, short-sighted. Most argued that security knows no price: "The cost of building a navy casts no perceptible burden upon a country of our vast resources. It is the premium paid by the United States for the insurance of its acquired wealth and its growing industries. It is a cheap price to pay for safety."[27] Even in the midst of the depression years of the mid-1890s, naval expansionists saw little need to revise their judgment about the economic benefits of naval spending. Speaking for many others in the House and Senate, Senator Orville Platt of Connecticut reminded the Navy's detractors that "[c]ompared with other nations we are richer than any. Our national debt is less in proportion to our ability to pay it than that of any other nation. Our opportunity to raise money without seriously taxing the people is greater than the opportunity of any other Government. We would do well not to forget that the United States is rich and able to build such a navy as it requires."[28] As for the notion that a large navy was incompatible with the nation's republican ideals, naval advocates were quick to respond that security is the handmaiden of liberty.

Sectional Bases of the Conflict

In view of such rhetoric, it is not hard to see why some scholars view the debate over naval expansion in terms of competing judgements about what was strategically necessary and politically acceptable.[29] At what point would the need to establish an American presence on the high seas conflict with the nation's long-standing tradition of avoiding foreign entanglements? Did America's growing interest in overseas commerce require, ipso facto, the development of a battleship navy? At the same time, the debate involved

questions of institutional power and constitutional authority. Would the creation of a large peacetime naval establishment subvert America's constitutional order? Would military expansion create an "imperial presidency" and
sap the power of Congress? These themes did run through the debate over
the new Navy. What such accounts cannot adequately explain is why the
issue of naval expansion split the country along sectional lines. Like so many
issues in late-nineteenth century America, naval expansion divided the country along industrial-agrarian or core-periphery lines. On vote after vote in the
Congress, politicians from the North and South clashed over a wide array
of issues linked directly and indirectly to the issue of naval expansion.

Figure 4.1 summarizes the pattern of voting in Congress on naval expansion. The vast majority of the rollcall votes on the Navy during the decade
dealt directly with appropriations for naval buildup.[30] Those concerning the
price of battleship armor-plating spoke to the issue of naval expansion while
raising Populist concerns about "price-fixing" and more broadly, the power
of the Eastern "trusts." Support for the new navy was strongest in the Northeast throughout the decade, especially among congressmen from the New

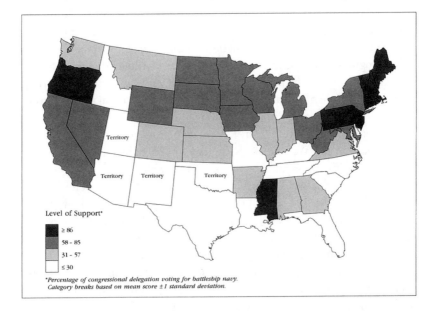

FIGURE 4.1 Support for Naval Buildup, 1890–1901

England and Middle Atlantic states.[31] This bloc of urban and coastal interests was opposed by one that was centered in the South.[32] The pattern of voting in the West is more mixed. Much of the region aligned with the Northeast in the fight over naval expansion. Western support for naval expansion was strongest along the Pacific Coast and in the upper Great Plains. Representatives from the lower Great Plains (Kansas, Missouri, Nebraska) and the Mountain West (Montana, Idaho, and Washington) were more likely to align with Southern lawmakers. Together, they waged a rearguard battle against the new navy, constantly searching for ways to slow the pace of warship construction.

The Northeast and Naval Buildup

An ambitious naval shipbuilding program served the interests of America's industrial heartland in three important ways.[33] First, a modern seagoing navy served the interests of industrialists and bankers who sought greater access to, and control over, markets in Latin America and Asia. These parts of the world were the focal points for America's growing trade in manufactured goods and direct overseas investment, as well as a focal point for Northern politicians looking for concrete ways to signal their commitment to solving the problem of domestic "overproduction" by opening new markets. Second, such a program promised high-wage jobs for the Northeast's workers, lucrative federal contracts for its shipyards and steel mills and gun foundaries, and business for many of its ancillary industries. Finally, naval expansionism proved to be enormously popular among the leaders of the Republican party.[34] Republicans used the Navy to create patronage, expand the party's political base in the Western states, and siphon off politically embarassing budgetary surpluses generated by the protective tariff.

It is clear that a larger, more powerful navy served the commercial interests of the Northeast. The late nineteenth century was an era of rapid growth in American exports, especially in manufactures.[35] More and more of the region's business community had a stake in overseas trade, and Latin America and Asia were areas of special interest to manufacturers.[36] The rapid growth in American exports of manufactures in the late nineteenth century was accompanied by a dramatic shift in the geographical pattern of trade: the share of American exports to Europe declined while exports to Latin America and Asia increased.[37] Before the Civil War, the bulk of America's export trade went to Europe, particularly Britain, which was the largest importer of American cotton and wheat. Europe continued to be the biggest export market for the United States in the postbellum period, but as America industrialized it sold an increasing proportion of its exports in North America, Asia, and South America. Manufactures, led by the sale of finished goods, accounted for the bulk of this trade with less developed nations.[38] Industrial exports to Europe also increased in the period but not nearly as sharply; raw materials continued to make up the single largest class of exports to the Old World.

Despite fears among European industrialists that the continent would be commercially "Americanized," it was becoming clear to some American economists that the real "commercial struggle between Europe and the United States centered not in the European market, but in the underdeveloped markets throughout the remainder of the world."[39] This view was shared by many congressional delegations from the Northeast who saw the acquisition of world class navy and overseas bases and coaling stations as a significant first step in winning this struggle. It is true, as Edward Rhodes points out, that industrialists overestimated America's need for markets in Asia and Latin America, but this is irrelevant. In the 1890s, the belief that the country would be running a permanent industrial surplus, well in excess of effective domestic purchasing power, was widespread in the Northern core. So was the notion that America's best trading partners were nations less developed than the United States:

> We know today that we can not successfully compete with England, France, and Germany in the manufacture of many goods that are sold in Europe. They have the markets there, and they hold the markets there. They are great manufacturing countries, and they can manufacture materials just as cheap if not cheaper than we can. They pay, as a general thing, less wages than we do, and their workmen and artisans labor more hours a day. We, too, are a great manufacturing country. We must find a market for our surplus goods. What we can not sell in Europe we must find a market for in Central and South America, in Asia and Africa, in the East Indies and the South Seas. Here is a new outlet and a great market. There is no doubt our merchants are aware of it and alive to its great advantages and rich opportunities.[40]

The New Navy served the interests of the Northeast in other ways as well. One need not attribute the naval buildup to the dominance of "big business" to recognize that shipbuilders and steel producers, among others, also had a considerable stake in the modernization of the Navy, and to see that these producers generally acted in ways that were consistent with their interests.[41] Shipyards clearly profited by the demand for a strong navy. Economists at the time went even further and gave the government credit for almost single-handedly creating the steel shipbuilding industry.[42] Steel producers also enjoyed handsome profits, and before the 1890s many were already "active lobbyists and propagandists for naval expansion."[43] At a time when rail and structural steel markets were poor, there was much to be said for a long-term, federally financed program involving large sums of money and little risk, even if it did involve some degree of government regulation.[44] Congress insisted that only domestic steel, which was more expensive than European steel, be used in the construction of American warships, and this fact only made the program more appealing to an industry that had massive capital requirements, and that therefore looked for ways to stabilize markets and allow for orderly debt amortization.

The geographic distribution of these industries all but guaranteed the Northeast the lion's share of the Navy's procurement budget. Nearly sixty percent of all naval contracts to shipbuilders during the decade went to Northeastern shipyards, almost three times the share that went to either Southern or Western shipbuilders. Similarly Northeastern steel producers won the bulk of the contracts for armor plating, gun forgings, steel projectiles, and other accoutrements of warship production.[45] The Middle Atlantic and Great Lakes regions accounted for more than four-fifths of the nation's iron and steel output, with major concentrations in Pittsburgh, Youngstown, Buffalo, Cleveland, Detroit, and Chicago. Even though one of the nation's newest and most prolific centers of steel production was located in Birmingham, Alabama, the South as a whole accounted for less than one-fifth of the nation's pig iron.

Northern politicians also had their own political reasons to push for a bigger navy. By increasing America's relative power in the international system, they would also be expanding their own power here at home. For starters, more federal money for shipbuilding meant more opportunities for patronage. Despite repeated calls to reform and clean up the navy yards located along the East and West coasts, the federal government's shipyards continued to function as patronage machines.[46] A reliable source of votes in good times, naval contracts were especially valuable during difficult years. As the naval historian Benjamin Franklin Cooling puts it, the new navy "was really a vast public works project designed to further stimulate the business community."[47] Such considerations were clearly at work during the depression-racked Cleveland years. Although he initially opposed Republican-style "pump priming," Cleveland relented in the face of mounting pressure, calling on Congress to fund the construction of three new battleships and twelve additional torpedo boats.[48] Meanwhile, naval appropriations could be tailored to serve the goals of coalition-building, especially with the West.

Winning the West

Navy contracts were one of many devices used by naval expansionists to weaken resistance in Congress, and to broaden the geographic bases of support for overseas expansion in the process. California, Oregon, and Washington were clearly the biggest beneficiaries of these efforts, and the Harrison administration's decision in 1890 to push for the development of two battleship fleets—one stationed in the Atlantic, the other based in the Pacific—was as political as it was strategic. Elected officials from these Western states had their own reasons for favoring naval buildup. Even before the 1890s, the Pacific Coast states reaped the largest share of the Navy's budget on a per capita basis.[49] Union Iron Works of California was one of the nation's largest shipbuilders, and there were many smaller ones stretching from San Pedro to Seattle.[50] Moreover, there was large carrying trade, and Latin America and Asia were areas of special interest to Western manufactures and merchants.[51] In the final analysis, that the Pacific Coast states aligned with the Northeast on the naval question is not surprising. By most measures of economic development, the states of the Far West had more in common with the Northeast than they did with the rest of the West.[52]

Naval expansion served even broader coalition-building strategies for Northern Republican leaders. The intertwined issues of naval reform, commercial expansion, and the bargaining tariff provided Republican leaders with the basis for an electoral alliance with politicians from the agrarian West. This was a clever strategy that not only dealt with the immediate problem of winning support for naval appropriations outside the Northeast, but also provided a means to counter the powerful and seductive appeal of agrarian populism. The populist insurgency posed a serious challenge to the

Republican party's dominance in the Great Plains and parts of the Mountain West.[53] The fear was not so much that the newly founded Populist party would replace the Republican party, but rather that the Democrats would be the beneficiaries of any three-way competition, picking up House and Senate seats. Republican leaders were looking for ways to forestall further party losses. Starting from the premise that low farm prices, one of the farmers' chief complaints, stemmed from overproduction, they argued that commercial expansion in Latin America and Asia was the remedy for the West's problems. Commercial expansion, in turn, required a more powerful navy. They were, Northern Republicans argued, two sides of the same coin:

> Not only respect for us depends upon the Navy, but commercial supremacy depends upon a proper and adequate naval force, a force proportioned to the magnitude of the country, to its resources, to its aims, to its purposes. No nation that does not maintain a navy can obtain commercial supremacy. Foreign trade flourishes where there is an adequate and proper navy to defend and protect it, or languishes where the navy is insufficient to protect and defend it. We of this country desire commercial supremacy."[54]

Many Westerners believed that the Republicans were up to no good. Some accused them of trying to divert the attention of the masses from the real problems—usurious interest rates, exorbitant prices for farm equipment, and greedy transportation rates. Others contended that the party of Lincoln was more interested in their votes than their well-being. Despite opposition, the Republican's "divide-and-conquer" strategy worked in Congress. Many lawmakers representing hard-pressed farmers in the trans-Mississippi West found the promise of new markets in Latin America and Asia hard to resist. Whatever suspicions Western farmers had about Eastern Republicans, they also held "deep misgivings" about their dependence on the British market and viewed the growing competition from other wheat exporters, most notably Russia, with alarm.[55] British efforts to reduce dependence on American wheat only seemed to confirm their worst fears about the future of the European market. As a result, by the mid-1880s Western farmers were already agitating for new markets in other parts of the world, particularly Latin America and Asia. Sensing the West's vulnerability on this issue, Republican leaders seized the opportunity, splitting the agrarians' ranks and winning crucial support for naval appropriations.

The Logic of Southern Opposition

Logic and circumstance led the plantation South, and its elected representatives, to view the issue of naval reform differently. While the Northeast could hope to realize gains from greater federal spending on the Navy, most of the agrarian South could not and, in fact, did not. In large part, of course, the regional bias in naval contracting was unavoidable: most defense-related sectors were located in the Northeast and the Pacific Coast. Compounding matters was the fact that Southern influence on the House and Senate Committees of Naval Affairs was quite limited.[56] On average, Southerners held only one-third of the seats on the House and Senate Committees.[57] Under such conditions, only those non-committee members who represented Southern constituencies around the navy yards in Norfolk and Pensacola, and perhaps the steel mills in Birmingham, could expect to win navy contracts and generate patronage. For most members from the Southern periphery there were few political rewards in supporting naval shipbuilding, regardless of which party occupied the White House, and perhaps more to the point, headed the Navy Department. If naval spending was warranted, and few were prepared to concede the point, it made more sense (i.e., politically) to limit the amount. One way to justify such limits was to stress the continuing viability of the more traditional and less costly naval missions of coastal defense and commerce protection.

Such considerations aside, the periphery did have a sizeable stake in foreign trade. And like their Northern and Western counterparts Southern politicians were very keen on expanding trade. In fact, the South was more dependent on foreign markets than either the Northeast or the West. Between 1870 and 1910, the region's exports averaged between 15 and 20 percent of its regional output (table 4.1). By contrast, the Northeast's ratio of exports to regional output was much closer to the national average of exports-to-GNP of between 5 and 6 percent.[58] Even the West, which specialized in the production of exportable foodstuffs such as wheat and cattle, was sending less than 10 percent of the regional gross product abroad by the 1890s. One important reason for the regional disparity was the high level of specialization and trade between the Northeast and the West.[59] Compared to the Northeast, the South was virtually self-sufficient in foodstuffs, which sharply limited its potential interregional links with the West.

Considering the South's heavy dependence on international markets, it is not surprising that Southern politicians were among the most vocal pro-

TABLE 4.1 Regional Export Dependence, 1870–1910

	Ratio of Regional Exports to Regional Output				
Region	1870	1880	1890	1900	1910
East	.017	.039	.023	.021	.024
Midwest	.029	.122	.036	.062	.034
South	.192	.264	.206	.146	.109
West	.166	.184	.059	.059	.032
United States	.049	.075	.049	.062	.039

SOURCES: Ratios were estimated from data in William K. Hutchinson, "Regional Exports to Foreign Countries: United States, 1870–1914," in *Research in Economic History*, ed. Paul Uselding (Greenwich, Conn., JAI Press, 1982), 7: 133–237. In the case of *Regional Exports*, estimates are based on those indicated in Hutchinson, Table 1, 145. *Regional Output* was calculated from Gross Regional Product Estimates of Hutchinson (200, table B.6), converting these from nominal to real terms using the GNP deflated index in Robert E. Lipsey, *Price and Quantity Trends in the Foreign Trade of the United States* (Princeton: Princeton University Press, 1963), 422–23, app. G, table G-8. Hutchinson's regional classification scheme differs from the one used here. In Hutchinson, states from the Great Lakes and Great Plains make up a separate category. In table above this category of states is referred to as Midwest. The "East" refers to the New England and Middle Atlantic regions.

ponents of expanded trade. For the South and its representatives, however, there was a key difference. Unlike the Northern core, the Southern periphery mainly produced raw materials (e.g., cotton, tobacco, minerals). True, the South's share of national manufacturing production had increased since the Civil War. But raw materials, especially cotton, were still the region's most important class of exports (table 4.2).[60] And markets for raw materials were not to be found in Latin America or Asia. Unlike the industrial Northeast or the agricultural West, the plantation South required industrial markets, either in the United States or Europe.[61] A large offensive navy might be useful in promoting expanded trade with non-industrialized countries that could import Northern manufactures, and even perhaps Western foodstuffs, but it held little promise for securing markets for Southern raw materials. Those markets already existed, and European demand for Southern

TABLE 4.2 Regional Exports by Commodity Type, 1870–1910 (percentage)

Region	Class[a]	Exports				
		1870	1880	1890	1900	1910
East	Materials	8.7	8.9	8.5	9.8	17.3
	Food	30.4	53.2	56.4	11.1	0.8
	Manufactures	60.9	37.9	35.2	79.2	79.9
Midwest	Materials	5.0	2.2	4.1	1.2	2.2
	Food	80.9	92.1	83.3	98.0	81.5
	Manufactures	14.2	5.6	12.6	0.9	16.4
South	Materials	98.5	86.4	89.8	81.5	85.6
	Food	1.0	11.9	9.2	15.1	9.0
	Manufactures	1.1	1.7	0.9	4.3	5.3
West	Materials	—	1.0	0.1	1.2	3.8
	Food	93.3	96.7	82.1	89.3	25.4
	Manufactures	6.7	3.7	17.8	10.1	70.7

SOURCES: Based on data in William K. Hutchinson, "Regional Exports of the United States to Foreign Countries: A Structural Analysis," in *Research in Economic History*, ed. Paul Uselding (Greenwich, Conn., JAI Press, 1986), 10: 131–54, 140, table 3. For each region and year the columns add to 100.0 percent except for rounding error. Hutchinson's regional classification scheme differs from the one used here. In Hutchinson, states from the Great Lakes and Great Plains make up a separate category. In table above this category of states is referred to as Midwest. The "East" refers to the New England and Middle Atlantic regions.

[a]The five standard commodity classes were organized as follows: materials (raw materials); food (crude and manufactured foods); manufactures (semi- and finished manufactures).

raw materials was strong at the time, accounting for almost 80 percent of Europe's cotton imports.

The Southern experience thus contradicted the notion that "trade follows the flag." A large and powerful navy was not required to guarantee access to overseas markets for the South. For this reason, many Southern lawmakers found arguments about the commercial value of a blue-water navy to be unpersuasive. One analyst puts the point this way: "While the Southerners were as interested in commercial expansion as other Congressmen, they doubted the need for a large naval establishment to implement commercial policy. Like Mahan, Southern Congressmen believed that commerce was the 'civilizing' factor that enabled the prosperous nations to help the unfortunate peoples of the world; unlike him, however, they were satisfied that commerce could perform this mission without the help of a new navy."[62] What was to be avoided were policies that might provoke or exacerbate tensions among industrial nations and thereby threaten American access to the great industrial markets of Europe. Southern politicians who stressed the dangers of naval arms races were well aware of the commercial issues at stake. For the South, a policy of free trade was the best way to promote regional prosperity.

Southern lawmakers were risk averse: they were more sensitive to possible losses than potential gains. To be sure, there were important exceptions like Congressman Hilary Herbert (D-AL) and Senator John Tyler Morgan (D-AL) who believed that commercial expansion in South America and Asia provided a key to curing the South's depressed, colonial condition. But these champions of Southern industry and overseas expansion were a distinct minority.[63] Most politicians saw whatever gains Southern industry could hope to reap through expanded trade in Latin American and the Pacific Basin as vastly outweighed by the needs of Southern agriculture. Old-line Democrats' attitudes toward naval expansion reflected this essential fact. Twenty-five years after the end of the Civil War, over two-thirds of the Southern labor force was still involved in agriculture, and most of these were engaged in the cultivation of cotton. Here lay the Democrats' core constitutency, not in the new urban, professional "business class" sprouting up in cities like Atlanta, Birmingham, and Charlotte.[64] Few Southern Democrats were prepared to compromise agriculture in the name of industrial progress, especially when such temporizing could open them to attack from Southern populists.

There was, however, a more immediate reason for Southern opposition to the development of a blue-water navy. To the extent that increased federal spending on the Navy could justify high tariff barriers, it was clearly damaging to Southern interests. The relationship between the Navy and the tariff was not lost on Southern politicians, many of whom viewed a vote for naval spending as a vote for high tariffs. The relationship between the naval expenditures and customs duties is not difficult to understand. Each year since the end of the Civil War, revenue generated by the tariff, the single largest source of federal revenue at the time, exceeded government expenditures.[65]

One of the continuing issues before Congress was how to deal with the politically embarrassing surplus. One option was to reduce it by cutting taxes, thereby lowering trade barriers to foreign goods. Southerners favored this option because it would lower the costs of goods that they consumed, and because a policy of free trade was the best way to promote regional prosperity. Another option was to maintain tariff barriers and increase federal spending. This alternative was much more attractive to Northern members of Congress.

The trade-offs were clear to political representatives from the Southern periphery. As William Oates of Alabama noted, it was hard not to view the naval buildup as anything other than "a well devised scheme to take advantage of that unsubstantial and transitory popular idea in favor of building a navy, to make a permanent disposition of the surplus revenue, and thereby dispense with the necessity of revising the tariff and reducing taxation."[66] He was not alone. Most of his Southern colleagues saw naval appropriations as a clever method for disposing of customs duties and redistributing wealth. In this regard, the naval build-up was not considered much different than the military pension, which also recycled revenues generated by the tariff.[67] Like the pension plan, the naval buildup disproportionately favored the Northeast. Disposing of government revenue by investing in the Navy was perhaps a more indirect and subtle means of redistributing wealth, but from the South's vantage point the underlying purpose was the same. The industrial core would prosper at the expense of the agrarian periphery.

Politicians from the Northeast vigorously denied any such motive. All parts of the country, they claimed, stood to benefit from efforts to improve the nation's ability to protect its coastlines and project power abroad. How, they asked, could farmers expect to sell their cotton and wheat overseas if America could not even protect its coastlines? Responding to criticisms from congressmen from agrarian states, William G. McAdoo (D-NJ), the future Assistant Secretary of the Navy, observed: "One month of blockade of our ports on the seacoast and you would burn more corn in Kansas than you now do. . . . One of the vessels thundering from her iron sides is defending the humblest homes out on the prairies in Indiana, the great cities in the Mississippi Valley, and the miners upon the Pacific coast just as much as she is the cities upon the Atlantic."[68] Naval enthusiasts warned that playing to divisive regional interests might be good politics, but it was damaging to the national interest. Sensing the danger and leaving nothing to chance, navalists called on their colleagues to take the high road and refrain from playing the sectional card. Paraphrasing Daniel Webster, Henry Cabot Lodge urged members to remember that in matters of state "all sectionalism ought to cease at the water's edge."[69] Such appeals may have struck a responsive chord in some quarters, but for those who opposed the naval buildup it was nothing more than self-serving rhetoric. One section's gain was another's loss:

> It is well to remember, that the sums of money Congress is called upon to appropriate for these purposes will be drawn from our people by excessive and exhaustive taxation, taxation not necessary for the national defense, and will be expended in a limited section of our country, a section said to be prosperous, drowning in the fruits of the labor of other sections of the Union for the local benefit of the favored section, and this, while the industries of the greater portion of our country, the great agricultural interests, are fearfully depressed.[70]

Conclusion

The modern American navy was forged in the crucible of regional political struggle. Often depicted as a contest between competing visions of America's role in the world, the conflict over naval reform was also a conflict of interests. The stakes were high. As countless historians have argued, the foreign policy choices that politicians faced at the end of the nineteenth century were also choices about how to restore domestic prosperity and social stability in the midst of what was then considered America's greatest depression. These choices entailed changes in the locus and scope of political authority at the federal level, and thus promised to alter the prevailing balance of power in the polity at large. More obviously, competing visions of the national interest carried with them different prescriptions for using the taxing, spending, and investment powers of the federal government. They implied choices about which overseas markets to pursue, which sectors of the economy to subsidize, and about whose blood and treasure should be invested in pursuit of these ends. Who wins? Who pays? These were the fundamental questions that divided the nation at the end of the nineteenth century.

The debate over the Navy was thus part of a larger struggle over whether the federal government should play a more active role in promoting American commercial interests overseas. Devising a more active role for government raised difficulties. The problem was not only that many Americans remained wedded to laissez-faire liberalism or feared that a more active foreign policy would mean a more powerful presidency. The more pressing concern was who would benefit from the adoption of a more activist, neo-mercantile strategy. The answer to this question did not turn simply on who won the naval contracts. Elected officials viewed the issue of military spending against a larger political canvass. The issue of naval reform was debated in terms of its impact on each region's overseas commercial interests and on postbellum political arrangements like the protective tariff that continued to make the agrarian South a "colony" of the industrial Northeast.

This approach to explaining conflict over American foreign policy contrasts sharply with cultural and institutional explanations. Those who favor cultural or institutional explanations must explain away the fact that where politicians' stand on questions of foreign policy is shaped by interests—their own, as well as those of the individuals and groups they represent. This is plainly evident in the case at hand. Politicians who championed a blue-water navy came from parts of the country that had the most to gain from an expansionist or imperialist foreign policy and the centralization of power that would accompany it. Those who remained wedded to the liberal or Jeffersonian ideal of a small brown-water navy and expressed fears about the "excessive growth of the state" were the ones who knew they would have little control over, and derive little benefit from, the strong state. Ideas were grounded in interests, and institutional conflict between the executive and legislative branches (and the Democratic and Republican parties) reflected patterns of competition that were grounded in deeper and broader societal conflicts.

Explanations of American foreign policy that rest on ideas and institutions confuse symptoms with causes. Each approach is handicapped by its view of politicians. Cultural explanations view America's elected officials as though they were little more than surrogates of the Founding Fathers: poor substitutes to be sure, but substitutes nonetheless. Politicians are reduced to ideas, and politics is reduced to the clash of ideas. This is a very apolitical view of politics. Politicians may have strongly held beliefs but they also have interests. For them, ideas are also political resources: instruments for mobilizing voters, building coalitions, and translating interests into foreign policy. When naval enthusiasts like Republican Henry Cabot Lodge waxed Hamiltonian, linking naval expansion to national greatness, they were also playing politics, searching for ways to divide Democrats along sectional lines and strengthen the party's control over the machinery of national government.

Many institutionalists recognize that there is a strategic dimension to politics. They see political leaders, executives as well as legislators, as strategic actors who are self-interested. Politicians seek power, influence, and approbation (votes) first; matters of principle come second. The problem with this view is not that it focuses on institutions per se, or that it insists that presidents and congressmen seek to protect and expand their institutional prerogatives and resources. Analysis of institutions is necessary; assumptions about political self-interest are sensible. The trouble with this view of American foreign policy is that it strips away the larger socioeconomic context within which fights over institutional prerogative are played out. Institutionalists flesh out the "agents" that culturalists caricature, but like culturalists, their conception of "structure" is narrow and insufficiently contextualized. In the 1890s, politicians were constrained by the harsh realities of economics. Their views about naval expansion and more generally, the national interest reflected this essential but often disregarded fact.

The analysis of America foreign policymaking at the end of the nineteenth century also tells us something about the limits of more traditional Realist explanations of strategic adjustment. Those accounts give pride of place to the "external" environment in explaining strategic change. They argue that America did not so much seek empire at the end of the nineteenth century as have empire thrust upon it.[71] For much of its history, the United States had lived in "splendid isolation," free of internal discord and unfettered by the miseries of European strife. But by the late nineteenth century the geopolitical conditions that assured American safety in the past—geographical isolation, British naval power, and the balance of power in Europe—were rapidly disappearing. "The era which had seen the new world fattening on the follies of the old," writes British historian John A. S. Grenville, "was coming to an end; soon the follies of the old world impinged on the peace and prosperity of the new."[72] In the traditional geopolitical account, the United States, no longer able to assume the safety of the Western Hemisphere, was forced to respond by developing new means to deal with the new external realities. America adjusted, reluctantly and with periodic lapses, but it adjusted all the same.

Such accounts remind us of the importance of the international environment in explaining strategic change. Where Realists go astray is in assuming that the internal consequences of international forces are spatially uniform. They are not, especially in countries as regionally diverse as the United States. In the 1890s, as in other eras, uneven growth meant that the implications of external developments varied internally within the United States. One region's strategic imperative was another's economic albatross. For Northern industrialists and Southern cotton growers in the late nineteenth century, for example, the decline of British hegemony and the rise of imperial rivalry meant very different things: for the former, it opened possibilities for commercial expansion; for the latter it threatened an already-weakened liberal trading order on which the South was vitally dependent. The point is this: the implications of changes in the external environment are indeterminate when it comes to explaining grand strategy. International affects vary regionally, and must be translated into policy via a complex and competitive political process.

During periods of transition in American security policy like today, this indeterminacy is conspicuous. It is manifest in bitter domestic struggles over policy and, at a deeper level, in conflicts over the very meaning of "the national interest." Because Realists cast their analysis at the national level, and miss crucial geographic variations in the effects of external forces, they cannot explain how changes on "the outside" produce big changes on "the inside." They assume what needs to be shown: why one view of how America should respond to changing international conditions and circumstances triumphs over another. Without a model that shows how conflicts over the meaning of international trends and events are mediated politically, they cannot account for what they purport to explain: programmatic changes in strategy. In the final analysis, it is the realities of power inside a country, not the distribution of power in the international system, that determine the course of the nation's grand strategy. In the 1890s, it was Northerners' ability to prevail in Washington that produced a mighty blue-water navy—without this Captain Mahan's ideas about American naval mastery might well have gathered dust on the shelves.

Acknowledgment

I wish to thank Catherine Boone, Lynn Eden, Emily Goldman, Timothy McKeown, Edward Rhodes, and Mark Shulman for their comments and suggestions.

Notes

1. Alexis de Tocqueville, *Democracy in America*, 2 vols. (New York: Alfred Knopf, 1945); Walter Lippmann, *The Public Philosophy* (Boston: Little, Brown, 1955); and George F. Kennan, *The Cloud of Danger: Current Realities of American Foreign Policy* (Boston: Little, Brown, 1977). For a general overview of this and related literature see Miroslav Nincic, *Democracy and Foreign Policy: The Fallacy of Political Realism* (New York: Columbia University Press, 1992), 1–24.

2. The standard references on the consequences for American diplomacy are Hans J. Morgenthau, *In Defense of the National Interest* (New York: Alfred Knopf, 1951); Henry Kissinger, *The Necessity for Choice: Prospects of American Foreign Policy* (New York: Harper and Row, 1960); George F. Kennan, *American Diplomacy: 1900–1950* (Chicago: University of Chicago Press, 1950); and Stanley Hoffmann, *Gulliver's Troubles, or the Setting of American Foreign Policy* (New York: McGraw-Hill, 1968); For a contrary view, see Kenneth N. Waltz, *Foreign Policy and Democratic Politics: The American and British Experience* (Boston: Little, Brown, 1967).

3. This formulation is best expressed in Felix Gilbert's classic *To the Farewell Address: Ideas of Early American Foreign Policy* (Princeton: Princeton University Press, 1961). See also Samuel Huntington, *American Politics: The Promise of Disharmony* (Cambridge: Harvard University Press, 1981); Robert A. Isaak, *American Democracy and World Power* (New York: St. Martin's Press, 1977); Walter A. McDougall, *Promised Land, Crusader State: The American Encounter with the World Since 1776* (Boston: Houghton Mifflin, 1997); Robert Osgood, *Ideals and Self-Interest in America's Foreign Relations* (Chicago: University of Chicago Press, 1953); Paul Seabury, *Power, Freedom, and Diplomacy: The Foreign Policy of the United States* (New York: Random House, 1963); and Robert Strausz-Hupé, *Democracy and American Foreign Policy: Reflections on the Legacy of Alexis de Tocqueville* (New Brunswick, N.J.: Transaction, 1995). See also the chapters by Edward Rhodes and Mark Shulman in this volume.

4. Edwin Corwin's *The President's Control of Foreign Relations* (Princeton: Princeton University Press, 1917) is the touchstone here. See also Louis Henkin, *Foreign Affairs and the Constitution* (New York: Norton, 1972); George C. Edwards, III and Wallace Earl Walker, eds, *National Security and the U.S. Constitution: The Impact of the Political System* (Baltimore: Johns Hopkins University Press, 1988); Harold Hongju Koh, *The National Security Constitution: Sharing Power After the Iran-Contra Affair* (New Haven: Yale University Press, 1954); and Theodore J. Lowi, *The End of Liberalism: The Second Republic of the United States* (New York: Norton, 1969). For a good discussion

of the relationship between American institutions and American strategy in the current period, see Aaron Friedberg, "Is the United States Capable of Acting Strategically?," *The Washington Quarterly* 14 (Winter 1991), 5–23.

5. On this distinction, and its impact on foreign policymaking, see Stephen D. Krasner, *Defending the National Interest: Raw Materials Investments and U.S. Foreign Policy* (Princeton: Princeton University Press, 1978), 63–64; David A. Lake, *Power, Protection, and Free Trade: International Sources of U.S. Commercial Strategy, 1887–1939* (Ithaca: Cornell University Press, 1988), 69–72; and Jack Snyder, *Myths of Empire: Domestic Politics and International Ambition* (Ithaca: Cornell University Press, 1991), 51.

6. See Peter Trubowitz, *Defining the National Interest: Conflict and Change in American Foreign Policy* (Chicago: University of Chicago Press, 1998).

7. See, for example, Robert A. Bernstein and William A. Anthony, "The ABM Issue in the Senate, 1968–1970: The Importance of Ideology," *American Political Science Review*, 68 (September 1974), 1198–1206; James Clotfelter, "Senate Voting and Constituency Stake in Defense Spending," *Journal of Politics*, 32 (November 1970), 979–83; James M. Lindsay, "Parochialism, Policy, and Constituency Constraints: Congressional Voting on Strategic Weapons Systems," *American Journal of Political Science*, 34 (November 1990), 936–60; and Kenneth R. Mayer, *The Political Economy of Defense Contracting* (New Haven: Yale University Press, 1991).

8. See John Agnew, *The United States in the World-Economy: A Regional Geography* (Cambridge: Cambridge University Press, 1987); Ann Markusen, *Regions: The Economics and Politics of Territory* (Totowa, N.J.: Rowman & Littlefield, 1987); and Richard Bensel, *Sectionalism and American Political Development, 1880–1980* (Madison: University of Wisconsin Press, 1984).

9. For a discussion of the various approaches see Michael J. Healey and Brian W. Ilbery, *Location and Change: Perspectives on Economic Geography* (Oxford: Oxford University Press, 1990).

10. For a more extensive discussion see Trubowitz, *Defining the National Interest*, pp. 13–18.

11. Export dependence refers to the net balance of regional exports to regional imports, as well as to the relative importance of these exports vis-a-vis total regional production. Thus, a region's export dependence measures its sensitivity to reductions in regional sales abroad.

12. The logic here is similar to that developed in sectorally-based models of foreign economic policy. See, for example, Peter Gourevitch, *Politics in Hard Times: Comparative Responses to International Economic Crises* (Ithaca: Cornell University Press, 1986), especially 55–60; Jeffry A. Frieden, "Sectoral Conflict and U.S. Foreign Economic Policy, 1914–1940," *International Organization* 42 (Winter 1988), 59–90; and Thomas Ferguson, "From Normalcy

to New Deal: Industrial Structure, Party Competition, and American Public Policy in the Great Depression," *International Organization* 38 (Winter 1984), 41–94.

13. See Ann Markusen, Peter Hall, Scott Campbell, and Sabina Deitrick, *The Rise of the Gunbelt: The Military Remapping of Industrial America* (New York: Oxford University Press, 1991) and Brendan O hUallacháin, "Regional and Technological Implications of the Recent Buildup in American Defense Spending, *Annals of the Association of American Geographers* 77 (Spring 1987), 208–23.

14. On this point see the discussion and analysis in Peter Trubowitz and Brian Roberts, "Regional Interests and the Reagan Military Buildup," *Regional Studies* 26 (October 1992), 555–67. See also Ben Baack and Edward John Ray, "The Political Economy of the Origins of the Military-Industrial Complex in the United States," *Journal of Economic History* 45 (June 1985), 369–75.

15. Politicians, of course, have other goals, such as achieving political influence and making "good" foreign policy. Re-election, however, is a necessary precondition for pursuing these other goals. On this point see David Mayhew, *Congress: The Electoral Connection* (New Haven: Yale University Press, 1974).

16. On the changing role of the national government in foreign affairs during the 1890s, see Robert Wiebe, *The Search for Order, 1877–1920* (New York: Hill and Wang, 1967); Emily S. Rosenberg, *Spreading the American Dream: American Economic and Cultural Expansion: 1890–1945* (New York: Hill and Wang, 1982); and Robert L. Beisner, *From the Old Diplomacy to the New, 1865–1900* (Arlington Heights, Ill: Harlan Davidson, 1986).

17. *The New Empire: An Interpretation of American Expansion, 1860–1898* (Ithaca: Cornell University Press, 1963), 58.

18. Historians generally regard 1890 as the "pivotal" or "benchmark" year in the development of the modern American navy. On the distinction between the navy of the 1880s and 1890s see George W. Baer, *One Hundred Years of Sea Power: The U.S. Navy, 1890–1990* (Stanford: Stanford University Press, 1994), 1–2, 9–26; Robert L. O'Connell, *The Cult of the Battleship and the Rise of the U.S. Navy* (Boulder, Colo.: Westview, 1991), 60–71; Benjamin Franklin Cooling, *Gray Steel and Blue Water Navy: The Formative Years of America's Military-Industrial Complex, 1881–1917* (Hamden, Conn.: Archon Books, 1979); and Harold Sprout and Margaret Sprout, *The Rise of American Naval Power, 1776–1918* (Princeton: Princeton University Press, 1939), 213.

19. Lightly armored cruisers were "useful in deterring commercial states from aggression," but they did not, the Secretary argued, "constitute a fighting force." To wage "even a defensive war with any hope of success," he continued, "we must have armored battleships." What was needed was a fleet "able to

divert an enemy's force from our coast by threatening his own, for a war, though defensive in priciple, may be conducted most effectively by being offensive in its operations." See *Annual Report of the Secretary of the Navy, 1889*, 51st Cong. 1 Sess., H. Ex. Doc. No. 1, Pt. III. The Secretary's report was premised on the notion that the very character of naval warfare was undergoing a "seachange," and that in the near future only seagoing, capital-ships would provide a credible deterrent to foreign pressure and aggression. Along these lines, the report also marked a significant change in how naval requirements were to be determined in the future. They would be based on comparisons of relative strength with selected foreign navies. On the significance of Secretary Tracy's report see Benjamin Franklin Cooling, *Benjamin Franklin Tracy: Father of the Modern American Fighting Navy* (Hamden, Conn.: Archon Books, 1973), 75–78 and Walter R. Herrick, Jr., *The American Naval Revolution* (Baton Rouge: Lousiana State University Press, 1966), 54–68.

20. As a share of the total naval budget, the procurement of steel ships rose from a little over 13 percent in 1885 to 35 percent in 1895. By 1905, roughly 39 percent of the Navy's annual budget was spent on the construction of new steel ships. By comparison, military pay's share of the naval budget dropped from 43 percent in 1885 to just over 26 percent in 1895. By 1905, military pay accounted for a little less than 17 percent of the Navy's budget. See Ben Baack and Edward John Ray, "Special Interests and the Nineteenth-Century Roots of the U.S. Military-Industrial Complex," *Research in Economic History*, ed. Paul Uselding, Vol. 11 (Greenwich, Conn.: JAI Press, 1988), 153–69, 156.

21. Secretary Tracy quoted in LaFeber, *New Empire*, 127.

22. On the initial debate over the relative advantages of an offensive battleship and coastal defense navy see *Congressional Record*, 51st Cong., 1st sess., 1890, 21, pt. 4, 3161–72, 3216–23, and 3256–74.

23. For a discussion of Mahan's ideas and their impact see Baer, *One Hundred Years of Sea Power*, 1–2, 9–33; LaFeber, *New Empire*, 85–89; and Sprout and Sprout, *Rise of American Naval Power*, 202–22.

24. Representative Thomas A. E. Weadock of Michigan, *Congressional Record*, 53rd Cong., 3d sess., 1895, 27, pt. 3, 2259.

25. There is a large literature on the "overproduction thesis" and its impact on American politics at the end of the nineteenth century. See LaFeber, *New Empire*; Thomas J. McCormick, *China Market: America's Quest for Informal Empire, 1893–1901* (Chicago: Quadrangle Books, 1967); William Appleman Williams, *The Roots of the Modern American Empire: A Study of the Growth and Shaping of Social Consciousness in a Marketplace Society* (New York: Random House, 1969); and James Livingston, *Origins of the Federal*

Reserve System: Money, Class, and Corporate Capitalism, 1890–1913 (Ithaca: Cornell University Press, 1986).

26. *Congressional Record*, 53rd Cong., 3d sess., 1895, 27, pt. 3, 2242.

27. Secretary of the Navy Benjamin Franklin Tracy, *Congressional Record*, 51st Cong., 1st sess., 1891, 21, pt. 11, app., 3171.

28. Ibid., 3045.

29. See, for example, the chapters by Edward Rhodes and Mark Shulman in this volume. See also Lance Buhl, "Maintaining 'An American Navy,' 1865–1889," *In Peace and War: Interpretations of American Naval History, 1775–1984*, ed., Kenneth J. Hagan (Westport, Conn.: Greenwood, 1984), 145–73 and Allen R. Millett and Peter Maslowski, *For the Common Defense: A Military History of the United States* (New York: Free Press, 1984), 233–66.

30. Principal components analysis was used to construct an index or scale of state support for naval buildup. Only votes that loaded on the first component (i.e., where the loading was greater than 0.60) were used to construct the voting support scale. (A total of 18 votes made the cutoff.) One vote was then selected to define support for the naval buildup. The direction of every other roll call vote was determined by its sign of correlation with this roll call. The position of each representative on the votes in the analysis was then identified and a mean support score was calculated for the representatives for each state. Following convention, paired votes and announced positions were treated as formal votes. Territories that were not already incorporated as states by 1890 are not included in the analysis.

31. The Northeast refers to states in New England, the Middle Atlantic, and the Great Lakes areas: Connecticut, Delaware, Illinois, Indiana, Maine, Maryland, Massachusetts, Michigan, New Hampshire, New Jersey, New York, Ohio, Pennsylvania, Rhode Island, Vermont, and Wisconsin. The South includes states from the Southeast and Southwest: Alabama, Arkansas, Florida, Georgia, Kentucky, Louisiana, Mississippi, North Carolina, South Carolina, Tennessee, Texas, Virginia, and West Virginia. The West refers to states from the Great Plains, Mountain West, and Pacific Coast: California, Colorado, Idaho, Iowa, Kansas, Minnesota, Missouri, Montana, Oregon, Nebraska, Nevada, North Dakota, South Dakota, Washington, and Wyoming.

32. The mean for Northeastern and Southern states is 78.8 and 33.1 percent respectively.

33. Much of the following discussion is derived from Trubowitz, *Defining the National Interest*.

34. Edward Rhodes argues in this volume that Republicans before 1890 opposed naval expansion. The voting record in Congress suggests otherwise. While there were certainly exceptions, the vast majority of Republicans favored increased spending on the Navy as early as 1883. See Baack and Ray, "The

Political Economy of the Origins of the Military-Industrial Complex in the United States."

35. Between 1865 and 1898, exports expanded from $281 million to roughly $1,231 million, making America the third greatest exporter in the world behind Britain and Germany. While most of this increase was due to the steady expansion of agricultural production, by the late 1890s manufactures accounted for fully 35 percent of the country's export trade. U.S. Bureau of the Census, *Historical Statistics of the United States, Colonial Times to 1970*, 2 vols. (Washington, D.C.: GPO, 1975) Series U 213–224.

36. For a discussion of the commercial preferences of the American business community during this period see David Healy, *US Expansionism: The Imperialist Urge in the 1890s* (Madison: University of Wisconsin Press, 1970), 159–77. More generally, see William H. Becker, *The Dynamics of Business-Government Relations: Industry and Exports, 1893–1921* (Chicago: University of Chicago, 1982).

37. On this point, and its relationship to the naval buildup, see Baack and Ray, "Special Interests and the Nineteenth-Century Roots of the U.S. Military-Industrial Complex," 162.

38. On the changing regional composition of American trade see Emory R. Johnson, T.W. Van Metre, G.G. Huebner, and D.S.Hanchett, *History of Domestic and Foreign Commerce of the United States*, vol. 2 (New York: Burt Franklin, 1915), 64–97. See also Matthew Simon and David Novack, "Some Dimensions of the American Commercial Invasion of Europe, 1871–1914: An Introductory Essay," *Journal of Economic History* 24 (December 1964), 591–605.

39. See Johnson, et al., *History of Domestic and Foreign Commerce of the United States*, 90.

40. Representative William Sulzer (D-NY), *Congressional Record*, 55th Cong., 2d sess., 1898, 31, pt. 6, 5905.

41. This is a prominent theme in Benjamin Franklin Cooling's account of the steel industry and its role in the naval buildup in *Gray Steel*.

42. J.F. Crowell, "Shipping Industry of the United States; its Relation to the Foreign Trade," in *Monthly Summary of Commerce and Finance of the United States* (Washington, D.C.: GPO, 1901), 1373–1411.

43. Sprout and Sprout, *Rise of American Naval Power*, 194. See also Walter LaFeber, *The American Search for Opportunity, 1865–1913* (Cambridge: Cambridge University Press, 1993), 31–36.

44. The value of heavily armored battleships was certainly not lost on Andrew Carnegie, the voracious Captain of Industry, who candidly observed, "there may be millions for us in armor." Cited in Cooling, *Benjamin Franklin Tracy*, 92. The irony here is that Carnegie was a vocal opponent of imperialist ex-

pansion. Apparently, he mastered the distinction between the "need" to develop tools of war and decisions to actually use them.

45. See Cooling, *Gray Steel*, Tables 5, 6, and 9. Estimates for regional steel output (measured in pig iron) are from Harvey S. Perloff, Edgar S. Dunn, Jr., Eric E. Lampard, Richard F. Muth, *Regions, Resources, and Economic Growth* (Baltimore: Johns Hopkins University Press, 1960), 210.

46. For a discussion of this issue, see Cooling, *Benjamin Franklin Tracy*, 102–24.

47. Cooling, *Gray Steel*, 88.

48. For a discussion of the impact of the depression on the Cleveland administration, and the naval buildup more generally, see LaFeber, *New Empire*, 231–35. See also Cooling, *Gray Steel*, 120–21.

49. See John Legler, *Regional Distribution of Federal Receipts and Expenditures in the Nineteenth Century: A Quantitative Study* (New York: Arno, 1977), Table 24, 77.

50. J.F. Crowell, "Shipping Industry of the United States," 1411.

51. On Western attitudes toward overseas commerce see Salvatore Prisco III, *John Barrett, Progressive Era Diplomat: A Study of a Commercial Expansionist, 1987–1920* (Tuscaloosa: University of Alabama Press, 1973), 13–30.

52. While these states were still major raw materials producers, by 1870 they had also achieved the greatest concentration of manufacturing-service activities outside the Northeast. For supporting data see Perloff, et al., *Regions, Resources, and Economic Growth*, 170–90, especially 182–84.

53. The following discussion owes much to William Appleman William's cogent analysis. See his *The Roots of the Modern American Empire*, 319–37.

54. Senator Orville Platt (R-CT), *Congressional Record*, 53rd Cong., 3d sess., 1895, 27, pt. 4, 3045.

55. On Western attitudes toward the British market see Morton Rothstein, "America in the International Rivalry for the British Wheat Market, 1860–1914," *Mississippi Valley Historical Review* 47 (December 1960), 401–18.

56. An obvious exception here was Congressmen Hilary Herbert of Alabama who was Chairman of Naval Affairs Committee in the early 1890s. A convert to Secretary Tracy's naval reform program, Herbert went on to assume the position of Secretary of the Navy during the Cleveland administration. As Secretary, Herbert used his considerable influence to move a somewhat reluctant Cleveland to pursue the program begun by the Harrison administration. For an account of Secretary Herbert's tenure in office see Herrick, *The American Naval Revolution*, 153–92.

57. Computed by author from *Congressional Directory*, selected years.

58. William K. Hutchinson, "Regional Exports to Foreign Countries: United States, 1870–1914," in *Research in Economic History*, ed. P. Uselding, (Greenwich, Conn: JAI Press, 1982), 7: 133–237, 156.

59. David F. Good, "Uneven Development in the Nineteenth Century: A Comparison of the Habsburg Empire and the United States," *Journal of Economic History* 96 (March 1986), 147.

60. William K. Hutchinson estimates that cotton accounted for roughly 50 percent of Southern exports in the late nineteenth century. See his "Regional Exports to Foreign Countries," 155.

61. On the South's dependence on European markets see Morton Rothstein, "The New South and the International Economy," *Agricultural History* 57 (October 1983), 385–402.

62. Thomas Coode, "Southern Congressmen and the American Naval Revolution, 1880–1889," *Alabama Historical Quarterly* 30 (Fall–Winter 1968), 108–09.

63. As Joseph Fry repeatedly points out in his excellent biography of John Tyler Morgan, Chairman of the Senate Foreign Affairs Committee and a champion of imperialism, such views were exceptional in the South, lying outside the mainstream of Southern opinion. See his *John Tyler Morgan and the Search for Southern Autonomy* (Knoxville: University of Tennessee Press, 1992).

64. Treatments of Southern politics after Reconstruction revolve around C. Vann Woodward's *Origins of the New South, 1877–1913* (Baton Rouge: Louisiana State University Press, 1951). Woodward's account, which emphasized the demise of the old planter elite and the rise of a new urban, industrial, professional elite in explaining post-Civil War politics in the South, has been repeatedly challenged. It now seems clear that Woodward's view of the disjuncture in Southern political life was overstated, that the planter class was still a powerful political force in Southern society, and that in most cases southern Democrats in Congress aligned themselves with agrarian-minded interests rather than industrially oriented ones. See, for example, James Tice Moore, "Redeemers Reconsidered: Change and Continuity in the Democratic South, 1870–1900," *Journal of Southern History* 44 (August 1978), 357–78 and William Cooper, *The Conservative Regime: South Carolina, 1877–1890* (Baltimore: Johns Hopkins University Press, 1968). For a balanced survey of this issue and the relevant literature see Howard N. Rabinowitz, *The First New South, 1865–1920* (Arlington Heights, Ill.: Harlan Davidson, 1992), 72–131. On the political orientation of Southern Democrats during this period see Carl V. Harris, "Right Force or Left Fork? The Section-Party Alignments of Southern Democrats in Congress, 1873–1897," *Journal of Southern History*, 42 (November 1976), 471–506.

65. The surplus, and more generally the tariff, was a persistent theme in the debates over the Navy. Even in the mid-1890s, when many contended that government revenues were no longer sufficient to cover increased naval expenditures, the issue continued to provoke heated debate. See, for example,

the speeches in the *Congressional Record*, 54th Cong., 1st sess., 1896, 28, pt. 4, 3193–203; pt. 5, 4502–23; pt. 5, 4847–56.

66. Oates, a leading opponent of the battleship navy, continued: "The right thing to do is to revise the tariff and reduce taxation and modify the internal-revenue laws so that there will be no surplus in the Treasury; leave the surplus in the pockets of the people, where it rightly belongs." *Congressional Record*, 51st Cong., 1st sess., 1890, 21, pt. 4, 3259.

67. For a similar interpretation see Baack and Ray, "Special Interests and the Nineteenth-Century Roots of the U.S. Military-Industrial Complex," 167. On the relationship between the protective tariff and veteran's pensions, see Bensel, *Sectionalism and American Political Development*, 62–73.

68. *Congressional Record*, 51st Cong., 1st sess., 1890, 21, pt. 4, 3169.

69. Ibid., 3268.

70. *Congressional Record*, 51st Cong., 1st sess., 1890, 21, app., 178

71. See John A. S. Grenville and George B. Young, *Politics, Strategy and American Diplomacy* (New Haven: Yale University Press, 1966); Ernest May, *Imperial Democracy: The Emergence of America as a Great Power* (New York: Harper and Row, 1961); and Julius W. Pratt, *Expansionists of 1898: The Acquisition of Hawaii and the Spanish Islands*, 2d edition (Chicago: Quadrangle, 1964).

72. "Diplomacy and War Plans in the United States, 1890–1917," in *Essays on the History of American Foreign Relations* ed. Laurence B. Gelfand (New York: Holt, Rinehart, and Winston, 1972), 240.

5 Strategic Adjustment and the U.S. Navy: The Spanish-American War, the Yellow Press, and the 1990s

Bartholomew H. Sparrow

> Newspapers are made to sell and for this purpose there is nothing better than war. War means daily sensation and excitement. On this almost any kind of newspaper may live and make money. . . . [I]t cannot but follow, that it is only human for a newspaper proprietor to desire war, especially when he feels sure that his own country is right and its opponents are enemies of civilization.
>
> —E. L. Godkin[1]

Because Cold War expectations no longer obtain in the currently unipolar or unevenly multipolar world order, the United States, as the predominant world power, faces a period of strategic adjustment. Despite the many attempts that have been made to categorize the present international position of the United States, there are no obvious parallels between the United States today and prior eras of strategic adjustment, such as the late 1940s, the interwar 1920s and 1930s, the 1890s, the Civil War years, or the founding.[2]

Unlike the latter half of the 1940s, the United States does not confront a formidable military and ideological antagonist of the stature of the Soviet Union. Its defense budget cuts and personnel reductions scarcely match those after 1945. Most of the major powers with the capacity to threaten the United States—Great Britain, France, Germany, and Japan—happen to be its allies. Unlike the 1920s and 1930s, the United States does not face other major powers of equivalent capability. And unlike the 1890s and preceding eras, the United States is a major world power. In contrast to the decline of the British Empire, moreover, there is no emerging power to whom the baton of world leadership can be passed.[3] The United States finds itself in uncharted territory, in a "fog of peace."

Yet, there may be an important parallel between the present strategic situation of the United States and that of a century ago with respect to the role of the news media. An examination of the 1890s is instructive as an example of the potential influence of the press (or news media) on U.S. foreign policy. The yellow journalism of the late 1890s exerted its own separate impact on national politics.[4] The sensational press fanned the flames of the Cuban issue and provoked a national outcry that neither the Congress nor the President could ignore. As historian David Trask concludes: "compelling domestic influences were more important than international considerations in dictating McKinley's decision for war."[5] National politics and societal interests, rather than changes in the international system, provided the grounds for the American war with Spain and for the accompanying U.S. strategic adjustment at the end of the nineteenth century.

With the quick and easy victory over Spain, the United States acquired Puerto Rico, Guam, Wake Island, Eastern Samoa, the Philippines, and shortly thereafter (and as a direct consequence of the war), the Hawaiian islands. Americans experienced "a new consciousness of international empire and world-wide power" as a result of their victory in 1898. The United States entered the ranks of world powers, complete with international ambitions and international obligations. The U.S. Navy became responsible for American interests that encompassed the Caribbean and stretched across much of the Pacific.

In the 1990s U.S. foreign policy has once more become tied to the news media, specifically in the case of the "CNN Effect." The speed and impact of the televised image is forcing American decisionmakers to formulate policy on the run, before diplomatic communications and intelligence reports are in, and before the president has time to consult with his executive aides and congressional allies. The news media, and television in particular—rather than the White House, the Congress, or either of the political parties—often appear to be initiating government action and setting the political agenda.[6] Pictures of starving children got the United States into Somalia and televised pictures of a soldier being dragged through Mogadishu streets forced U.S. troops out. Similarly, news of Iraq's treatment of the Kurds at the close of the Gulf War forced a change in the U.S. plans for withdrawal from the region.[7]

The argument in this chapter is that the strategic adjustment of the United States in the 1890s—i.e., the rise of U.S. global strategic, economic, political, and humanitarian interests—hinged upon the occasion of the Spanish-American War of 1898. In order to understand the U.S. decision to go to war against Spain, however, we have to look at the sensational journalism of the late 1890s—the yellow press—and at why it was so able to affect American policy, and ultimately American strategic adjustment.

I define "strategic adjustment" as an enduring and significant change (although not necessarily a permanent change) in the ends and means of statecraft, i.e., in the definition and pursuit of the national interest. I operationalize "strategic adjustment" in terms of the changes in the ideas, institutions, and capabilities of the U.S. Navy. My assumption is that the strategic adjustment evident in naval affairs was consistent with and reflective of a more comprehensive strategic adjustment taking place in national politics and throughout the federal government. Section 1 establishes the central role of the Spanish-American War in the strategic adjustment of the United States at the end of the nineteenth century, as manifest in the case of the ideas, organizations, and material resources of the U.S. Navy. Section 2 presents an institutional explanation for the short-lived impact of the yellow press on national politics in the 1890s. It is based on theory that focuses upon the fluidity of institutions. Section 3 reconsiders the news media as an institution in the 1990s in light of the history of the 1890s.

Strategic Adjustment and the U.S. Navy in the 1890s

The complex process of strategic adjustment may take years to accomplish. Even the rearming and mobilization of the U.S. economy and society during the 1940s, perhaps the single greatest economic transformation and societal reorientation in American history, was a lengthy process. The rearmament period began in earnest after the fall of France, in June 1940. It would not be until after the invasion of South Korea, in June 1950, that the American military, industry, and scientific communities achieved their Cold-War standing.[8]

The strategic adjustment of the late 1890s and early 1900s was a similarly drawn-out process, with roots in the 1880s and extensions into the 1910s.

Alfred Thayer Mahan's *The Influence of Sea Power on History* was published in 1890; Navy Secretary Benjamin Tracy called for the construction of a battleship navy at the end of 1889. Total navy budgets grew rapidly in the 1880s, rising from $6.6 million in 1886 to $8.5 million in 1888, and then to $11.4 million in 1890. A battleship-based, blue-water fleet would eventually replace the U.S. Navy's former and exclusive dependence on cruisers and coastal-defense vessels.[9]

The Spanish-American War accelerated and consolidated this process of strategic adjustment. Lectures, discussions, and popular articles on navalism were prevalent in the United States during the 1890s, even before 1890, but it was not until after the Spanish-American War that there was an across-the-board acceptance of Mahan's ideas. Similarly, while a limited set of organizations necessary for conducting naval warfare were already in place, it was not until mid-1898 that the United States reinforced and created the naval institutions appropriate for a world power. And it was not until the war with Spain, and its aftermath, that the United States permanently dedicated the budgetary resources necessary for the construction of a formidable ocean-going navy.

Naval Strategy

Ideas of what the Navy should *do* constitute naval strategy. In peacetime, U.S. naval strategy was to implement foreign policy; in wartime, it was to decide where conflict would be engaged and how it would be pursued. Here, the success of the U.S. Navy in the Spanish-American War legitimated Mahan's naval strategy. Mahan argued that command of the sea was essential to a nation's success in the "harsh competition of international life." The "denial of safe transit" was the key to victory in modern warfare. For the defense of the merchant marine and for keeping trade routes open, maritime strategy demanded a force capable of being trained on rival fleets or on the "highways of commerce." Naval fleets should be kept intact, and not dispersed, if they were to achieve this concentration of power. "The most important units of the fleet were those which would contribute most directly to a decisive outcome"—the capital ships, the battleships.[10]

The victory over Spain in 1898 marked the changeover in U.S. naval strategy, from commerce raiding and coastal defense to Mahan's blue-water strategy that required capital ships, fleet engagements, and command of the sea. Future naval conflicts would be in the open water, away from American shores. The destruction of the Spanish fleets in Manila harbor and off Santiago de Cuba demonstrated the efficacy of the ocean-going navy as a gun platform and means of sea control. After the war most Americans would consider the United States to be a maritime nation, dependent on an offensive battleship fleet for its security and prosperity. Before the war, few Americans had thought of the United States and the U.S. Navy in such terms.[11] The success of the naval war with Spain provided an emphatic confirmation of the naval doctrine espoused by Mahan, Stephen Luce, Theodore Roosevelt, Carl Schurz, Senator Henry Cabot Lodge, and others.[12]

Naval Institutions

Several institutions of the U.S. Navy were affected by the war: the Naval Institute, the Office of Naval Intelligence, the Naval War College, the Naval War Board, and the General Board. The Naval Institute, founded in 1873 by Stephen Luce, served as a forum for ideas about the Navy. It awarded prizes, published journals, and sponsored conferences on matters of "policy, materials, strategy, tactics, organization, administration, education," and naval developments abroad.[13] The Office of Naval Intelligence (ONI), created in 1882 by Navy Secretary William Hunt and located within the Bureau of Navigation, was the first U.S. agency to be organized explicitly for the purpose of collecting and classifying information on military affairs abroad, on "all information that may be of value to the Navy in the event of hostilities."[14] Two years after the creation of the ONI, Navy Secretary William Chandler established the Naval War College (again in response to Luce's initiatives) for the education of naval officers on technology, strategy, tactics, and logistics, as well as history, geography, and international law. President Cleveland's Secretary of the Navy, Hilary Herbert, used the Naval War College as a general staff for drawing up a war plan against Britain, given the possibility of war with Britain over the Venezuelan-British Guianan boundary dispute.[15] It was Naval War College's staff which, together with naval intelligence personnel, drew up the plan for Commodore Dewey's attack on the Spanish Pacific fleet in Manila Bay—the "Kimball plan."[16]

The successful conduct of the Spanish-American War marked the fruition of the efforts of the Naval Institute, the ONI, and the Naval War College. Besides legitimating the existing institutions of the Navy, however, the war

with Spain also fostered a demand for new institutions. The McKinley administration established the Naval War Board to serve as an advisory body
to the Navy Secretary and to coordinate war planning and operations. Ten
days after the signing of the armistice, on August 12, 1898, the Naval War
Board advised that the United States should control the Caribbean and the
Central American isthmus; it recommended the construction of the Panama
Canal (consistent with Mahan's precept that the fleet should not be divided
but be able to go between the Atlantic and the Pacific Oceans). It called for
the acquisition of naval stations on Cuba, Puerto Rico, St. Thomas, and on
either end of the proposed Panama canal; it also called for the establishment
of naval bases on Pago-Pago, the Samoan islands, the Hawaiian islands,
Guam, Manila, and the Chusan islands. Most of this would come to
pass. The Spanish-American War also "revealed the need for a naval general
staff." Navy Secretary John D. Long therefore created the General Board in
1900 for strategic planning, modeled after the Prussian general staff (and the
Naval War Board). The General Board became "the senior military council
of the nation" and was mandated to advise the Navy Secretary on "any matter
it deemed important" as well as on the annual construction needs of the
fleet.[17]

Other institutional developments followed quickly: the creation in 1903
of the Joint Army-Navy Board for the purpose of interservice planning; the
formation of an independent Marine Corps within the Navy Department
between the years 1900 and 1920; and the establishment of the Office of
the Chief of Naval Operations in 1915. These institutions contributed to the
strategic adjustment of the 1890s both directly (by serving as forums for
planning and strategy) and indirectly (by serving as the loci for the creation
and dissemination of new ideas concerning the American Navy). The Spanish-American War proved the worthiness of naval organizations established
for the instruction of personnel, collection of information, planning of operations, and coordination of tactics. The war also prompted the creation of the
Naval War Board and the General Board.

Naval Capabilities

Indicators of the Navy's capabilities further point to the significant impact
of the Spanish-American War on strategic adjustment. Whereas the U.S.

Navy of 1890 ranked twelfth in the world, by 1915 it was "one of the world's most powerful fleets," able "to project immense power abroad."[18] The biggest changes in naval spending and shipbuilding coincided with and followed the Spanish-American War. The figures below (see table 5.1) illustrate the growth of naval spending. Spending on new construction rose from $5 million in 1890 to $22 million in 1898, and to between $20 and $32 million annually in the early 1900s. Spending on maintenance and operations rose from around $7 million a year in the early 1890s to more than double that by 1900. Aggregate Navy Department outlays soared in 1898 and in the years following.

Once the war ended, the government quickly moved to expand the U.S. naval fleet. Congress lifted the range restrictions and tonnage limitations on

TABLE 5.1 The Cost of the New Navy (millions)

Fiscal Year	New Construction	Maintenance and Operation	Total Navy Outlays	Ships Added
1890	$4.8	$6.6	$22.0	3 battleships
1892	10.8	7.1	29.2	1 battleship
1894	12.5	7.2	31.7	0 battleships
1896	7.7	8.3	27.1	3 battleships
1898	22.2	15.0	58.8	3 battleships, 3 monitors
1900	10.7	15.9	56.0	2 battleships, 2 cruisers
1902	14.4	20.2	67.8	2 battleships, 2 cruisers
1904	32.4	27.9	103.0	1 battleship, 1 cruiser
1906	31.8	29.2	110.5	1 dreadnought
1908	20.2	45.3	118.0	2 dreadnoughts
1910	24.7	48.8	123.2	2 dreadnoughts

SOURCES: New Construction and Maintenance and Operations expenditures are from *Report of the Secretary of the Navy*, 1917, 276, cited in Paolo E. Coletta, *A Survey of U.S. Naval Affairs 1865–1917*, (Washington, D.C.: University Press of America, 1987) Appendix H, 238; Navy Department outlays are from Series Y 457–465, "Outlays of the Federal government: 1789 to 1970," Bureau of the Census, *Historical Statistics of the United States*, Colonial Times to 1970, 2 vols. (Washington, D.C.: GPO, 1975), 1114–5; and shipbuilding figures are from George C. Davis, *A Navy Second to None* (New York: Harcourt, Brace, 1940), 168, cited in Coletta, *A Survey of U.S. Naval Affairs*, Appendix F, 237.

battleships in 1899, and the $78 million appropriation bill passed in 1900 was the largest in the history of U.S. peacetime expenditures. By 1900 the United States stood sixth among the world's naval powers in battleships commissioned or under construction, and by 1902 the U.S. Navy was rated fourth in the world (behind Great Britain, France, and Russia). Soon thereafter, in 1906, Congress called for the construction of the most powerfully armed, most heavily armored, and longest-range battleships ever: the dreadnoughts.[19]

In sum, the events of 1898 resulted in strategic adjustment in terms of lasting changes in the allocation of national resources, improvements in the quality and functions of naval institutions, and the redefinition of American grand strategy.

Historians show an overwhelming consensus on the importance of the Spanish-American War and the year 1898. The war with Spain was "a turning point in American history," one which forced a "revolution in foreign affairs" and caused a "radical" reassessment of U.S. defense policy. The Spanish-American War forged a "new empire" for the United States; it marked the "acquisition of empire" which "placed new demands on the navy."[20] After 1898, European writing on the "American peril" would no longer use the future tense. The historian Ernest R. May notes that whereas "diplomats and writers rarely spoke of the United States in the same breath with the six recognized great powers—Britain, France, Germany, Austria-Hungary, Russia, and Italy" in the 1890s, by "the beginning of the twentieth century they included it almost invariably."[21]

Yellow Journalism as a New Institution

If the Spanish-American War both accelerated and consolidated U.S. strategic adjustment in terms of the historical changes in the ideas, institutions, and capabilities of the U.S. Navy, then we need to understand the reasons behind the war.

Partisan politics cannot explain the decision to go to war, despite the prominence of party politics and partisan differences in the late nineteenth century—a time when the Republican party controlled the presidency and both houses of Congress. Although they were supporters of American manifest destiny and economic internationalism, the Republicans were cautious about interfering in Spanish-Cuban relations and reluctant to go to war.[22] It was the minority-party Democrats who advocated U.S. intervention in Cuba and who had used the Cuban issue for partisan reasons since 1896.

Nor can an argument based on economic interests account for the decision. Business interests and conservative newspapers resisted American intervention in Spanish colonial relations. Indeed, Mark Hanna and the conservative *Journal of Commerce* consistently opposed American belligerence. One study that looked at the effect of news about U.S.-Spanish relations and changes in stock prices found that in eight instances of news about increasing tensions with Spain (between February 1896 and March 1898) stock prices fell, and in five instances where peaceful settlements were reported as news (between March and December 1896) stock prices rose.[23] Military intervention by the United States would put the $50 million of American investment in Cuba at risk.[24] Indicatively, the Spanish blamed jingoes and jingoism — and not American businessmen or economic imperialism — for the U.S. intervention in Cuban affairs. Nor was the Spanish-American War managed by President McKinley as others contend, as will be argued below.

If the war cannot be explained by party politics, economic forces, or presidential design, how then do we explain the impact of the yellow press? An application of the new institutionalism to the political communication of the 1890s provides some answers, I suggest.

Several characteristics distinguish the historical (or sociological) version of the new institutionalism.[25] For one, history is not efficient. The normal state of affairs is more likely to be one of disorder, dissonance, inconsistency, and incongruity than one of a singular "order." Politics "is essentially *open-ended* and *unsettled*" given the number, interrelation, and complexity of human institutions. Political life manifests multiple, clashing institutions.[26] The new institutionalism attends to matters of timing (the conjuncture of one institution with another) and temporality (the impermanence of institutions).[27] Institutions exist in no necessary relationship with other institutions; they have different origins and founding periods; they are nonsimultaneous.[28] The new institutionalism is also cognizant of power—i.e., the institutions' "purposive or intentional" quality. Institutions exist in relation to elites, interests, and other institutions, and they "control (or attempt to control) the behavior of persons or institutions other than themselves." The constructed and reconstructed rules of institutions are the product of human intent, aimed at particular ends. The rules of institutions "partake of the actors' personal motives and ambitions."[29] Applied to the sensational press at the end of the nineteenth century, the new institutionalism directs our attention to the changing and interconnected institutional orderings in the sphere of political communication,[30] to the timing and temporary quality of institutions, and to the use of power within them.[31] I take up each of these in turn.

Four "relatively independent" orderings figured in the political communication of the late nineteenth century. One ordering that factored into the emergence of the yellow press as an institution was the means by which the electorate learned of politics. Newspapers became independent of political parties as sources of publicly available information about politics and government. A second ordering was the commercialization of the news business as newspaper publishing became highly profitable. A third ordering was the working relationship between journalists and politicians—the standard practices of government public relations as they were at the time. A fourth ordering consisted of the content of the press—the political information being communicated by the press—in this case, the sensational content of the news. The particular conjunction of these orderings in the late 1890s allowed the yellow press to influence U.S. politics and American expansionism. In neither the decades immediately preceding the 1890s nor those immediately following was the sensational press so able to influence national affairs.[32]

Newspapers and Political Communication

Americans of the 1890s read their newspapers. The literacy rate approached 90 percent. There were about 1,900 daily newspapers and 14,000 weekly newspapers then in circulation.[33] With the high rates of voter turnout in the 1890s (turnouts ranged between 70 and 80 percent of eligible voters from 1840 through 1896), the press was in a position to exert considerable pressure on public opinion.[34] The competition for voters was especially intense in the larger cities of the East and Midwest, where 46 percent of Americans in 1900 were either first-generation citizens or immigrants themselves (36 million of the country's population of 76 million).[35]

Newspapers had been conduits of political information for a long time, of course; they had been explicitly affiliated with the political parties since the 1830s. Newspapers, not very profitable for most of the nineteenth century, needed the capital provided by political advertisements, and political parties needed the forum provided by the newspapers for publicizing rallies, informing voters, and explaining politics to their partisans. Loyal editors were rewarded with patronage jobs.[36] These press-party ties began to deteriorate over the latter half of the century, however, such that newspaper partisanship by the 1890s evolved into "a new style of limited partisanship," one independent of political party.

The press could thus serve as an instrument of reform. Newspapers would be "the master, not the tool, of party." Newspapers could present facts and relevant arguments, and thereby facilitate the education of voters. If political position could be determined by reason—rather than by heritage or emotion (to exaggerate somewhat)—then party affiliation no longer had to be reflexive. Newspapers, like the voters themselves, would be party members by choice, according to the interests of their editors and publishers.[37]

As the newspapers grew independent and became to varying degrees part of the reform movement, they reinforced the educational and reformist movements within the two parties. Grover Cleveland used educational politics to win the presidential election of 1892 (rather than relying on the torchlight marches typical of former elections); he was aided by the reformist Mugwumps in his electoral victory. Once in office he promulgated reforms of the civil service and of the tariff system. The Republican party also relied heavily on newspapers in response to the surge of educational politics and the weakening of party ties. It set up a "literary bureau" for disseminating information on the tariff in the 1888 election, and in the 1892 election established a newspaper office which clipped and sent out newspaper articles to party papers around the country.

As the historian Michael McGerr reports, "the papers of both parties" in the election of 1892 "applauded the campaign of education" and the focus on the "facts." Indeed, McGerr finds that "traditional party journalism was crippled" by the end of the nineteenth century.[38] It is indicative of this newfound independence that a number of Republican papers—including the *New York Times*, the *New York Evening Post*, and the *Boston Herald*—deserted the 1884 Republican presidential ticket, just as a number of prominent Democratic papers would later bolt from the presidential ticket of the Democratic Party in 1896.[39]

In short, in a world of educational politics with newspapers independent of political party, the overwhelming majority of Americans in the second half of the 1890s were learning about politics and foreign affairs only as mediated by the press. The press was poised to play an independent role in political communication, capable of affecting national politics as it had not previously.

The Structure of the News Industry

A second ordering of political communication of the 1890s was the commercial status of the U.S. newspaper industry: newspaper publishing was becoming big business. Advertising sales were for the first time being based on actual circulation figures. Advertisers were no longer being penalized for using pictures rather than copy; and advertising in newspapers was becoming very attractive to businesses, given the rise of the middle class and a national market for goods and services. The ratio of advertising content to newspaper editorial matter changed from about 30:70 in 1880 to about 50:50, and above, by 1900. Newspapers' advertising revenues rose sixfold in just thirty years' time, from a total of $16 million in 1870 to more than $95 million by 1900.[40]

Technological developments made the growth in circulation and profitability possible, and the new production methods provided another incentive for the move away from partisanship: with a partisan press, newspapers' markets were limited *a priori* to a little more (or less) than 50 percent of potential customers, whereas the logic of news production was to maximize circulation and minimize per-copy costs.

The new economics of the news industry—derived from the technological improvements, the inflow of advertising dollars, and the increase in newspaper circulation—made newspaper publishing extremely competitive. New York City alone had eight morning newspapers, seven evening papers, and more than fifteen weekly papers of general interest. Newspapers hired star reporters, vigorously promoted their own publications, and priced their newspapers at one or a few cents each (in contrast to the "six cent" business and financial papers) in order to gain greater circulation and an edge on their rivals.[41] Newspapers, which previously had hired few reporters, began to fill their staffs with them, since news stories had begun to replace editorials as newspapers' most important feature. The new reporters were more likely than their predecessors to view journalism as a profession, to have gone to college, and to believe in the desirability of professional training.

Given the size of metropolitan New York and the resources—and ambitions—of Joseph Pulitzer and William Randolph Hearst, Pulitzer's *New York*

World (purchased in 1883) and Hearst's *New York Journal* (purchased in 1895) competed vigorously and viciously.[42] The two papers introduced the use of banner headlines set in heavy type and spanning several columns; they were the first to use line drawings and illustrations in their papers and hired portrait artists and cartoonists to this end; they invested in faster telegraph transmission of images and copy; they hired the best talent (Richard Harding Davis, Sylvester Scovel, Frederic Remington, Stephen Crane, and James Creelman, among others); and they constantly advertised their own news coverage and circulation figures. What the *Journal* and the *World* began became standard industry practice.[43]

Politicians and the Press

A third ordering of political communication was the relationship between public officials and members of the press: journalists rather than politicians set the agenda with respect to U.S. policy on Spain and Cuba. White House press relations were "somewhat haphazard" under McKinley, one historian of journalism, Robert Desmond, reports. "Even with the Spanish-American War in progress [the White House] was not regarded as a source of news warranting special coverage." Reporters infrequently went to the White House and rarely saw the President.[44] Not until the war was underway did the President and his staff develop some of the standard public relations practices assumed today as a matter of course: centralizing the control of information, regulating correspondence (specifically, that originating from the Caribbean and the Philippines), dedicating space in the White House for reporters' use, and observing unwritten conventions in their relationship with the press.[45]

Before the war the White House had no public relations apparatus. Neither the President and his staff nor the federal government as a whole was equipped to assemble basic information, distribute within the government that information which did arrive, or inform the public of government policies and actions. Public officials responded neither quickly nor emphatically to false and misleading news coverage, and only occasionally did government personnel use the news media to promote their own positions. "Politicians showed deference to the press," and used the newspapers for gathering information for their own use.[46] The press, and not government public relations, determined what voters knew about their government. And it was the press, and not private consultants or opinion polls, that provided politicians with a gauge of public opinion.

The press's domination of political communication was especially striking after the sinking of the *Maine*. The overwhelming sentiment in the nation's newspapers was one of retribution. The sensational press, calling for action against Spain, roiled public opinion, incited a majority of Congressmen to act (Congressmen who faced elections in the fall of 1898), and condemned the caution shown by the President.[47] Indeed, when the Naval Board of Inquiry concluded that the *Maine* had been sunk by a mine, "Republican congressmen and editors warned the President that if he did not lead the country into a popular war, others would."[48] No community or occupational group was immune to the "war fever." Not even the vocal opposition of much of the clergy and religious press, a silence on the part of Civil War veterans (the Grand Army of the Republic), and the disapproval of many successful businessmen could check what had become the "unshakable conviction" of the necessity of war. Congressional Republicans abandoned their support for McKinley to join their partisans across the aisle in support of Cuba.[49]

Government spending followed the reporting of the sensational press. Whereas Congress had cut back expenditures from the levels of previous years in early 1898, after the sinking of the *Maine* Congress approved additional government spending for two extra artillery regiments, new buildings, the manufacture of smokeless powder, and the arming of the navy militia.[50] And when the President proceeded on May 6 to ask Congress for $50 million in emergency defense appropriations, the House and Senate passed the measure unanimously.[51]

But President McKinley equivocated over the decision to go to war. On the one hand, McKinley was an extremely astute politician. He did ultimately inform the Congress of the nation's readiness to go to war. And the war with Spain did take national politics beyond the North-South divide and did result in a more internationally minded Republican party and United States, both objectives of the President. The Spanish-American War was perhaps also the most popular war in U.S. history, and one with obvious, long-term international significance.

On the other hand, McKinley was loath to go to war. A devout Methodist, the President made repeated statements in his speeches and conversations, both before and after the war, in opposition to armed conflict. He was "anxious to do the right thing, what the country and the world would consider just and honorable."[52] The President made a number of attempts to settle the Cuban issue peaceably (once through a cash settlement with Spain, another time with the intercession of the Vatican). Nor did McKinley do much to prepare the Army or the Navy for any forthcoming conflict. The President's health also deteriorated considerably in late March and early April 1898.[53]

The combination of an increasingly impatient Congress, an outraged public—both excited by the yellow press—and an intransigent Spain demanded that the President advocate military intervention if he were to hold the Republican party, and the country, together.[54] The President may have carefully and artfully steered the United States toward war against Spain, but it was the yellow press that created the political environment forcing McKinley to act.[55] The press, rather than the President, the Republican party, or the State Department, incited the United States to go to war.[56]

The Content of the Press

Newspapers, becoming a medium of popular entertainment, began moving away from exclusive coverage of politics and commerce to emphasize crime, sex, sports, women's features, and comics.[57] Leading the way in the publication of newspapers that appealed across gender, social class, and ethnic background were Pulitzer (and the *New York World*) and Hearst (and the *New York Journal*).[58] Pulitzer and his imitators represented the "new journalism," one that sought out unusual and dramatic incidents to report to their wide-cast audiences. They did not see entertainment as inconsistent with the presentation of facts (in contrast to the present-day ethos of "responsible journalism"). The new journalism was also called "the journalism that acts"—or, more typically, "yellow journalism."[59]

About one-third to one-half the newspapers in the United States in 1896 had been characterized as "yellow." St. Louis had three newspapers that could be labeled as sensational; Boston had five; Philadelphia had four; and Chicago had three. Significantly, none of these cities had newspapers that could be called "conservative." Even the newspapers that were neither explicitly sensational nor conservative in outlook were influenced by the yellow press into changing their editorial positions in the direction of sensational reporting.[60]

Pulitzer and Hearst turned the Cuban issue, culminating in a series of sensational events in 1897–1898 and then the sinking of the *Maine,* into high drama. The two publishers (who also believed in the liberty of Cuba and of the Cubans) were able to use the Cuban situation to alter the content of newspapers.[61] When the *World* reported the capture of American citizens on the schooner *Competitor* in 1896 (playing up the barbarism of the Spanish governor and the right of U.S. citizens to due process), its weekly circulation rose by an average of more than 216,000 newspapers *a day* (in comparison to the same week of the preceding year) and other newspaper editors across the country expressed similar outrage over Spanish policies.[62] Next came the arrest of star *World* correspondent Sylvester Scovel and the death of dentist Ricardo Ruiz, both in February 1897; the imprisonment and rescue of Evangelina Cosio y Cisneros in August 1897; and the publication of the de Lôme letter on February 10, 1898.[63] The *World* and the *Journal* featured these stories, and they were also picked up by the Associated Press wire as well as disseminated across the United States via the two papers' news services. Both Ruiz's widow and Cisneros received the audience of President McKinley at the White House.[64]

No story was bigger than the sinking of the *Maine*. Newspaper headlines around the country cried out for war: "Destruction of Warship Maine Was the Work of an Enemy"; "American Women Ready to Give Up Husbands, Sons, and Sweethearts to Defend National Honor"; and "Wherever Americans Gather, the Word 'War' Awakens Wild Enthusiasm." More than one hundred newspapers around the country exhibited pro-war headlines in the days immediately following the sinking of the *Maine*. The *World* used pictures of maimed victims and cartoons to emphasize the point that "Uncle Sam" had to settle the Cuban issue; it carried a questionable story about an English munitions expert who had patents on mines made for Spain; and it ran a daily count of the total number of days since the disaster, accompanied by editorial criticism of McKinley's inactivity. One headline, asked, referring to the President: "Will Anything Make Him Fight?"

The *Journal*, the *World*'s rival, went further. When a dubious story smuggled out of Havana reported that divers had found an eight-inch diameter hole in the *Maine*, the *Journal* jumped on the story with its biggest available headline: "War! Sure!" and beneath this "*Maine* Destroyed by Spanish. . . . This Proved Absolutely by Discovery of the Torpedo Hole." Other *Journal* headlines read "The Maine was Destroyed by Treachery" and "Whole Country Thrills with War Fever." The *Journal* also employed artists' sketches to *imagine* what the *Maine* looked like under water; it offered a $50,000 reward for information on the perpetrator of the deed; and it began to raise funds for the building of a monument for the 266 victims of the *Maine* explosion and, to this end, established a committee of "the governors of fifteen states, the mayors of fifty-two cities," and other prominent public and private persons. All of this took place before the official investigation had even started.[65]

The *Journal* dedicated an average of *eight and a half pages* a day during the week of February 17, 1898, to news, editorials, and pictures of the *Maine* disaster. Indeed, the *Journal*'s circulation more than doubled after the sinking of the *Maine*, going from an average of 417,000 newspapers a day during the week of January 9, 1898, to an average of more than a million newspapers a day on the 17th and 18th of February. The *Journal*'s circulation averaged just under a million newspapers a day in early April 1898.[66]

In short, the condition of political communication in the 1890s enabled the yellow newspapers to sensationalize the Cuban issue in the competition for circulation. In so doing, the New York and national press was able to drive U.S. foreign policy and, given the diplomatic stalemate between the United States and Spain, induce the American public and the U.S. Congress to support intervention.[67]

Timing

None of these four orderings—of the role of the press in political communication, the structure of the news industry, government-press relations, and the standard content of the news—exhibited the above characteristics in either the period before or after the 1890s. The stars sometimes come into line, as Orren and Skowronek suggest.[68]

Before the late nineteenth century, newspapers were in a less advantaged position for mobilizing the electorate: there were fewer immigrants, lower literacy rates (20 percent illiteracy in 1870) and lower turnout rates in federal elections. Then, with the turn of the century, came restrictions on immigration, further political reform, a drop in voter turnout (falling from 73 percent in 1900 to 61 percent in 1920), and the rise of other news media.

As economic enterprises, newspapers were distinctly smaller, less profitable, and less sophisticated technologically and editorially prior to the 1890s. After 1900, the more conservative and more responsible newspapers began to regain the ground they had lost to the yellow press. Indicatively, the daily circulation of the *New York Times* rose from 9,000 papers in 1895 to 25,000 in 1897, 82,000 in 1900, and 192,000 in 1910.[69]

Government-press relations also changed with the advent of the Theodore Roosevelt and Wilson presidencies. These and later presidential administrations were able to use the power of publicity to their own advantage.[70] It may even be argued that the transition to the modern presidency in the sense of a public and open presidency began with McKinley himself, as Lewis Gould, Robert Hilderbrand, and Martha Kumar suggest. They note McKinley's explicit use of public relations strategies, his speaking tours, and the use of White House staff for public relations purposes.[71] After the Spanish-American War, the White House and federal government would no longer be content to stand passive vis-à-vis "active" journalism. Instead, government officials used public relations and courted members of the press in the attempt to control political communication.

Finally, the content of newspapers changed. Whereas Pulitzer and Hearst had initiated the sensational journalism of the 1890s, the yellow press fell out of favor in the twentieth century with the further spread and acceptance of professional standards and the continued rise of objective science. News coverage became less partial and more balanced. A turning point in the history of the yellow press came with the death of President McKinley in 1901. Before he was assassinated the *New York Journal* had printed editorials, cartoons, and a poem endorsing the use of violence against the President. Hearst's *Journal* and the yellow journalism in general quickly fell out of favor with the public.[72] By the 1920s what remained of the sensational press occupied a distinct, separate niche: tabloid journalism.[73]

In sum, the yellow press was able to play the part it did in American politics in the 1890s because of the simultaneous development and interrelationship of the role of newspapers as a medium of communication in a highly mobilized American society, the development of newspaper publishing as a large and profitable commercial enterprise, the condition of government public relations, and the dramatic content of newspapers. For a short while, at least, the yellow press was able to dominate political communication for millions of voters, members of Congress, and even a politically adept President.[74]

There were also larger structural conditions that made Americans receptive to sensational reporting. One was the growing military and economic threat posed by the existing great powers. The European powers were vigorously exploring further colonial and commercial opportunities. Their growing fleets, those of Britain and Germany especially, posed increasing dangers to American coastal cities.[75] The other structural condition was the industrialization and internationalization of the U.S. economy, in conjunction with the economic depression of the 1890s. International markets could provide the salve for the economy by consuming (excess) American goods.[76] The U.S. trade balance in merchandise turned positive for the first time in 1894 (and would remain positive until 1971), and Latin America and the Far East were the most promising regions for economic expansionism.[77] The transformation of American foreign relations "reached its climax in the 1890s," remarks Walter LaFeber.[78] The structure of the international system and the economic reorientation of the United States at the end of the nineteenth century provided the larger political context that enabled political communication about U.S. foreign policy—specifically, the interventionist sentiment expressed by the yellow press—to play a distinct role in American political development.[79]

Power

The yellow press was the creature of Hearst and Pulitzer, their own editors and reporters, and their imitators. Pulitzer and Hearst were intent on outdoing each other and their fellow New York newspaper publishers. Their ambitions altered an industry, just as the efforts of their editors and reporters changed conventions of news reporting and newspaper content. Editors wanted themselves to decide what was interesting or important political news (rather than have the political parties decide for them); publishers wanted higher circulation and increased revenues; reporters aggressively sought out news stories in their quest for prominence (e.g., by going to Cuba themselves rather than depending on government officials as news sources); and editors and reporters alike sought to grab the attention of their reading audience through provocative writing, the unprecedented use of headlines, and the new employment of pictures.

It is therefore a mistake to claim that "sensational journalism had only a marginal impact," on national politics because of the split between the conservative and sensational newspapers over U.S. foreign policy toward Cuba and the implications of the *Maine* disaster.[80] The division in the American press cannot explain the "emotionally intense and threatening" response of members of Congress to the *Maine* disaster. Nor does the presence of opposing styles and editorial positions of American newspapers in the 1890s effectively cancel out the press's influence: the yellow press had the greater circulation, enjoyed the larger circulation growth, and set the new technical and reporting standards for the news industry. To say that absent the sensational press McKinley would not have acted otherwise[81] ignores the effect the cumulative coverage of the Cuban issue, culminating in the reporting on the *Maine* explosion, had on both the public and Congress after the death of José Marti in 1895.

"The journalism that acts" acted. It was the press—not public officials and not the voters—that was determining political communication. The yellow press did not simply relay presidential and congressional policy to the public, nor did it merely respond to popular demands. Instead, the sensational newspapers reported actual, distorted, and fabricated stories about the situation in Cuba in order to catch the attention of their readers and thereby gain circulation.

Nor is it accurate to claim that "Hearst played on American prejudices" and "did not create them."[82] The press could not "reflect" what the public had no prior knowledge of, and had not previously articulated.[83] It was the "new journalism" that gave specific form, content, and direction to vague and unspecified public sentiment. Even were one to accept the claim that the newspapers "did not fabricate the major events that moved the United States"—such as the de Lôme letter and the *Maine* explosion[84]—the yellow press was able to heighten the public's awareness of and reactions to these "major events" and link them with the preceding news of Cuba. In fact, as late as December 1897 it could be claimed that the McKinley and Cleveland positions were identical, but that American nonintervention could not persist if "some satisfactory end to the struggle is not reached before long." The yellow press brought an end to American patience.[85] It was not that the Spanish-American War was "an unwanted war"; it was a war that the yellow press wanted, the American people wanted, and the Congress and the President both eventually wanted.

The Press of the 1890s as a New Institution

The press—and not President McKinley, not the Republican majorities in the House and Senate, not economics, and not predestiny—succeeded in initiating the war against Spain.[86] Although it is true that the origin of the American war with Spain had little relation to its actual consequences,[87] the press *was* able to tell a story, a tale of American manifest destiny, that was capable of bridging the pre-war and post-war experiences. The wave of hysteria accompanying the *Maine* explosion continued on as "delirium" over the victory of Commodore Dewey in Manila harbor and intense popular enthusiasm about the overall triumph of the Spanish-American War. The popular and political support for the acquisition of the Philippines, Hawaii, and other international territories allowed President McKinley to forge an imperial United States.[88]

The new institutionalism sheds significant light on the development and then decline of sensational journalism. In terms of the institutional orderings, the evolution of the party-newspaper relationship was distinct (albeit not wholly so) from the changing economics of the newspaper industry. Similarly, the altered conventions of newspaper content in the 1890s were phenomena separate from the norms of government-press relations. An emphasis on the incongruities and asymmetries of politics further allows us to appreciate the exceptional circumstances of the yellow press's emergence. It is not to be expected that a sensationalizing press would have powerfully affected members of Congress and the White House alike; it is novel for the editorial content of much of the press to run contrary to the policy preferences of the political party in control of the legislative and executive branches; it is highly unusual for new publications to determine news coverage at the expense of more respected older news organizations; and it is atypical for distorted and even fabricated news reporting to become accepted by much of the news industry.

We also see the contradiction between the realignment of partisan politics in 1894 and 1896 and the bipartisan support for intervention in Cuba and for American expansionism more broadly. Yet this contradiction is consistent with the new institutionalism's focus on the dissonance and disorder of political history.[89]

The study of the fluid and temporal quality of politics inherent in the new institutionalism allows us to appreciate the realm of the possible. The news media *may* constitute a distinct political actor, even if they do not exert significant independent effects. More usually, news coverage is the artifact of party balance, national security needs, and divisions within and between the legislative and executive branches of government.[90]

Strategic Adjustment and the Media of the 1990s

The orderings of political communication that enabled the press to incite the Spanish-American War, and that therefore led to the strategic adjustment of the 1890s, are once again in evidence.

With about two-thirds of Americans saying that the television is their primary source of news, and with more than 95 percent of Americans trusting what they see on television, the major over-the-air television networks and CNN are able to reach millions of Americans immediately and intimately. More than 90 percent of Americans saw televised broadcasts of the Gulf War, for instance. Television constitutes the most powerful and direct link between the electorate and political leaders, analogous, perhaps, to how the sensational papers of the late 1890s were able to reach out to a broad audience unheedful of the established "six cent" press. Now, as then, the newer media—television in the 1990s—are capable of driving public opinion.

The structure of the news industry is also conducive to the "CNN Effect," given the size and concentration of the media industry. Fourteen companies now control half or more of the daily newspaper business; three companies receive half or more of television revenues; and the total number of corporations dominating all media (newspapers, book publishing, television, and motion pictures) comes to just twenty-two (since corporations may be dominant in more than one medium). Nine out of the fourteen leading newspaper publishers are members of the *Fortune* 500. The telecommunications legislation of 1996 accelerates this trend. And CNN, despite its initial revolutionary promise, covers politics and government in much the same way as do the other major networks.[91]

The relationship between members of the new media and U.S. public officials shows a further parallel. Journalists have become increasingly critical of, even cynical about, national politics, politicians, and public policy. At the same time, they have become increasingly celebrated and affluent.[92] The result is that journalists, especially television personalities, enjoy increasing independence from any one politician or political party in their reporting of news about national politics and government.

Finally, the content of the news has changed. With the economics of the television industry and the smaller news hole that television allows have come brevity and sensationalism. The rise of "infotainment," television's abridged and sensationalized content, is increasingly evident in the news programs and such shows as *Dateline* or *60 Minutes*. Political news is less dominated by what is published in *The New York Times, The Washington Post,* and other prestige news organizations, and more determined by television; newspapers are forced to analyze news that has already been broken by the broadcast media. The hierarchy among news organizations typical of the postwar years, where the broadcast media followed and deferred to the print media, has eroded to the point that television is now seen as the more innovative and important medium, independent from and beyond the control of the prestige print media. Networks (and cable), like Hearst's *Journal* and Pulitzer's *World,* are in a position to dominate the political discourse that could define U.S. international interests.

Even the broader structural preconditions are aligned: the United States finds itself in an indeterminate international system that allows for considerable latitude in foreign policy. It again faces a period of wrenching economic change typified by growing gaps between the highest and lowest income groups, a large and controversial influx of immigrants, and an ongoing transformation of the workplace and economy that has created new technologies and accentuated international competition. The news media, and the televised media in particular, are thus in a position to exert significant, independent impact on U.S. strategic adjustment.[93]

All this suggests the probable influence of the CNN Effect. As former Secretary of State James A. Baker attests, "The 'CNN Effect' has revolutionized the way policymakers have to approach their jobs, particularly in the foreign policy arena." One scholar's study of the CNN Effect comes to the same point: "Virtually every official interviewed agrees that the rise of the Cable News Network has radically altered the way U.S. foreign policy is conducted."[94] Recent events, such as the Gulf War, the handling of North Korea, and the U.S. interventions in Somalia and Haiti suggest as much.[95]

One key consequence of the CNN Effect, it has been argued, is that large numbers of American casualties—not to mention wars of attrition—become increasingly unattractive to policymakers in a world where televised images of injured and killed Americans are subject to immediate national and even international publicity. It may also be the case that the distinct conditions of and the reporting on the Gulf War are partly responsible for delaying the implementation of the more fundamental changes and choices evoked by the new international environment. The coverage and framing of U.S. involvement in the Gulf War, Somalia, North Korea, Bosnia, and Haiti is no doubt setting the path for future naval and strategic developments.

Acknowledgments

I am grateful for the comments made on earlier drafts of this chapter by members of the workshops on the "Politics of Strategic Adjustment" held in Austin, Texas (April 1994) and Monterey, California (February 1995). I am especially grateful for the particular contributions of Chris Ansell, Russ Burgos, Walter Dean Burnham, Emily Goldman, Lewis Gould, Scott James, Patti MacLachlan, John Nerone, Ed Rhodes, Mark Shulman, Edward Smith, Peter Trubowitz, Harrison Wagner, Charles Whitney, Keith Whittington, and Wes Widmaier.

Notes

1. Godkin, a leading Progressive and founder of the *Nation,* is cited in Marcus M. Wilkerson, *Public Opinion and the Spanish-American War* (New York: Russell & Russell, 1932), 125.
2. David E. Jeremiah, "Beyond the Cold War," *Proceedings* (Naval Review 1992), 52–57; Ernest R. May , "National Security in America's History," in *Rethinking America's Security* eds., Graham Allison and Gregory Treverton (New York: Norton, 1992), 94–114; Colin Powell, "U.S. Forces: Challenges Ahead," *Foreign Affairs* 71 (Winter 1992/93), 32–45; Michael Vlahos, "Culture and Foreign Policy," *Foreign Policy* 82 (Spring, 1991), 59–78; Michael Vlahos, "A Global Naval Force? Why Not?" *Proceedings* (March 1992), 40–44; Paul D. Wolfowitz, "Clinton's First Year," *Foreign Affairs* 73 (January/February 1994), 28–43. Also see R. Harrison Wagner, "What was Bipolarity?" *International Organization* 47 (Winter 1993), 77–106.
3. Aaron L. Friedberg, *The Weary Titan* (Princeton: Princeton University Press, 1988); Paul Kennedy, *The Rise and Fall of Great Powers* (New York: Vintage Books, 1987).
4. For overviews of the press's (and news media's) impact on American history, see Douglass Cater, *The Fourth Branch* (Boston: Houghton Mifflin, 1959); Edwin Diamond and Robert A. Silverman, *White House to Your House* (Cambridge: MIT Press, 1994); William A. Gamson, *What's News?* (New York: Free Press, 1984); Bartholomew Sparrow, *Uncertain Guardians* (Baltimore: Johns Hopkins University Press, 1999).
5. David F. Trask, *The War With Spain in 1898* (New York: Macmillan, 1981), 475.
6. The networks themselves may also fail to take the time to check out their stories or their sources; the temptation is to go with the captivating visual image. Mort Rosenblum, *Who Stole the News?* (New York: Wiley, 1993), 180–

81; Ben Bagdikian in "Theodore H. White Seminar," November 19, 1993, The Joan Shorenstein Barone Center, Harvard University, p. 46.

7. This is not to say that the news media are the *only* cause of these actions. For a recent nuanced investigation of the CNN Effect, see Warren Strobel, *Late Breaking Foreign Policy: The News Media's Influence on Peace Operations* (Washington, D.C.: U.S. Institute of Peace, 1997).

8. For a study of the Navy's changes in organization and resources in response to the Second World War and then between 1945 and 1950, see Bartholomew Sparrow, *From the Outside In: World War II and the American State* (Princeton: Princeton University Press, 1996), 161–257.

9. In fact, by 1890 "American battleships compared quite favorably with the best in Europe's navies and in some cases, as in secondary batteries and armor, improved upon them"—and the U.S. Navy was using American (not foreign) ship designs. Paolo E. Coletta, *A Survey of U.S. Naval Affairs, 1865–1917* (Washington, D.C.: University Press of America, 1987), 52.

10. Friedberg, *Weary Titan*, 142–43; Harold Sprout and Margaret Sprout, *The Rise of American Naval Power* (Princeton: Princeton University Press, 1939), 203–5; Julius Pratt, *Expansionists of 1898* (Chicago: Quadrangle Books, 1964 [1936]), 12–17.

11. Robert E. Osgood, *Ideals and Self-interest in America's Foreign Relations* (Chicago: University of Chicago Press, 1953), 29; John A. S. Grenville and George Berkeley Young, *Politics, Strategy, and American Diplomacy* (New Haven: Yale University Press, 1966), 290, 307.

12. George W. Baer, *One Hundred Years of Sea Power* (Stanford: Stanford University Press), 27–31; Paolo E. Coletta, *A Survey of U.S. Naval Affairs*; Kenneth J. Hagan, *This People's Navy* (New York: Free Press), 228–29. Among the "others" was the U.S. Senator from Maine and former Secretary of State (under Benjamin Harrison) James G. Blaine. See Pratt, *Expansionists of 1898*, 22–25.

13. Coletta, *Survey of U.S. Naval Affairs*, 25. In the following year, 1874, Congress passed the Marine Schools Act, which set up a permanent system of naval training for both the Navy and Merchant Marine. (The Naval Academy had been established in 1845.)

14. Coletta, *Survey of U.S. Naval Affairs*, 27–28; Trask, *War With Spain in 1898*.

15. Coletta, *Survey of U.S. Naval Affairs*, 44. The Navy proceeded to send Commander Charles B. Gridley to the Great Lakes in order to secretly organize four squadrons of ships for the purpose of destroying the Welland Canal. Grenville and Young, *Politics, Strategy, and American Diplomacy*, 171–72.

16. The Kimball plan, contingent on the United States going to war against Spain, had been conceived in the mid-1890s and was reviewed in the summer

of 1897. Its objective was to neutralize the naval threat of the Spanish fleet in the Philippines. John Dobson, *Reticent Expansionism: The Foreign Policy of William McKinley* (Pittsburgh: Duquesne University Press, 1988), 79.

17.   Paolo E. Coletta, *The American Naval Heritage in Brief* (Washington, D.C.: University Press of America, 1978), 166; Grenville and Young, *Politics, Strategy, and American Diplomacy*, 299–300.

18.   Robert Greenhalgh Albion, *Makers of Naval Policy, 1798–1947* (Annapolis, Md.: U.S. Naval Institute Press, 1980), 205.

19.   Baer, *One Hundred Years of Sea Power*, 32–33; Hagan, *This People's Navy*, 232.

20.   James C. Bradford, "Introduction," in *Crucible of Empire: The Spanish-American War & Its Aftermath* ed., James C. Bradford (Annapolis, Md.: Naval Institute Press, 1993), xiii–xvi; Osgood, *Ideals and Self-interest in America's Foreign Relations*, 27; Trask, *War With Spain in 1898*, 486; Lewis L. Gould, *The Spanish-American War and President McKinley* (Lawrence: University of Kansas Press, 1982), 138; Grenville and Young, *Politics, Strategy, and American Diplomacy*, 290; LaFeber, *New Empire*, 416; Coletta, *Survey of U.S. Naval Affairs*, ii; Sprout and Sprout, *Rise of American Naval Power*, 223; Hagan, *People's Navy*, 228–29; Ernest May, *Imperial Democracy: The Emergence of America as a Great Power*, (New York: Harper and Row, 1963), 263–66. Nicolas Spykman sees the events of 1898 as a symbolic "turning point" in U.S.-British relations: Great Britain now recognized the supremacy of the United States in the Caribbean—the "American Mediterranean." Nicolas Spykman, *America's Strategy in World Politics* (New York: Harcourt, Brace and Company, 1942), 81–82.

21.   May, *Imperial Democracy*, 6.

22.   See, for example, LaFeber, *New Empire*; Pratt, *Expansionists of 1898*.

23.   Joseph E. Wisan, *The Cuban Crisis as Reflected in the New York Press* (New York: Columbia University Press, 1934), 456; Pratt, *Expansionists of 1898*, 22, 233–34. See Lewis Gould for a compelling case against the exaggerated influence ascribed to the Reick Telegram, which a number of scholars have argued proved the impact of big business on McKinley's decision to go to war. Gould, "The Reick Telegram and the Spanish-American War: A Reappraisal," *Diplomatic History* 3 (Spring 1979), 193–99.

24.   Lewis L. Gould, *The Presidency of William McKinley* (Lawrence: University of Kansas Press, 1980), 63.

25.   The historical or sociological strand of new institutionalism stands in contrast to the rational choice version of the new institutionalism, also referred to as the positive theory of institutions. The rational-choice institutionalism seeks to explain the endurance of political norms and processes through the accounts of individual decisionmakers. Institutions allow individuals to achieve

"structure-induced equilibria," according to this school; institutions furnish stability since stable equilibria are not to be found in individual "tastes." See William Riker, "Implications from the Disequilibrium of Majority Rule for the Study of Institutions," *American Political Science Review* 74 (1980), 432–46; Kenneth Shepsle, "Studying Institutions: Some Lessons from the Rational Choice Approach," *Journal of Theoretical Politics* 1 (1989), 131–47; Terry Moe, "Interests, Institutions, and Positive Theory: The Politics of the NLRB," *Studies in American Political Development* 2 (1987), 236–99; and Kenneth Shepsle and Barry Weingast, "The Institutional Foundations of Committee Power," *American Political Science Review* 81 (1987), 85–104).

26. Paul DiMaggio and Walter W. Powell, "Introduction," in *The New Institutionalism in Organizational Analysis* ed., Walter W. Powell and Paul DiMaggio (Chicago: University of Chicago Press, 1991), 1–38; James March and Johan Olsen, "The New Institutionalism: Organizational Factors in Political Life," *American Political Science Review* 78 (1984), 734–49; James March and Johan Olsen, *Rediscovering Institutions* (New York: Free Press, 1989); Karen Orren and Stephen Skowronek, "Beyond the Iconography of Order: Notes for a 'New Institutionalism,'" in *The Dynamics of American Politics: Approaches and Interpretations* eds., Lawrence C. Dodd and Calvin Jillson (Boulder, Colo.: Westview Press, 1994); Kathleen Thelen and Sven Steinmo, "Historical Institutionalism in Comparative Politics," in *Structuring Politics: Historical Institutionalism in Comparative Analysis* eds., Kathleen Thelen and Sven Steinmo (Cambridge: Cambridge University Press, 1992), 1–32.

27. March and Olsen, "The New Institutionalism"; Orren and Skowronek, "Beyond the Iconography of Order"; Thelen and Steinmo, "Historical Institutionalism in Comparative Politics."

28. Orren and Skowronek, "Beyond the Iconography of Order," 323–25.

29. Ibid., 325; DiMaggio and Powell, "Introduction"; Thelen and Steinmo, "Historical Institutionalism in Comparative Politics"; Ronald Jepperson, "Institutions, Institutional Effects, and Institutionalism," in *The New Institutionalism in Organizational Analysis* eds., Walter W. Powell and Paul DiMaggio (Chicago: University of Chicago Press, 1991), 143–64.

30. Orren and Skowronek refer to both "orderings" and "institutions." They imply that institutions are of a larger scale, when they write of the institutions of family organization, republicanism, and judicial regulation. "Beyond the Iconography of Order," 324.

31. In contrast to the "old institutionalism," the new institutionalism attends to the informal quality of institutions; it focuses on their interactions with other institutions; and it is more theoretically developed (and theoretically explicit). In contrast to behavioralism, the new institutionalism holds that institutions

do not necessarily allow for the optimization of individual preferences, that institutions may be inefficient, and that they cannot be reduced to the aggregate of individual behaviors.

32. In the polling data, and without a comprehensive study of the content of American newspapers at the time, I am necessarily making a structural argument about the probable influence of the yellow press consistent with the circumstantial evidence and the existing secondary literature available.

33. Charles H. Brown, *The Correspondent's War* (New York: Scribner's, 1967), 10. This compares to approximately 1,500 dailies today.

34. Turnouts in the non-Southern states were well in excess of 80 percent from 1876 through 1900, and in 1896 turnout in the five crucial Northeast and Mid-East states, including Iowa, exceeded 95 percent.

35. The U.S. population stood at 63 million persons in 1880 and rose to 72 million persons by 1890. The majority of Americans lived in the Northeast and Mid-East. There was also increasing urbanization. The number of Americans living in cities of one million or more almost doubled between 1890 and 1900 (from 3.6 to 6.4 million persons) and New York City itself included more than 3.4 million persons. Gould, *The Presidency of William McKinley*, 21–22.

36. Michael E. McGerr, *The Decline of Popular Politics: The American North, 1865–1928* (New York: Oxford University Press, 1986), 14–17.

37. Ibid., 58–59.

38. Ibid., 78, 120–21, 132–33.

39. Ibid., 114–16.

40. Michael Schudson, *Discovering the News* (New York: Basic Books, 1978), 93; Sidney Kobre, *The Yellow Press and Gilded Age Journalism* (Tallahassee: n.p., 1964), 7.

41. Brown, *Correspondent's War*, 10. As the great muckraker Lincoln Steffens summarized in 1897, "Journalism today is a business." Brown, *Correspondent's War*, 20. Also see McGerr, *Decline of Popular Politics*, 108.

42. Pulitzer and Hearst used the Cuban issue not only to outdo each other, but also as an opportunity to beat their other competition, which included the *New York Herald* and the *New York Sun*, among others. Brown, *Correspondent's War*, 126–27; Wilkerson, *Public Opinion and the Spanish-American War*, 115.

43. Brown, *Correspondent's War*, 132–34; Wilkerson, *Public Opinion and the Spanish-American War*, 101. The historian Lewis Gould notes that it is too simple to assign primary blame for the conflict to Hearst and Pulitzer, since they did not create the real differences between the United States and Spain and spoke for only a small part of the journalism community see his *Spanish-American War and President McKinley*, 24. Yet the *Journal* and the *World*

were at the vanguard of a broad and pervasive trend in American journalism as manifested in the Associated Press dispatches, the use of the *Journal* and *World* news services, and the imitation engendered in other, less sensational newspapers. Publications that followed the *Journal* and *World*'s lead included Dana's *New York Sun*, Bennett's *New York Herald*, and the *Chicago Tribune*. Other interventionist papers included the *New Orleans Times-Democrat*, the *Atlanta Constitution*, the *Indianapolis Journal*, and the *Charleston News and Courier*.

44. Robert W. Desmond, *Windows on the World: The Information Process in a Changing Society 1900–1920* (Iowa City: University of Iowa Press, 1980), 92. Also see Robert C. Hilderbrand, *Power and the People* (Chapel Hill: University of North Carolina Press, 1981), 8–9. Gould, Hilderbrand, and the historian John Offner each contend that McKinley was unaffected by the sensational press. Gould, *Spanish-American War and President McKinley*, 25; Hilderbrand, *Power and the People*, 27; John L. Offner, *An Unwanted War* (Chapel Hill: University of North Carolina Press, 1992), 158. Yet the President spoke frequently of the sensational press in early 1898. McKinley and his closest associates on numerous occasions referred explicitly to the "sensational newspapers" and the "blatherskite sheets." The sensational newspapers were "scavengers" and the product of "degenerate minds." The sensational papers published "falsehoods," they imagined events and influences where none existed, they made "vile slanders" against the President, and they exerted undue influence over members of Congress and "a too-easily-led public." See George B. Cortelyou, "March 16–December 13, 1898," Diaries of George B. Cortelyou, 1897–1901. Papers of George B. Cortelyou, Library of Congress. See also Cortelyou, Wednesday, February 15, 1899, Cortelyou Diaries.

45. Martha Joynt Kumar, "The President and the News Media," in *Guide to the Presidency* ed., Michael Nelson, 2d ed. (Washington, D.C.: Congressional Quarterly Press, 1996), 843–44; Hilderbrand, *Power and the People*, 11, 31.

46. Gerald F. Linderman, *The Mirror of War: American Society and the Spanish-American War* (Ann Arbor: University of Michigan Press, 1974), 153, 162.

47. The press was not all of a kind, of course. See note 80.

48. McKinley's assistant secretary remarked that the normally conservative (and Republican-controlled) Senate was being taken over by "a spirit of wild jingoism." George B. Cortelyou, "Transcript of shorthand notes of G.B.C. under date of Saturday, April 16, 1898, in Clayton's Quarto Diary 1898 by H.O.W.," Cortelyou Diaries. Cortelyou had earlier noted that "the report of the Maine disaster" had a "bad effect" on "the feeling in Congress." There was "a great deal of opposition to a suggested armistice or anything in the nature of delay." Cortelyou, Tuesday, March 29, 1898, Cortelyou Diaries.

49. Graebner, *Foundations of American Foreign Policy*, 331; May, *Imperial Democracy*, 137–47. Hilderbrand's claim that "the [P]resident felt little threatened by the readers of the yellow press, who lacked the political influence to harm his policy" ignores the voter demographics of the period and McKinley's responsibilities as head of the Republican party—with elections forthcoming in November of 1898. Hilderbrand, *Power and the People*, 27–28.

50. Wisan, *Cuban Crisis as Reflected in the New York Press*, 408–9.

51. Hilderbrand describes the President's proposal as an "aspect of McKinley's influence on public opinion." But Hilderbrand's portrayal of the early months of 1898 is one that is altogether too calm and too deliberate in the face of the vociferous yellow press. Hilderbrand's account gives short shrift to the *defensiveness* of McKinley's action. Nor does it convey much sense of the President's turmoil in the face of the increased likelihood that the United States would have to intervene militarily in Cuba. Hilderbrand, *Power and the People*, 20.

52. George B. Cortelyou, "Transcript of shorthand notes of G. B. C. under date of Sunday, March 27, 1898, in Clayton's Quarto Diary 1898 by H.O.W.," Cortelyou Diaries. McKinley himself was moved to say before the war that "should the cruelty be so long continued and revolting that the best instincts of human nature are outraged by it and should opportunity arise for bringing it to an end, and removing its cause without adding fuel to the flame of the contest, there is nothing in the law of nations which will condemn as a wrong doer, the State which steps forward and undertakes the necessary intervention" (undated, Subject File "Spain War, 1897–98 and undated," Papers of William R. Day, Library of Congress [William Day was Assistant Secretary of State, federal judge, and a close friend of the President]). As Trask points out, "nothing could have been more distasteful to the pacific McKinley than war." *War with Spain in 1898*, 474.

53. See George B. Cortelyou, "March 20–April 1898," Cortelyou Diaries. Also see Linderman, *Mirror of War*, 27–35.

54. See Brown, *Correspondent's War*, 140–41, 144–48; Offner, *An Unwanted War*, 150–57; Ephraim Smith, "William McKinley's Enduring Legacy: The Historiographical Debate on the Taking of the Philippine Islands," in *Crucible of Empire: The Spanish-American War & Its Aftermat*, ed., James C. Bradford (Annapolis, Md.: Naval Institute Press, 1993); Trask, *The War With Spain in 1898*, 31–44, 49–54; Wilkerson, *Public Opinion and the Spanish-American War*, 109–32; and Wisan, *Cuban Crisis as Reflected in the New York Press*, 422–42. Gould, Offner, Trask, and others cite the impressive speech made by Senator Redfield Proctor (R., VT) to explain the increased belligerence of Congress following the *Maine* disaster. Gould, *Presidency of William McKinley*, 77; Offner, *An Unwanted War*, 131–35, 229–32; Trask, *War With Spain*

in 1898, 36). (Proctor spoke on the deplorable condition of the *reconcentrados* and on the struggle of a million and a half Cubans for independence from Spain). Yet this belligerence on the part of Spain was amply manifest before the speech; the speech itself was widely covered in the press; and Proctor's address bought into the premise of the sensational newspapers—that the United States should for humanitarian reasons interfere in Spanish-Cuban relations.

55. The stories reported in the *Journal* and the *World* were also read out loud in Congress. "Staid newspapers that hesitated to repeat verbatim some particularly gruesome item from the *Journal* would relay it to its readers the next day as a statement read on the floor of the Senate or as testimony before the Senate Foreign Relations Committee." When a rebel general, Antonio Maceo, was killed in a skirmish, for instance, the press claimed "murder" and the Senate appointed a special committee to investigate the "Maceo Assassination." Walter Karp, *The Politics of War* (New York: Harper and Row, 1979), 58–59.

56. The President testified indirectly to the influence of the yellow press in a message delivered to Congress after the war: the destruction of the battleship *Maine* "stirred the nation's heart profoundly," and "[s]o strong" was the belief that United States-Spanish relations were at a crisis over the Cuban issue "that it required but a brief executive suggestion to the Congress to receive immediate answer to the duty of making instant provision for the possible and perhaps speedily probable emergency of war, and the remarkable, almost unique spectacle was presented of an unanimous vote of both house on the ninth of March, appropriating fifty million dollars 'for the national defense and for each and every purpose connected therewith, to be expended at the discretion of the president'." William McKinley, Message to Congress, December 5, 1898.

57. James Gordon Bennett's *New York Herald* was the original "penny press" paper, established in 1833. Other independent papers formed in the late 1870s and early 1880s in explicit rejection of party affiliation included the *Chicago Daily News*, the *Kansas City Evening Star*, and the *Newark Evening News*. These papers had neither the political commitment nor the mass audiences of Pulitzer's *New York World* or Hearst's *New York Journal*.

58. On Pulitzer, see George Juergens, *Joseph Pulitzer and the New York World* (Princeton: Princeton University Press, 1966). With their crusades against the trusts of the day, monitoring federal, state, and local government, and efforts on behalf of the workingman, Hearst and Pulitzer prepared the way for the muckrakers of the early twentieth century. Kobre, *The Yellow Press and Gilded Age Journalism*, 75–78.

59. Joyce Milton, *The Yellow Kids: Foreign Correspondents in the Heyday of Yellow*

Journalism (New York: Harper & Row, 1989), xiii; Wilkerson, *Public Opinion and the Spanish-American War*, 83. "Yellow" referred to the *New York World's* use of yellow ink, initiated in 1896, for printing "Hogan's Alley." The star of Hogan's Alley, the most popular cartoon comic in New York, was the impudent and hyperactive ringleader of the Hogan Alley gang, the "Yellow Kid."

60. Brown, *Correspondent's War*, 19; Linderman, *The Mirror of War*, 157; Milton, *Yellow Kids*, 43; Frank Luther Mott, *American Journalism: A History: 1690–1960*, 3d ed. (New York: Macmillan, 1962), 539–40.

61. Wilkerson, *Public Opinion and the Spanish-American War*, 131–32.

62. Ibid., 20–27.

63. Brown, *Correspondent's War*, 85–87, 95–102; Dobson, *Reticent Expansionism*, 56–57; Milton, *Yellow Kids*, 70–71, 196–202; Wilkerson, *Public Opinion and the Spanish-American War*, 11, 83–91; Wisan, *The Cuban Crisis as Reflected in the New York Press*, 222–24. Hilderbrand writes that Cuba "commanded virtually no public interest" in the summer of 1897. Hilderbrand, *The Power of the People*, 13. The de Lôme letter called McKinley "weak and a bidder for the admiration of the crowd" as well as a "would-be politician" (*politicastro*). Interestingly, de Lôme's letter not only attacked President McKinley but also criticized the *New York Journal*. See Gould on McKinley's interpretation of the de Lôme letter: that Spain was stalling for more time. *Presidency of William McKinley*, 73–74.

64. Edwin Emery and Michael Emery, *The Press and America: An Interpretive History of the Mass Media*, 4th ed. (Englewood Cliffs, N.J.: Prentice-Hall, 1978), 251; Kobre, *Yellow Press and Gilded Age Journalism*, 286–88; Linderman, *Mirror of War*, 158–59. The *Chicago Tribune* was as vehement as the *New York Journal* and the *New York World*. It used both papers' news services; the *San Francisco Examiner*, owned by Hearst, used the *Journal's* news. Both the *San Francisco Chronicle* and the *Chicago Times-Herald*, moreover, had to keep up with their competitors. San Francisco and Cincinnati were also centers of the yellow press. Smaller papers, on their part, naturally "tended to borrow some of the techniques and manners of the big journals." It is only a slight overstatement to claim that "readers everywhere got sensational, exaggerated accounts of the Cuban insurrection." Kobre, *Yellow Press*, 279; Mott, *American Journalism*, 548; Wilkerson, *Public Opinion and the Spanish-American War*, 6.

65. Brown, *Correspondent's War*, 123; Milton, *Yellow Kids*, 225–26; Wilkerson, *Public Opinion and the Spanish-American War*, 102–3; Wisan, *Cuban Crisis as Reflected in the New York Press*, 391–92. When the Spanish battleship *Vizcaya* made a reciprocal visit to New York on February 18, the *Journal* introduced its readers to a new card game, "The Game of War With Spain," the object of which was to sink the *Vizcaya*. The *Journal* thoughtfully pro-

vided its readers with a map to see if they were in range of the *Vizcaya's* guns. Meanwhile, the *World* published a Sunday feature reminding New Yorkers that the Spanish battleship could fire its shells all the way to the Harlem River and the "suburbs of Brooklyn." Milton, *Yellow Kids,* 228; Wisan, *Cuban Crisis as Reflected in the New York Press,* 393.

66.   Wisan, *Cuban Crisis as Reflected in the New York Press,* 388, 391.

67.   Gould, (*Presidency of William McKinley* and Trask, *War with Spain in 1898*) both emphasize the intransigence of the Spanish in their explanations of why the United States went to war. On the moral and religious dimensions of the American feelings toward Latin America and the Far East see Pratt, *Expansionists of 1898.*

68.   Orren and Skowronek, "Beyond the Iconography of Order," 322. I should point out that Orren and Skowronek use their framework to explain the *disorder* common in politics, whereas I use it to explain an instance of a temporary order (the yellow press) amid the disorder of conflicting multiple institutions in politics.

69.   Schudson, *Discovering the News,* 115; Brown, *Correspondent's War,* 18–19. There was also the matter of economics. Coverage of the Spanish-American War, with the extra transportation and transmission costs, the large numbers of reporters employed, and the extra editions was expensive; the *World* lost money in 1898.

70.   Desmond, *Windows on the World,* 94–96; Michael Bernard Grossman and Martha Joynt Kumar, *Portraying the President: The White House and the News Media* (Baltimore: Johns Hopkins University Press, 1981), 20–21; Samuel Kernell, *Going Public: New Strategies for Presidential Leadership* (Washington, D.C.: Congressional Quarterly Press, 1986), 59–63, 224–25. Theodore Roosevelt was already a master of public relations as a member of the McKinley administration, where Roosevelt was assistant secretary of the Navy. Roosevelt appears to have successfully covered up the Navy's investigation of the *Maine* explosion, for instance, and he was proficient at leaking information to the press and then vehemently denying doing so. Milton, *Yellow Kids,* 221–22, 235; Offner, *An Unwanted War,* 123.

71.   See Hilderbrand, *Power and the People*; Gould, *Presidency of William McKinley*; Kumar, "The Presidency and the News Media."

72.   See Emery and Emery, *Press and America,* 265; Linderman, *Mirror of War,* 169–70; Mott, *American Journalism,* 540–41. The editorial statement found on the body of Leon Czolgosz, the assassin, read "If bad institutions and bad men can be got rid of only by killing, then the killing must be done." Ambrose Bierce's quatrain published in the *Journal* read as follows: "The bullet that pierced Goebel's breast/Can not be found in all the West/Good reason, it is

speeding here/To stretch McKinley on his bier." (Kentucky Govenor Goebel had been assassinated in 1900).

73. The yellow press was *not* the tabloid press—publications not taken seriously by either politicians or serious readers, and recognized as containing stories known to be untrue. The yellow press well preceded the tabloids (referring to the actual size of the newspaper pages); the tabloids dated from the 1920s. The tabloids were also far less political than the yellow press. The *New York Daily News* had front-page stories on politics in only two editions throughout all of 1924, for example; it featured scandal, sports, and sex instead. Furthermore, the tabloid press deliberately promoted falsehoods. The yellow press, in contrast, may have contained inaccurate or deliberately misleading reporting, but was published with the understanding that distortion or misrepresentation was justified as long as it was consistent with the truth (e.g., of Spanish cruelty, the virtue of the American people). Emery and Emery, *Press and America*; 363–68; Mott, *American Journalism*, 666–73.

74. The argument for the singular impact of the yellow press is also consistent with the works of May, Grenville and Young, Graebner, Osgood, Trask, and others that refer to the importance of "irrational public opinion," "national outrage," the "new consciousness," "congressional impatience," "an ungovernable burst of popular emotion," and a "fire-storm of political emotion." But these terms are not assigned any historical or theoretical significance. Much of John Offner's history is in fact consistent with the argument offered here. See his *An Unwanted War*, xi, 117, 122, 230, 232. See also Gould, *Presidency of William McKinley*, 75.

75. Graebner, *Foundations of American Foreign Policy*, 305–6; Grenville and Young, *Politics, Strategy, and American Diplomacy*, 208–10; Coletta, *American Naval Heritage in Brief*, 147–48; Coletta, *Survey of U.S. Naval Affairs*, 44; LaFeber, *New Empire*, 363–64, 377.

76. LaFeber, *New Empire*, 326. Also see ibid., 172–75, 184–96, 326–27, 370–79.

77. The value of U.S. exports of manufactured goods rose from $112 million in 1887 to $213 million in 1897, and that of semi-manufactured goods rose from $37 million in 1887 to $98 million by 1897. The total value of U.S. exports rose from $703 to $1,032 million over the same period. Bureau of the Census, *Historical Statistics of the United States, Colonial Times to 1970*, 2 vols. (Washington, D.C.: GPO, 1975), Series U 213–224. Exports to the Far East, although smaller, rose from $20 million in 1887 to $39 million by 1897.

78. LaFeber, *New Empire*, 326.

79. Thelen and Steinmo note that institutional change or a new salience accruing to institutions can emerge as a result of "broad changes in the socioeconomic or political context." Thelen and Steinmo, "Historical Institutionalism in Comparative Politics," 16.

80. Offner, *An Unwanted War*, 123, 229; Gould *Presidency of William McKinley*, 62–63, 90; Gould, *Spanish-American War*, 24; Hilderbrand, *Power and the People*, 27; Schudson, *Discovering the News*, 88–120. The *New York Tribune*, the *New York Evening Post*, the *New York Times*, the *Journal of Commerce*, the *Chicago Daily News*, and the *Boston Transcript* among other papers all opposed war with Spain. Kobre, *Yellow Press and Gilded Age Journalism*, 291–92; Mott, *American Journalism*, 532. The communications scholar Michael Schudson also rejects the argument of a powerful yellow press. See Schudson, *The Power of News* (Cambridge: Harvard University Press, 1995), 23. Schudson dismisses the independent role of the press by arguing that explanations of the Spanish-American War by contemporary historians made no mention of the special impact of the press. Yet the timing of an argument would seem to be unrelated to the matter of its validity.

81. Offner, *An Unwanted War*, 123.

82. Offner, *An Unwanted War*, 229. Yellow journalism was much more than Hearst, of course. It was the rivalry between Pulitzer and Hearst; it was the influence of the *Journal* and the *World* on other newspapers in New York, such as the *Sun*, the *Herald*, and the *Tribune*, and throughout the United States; and it was the effect of the editorial and marketing leadership of the Pulitzer and Hearst newspapers on the U.S. newspaper industry. Schudson also finds that "there is little indication" that the yellow press influenced policymaking. He consults two sources in support of his contention: Lewis Gould's *Spanish-American War and President McKinley*, and an unpublished dissertation on Minnesota newspapers and the Cuban issue. Schudson, *Power of News*, 24.

83. Gould, *Presidency of William McKinley*, 63; Offner, *An Unwanted War*, 229.

84. Offner, *An Unwanted War*, 229. But even this claim is wrong: it was the *Journal* that published the de Lôme letter; it was the *Journal* staff who rescued Evangelina Cisneros to great popular acclaim; and one of the prominent Americans arrested in Cuba, Sylvester Scovel, was himself a newspaper reporter.

85. *Outlook Magazine* 54 (December 4, 1897), 795, quoted in Dobson, *Reticent Expansionism*, 45.

86. The press also made a difference by neglecting potential news. A number of important diplomatic developments that took place in the six (crucial) weeks following the destruction of the *Maine* went unreported, and there was almost no reporting of the fact that the Spanish government requested a joint investigation of the wreck, a request rejected by the U.S. government. Wisan, *Cuban Crisis as Reflected in the New York Press*, 417–19; also see Milton, *Yellow Kids*, 334.

87. Osgood, *Ideals and Self-interest in America's Foreign Relations*, 42; Trask, *The War with Spain in 1898*, 476.

88. See Richard Hofstadter, "Manifest Destiny and the Philippines," in Daniel Aaron, *America in Crisis* (New York: Alfred Knopf, 1952), 187–90; Gould, *Spanish-American War and President McKinley*, 84, 105; Grenville and Young, *Politics, Strategy, and American Diplomacy*, 286–88, 298; Milton, *Yellow Kids*, 265; Smith, "William McKinley's Enduring Legacy"; and Trask, *War With Spain in 1898*, 452–56. As McKinley told an aide soon after the war: "We need Hawaii just as much and a good deal more than we did California. It is manifest destiny." George B. Cortelyou, Monday, June 8, Cortelyou Diaries. The historian Graebner notes that "Few Americans attempted to justify the war against Spain except in terms of humanitarianism," and that the religious press was a part of this wave of humanitarian sentiment. Not only was President McKinley himself religious, but also all the religious press except for the Quaker and the Unitarian publications were for the annexation of the Philippines and Hawaii. The "dictates of civilization and humanity impelled" the United States to assist the Cuban revolution, annex Hawaii, keep the Philippines, and intervene in China. Graebner, *Foundations of American Foreign Policy*, 352–53 and Grenville and Young, *Politics, Strategy, and American Diplomacy*, 266.

89. See especially Orren and Skowronek, "Beyond the Iconography of Order."

90. On the *lack* of political independence typical of the news media, see W. Lance Bennett, "Toward a Theory of Press-State Relations in the United States," *Journal of Communication* 40 (1990), 103–25; Daniel C. Hallin, *The "Uncensored War"* (New York: Oxford University Press, 1986); and Leon V. Sigal, *Reporters and Officials: The Organization and Politics of Newsmaking* (Boston: D. C. Heath, 1973).

91. See Ben Bagdikian, *The Media Monopoly*, 4th ed. (Boston: Beacon Press, 1992), 18, on the concentration in the news industry. See Matthew Robert Kerbel, *Edited for Television: CNN, ABC, and the 1992 Presidential Campaign* (Boulder, Colo.: Westview Press, 1994), on the similarity of CNN with ABC and the other major television networks in election campaign coverage.

92. See David Broder, *Behind the Front Page* (New York: Simon and Schuster, 1987); Mark Hertsgaard, *On Bended Knee* (New York: Farrer, Straus, and Giroux, 1988); Howard Kurtz, *Media Circus* (New York: Times Books, 1993); and Thomas Patterson, *Out of Order* (New York: Knopf, 1994). It should also be admitted that public officials have learned how to use media practices and routines to their advantage (recall the Nixon administration's "Deep Throat," the Reagan administration's handling of the news media during the early and mid-1980s, and the facility by which the Bush administration conducted its public relations campaign against Iraq before and during the Gulf War).

93. There is, of course, no analogous economic depression at this time of writing.
94. James A. Baker III, "Report First, Check Later," *The Harvard International Journal of Press/Politics* 1 (Spring 1996), 7; Warren P. Strobel, "The CNN Effect," *American Journalism Review*, May 1996, 34. Strobel goes on to argue that the existence of the CNN Effect does not mean that it *determines* policy.
95. Bartholomew Sparrow, "The Presidency and the World," in *The Presidency and the Political System*, ed. Michael Nelson, 4th ed. (Washington, D.C.: Congressional Quarterly Press, 1995).

6 The Social Foundations of Strategic Adjustment

Miroslav Nincic, Roger Rose, and Gerard Gorski

If the purpose of grand strategy is to marshal and employ a nation's resources in the manner most conducive to its security objectives, then strategic adjustment is the business of redefining security objectives when established ends no longer bear a compelling relation to evolving circumstances, and of altering the relations between ends and means, resources and security needs, when changing conditions make these relations obsolete. As grand strategy is a reflection of national needs and values, on the one hand, and of international circumstances, on the other, an understanding of the shape that strategy assumes must be attentive to both domestic and external forces.

The end of the Cold War marks the first truly significant transition for postwar U.S. foreign policy, with implications as substantial as those that attended the beginning of the Cold War and the decisive abandonment of isolationism in the mid-1940s. Forced to find new guidelines for its foreign and military policy, the nation currently finds itself in a situation with no clear parallels in its experience. While the United States no longer confronts a serious challenge to its physical security or fundamental values, in contrast to its isolationist period it retains massive power acquired to deal with the Communist threat, as well as a conception of itself as the international community's leader in the pursuit of fundamental common objectives. Having dispensed with the concerns that dominated its policy during nearly half a century, it has not yet articulated a new sense of priorities, a firm conception of its place within the international community, or of the instruments, including military tools, of national policy appropriate to the new circumstances.

Recent reviews of U.S. military force structure provide the first wave of thinking on how military resources and planning should be adjusted to post-Cold War circumstances.[1] Their common feature is the recognition that international circumstances no longer provide a reliable guide to strategic planning, implying that, in the absence of clearly etched external priorities, societal pressures may play a significant role in guiding U.S. strategic adjustment. The significance of the domestic setting to national strategy is not a recent revelation. In addition to his dictum that armed force should be used with due regard to the political purposes it is intended to serve, Clausewitz drew attention to the societal forces upon which military success ultimately rests—especially in his comparison of the wars of the French Revolution with those of Frederick the Great.[2] More recently, Michael Howard, writing on "The Forgotten Dimension of Strategy,"[3] emphasized the dependence of military planning on its social underpinnings (the "forgotten dimension"), especially on the attitudes of the people upon whose "commitment and readiness for self-denial" the efficacy of its logistical, operational, and technological dimensions ultimately depend.

Pressures come from various political institutions and segments of society. While one could examine the role of interest groups or bureaucratic and institutional politics, this essay focuses on aggregate public preferences relevant to strategic adjustment, since the legitimacy of democratic policy ultimately requires the active support, or at least the passive acquiescence, of the national public.[4] While popular opinion plays some role in virtually all modern nations, its effect is strongest in systems where tenure of the top political office depends on the public's good will and where, even between elections, anticipated public responses govern so many presidential policy choices.[5] On many issues, the general public rarely does more than set the broad boundaries in which leaders conduct policy; on others, however, its strictures are more sharply defined. In either case, political leaders violate these boundaries at considerable political risk, and, on those exceptional occasions when foreign policy issues are highly salient, as when Americans are sent to fight on foreign shores, democratic public opinion must be, and generally is, monitored and consulted on a continuous basis.[6] Accordingly, we will examine the extent to which public view and preferences may help mold the process of strategic adjustment. Unlike the other contributions to this volume, which seek to shed light on the lessons of history, we will examine the guidelines that certain socio-psychological processes, when applied to the analysis of public opinion, may provide to U.S. leaders.

The Forms and Nature of Public Influence

The influence of social forces on strategic policy decisions can be felt in at least three ways. To begin with, strategic needs are tethered to political goals which, in turn, are rooted in the interests and preferences of relevant social actors. Beyond immediate threats to national survival, the definition of political, and hence strategic, goals will vary according to constellations of social forces and preferences, and strategic adjustment must be alert to these constellations. Second, because new strategic ends, like the old ones, imply material and other costs, the concurrence of those who are called upon to foot the bill is a necessary part of strategic calculations, while society's "commitment and readiness for self-denial" depend on the public's political priorities. Finally, the extent and the nature of military operations depend on societal acquiescence with the methods involved, since certain military options may be precluded by societal ideas, rooted in culture and ethics, of what is proper and acceptable; and means considered appropriate under one set of security challenges may appear unsuited to other circumstances.

Much of the empirical work on the form and nature of public influence concludes that foreign and national security policy is closely responsive to popular sentiment. A study conducted in the early 1970s comparing public preferences revealed by polling data on several national issues with actual policies, concluded that the degree of congruence on foreign policy matters was roughly comparable to that encountered for domestic issues.[7] Another study found that the correlation between public opinion and government policy was even more pronounced in the case of foreign policy.[8] Both studies sought only to establish a correlation between public opinion and policy, leaving open the issue of causal direction. More recent research has compared policy changes with opinion shifts at various points in time, establishing that, for foreign as well as domestic affairs, opinion shifted *before* policy changed in the majority of cases.[9] On a subject of particular relevance to strategic adjustment, Bruce Russett has inquired whether governmental decisions on levels of military spending followed or preceded shifting public views on whether increases were necessary. He found that the statistically strongest relation linked popular attitudes in a given year and changes in actual spending in the subsequent year.[10]

Since some scholars argue that the public's view is primarily a function of elite discourse and media coverage,[11] it is worth asking how malleable public priorities may be to influence from above. Research has shown that, the greater a citizen's political awareness, the more likely that person is to adopt elite and media views, especially when elites are united in their position.[12] When elites are divided along partisan or ideological lines, politically attentive citizens tend to align their views with those elites that share their broad values.

It is not surprising that the attentive public takes its cues from elites to whom its members are philosophically or socially proximate. But this also implies that the views of the poorly informed and politically inattentive *majority* are not easily molded from above, especially when, as is currently the case, there is considerable division within elite opinion itself. Under the circumstances, political leaders are wise to view the attitudes of the general public as relatively settled parameters, at least in the short- to medium-term. Furthermore, electoral considerations and the impact of mass opinion upon a president's congressional support suggest that, at least in the broad outlines of presidential foreign policy, the opinion of the *general* public matters very much.[13]

The specific impact of public priorities depends on the respective influence of societal and international pressures upon the formulation of national strategy.[14] The more serious the external threat, and the greater its clarity, the less do domestic social and political calculations dominate the thinking of policymakers. The greater the threat, the more the imperative of domestic solidarity asserts itself. Moreover, the clearer the cues provided by the international environment, the slighter the domestic dissension concerning their interpretation. Thus, threat and clarity imply an ability to focus strategic planning almost exclusively on the external world. It is not that strategic policy is any less a resultant of various vectors of domestic societal interest and preference, it is just that most of the relevant vectors point in the same direction, and decisionmakers are spared the effort of groping for the outlines of a domestic consensus. But when there is uncertainty about security threats and objectives, about the acceptable tradeoffs between wholly or partially incompatible goals, and about the proper relation of means to ends, a prior task of strategic adjustment is to devise the outlines of the necessary societal consensus. This is the position at which the United States currently finds itself.

The challenge, then, is to establish what guidance the U.S. public may offer its policymakers as they strive to design a national strategy for the post-Cold War era. The question guiding our inquiry is whether the general public provides its policymakers with clear and consistent cues, and whether there is an understandable and predictable structure to these cues. More particularly, we ask: do specific military and political preferences displayed by Americans follow from their more general principles and priorities? In other words, are these preferences governed by a discernible pattern of "vertical constraints"?[15] For example, vertical constraints would be operating if a person's support for local expenditure on public schools were predictable from that person's overall feelings about the value of education. During the Cold War years it may well be that the average American's attitudes on foreign policy and defense issues followed from more general attitudes toward communism, or about the primacy of national security. Correspondingly and in the wake of the Cold War's demise, it is important to ask whether a new structure of vertical constraints has emerged, one that might allow decisionmakers to anticipate specific positions from a grasp of general postures.

It may also be that certain overarching psychological inclinations, having little or nothing to do with the logic of vertical constraints, impart a predictability to popular stances on specific issues, providing policymakers with guideposts to what may or may not be popularly acceptable in the post-Cold War era. In particular, we will explore whether a dominant tendency to loss aversion—i.e., to weigh losses to acquired positions more heavily than comparable gains in the form of new positions—may also provide policymakers with clues useful in designing acceptable international security postures.

What we ultimately find is that, while the governed desire to keep their government on a short leash on matters of foreign and defense policy, they provide it with very little guidance about the specific ends that these policies should serve. Although the desire for a meaningful level of international involvement has not markedly decreased since the end of the Cold War, the public's foreign policy priorities in concrete applications are hard to infer from its overall policy predilections, contrary to what a belief in vertical constraints would suggest. Its attitudes toward military force are predictable to some degree on the basis of whether the goal is to expand or protect U.S. interests (an implication of loss aversion). Yet, even here, as we shall see, specific policy implications remain murky. A fairly tentative, case-by-case, and low cost approach to the nation's foreign and security goals may be what the domestic setting is more prone to encourage.

Before turning to the current period, it is useful to review the way in which the Cold War projected itself on the public's thinking, creating a consistent pattern of support for an activist, largely unilateral, and security-oriented grand strategy.

The Pattern of Cold War Preferences

At the height of the Cold War, the magnitude of the Soviet threat, the fundamental national values against which it seemed directed, and the monolithic character of the adversary bloc established a temporary, but stable, national consensus regarding the nature of the peril and the level of the necessary response. Though public pressure retained the ability to check policy, the agreement between government and governed on these matters meant that it rarely wished to do so. This was a time when a majority of Americans considered foreign affairs, the Communist threat especially, as the most important problem facing the nation, and there was little dissension on the need for toughness. According to a Gallup survey in 1946, 62 percent of the public opposed the notion of arms control with the Soviet Union.[16] A poll conducted two years later revealed that 34 percent of the respondents to the question "What policy do you think we should be following toward Russia?" thought that the U.S. should either prepare to fight or go to war.[17] Support for defense spending was correspondingly high. When asked, in 1951, whether the U.S. defense program should be reduced if the Korean war were brought to an end, only 12 percent of the public concurred, while a massive 82 percent opposed reductions.[18] Finally, public support for the use of force by the U.S. abroad was high and remained vigorous, particularly when measured in terms associated with Cold War objectives. In September 1950, 66 percent of the public expressed support for defending other countries against communism "like we did in Korea." Even though support for this notion declined somewhat as the war progressed, it never fell below 45 percent; remarkably, once the war was over public support for this idea rebounded to over 50 percent.[19]

By 1960, Cold War thinking was virtually unchallenged in popular politics. The presidential election campaign of that year reflected this consensus.

Both Nixon and Kennedy were ardent cold warriors and spent a significant portion of the 1960 campaign attempting to "one-up" each other as the strongest, toughest, and most dedicated anti-Communist.[20] The campaign rhetoric apparently struck a responsive chord among the public, for, by election day, 63 percent agreed strongly that "the United States should keep soldiers overseas where they can help countries that are against Communism" (up from 55 percent in 1958 and 49 percent in 1956).[21] This foreshadowed a general preoccupation with the Cold War, driven by events of the next few years.[22] When Gallup inquired in 1960 and 1961 about the most important problem facing the nation, the response was so overwhelmingly colored by concerns for foreign affairs that the pollster chose, uncharacteristically, not to report percentages in its annual yearbook. Subsequently, in 1962 and 1963 the percentages naming foreign affairs averaged over 60 percent.

Reflecting the popular mood, Congress was loath to question presidential initiatives in foreign policy, especially on matters of national security. The concept of "Two Presidencies" was coined, to distinguish a domestic presidency, girded by the usual forms of democratic control, and a foreign-policy presidency within which the Chief Executive enjoyed surprising autonomy.[23] As Senator William Fulbright maintained at the time, "The price of democratic survival in a world of aggressive totalitarianism is to give up some of the democratic luxuries of the past."[24]

Still, the period of consensus represented a relatively brief chapter in U.S. political history. By the late 1960s, the Vietnam debacle had demonstrated to many Americans that their government could not always be relied upon to define the national interest appropriately, or to pursue it effectively. In addition, by weakening the perceptions of threat upon which the Cold War consensus rested, the détente of the late sixties and early seventies produced a greater plurality of societal perspectives on foreign and defense policy.

To examine whether these were changes of degree, rather than of fundamental substance, we consider public attitudes toward the Soviet Union as an indicator of Cold War sentiment. Figure 6.1 displays three series of data points bearing on the issue. The longest, spanning the period from 1953 to 1990 represents general negative perceptions of the USSR[25] Two others are more particular but less complete. One charts the public's assessment of the U.S./ Soviet relationship;[26] the other indicates how the public has viewed Soviet intentions.[27] Each of these measures exhibit considerable fluctuation after the period of U.S./Soviet détente during the early 1970s, at

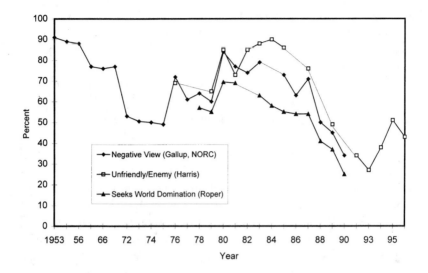

FIGURE 6.1 Negative Views of Russia/Soviet Union, 1953–1996
SOURCE: Gallup, NORC, Harris

times tilting significantly in the direction of the old Cold War consensus. Also in evidence is the marked decline of all indicators as the Cold War wound to a close and the Soviet Union dissolved. Accordingly, the first major and unambiguous shift in the nature and perception of external threat coincides with the end of the Cold War.

The General View: Internationalism After the Cold War

Since the Cold War witnessed a shift from traditional isolationism to vigorous internationalism, one may ask whether the process operates symmetrically: whether a retreat to isolationism has followed the disappearance of direct Cold War-related threats to the United States. This has been the fear of policymakers and commentators. In 1993, political commentator Ben Wattenberg cautioned against America's habit of "playing ostrich when danger recedes," a tendency that has "led to tragedy, both American and global."[28] Following the 1994 midterm elections, George Bush warned against the rising influence of isolationism, urging Americans to resist "that faulted sirens' call."[29] Similarly, former Chairman of the House International

Relations Committee Lee Hamilton worried that "the public is, at best, ambivalent about an active U.S. role in the world . . . This makes it much more difficult for the President to conduct U.S. foreign policy during this time of transition."[30]

The concerns of pundits notwithstanding, the data provide only very limited evidence of resurgent isolationism; the more accurate characterization of public sentiment is one of *qualified* internationalism. Examining, in figure 6.2, responses to the question "Do you think it will be best for the future of the country if we take an active part in world affairs or if we stay out of world affairs?"[31] we find that the percentage preferring the former to the latter alternative was not very different in 1994 than in the mid-1940s. On average, over the entire period, only 25 to 30 percent expressed a preference for staying out, and the range of variation in this sentiment has been slight. The extent of current isolationism seems no greater than during the late 1970s and early 1980s, which is somewhat surprising, since that period was characterized by increased U.S.-Soviet tension, and since the public was gener-

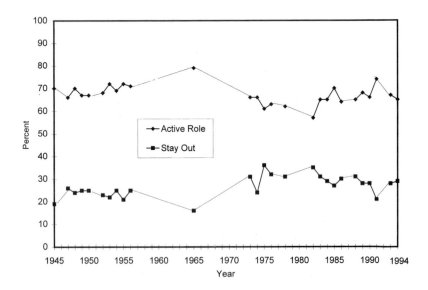

FIGURE 6.2 Attitudes Toward International Involvement, 1945–1994
(Annual Average)
SOURCE: Gallup, NORC

ally supportive of increased defense spending. If anything, this indicates that internationalism and perception of external peril do not necessarily go hand in hand, suggesting, in turn, that a return to isolationism need not be a consequence of the Soviet Union's collapse.

Two other measures of opinion on an isolationist-internationalist continuum are provided by the Times Mirror Center for the People and the Press.[32] While both suggest that isolationism has gained ground with respect to the pre-détente period, they reveal no substantial change since the mid-seventies.

Measure 1 is based on public responses to the following statement: "The US should mind its own business internationally and let other countries get along the best they can on their own." As figure 6.3 demonstrates, the percent concurring with this view in 1995 is a little more than twice as high as it was in 1964 and about what it was in 1976. A rejection of the isolationist position did coincide with the worsening of U.S.-Soviet relations during the late 1970s and early 1980s, but the overall trend in this measure is a rather

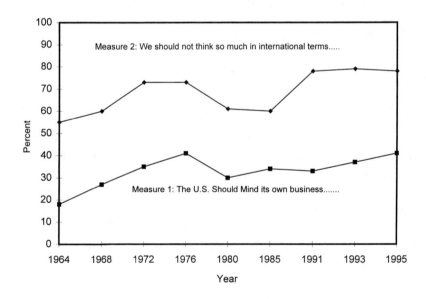

FIGURE 6.3 Measures of Internationalism, 1964–1995
SOURCE: Times Mirror

slow gradual return to the level of the mid-seventies. Absent is any indication of a precipitous increase in isolationist sentiment following the end of the Cold War.

Measure 2 involves public reactions to the statement "We should not think so much in international terms but concentrate more on our own national problems and building up our strength and prosperity here at home." Although the two trend-lines trace a roughly comparable trajectory, the *level* of apparent isolationism is much greater in the second case than in the first. Measure 1 implies that about 2 in 5 Americans have opted for isolationism after the Cold War; Measure 2 implies that the figure is nearly twice as high!

The discrepancy, although large, may result from the wording of the two statements: the first refers to international involvement in an absolute sense, with no reference to its domestic consequences; the second implies a necessary tradeoff between internationalism and an ability to address pressing domestic problems. This suggests that isolationism is apt to be greatest when people believe that international challenges can be met only at the expense of domestic needs, and that support for foreign involvement may hinge on the extent to which these costs are perceived as: (a) slight in absolute terms, and/or (b) being shared with other nations.

Our view of the public finds additional support in recent scholarship. In a study, covering the 1947 to 1991 period, Alvin Richman found that the Cold War's demise brought no significant change in public attitudes toward involvement in world affairs.[33] Examining 13 trend measures of U.S. internationalist sentiment, he detected no meaningful difference for six; five of the measures actually showed an increase in internationalism, while only two reflected a decline. Revisiting this question three years later, Richman updated and reconceptualized his examination. While this produced a more nuanced discussion, his basic conclusions remain unchanged.[34] In the more recent work Richman identifies four dimensions (factors) of internationalist sentiment derived from his examination of the October 1994 Chicago Council on Foreign Relations Survey. He argues that opinions vary separately across each of these dimensions, and while changes along one of them, "global altruism" can be read as a decline in internationalist sentiment, shifts in the other three suggest, instead, adjustments of substantive and regional priorities. Moreover, Richman finds, as we do, that for the most part general measures of internationalism have remained relatively constant.

All in all, then, it appears that internationalism has not so much been replaced by staunch isolationism as tempered by a concern with the domestic opportunity costs of international activism. The lack of strong isolationist sentiment may be natural, since the nation as a whole has become increasingly aware of the extent of international interdependence and of the futility of insulating U.S. interests from external influences and developments. Nevertheless, concern with the costs of involvement may have limited the public's appetite for foreign engagements to those that do not carry meaningful domestic costs or to those that enhance the domestic economic and social agenda; and if popular thinking on foreign policy is indeed vertically constrained, some guidelines for strategic adjustment may be inferred from general priorities and preferences.

The Emerging Structure of Priorities: Domestic Priorities and Foreign Policy Objectives

A common feeling, consistent with observations on internationalism, is that, in the post-Cold War era, external goals are defined by domestic needs, and that the rank ordering of these goals reflects the structure of domestic priorities. For example, Andrew Kohut, Director of the Times Mirror Center for the People and the Press, observed in his 1993 testimony before the House Foreign Affairs Committee that "The public wants a foreign policy agenda that serves its domestic agenda."[35] This preference could certainly be inferred from what the average American defines as the most important national problem, and by observing the respective movements of domestic and international concerns (as shown in figure 6.4). The graph traces the percentage of the public that identified foreign and defense issues as the nation's most important problem. As one can see, throughout the 1950s and 1960s foreign policy ranked even with, and often higher than, domestic policy concerns.[36] But since the Vietnam War, foreign policy problems consistently track far below domestic issues in the public's mind, except in times of immediate foreign policy crises like the Iran Hostage Crisis (1979) and the Persian Gulf War (1991).

One would anticipate, along with Kohut, that an altered sense of national challenges, where domestic problems have superseded international problems in the hierarchy of popular concerns, should now cause a good foreign

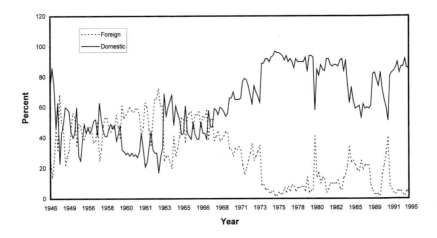

FIGURE 6.4 Most Important Problem, 1946–1995
SOURCE: *Gallup Monthly*, vars. eds.; Smith, *Public Opinion Quarterly*, 1985

policy to be defined as one that advances important domestic needs. This is what effective vertical constraints would lead us to expect, and this is substantially what surveys by the Chicago Council of Foreign Relations (CCFR) reveal in table 6.1.[37]

In each of the five surveys, the two highest ranking foreign policy goals have involved objectives directly related to domestic needs: protecting U.S. jobs and securing adequate energy supplies (in 1990, protecting U.S. business interests), objectives with a pronounced "bread and butter" content. Interestingly, the support for these objectives may not even be associated with post-Cold War priorities. The 1978 and 1982 surveys, conducted in the throes of a new chill in U.S.-Soviet relations and amid heightened security anxieties, reveal that the public deemed domestic goals as more important than containing communism, defending our allies' security, and matching Soviet military power. It is quite possible that identical surveys conducted between the late-1940s and early 1960s would have reflected a greater relative concern for Cold War objectives, but it is hard to escape the conclusion that, more recently and especially since the Soviet Union's collapse, the measure of a good foreign policy, from the perspective of the average American is how well it promotes domestic prosperity and well-being.[38]

TABLE 6.1 Public Support for Various U.S. Foreign Policy Goals
(Percentage of public agreeing that objective is "very important")

Year	1994	1990	1986	1982	1979	Mean
Mainly Protective						
Protecting U.S. Jobs	(1) 83	(1) 65	(1) 78	(1) 77	(1) 78	76
Securing Energy Supplies	(2) 62	(3) 61	(2) 69	(2) 70	(1) 78	68
Protecting U.S.						
Business Interests	(3) 52	(2) 63	(8) 43	(8) 44	(7) 45	49
Containing Communism	—	(7) 56	(4) 57	(4) 59	(4) 60	58
Defending Allies' Security	(5) 41	(3) 61	(5) 56	(5) 50	(5) 50	52
Matching Soviet						
Military Power	—	(7) 56	(6) 53	(6) 49	—	53
Protecting Weaker Nations						
from Aggression	(8) 24	(6) 57	(11) 32	(11) 34	(9) 34	36
					Mean	56
Mainly Promotive						
Strengthen United Nations	(4) 51	(10) 44	(7) 46	(7) 48	(6) 47	47
Protect & Defend						
Human Rights	(6) 34	(5) 58	(9) 42	(9) 43	(8) 39	43
World-wide						
Arms Control	—	(9) 53	(2) 69	(3) 64	(3) 64	63
Improve Living						
Standards Abroad	(9) 22	(11) 41	(10) 37	(10) 35	(10) 35	34
Promote Democracy						
Abroad	(6) 34	(12) 28	(12) 30	(12) 29	(11) 26	29
					Mean	43

SOURCE: Chicago Council of Foreign Relations
NOTE: Number in parentheses indicate rank-ordering of objective within the survey.

While distinctions based on the substance of the goals pursued—on the assumption that general objectives shape specific priorities—are valuable, a classification of foreign policy objectives based on the notion of loss-aversion is revealing as well. In this regard, it is useful to distinguish between two broad categories of foreign policy goals: those protecting objectives that the United States had pretty much attained, and those involving the pursuit of ends that are, as yet, unattained. The first will be termed *protective*, the second *promotive*.[39] The expectation is that the public's responses to loss and gain respectively may, in addition to vertical constraints, provide a basis for structuring foreign policy attitudes. A close examination of the results of the CCFR surveys confirms the hypothesis (table 6.1).

We have distinguished, among the survey questions, those in which the wording would qualify the associated goals as "promotive" from those which would be properly be classified as "protective." The explanation, consonant with the premises of prospect theory, is that the latter would evoke significantly more popular enthusiasm than the former.[40] The data support the hypothesis. We have computed the mean values for response considering the foreign policy objective "very important" in the rightmost column. As can be seen, the mean support score for the protective goals is 56, for promotive goals is 43. The dominance of protective over promotive goals is evident throughout the surveys. Protecting that which we have attained seems a more worthy objective to most Americans than attaining new goals.

Accordingly, the public appears to want a foreign policy pragmatically related to its domestic concerns, and one that is essentially protective rather than promotive. In and of themselves, these desiderata do not seem fully compatible with a role of vigorous international leadership. Nevertheless a look at the even more restricted set on military and national security goals furnishes further insight into the American public's ability to provide its leaders with cues as to which sorts of policies are likely to be most acceptable in terms of societal preferences.

The Absence of Security Threats

External threats provide the context for force postures and military activities, and one may ask what purpose armed force serves from the public's viewpoint if there is *no* compelling foreign peril. In this regard, the impact of the Cold War's demise cannot be overstated. In 1946, 69 percent of the population anticipated finding itself in another war within twenty-five years;[41] by 1993, 87 percent of the public was entirely or fairly satisfied with the nation's military security.[42] Indeed, as William Schneider observes, "sometime during the 1980s, people started to consider non-military issues a more serious threat to our national security than military issues."[43] Looking ahead to figure 6.5 provides additional evidence that the importance of an external peril has diminished, as it displays the decline in public concern with the Soviet threat.

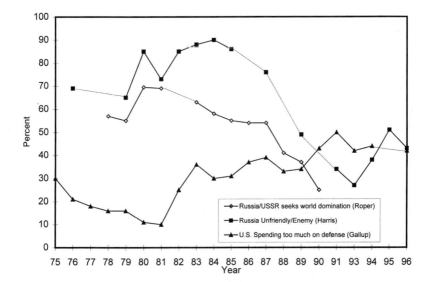

FIGURE 6.5 Russian/Soviet Threat and Attitude on Defense Spending
SOURCE: Gallup, NORC, Harris, Times Mirror

When queried about external threats to the United States, the public appears hard-pressed to name an overriding peril, and none dominates popular concerns. Predictably, when asked to identify the greatest threat to the international order (rather than directly to the United States), the public's views are likewise fragmented.

Times-Mirror asked the public to identify the greatest threat to world stability, but no single peril was mentioned by a majority, or even a strong plurality of the respondents, as their first choice, as indicated in table 6.2. Just over a quarter of the public identified interethnic hostility, and just under one quarter chose the (logically unrelated) problem of nuclear proliferation. The third choice (18 percent) was environmental pollution, while remaining opinion was divided between three other (and, again, largely unrelated) issues.

The Chicago Council on Foreign Relations' 1995 poll, reveals a greater number of people identifying a "critical threat" to U.S. interests, but, again, with no dominant threat. In fact, examining table 6.3, we observe that more than 50 percent of the respondents considered any of five more or less unrelated threats "critical" in this sense. This suggests that there is no vertically

TABLE 6.2 Public's View of Top Dangers to World Stability
(Percentage of Respondent's First Choice)

Nationalism and Ethnic Hatreds	27%
Proliferation of Weapons of Mass Destruction	24%
Environmental Pollution	18%
Religious Fanaticism	11%
Population Growth	10%
International Trade Conflicts	7%

SOURCE: Times Mirror, 1993.

TABLE 6.3 Threats to Vital U.S. Interests
(Percentage of Respondents who Consider Items as "Critical Threat")

Possibility of Unfriendly Countries Becoming Nuclear Powers	72%
Large Numbers of Immigrants and Refugees Coming to the U.S.	72%
International Terrorism	69%
Economic Competition from Japan	62%
The Development of China as a World Power	57%
Possible Expansion of Islamic Fundamentalism	33%
The Military Power of Russia	32%
Economic Competition from Europe	27%

SOURCE: Chicago Council of Foreign Relations, 1995.

structured thinking in this area. Moreover, the second and fourth ranked threat have little connection to security as it is traditionally conceived, and no logical connection to military force.

The Public and Military Power

The implications for strategic adjustment of a public that is, with the possible exception of nuclear proliferation, unable to identify a compelling common threat, are substantial, since this undermines national willingness to bear many of the costs of military power. These implications are apparent for three issues pivotal to strategic adjustment: (a) military spending; (b) multilateralism and burden-sharing, and (c) the use of force abroad.

Military Spending

Under the new international circumstances, it is not surprising that there should be limited enthusiasm for expanding military budgets, and examination of figure 6.5 reveals a strong inverse relationship between the public's sense of external threats and its support for defense spending.[44]

While only about one out of six Americans reckoned that the United States was spending too much on defense in the mid-1960s, since the early 1970s almost twice that number has felt that too much is lavished on defense. More recently, that percentage has increased from an average of 29 percent in the eighties, to more that 40 percent for every year of this decade.

Having paid the bill for the Cold War, the public displays little sympathy for extensive defense spending without a major threat to arm against. This does not mean that military spending is likely to decrease, in either real or nominal terms; but it does indicate that little real growth in defense outlays can be realistically expected in the foreseeable future. And it means that major new missions and weapons systems are likely to be purchased at the expense of existing programs. With regard to the size of the U.S. military, 58 percent of the public is willing to support a military force large enough to fight a war the size of the 1991 Gulf War. However, it is skeptical of the need for a force capable of fighting two regional wars simultaneously.[45]

Burden-sharing

In the wake of the Cold War, the public displays little attachment to pursuing security objectives unilaterally. Not surprisingly, it is unwilling to shoulder the costs of major international military operations whenever security objectives can be said to concern others as well. Further, most Americans favor having U.S. allies assume more of the responsibilities. Ninety percent of the public agreed that other countries should pay a share of the costs of intervention (even when the question suggests that outside support may "compromise our moral leadership and make us seem too mercenary).[46]" With regard to the United Nations, a Times Mirror poll portrays a public sympathetic to some notion of "*multilateral*" internationalism, and support for the statement "The United States should cooperate fully with the United Nations" has remained consistently above 60 percent since the mid-1980s.[47] Moreover, while some conservative policymakers disparage the idea of strengthening the United Nations, 57 percent of the public believes strengthening the UN would not interfere with the ability of the U.S. to pursue its interests.[48] In fact, strengthening the UN appears, according to one survey, to include contributing troops to UN efforts to defend other UN members from attack.[49]

Generally, the public overwhelmingly supports maintaining existing alliance commitments and, whenever possible, calling upon others to act jointly with the U.S. And, despite the demise of its original mission, 61 percent of Americans felt, in early 1997, that NATO should be maintained.[50]

Finally a series of polls on possible use of force in the Korean Peninsula and Saudi Arabia, two areas the U.S. has long pledged to defend on its own, show that the public supports using force in those areas only if the UN or U.S. allies also participate; 68 percent and 76 percent of the public supports joint military action to defend Saudi Arabia and South Korea, respectively, from attack. However, when the same poll asks respondents who favor these joint military operations if they would support unilateral action by the U.S., support drops to 44 percent for Saudi Arabia and 31 percent for South Korea.[51]

In sum, continued support for the U.S. resort to force abroad implies that the costs and responsibilities be shared with other nations.

Justifications for Resort to Force

Do public preferences indicate to what specific purposes military power should be applied? One might assume, by the logic of vertical constraints, that the specific ends the public feels should be addressed through armed force are directly implied by its sense of leading national priorities. But this is not entirely so. Table 6.4 displays the result of a 1993 poll on justifications for military intervention.

Interestingly, and quite contrary to what the public's domestic priorities would lead us to anticipate, economic interests do not head the list. After the need to fend off direct threats to American lives, the humanitarian objective of preventing mass starvation is regarded as the strongest justification for military intervention. This is followed by guaranteeing peace and security in important regions. Neither of the latter two were high on the general lists of foreign policy priorities. Economic interests rank only fourth here. (The only ranking that is expected in terms of more general priorities involves the promotion of democracy which, again, is at the bottom of the list.) Clearly,

TABLE 6.4 Justifications for Military Intervention
(Percentage Respondents Agreeing with Item)

U.S. Under Direct Military Attack	94%
To Prevent Large Numbers from Starving to Death	67%
To Guarantee Peace and Security in an Important Region	63%
Important U.S. Economic Needs Are at Stake	60%
One Nation Destroying Another by Killing People/Driving Them from Their Homes	57%
To Guarantee Democratically Elected Leaders Can Govern	47%

SOURCE: Wall Street Journal/NBC, 1993.

this is not the order of justifications for resort to force that the more general preferences would predict.

It is noteworthy that humanitarian goals, although they have no direct bearing on U.S. domestic needs, win the approbation of a majority of Americans. For example, fully 71 percent of those asked said they would favor sending U.S. troops "to save lives and help distribute food in countries where people are starving, but where U.S. national security is not involved," while only 22 percent were opposed.[52] In early 1994, a majority (59 percent) of respondents disagreed with the statement that "the US needs to be involved in Bosnia in order to protect its own interests." Nevertheless, a plurality of respondents concurred with the feeling that "the US has a moral obligation to stop Serbian attacks on Sarajevo."[53] Again, in June 1995, 63 percent of the respondents in a USA Today-CNN Poll estimated that the United States need not be involved in Bosnia "to protect US interests," although an identical percentage felt that the United States does have "a moral obligation to protect Bosnian civilians from Serbian attacks."

The public likewise failed to endorse domestic reasons for involvement in the most significant military action in recent years—the Gulf War. Despite President Bush's several attempts to justify the 1991 Persian Gulf War in terms of the economic consequences for the U.S. if major oil fields fell into Iraqi hands, the public seems not to have considered economic imperatives a sound rationale for military action. A few weeks before Operation Desert Storm was launched, most citizens felt that the goal of maintaining U.S. oil supplies would not justify armed intervention (though 62 percent endorsed military force to serve notice on Iraq and other potential aggressors that such behavior does not go unpunished.)[54] Probably taking his cue from the polls, the President began stressing the normative principle of nonaggression as a justification for U.S. military action.

Though some cases of promoting peace and thwarting aggression matter enough to most Americans to justify resort to force, the situation is very different when it comes to shaping the domestic politics of other nations. For example, in the same Harris survey that showed a strong majority in favor of using troops to help starving people, only 48 percent favored sending American troops to "help restore order and save lives in war-torn countries where effective government has broken down."[55] Similarly, before U.S. forces were dispatched to Haiti, a majority of Americans opposed the idea of sending U.S. troops to Haiti to "restore the elected government."[56] (Although, in another poll, 69 percent of the public was willing to support the Haiti intervention if the issue was to prevent the illegal immigration that might follow from a failure to restore democracy).[57] These findings are consistent with Bruce Jentleson's conclusions, based on popular attitudes toward a number of U.S. military interventions, that the U.S. public is more likely to endorse the use of force when the objective is to deal with another country's external behavior than when the purpose is to change its domestic order.[58]

The Costs of Military Intervention

We must distinguish support for the mere prospect of intervention from the attitudes that emerge once that prospective intervention has become a reality. While endorsement of intervention in the abstract may be based largely on the issues at stake, attitudes toward an intervention that is underway are at least as likely to be governed by its costs. For example, although most Americans initially supported the intervention in Somalia, enthusiasm quickly waned after the first U.S. casualties were reported. If many Americans felt that the U.S. had a "moral obligation" to stop Serbian attacks on Sarajevo, they endorsed only the most costless and riskless forms of achieving this (going as far as air strikes, but not the dispatching of U.S. ground troops).

The U.S. experiences in Korea and Vietnam demonstrated a clear link between decline in approval for the wars and their costs, especially their human toll,[59] and the overwhelming enthusiasm for the Gulf War must, in large part, be explained by the relatively small number of American casualties it claimed. In fact, some notion of how dependent approval of the war was on casualty levels is acquired when the link between support and hypothetical casualty levels is examined. The *Los Angeles Times* in January 1991 explored whether the public's perception of success in the war with Iraq would be influenced by the number of U.S. soldiers killed. The relationship between costs and support emerges clearly in figure 6.6.[60]

And, in a mission more similar to Somalia than to the Gulf War, Americans are again, as shown in figure 6.7, cost sensitive toward U.S. casualties in the case of Bosnia.[61]

The relevance of costs also extends to the economic realm. According to a Time/CNN poll conducted a few days before the start of the Gulf War, two-thirds of the public declared that Kuwait was worth fighting for. Attitudes shifted, though, when the issue of economic costs was explicitly introduced. A five to four negative answer was evoked when the following question pointed out economic costs: "Going to war against Iraq will cost this country billions of dollars. Given our current economic problems, do you think going to war against Iraq is worth the billions of dollars in costs?"[62]

In sum, military intervention that does not adequately consider public sensitivity to U.S. costs is likely to create pressures for a resolution of the involvement that may be at variance with its political objectives or, at least, with guiding conceptions of the proper relation of means to ends. In this regard, the current interest of defense planners in the technology of nonlethal conflict, within the context of a potential Revolution in Military Affairs, may have considerable implications—since, in the absence of significant human costs, the public constraints on national decisionmakers with regard to military involvements are likely to be considerably looser than ever before.[63]

The Hazards of Inferring Specific Preferences from General Priorities

As we have seen, vertical constraints operate clearly with regard to some issues and, at other times, especially with the use of force, appear sporadically, if at all. We started with most general principle: the commitment to internationalism, and while we found continuing support for international involvement, it appears domestically driven and cost-sensitive. A more general examination of the public's foreign policy priorities revealed that they were substantially tethered to domestic concerns. Moreover, when asked

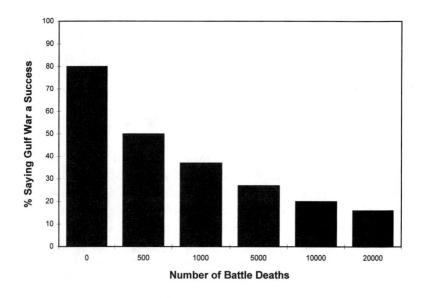

FIGURE 6.6 Casualties and Perception of Success in Gulf War
SOURCE: Los Angeles *Times*, January 17–18, 1991

about military spending and burden-sharing, the public again shows an alertness to domestic needs and a corresponding sensitivity to costs.

The public's apparent priorities may also account for the emphasis placed by both post-Cold War presidents on job-creation as a leading foreign policy objective. Evidence of a link to domestic priorities is found in President Clinton's claim, in his report entitled A *National Security Strategy of Engagement and Enlargement,* that his approach to strategy is: "premised on the belief that the line between our domestic and foreign policies has increasingly disappeared—that we must revitalize our economy if we are to sustain our military forces, foreign initiatives and global influence, and that we must engage actively abroad if we are to open foreign markets and create jobs for our people."[64]

At the same time, and surprisingly, public willingness to commit troops abroad seems largely unrelated to the more general domestic priorities. When it comes to looking at public support for specific decisions, the principle of restraint and domestic economic health does not trump humanitarian issues as often as we would expect. Further, it cannot be assumed that foreign policy and security decisions will be rewarded by the public to the

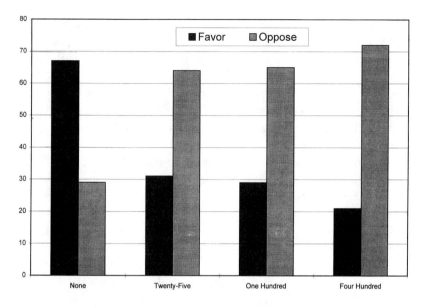

FIGURE 6.7 Casualties and Public Support for U.S. Involvement in Bosnia
SOURCE: Gallup/CNN/USA Today Poll, October 19–22, 1995

extent that they reflect its domestic priorities, even in the less threatening, less crisis-prone realm of diplomacy. We have seen that the public claims to place job promotion at the pinnacle of its foreign policy objectives, while ranking the support of human rights abroad very low. Accordingly, when a presidential choice must be made between the two, one expects jobs to be favored. This was the case when President Clinton opted, in May 1994, to maintain China's Most Favored Nation status despite its shoddy human rights record. But this does not appear to be what most Americans really wanted. A few months before the President's decision, the public was asked whether we should "maintain good relations with China despite disagreements we might have with its human rights policies, or should we demand that China improve its human rights policies if it wants to continue to enjoy its current trade status with the United States?" Less than one-third (29 percent) of the respondents opted for unconditional trade relations, while nearly two-thirds (65 percent) favored an insistence on human rights.[65]

The discrepancy between public sentiment on general preferences and specific decisions, therefore, needs clarification, and at least three reasons account for the occasional slippage between general priorities and specific preferences. To begin with, if the specific case involves a concrete foreign country, it invokes thoughts about that nation and society. Depending on how an event and its participants are portrayed, the standards of evaluation the public applies to the concrete case may get modified. Secondly, the particular policy will usually involve consideration not just of the foreign policy end, but also of the means by which it is pursued. This adds additional complexity to popular thinking, since certain means are, culturally or ethically, considered more suited to some ends than others. The "blood for oil" theme resonated ill with most Americans during the Gulf War (armed force seemed more appropriate to loftier objectives); and the notion of granting inducements to terrorists ("arms for hostages") in dealings with Iran seemed wrong to many, since bad behavior, in the public mind, is supposed to be punished, not rewarded. Last, as our references to war casualties suggest, the specific case draws public attention to the policy's costs, and cost-benefit calculations may not lead to the same conclusions about the policy's desirability as mere evaluation of the objective involved. But the discrepancy between endorsement of general objectives and support for the specifics of their implementation suggests limits to the extent to which a consistent national strategy can be devised in the post-Cold War era.

Conclusions

It bears reiterating that the country's leaders do not shape strategic adjustment exclusively, or even predominantly, around shifts in public preferences. Indeed, as Captain Ed Smith's contribution to this volume shows, the Navy's *From the Sea* review was a response to the collapse of the Cold War and the Soviet Union, the growth in global interdependence, and the pace of technological change. The public's role was indirect. Still, as we argued in the beginning of this essay, at least a passive public acquiescence is required for major changes in national policy, and no significant commitment of economic or human resources can be contemplated in the face of popular opposition.

Consequently, the most important questions asked in the Department of Defense's *Bottom Up Review*—How do we structure our armed forces for the future? How much defense is enough under the new circumstances? What, now, is the major purpose of military force?—must be answered with the public in mind. At the same time, when foreign threats seem neither clear nor pressing, the rules guiding popular thinking on political-military issues are poorly understood. Unfortunately, our own examination provides, at most, partial help in this regard. Three conclusions have a particularly significant bearing on the issue of strategic adjustment.

The first is that, while there are general objectives that seem more important than others, and while protective goals dominate those of a promotive nature, it is not easy to predict support for concrete policies from general public priorities, contrary to what the theory of "vertical constraints" on the public's political thinking may have led us to expect. The emphasis on domestic (especially economic) goals is not always present in specific cases, while an interest in general humanitarian and world order goals sometimes makes an unexpected appearance. Moreover, public views are quite fragmented with regard to potential external threats.

Slippage in vertical constraints from the general principles to the specific may be understandable, at least in the short term. A search for consistent policy requires an effort by policymakers to mobilize support by framing policies appropriately, by generating supportive media coverage, and by rallying important segments of the political establishment. At the same time, leaders have a limited ability to impose consistency. For example, they can only move the public to support humanitarian objectives as long as the costs remain low and, in several recent cases, popular feelings about specific actions have not proven to be malleable. There has never been great enthusiasm for interventions that seek to promote internal political change[66]

Second, and related to the above, the public is not inclined to accept significant costs for foreign policy goals. There is no sign the public will change its preference for modest levels of defense spending, and, unlike the late 1970s, no major threat appears on the horizon that could alter popular sentiment. Major new military programs are unlikely to evoke much popular enthusiasm, and international goals are more likely to be supported if pursued multilaterally than unilaterally. The costs of actual military intervention, if greater than the public is willing to bear, create pressures to redirect the intervention away from its original goals, possibly at the expense of U.S. credibility.

Third, and related to the first two observations, there is little in the structure of public preferences to indicate the outlines of a "Grand" strategy—in the sense of a comprehensive long-term blueprint directed at a limited set of stable, dominant goals. A strategy of flexible and incremental adjustment to changing international realities, assuming modest public cost-tolerance, may be all that is realistically feasible, at least to the extent that public moods are taken as a guide. Moreover, as elites have shown considerable inertia in their thinking on many defense and security issues, it is unlikely that many clear policy signals have been transmitted from the pinnacle of U.S. society to its base.[67] Thus, if the process of U.S. strategic adjustment has not progressed very far since the end of the Cold War, the lack of societal guidance, as well as the ambiguity of international challenges, must provide the explanation.

At a more general level, it seems that the most appropriate characterization of the popular mind is one of "principled pragmatism," encouraging a world vision closer to that of William James and John Dewey than of Machiavelli and Morgenthau.[68] Nevertheless, in the absence of compelling systemic imperatives and as the costs of the policy begin to mount, the pragmatism rather than the principles are likely to dominate.

The implications of public opinion should be placed in proper political context, since foreign policy's domestic setting encompasses other social entities as well—economic groups, single-agenda lobbies, political parties, and bureaucratic interests. As various domestic forces are often groping to identify their own foreign policy and security objectives, and since the priorities of different segments and levels of society need not be compatible, strategic adjustment cannot proceed in a smooth and uncomplicated manner. In particular, the lack of a public consensus on basic international challenges and security objectives deprives the political process of a substratum of agreement that might otherwise limit the scope for dissension among other politically relevant social entities. Additionally, the growing salience of economic objectives suggests that foreign policy debates may be increasingly connected to the interests of lobbies and specific congressional constituencies, with shifting coalitions waging short-term battles over specific policy goals or economically consequential military programs. Under the circumstances, the conduct of grand strategy may well simply come to resemble domestic politics, i.e., "politics as usual."

None of this is especially lamentable. Under post-Cold War international circumstances, it is natural that the aggregation of policy preferences should reflect the rough and tumble of democratic politics, and that it should be guided largely by domestic needs. As George Kennan accurately pointed out, the national interest "is *not* a detached interest in our international environment pursued for *its own sake*, independent of our aspirations and problems here at home. It does not signify things we would like to see happen in the outside world primarily for the sake of the outside world . . . It is the function of our duty to ourselves in our domestic problems."[69]

Notes

1. See Les Aspin, *Report on the Bottom Up Review* (Washington, D.C.: United States Department of Defense, October 1993); Dov Zakheim and Jeffrey M. Ranney, "Matching Defense Strategies to Resources," *International Security*, 18 (Summer 1993), 51–78; and Secretary of Defense, *Base Force Plan*, Annual Report to the President and the Congress (Washington D.C.: GPO, February 1992).

2. Karl von Clausewitz, *On War* (Princeton: Princeton University Press, 1976).

3. In Michael Howard ed., *The Causes of War and Other Essays* (Cambridge: Harvard University Press, 1983), 101–15.

4. We emphasize that our focus here is on public opinion in the aggregate. We do not disaggregate in our discussion even though we recognize that opinions on foreign policy and security issues vary across recognized constituent groups. (Examinations across race, gender, and or age can be particularly illuminating.) In practical terms policymakers must present foreign and se-curity policies, particularly in their most general forms, as public goods. This notwithstanding we believe it reasonable, appropriate, and prudent for poli-cymakers to be attentive to public opinion as a collective. See Miroslav Nin-cic, *Democracy and Foreign Policy* (New York: Columbia University Press, 1992), chapter 1; also: Benjamin I. Page and Robert Y. Shapiro, *The Rational Public* (Chicago: University of Chicago Press, 1992), chapters 1, 5, 6, 10.

5. In this sense, Theodore J. Lowi refers to the "plebiscitary presidency," in *The Personal President: Power Invested, Promise Unfulfilled* (Ithaca: Cornell Uni-versity Press, 1985), chapters 2 and 3. See also, Samuel Kernell *Going Public: New Strategies of Presidential Leadership*, (Washington D.C.: Congressional Quarterly Press, 1986).

6. For example, the Carter administration's decision to forgo building the neu-tron bomb provides a case where a specific weapons decision became highly salient to the attentive public. The public's strong discomfort with the weapon, along with strong public condemnation in Europe, brought a halt to its development.

7. Robert Weissberg, *Public Opinion and Popular Government* (Englewood Cliffs, NJ: Prentice Hall, 1976), 19–20.

8. Alan D. Monroe, "Consistency Between Public Preferences and National Policy Decisions," *American Politics Quarterly*, 7 (January 1979), 3–19.

9. Benjamin I. Page and Robert Y. Shapiro, "Effects of Public Opinion on Pol-icy," *American Political Science Review*, 7 (March 1983), 175–90.

10. Bruce M. Russett, "Democracy, Public Opinion, and Nuclear Weapons," in Philip Tetlock et. al., eds., *Behavior, Society, and Nuclear War* (New York: Oxford University Press, 1989).

11. See, for example, Benjamin Ginsberg, *The Captive Public* (New York: Basic Books, 1986).

12. See John R. Zaller, *The Nature and Origins of Mass Opinion* Cambridge: Harvard University Press, 1992). For a specific application to public opinion during the Gulf War, see John R. Zaller, "Elite Leadership of Mass Opinion," in *Taken By Storm: the Media, Public Opinion, and U.S. Foreign Policy*, eds. W. Lance Bennett and David L. Paletz, (Chicago: University of Chicago Press, 1994), 186–209.

13. See George Edwards, *At the Margin: Presidential Leadership* of Congress (New Haven: Yale University Press, 1989).

14. For a discussion of the relation between values and interests in U.S. foreign policy, see Miroslav Nincic, Gerard Gorski, and Roger Rose, "Values, Interests, and Foreign Policy Objectives," paper presented at the Annual Meeting of the American Political Science Association, New York City, September 1–4, 1994.

15. See Jon Hurwitz and Mark Peffley, "How are Foreign Policy Attitudes Structured? A Hierarchical Model," *American Political Science Review*, 81 (December 1987). See also Pamela Johnston Conover and Stanely Feldman, "How People Organize their Political World," *American Journal of Political Science*, 28 (February 1984); and Robert E. Lane, *Political Ideology* (New York: Free Press, 1962).

16.. *The Gallup Poll: Public Opinion 1935–1971* (New York: Random House, 1972), 566.

17. Another 22 percent advocated "be firm, no appeasement." Only two percent suggested "get together, work things out." *Gallup Poll: Public Opinion 1935–1971*, 721.

18. *Gallup Poll: Public Opinion 1935–1971*, 923.

19. In the years 1950–1956 NORC asked "If Communist armies attack any other countries in the world, do you think the United States should stay out of it, or should we help defend the countries like we did in Korea?" For ten polls taken during this period, on average 51% of the respondents said the U.S. should "help defend." Each of three polls taken in 1952 and 1953 record the lowest level of support at 45%. See John E. Mueller, *War Presidents and Public Opinion* (Lanham: University Press, 1985), 111.

20. See Christopher Matthews, *Kennedy and Nixon* (New York: Simon and Schuster, 1996), 150–69.

21. NES data as cited in Page and Shapiro (1992), 227.

22. Those events being: the Soviet downing of a U.S. U-2, the Berlin Blockade, and the Cuban Missile Crisis.

23. Aaron Wildavsky, "The Two Presidencies," *Transaction* 4 (December 1966).

24.   J. William Fulbright, "Congress and Foreign Policy," United States Commission on the Organization of Government for the Conduct of Foreign Policy," *Congress and Executive-Legislative Relations* 5 (June 1975), 58.

25.   Data points represent total percentages of negative responses on a 10 point "scalometer." Data are drawn from Gallup surveys, except for the years 1974, 1975, 1977, 1985–1988, where NORC data are used. Only in 1982 and 1983 are data available from both organizations. 1982 values are the same, 74%. 1983 values are Gallup, 84% and NORC 74%, Figure 6.1 shows the average. When more than one Gallup data point for a given year is available Figure 6.2 shows an average for that year. Gallup asked: "Here is an interesting experiment. You will notice that the 10 boxes on this card go from the highest position of 'plus five' –or something you *like* very much– all the way down to the lowest position of 'minus five'– or something you *dislike* very much. Please tell me how far up the scale or how far down the scale you would rate . . . Russia." In one of two polls in 1973, and in 1980–1987 Gallup posed the question using "Soviet Union." NORC used only a slightly different question: "You will notice that the 10 boxes on this card go from the highest position of 'plus five' for a country you *like* very much, to the lowest position of 'minus five' for a country you *dislike* very much. Please tell me how far up the scale or how far down the scale you would rate the following countries . . . Russia.

26.   Data points for the series marked "Unfriendly/Enemy" represent the total percentage of respondents who labeled Russia as unfriendly or an enemy and are drawn from Harris surveys.

27.   Data points for the series marked "Seeks world domination" represent the total percentage of respondents who choose responses "C" and "D" to the following question: "In your opinion, which of the following best describes Russia's primary objective in world affairs?

      A. Russia seeks only to *protect* itself against the possibility of attack by other countries.

      B. Russia seeks to *compete* with the U.S. for more influence in different parts of the world.

      C. Russia seeks *global domination*, but not at the expense of starting a major way.

      D. Russia seeks *global domination*, and will risk a *major war* to achieve that domination if it can't be achieved by other means.

      These data are from Roper as quoted in Alvin Richman, "Changing American Attitudes toward the Soviet Union," *Public Opinion Quarterly* 55 (Spring 1991), 135–48.

28.   "As the Dust Settles a Troubling Medley," *Washington Times*, July 1, 1993.

29.   "Bush Warns U.S. Against the Rise of Isolationism," *Los Angeles Times*, November 24, 1994.

30. Committee on Foreign Affairs, U.S. House of Representatives, Hearings on
     Public Attitudes Toward American Foreign Policy, July 27, 1994.
31. Data are drawn from Gallup and NORC as quoted in Richman, "Changing
     American Attitudes toward the Soviet Union" "American Support for Inter-
     national Involvement," *Public Opinion Quarterly* 57 (Summer 1993), 264–
     76. 1994 data are taken from *The Gallup Yearbook* When more than one data
     point per year is available figure 6.2 shows an average.
32. *America's Place in the World,* Times Mirror Center for the People and the
     Press, November 1993. Times Mirror commissioned Gallup surveys on these
     questions in 1993 and 1995. Additional trend data represent other Gallup
     sources as quoted by Times Mirror.
33. "American Support for International Involvement," *Public Opinion Quarterly*
     57 (Summer 1993), 264–76.
34. Alvin Richman, "American Support for International Involvement: General
     and Specific Components of Post-Cold War Changes," *Public Opinion Quar-
     terly* 60 (Summer 1996), 305–21.
35. Hearings on Public Attitudes Toward American Foreign Policy, 6
36. For a discussion of Gallup's Most Important Problem data series, see John
     Smith, "The Polls: America's Most Important Problems Part I: National and
     International," *Public Opinion Quarterly* 49 (Summer 1985), 264–74.
         It is entirely reasonable, as John Mueller argues, that the average citizen
     should value domestic concerns far above international ones. Indeed, absent
     a compelling and immediate threat, it is unreasonable to expect people to
     value distant concerns more than issues closer to their physical and emotional
     lives. See his "Fifteen Propositions about American Foreign Policy and Public
     Opinion in an Era Free of Compelling Threats," paper prepared for National
     Convention of the International Studies Association, San Diego, April 16–
     20, 1996.
37. For discussions of each of the CCFR surveys, see John E. Reilly in *Foreign
     Policy,* various years. The results are not limited to the CCFR surveys. Similar
     findings have been reported by the Times Mirror group in 1993 and 1995.
38. In 1995, for example, 64 percent of Americans favored the use of U.S. military
     and drug enforcement advisers in foreign countries to deal with drug traffick-
     ers. *The Gallup Monthly,* December 1995, 19.
39. This distinction was first made in Miroslav Nincic, "Loss Aversion and the
     Domestic Context of Military Intervention," *Political Research Quarterly,* 50
     (March 1994), 97–121.
40. For a description of these premises, see Daniel Kahneman and Amos Tversky,
     "Prospect Theory: an Analysis of Decision Under Risk," *Econometrica* 47
     (March 1979), 263–91, as well as Jack Levy, "An Introduction to Prospect
     Theory," in *Avoiding Losses/Taking Risks: Prospect Theory and International*

Conflict, ed. Barbara Farnham (Ann Arbor: University of Michigan Press, 1994), 7–22.

41.   *Gallup Poll: Public Opinion 1935–1971*, 566.

42.   *Gallup Poll Yearbook 1993*, 223.

43.   "The Old Politics and the New World Order," in *Eagle in a New World* eds. Kenneth Oye, Robert Lieber, and Donald Rothchild (New York: Harper Collins, 1992), 55.

44.   Data for "Russia/USSR seeks world domination" and "Russia Unfriendly/Enemy" are a subset of those used in Figure 6.1 above. Data for "Spending too much on defense" are drawn from Gallup, Roper, and NORC as quoted in Thomas Hartley and Bruce Russet, "Public Opinion and the Common Defense: Who Governs Military Spending in the United States," *American Political Science Review* 86 (December 1992), 905–16. Data for the years 1991–1993 are drawn from *America's Place in the World*, Times Mirror 1993, and *Gallup Yearbook*(s) 1994–1995. Question wording is as follows:

Gallup and Times Mirror: "There is much discussion as to the amount of money the government in Washington should spend for national defense and military purposes. How do you feel about this: Do you think we are spending too little, too much, or about the right amount?" or an alternate version "Do you think that we should expand our spending on national defense, keep it about the same or cut back?"

Roper: "Turning now to business of the country—we are faced with many problems in this country, none of which can be solved easily or inexpensively. I'm going to name some of these problems, and for each one I'd like you to tell me whether you think we're spending too much money on it, too little money, or about the right amount. Are we spending too much, too little or about the right amount on. . . . the military, armaments and defense?"

NORC: "We are faced with many problems in this country, none of which can be solved easily or inexpensively. I'm going to name some of these problems, and for each one I'd like you to tell me whether you think we're spending too much money, too little, or about the right amount. . . . military, armaments and defense?"

45.   See Americans on Defense Spending Survey, Dec. 16, 1995. Of the subsample who support a force size adequate to fight another Gulf War, only 38% support a force size large enough for two regional wars.

46.   *Americans Talk Issues*, "Survey #28," June 21, 1995, and "Americans on Defense Spending Survey," Dec. 16, 1995.

47.   Richman, "American Support for International Involvement." Increased support for action via the United Nations has not extended to a public willingness to have U.S. troops serve under non-U.S. United Nations commanders.

48.   Americans on Defense Spending Survey, Dec. 16, 1995. 37 percent agreed

with the notion that a stronger UN means "U.S. could become entangled in a system that would inhibit it from full freedom of action to pursue its interests."

49. Sixty-nine percent agreed with the statement the U.S. should contribute troops. Americans Defense Spending Survey, Dec. 16, 1995. The question offered was: "Some say the U.S. should contribute its military forces to such UN efforts because then potential aggressors will know that aggression will not succeed. Others say the U.S. should not contribute troops to such efforts because American Troops may be put at risk in operations that are not directly related to U.S. interests. Do you think the U.S. should or should not contribute troops to UN efforts to help defend UN members if they are attacked?"

50. "Public Indifferent about NATO Expansion," Pew Research Center for the People and the Press. Jan. 9–12, 1997.

According to *The Gallup Poll Monthly*, 70 percent of people supported maintaining NATO in January 1994, (p. 38).

When asked if the U.S. should spend only enough on defense to do its share, only 52 percent of the public agrees. This suggest there is still substantial support (45 percent in the survey) for aiding allies. "Americans on Defense Spending, Survey" Dec. 16, 1996.

One further point on alliances. There is no longer much reluctance to see both Germany and Japan contribute troops to the use of force in places like the Persian Gulf. 63 percent and 70 percent favor having Japan and Germany, respectively, contribute forces. "Americans on Defense Spending Survey," Dec. 16, 1996.

51. "Americans on Defense Spending Survey," Dec. 16, 1995.

52. *The Harris Poll,* December 10, 1992.

53. *The Gallup Poll Monthly,* July 1994.

54. *The Harris Poll,* September 16, 1990, 2.

55. *The Harris Survey,* December 10, 1992, 3.

56. *Harris Poll,* September 22, 1994, 4.

57. "Opinion Outlook," *National Journal,* October 30, 1993, 2616.

58. Bruce Jentleson, "The Pretty Prudent Public," *International Studies Quarterly* 36 (March 1992), 49–73.

59. John Mueller, *War, Presidents, and Public Opinion* (New York: Wiley, 1972), and Donna J. Nincic and Miroslav Nincic, "Commitment to Military Intervention: The Democratic Government as Economic Investor," *Journal of Peace Research,* 32 (November 1995), 413–26.

60. The Los Angeles Times question asked: "Assuming Iraq leaves Kuwait would you consider the war with Iraq a success if 500 American troops died, or not? . . . " (If respondents answer yes, the questioner moves to the next level of troops killed. The response of "no troops killed" was volunteered by respon-

dents.) Full text in Mueller, *Public Opinion and the Gulf War* (Chicago: University of Chicago Press, 1994) 235.

61.   The Gallup question asked: "Suppose you knew that if the United States sent US troops to Bosnia as part of an international peacekeeping force, that no American soldiers would be killed. With this in mind, would you favor or oppose sending US troops to Bosnia?" Question asked of a quarter of the survey sample, with each quarter being given a different level of troops killed.

62.   Time/CNN, January 1991. It is habitually assumed that increasing disenchantment with a war leads the U.S. public to want to cut its costs and withdraw from the ill-judged military venture. Not only have many Americans thus interpreted the relation between costs and commitment, but U.S. adversaries have as well. For example, Saddam Hussein threatened to turn the Kuwait into a "killing field" for U.S. soldiers, hoping that the threat would either dissuade U.S. intervention or, if the intervention did occur, that massive loss of American lives would rapidly undermine domestic support for the war and cause an early U.S. withdrawal. Similarly, Radovan Karadzic, leader of the Bosnian Serbs, has warned NATO and the United States that they would be unable to bear the casualties that intervention in the Bosnian war would entail for them.

63.   See John Alexander, "Non-Lethal Weapons & the Future of War," Los Alamos National Lab, LA-UR 95–699.

64.   President William J. Clinton, *A National Security Strategy and Engagement and Enlargement,* (Washington D.C.: GPO, 1994), 1

65.   NBC-Wall Street Journal. Reported in *National Journal,* "Opinion Outlook," January 1, 1994, 42.

66.   See Jentleson, note 58, above.

67.   Bruce Russett, Thomas Hartley, and Shoon Murray, "The End of the Cold War, Attitude Change, and the Politics of Defense Spending," *PS,* 27 (March 1994), 17–21.

68.   Miroslav Nincic, *Democracy and Foreign Policy: the Fallacy of Political Realism* (New York: Columbia University Press, 1992), 168–70.

69.   George F. Kennan, "Lectures on Foreign Policy," *Illinois Law Review* 45 (1951), 723.

Part IV

The Institutional Dimension

7 Technological Change and the New Calculus of War: The United States Builds a New Navy

Jan S. Breemer

> The battleship, engine of destruction, compact of scientific law's inevitable resultants, steel-chilled to defy severest impact, perfectly controlled, moved at instantaneous wish, responsive to the slightest velvet-finger pressure to annihilate . . ."
>
> —Edward Kirk Rawson, *Twenty Famous Naval Battles: Salamis to Santiago* (1899)

Earlier contributors to this volume have focused on the role of cultural and domestic political forces in stimulating and shaping American strategic adjustment. At best, however, the resulting spotlight on ideas and domestic interests illuminates only part of the historical tableau, and reveals only a partial picture of how and under the influence of what forces the United States will likely adapt to the circumstances confronting it as the twenty-first century opens.

To understand the phenomenon of strategic adjustment it is necessary to appreciate the process by which change occurs; this must include an exploration of the dynamic interaction between evolving technological, economic, and external political realities on the one hand and political institutions on the other. When it comes to strategic adjustment, the most important of these institutions are the military services themselves. In the two chapters that follow Emily Goldman and Ed Smith examine the capacity of the military services to adapt to changes in their environment and initiate and implement strategic adjustment. This chapter considers the other side of the relationship: it looks at the power of technological change to alter how individuals and institutions think about and prepare for war. There is a cautionary note here, especially as the United States explores the potential for new communications and computer technology to create a "Revolution in Military Affairs." Culture and politics may well be consequential, as earlier contributors have argued, but the logic implicit in technological developments may have the power to override both. To understand the ability of technology to shape national strategy, it is useful to return, once again, to the late 1880s.

America Builds a New Navy

In 1898, thanks to its victory in the war with Spain, the United States became a "complete" great power. Realists would argue that, after a century of "free security," the nation had finally acknowledged and come to terms with the zero-sum rivalry they claim marks the relations between nations; that the United States had finally recognized that survival in such a world demanded a military prowess commensurate with its growing economic and industrial strength. The country's transition to great power status, complete with overseas possessions, was made possible by the guns of the "New Navy," born only a decade before.

National strategy-making is about balancing the relationship between national goals, national interests, and national resources, including military. The rational model of strategy-making proposes that states adjust their strategies, that is to say, redefine their aspirations and/or recalculate the resources required to support those aspirations, when the two sides in the equation are found to be out of balance. Also rationally—and ideally—strategic adjustments, especially changes in military force postures, are made in a top-down fashion, i.e., as the logical product of changes in national goals, which themselves are commonly thought of as the result of changes in the external security environment. As rational, but less than ideal, is the obverse, bottom-up, relationship between ends and means. In this case, resources, or better put perhaps, *changes* in resources, can drive a state to raise or lower its external ambitions. The relationship between America's new naval prowess and the country's "imperial urge" is a case in point: the New Navy created the opportunity for the United States to expand its aspirations beyond safeguarding the continent and the adjacent seas. To paraphrase Harold and

Margaret Sprout, the New Navy became the means that "launch[ed] the American ship of state upon [a] much bolder and more comprehensive program of politico-naval imperialism" than most of its creators had envisaged ten years before.[1] But what were the strategic goals that prompted the transformation of the U.S. Navy from a motley collection of obsolete coastal defense craft and cruising ships to a fleet of battleships that was patently offensive? Why was it that a board of six naval officers convened by Secretary of the Navy Tracy could conclude in 1890 that the United States faced no plausible threat, yet recommended the immediate construction of more than 200 warships, including battleships with sufficient range to attack "points in the other side of the Atlantic"?[2] It is true that Tracy quickly disavowed his board's ambitious building plan; suddenly, his own call for a two-ocean navy with eight battleships in the Pacific and twelve in the Atlantic seemed modest. Yet, he too urged that a modern American fleet must be designed for offensive operations off the enemy's coast. Even more, such operations might have to be launched pre-emptively for, Tracy concluded, "The nation that is ready to strike the first blow will gain an advantage which its antagonist can never offset."[3]

In the end, the Naval Act of 1890 approved the construction of three "sea-going coast-line battleships" with only one-third of the 15,000 nautical miles' endurance the Tracy Board had asked for.[4] Nevertheless, the act was a victory for big navy proponents. The country had finally turned its back on the Navy's "dark age," and taken the first step toward a "proper" fleet, complete with the high-technology guns and armor plating that had long made the navies of Europe's great powers the envy of most American naval officers. Secretary Tracy could rightfully boast in an interview in 1891 that, "The sea will be the future seat of empire. And we shall rule it as certainly as the sun doth rise."[5] In an amazingly few short years, the United States Navy gave itself a brand new purpose, rethought its strategy, doctrine and concepts of operations, and revolutionized its force structure.[6]

Explaining American Navalism

The literature on this period of American naval history is dominated by three explanations for the transformation of the U.S. Navy from a fleet meant largely for commerce protection to one aimed at underwriting national security.[7] The first cites what may be called the power of the idea, that is to say, mainly Alfred Thayer Mahan's idea of sea power as the royal road to national glory and greatness. George Baer, for example, reports that, "The transformation of the Navy from a force of cruisers to one of battleships, from a defensive force to an offensive one, was based on arguments put forward by a group of navalists who sought no less than to change the country's strategic culture."[8] Most historians acknowledge Mahan's contribution to the era's navalism, but propose that his writings were merely a symptom of national and naval professional expectations that, in Kenneth Hagan's words, "change was in the air."[9] Their basic thesis is that Mahan's discovery had less to do with unlocking the secret to what he claimed was the historical decisiveness of sea power than the timing and cogency of his argument.[10]

The claim that Mahan was merely the most persuasive spokesman for the expansive navalism that pervaded the era's *esprit du temps* is central to the other two explanations that have been offered for the New Navy. The first, which is associated with the Realist school in international relations, proposes that the decision to build a blue-water fleet was a logical and necessary adjustment to shifts in the external security environment. Baer, for example, reports that the U.S. Navy was "forced" to rethink its purpose because of related changes in naval engineering and international affairs. The advent of the steamship, he writes, triggered a race for overseas coaling stations, which put America's vulnerable coastlines within reach of heavily armed foreign fleets, thus compelling the Navy to transform itself from an instrument for the protection of commerce to one designed for the defense of the nation's security.[11] Hagan, too, cites destabilizing changes in the international system, or what he termed "geopolitical realignments," as a key reason for the Navy's transformation.[12] In the Far East, Japan was "awakening" but, more important, on the other side of the globe, Germany had emerged as Europe's leading Continental power, upsetting the Continent's traditionally Franco-British dominated balance of power. This shift had worldwide implications. Not satisfied with continental dominance, Germany's leadership aspired to *Weltpolitik*—and global power meant overseas colonies and a fleet. The first hint that German-American relations, which had so far been amicable, were taking a turn for the worse came in 1889 in the harbor of a small atoll in the southwest Pacific. Warships of three nations—the United States, Britain, and Germany—watched each other warily in the Samoan harbor of Apia while the three nations' diplomats met in Berlin to negotiate the partition of the archipelago. The standoff ended without a shot being fired, but attentive Americans concluded that, like it or not, their country could no longer stay aloof from the Old World's rivalries.[13] More than that, Congressmen and Senators who were outraged by Germany's alleged insults in Samoa insisted that it was nothing less than dishonorable for the United

States not to underwrite its expanding overseas economic interests from behind the barrel of a naval gun. Only "sufficient naval power," said New Jersey Congressman William McAdoo, could protect the United States against foreign insults. "If the United States were a naval power . . . Bismarck would never have allowed the landing of a single German soldier on the Samoan Islands."[14]

George Quester's book, *Offense and Defense in the International System*, offers an interesting variant to the Realist argument that the decision to build a battlefleet was spurred by changes in America's external security environment. He does not deny that competition among the great powers was on the rise, but points out that the technical characteristics of the machine-age fleets in the late nineteenth century had actually served to make the United States much safer from attack. He notes how the replacement of sails by coal-fueled machinery had severely restricted the warship's strategic reach, and, as a consequence, had made the United States much less vulnerable to the projection of European military power. Quester proposes that the relative decline of Europe's global reach created the *opportunity* for newcomers, such as Japan and the United States, to build up locally superior fleets.[15]

Students of the domestic determinants of military policy have offered a third explanation, citing the lobbying influence of America's industrial interests, notably the iron and steel industry.[16] This line of reasoning is only partially convincing. It is true that a big fleet clad in iron and steel could be a profitable source of income, but this alone does not explain the long-range offensive navy the United States chose to build. Ton-for-ton, it made little profit-making difference whether coastal monitors for defensive purposes or high-seas battleships were built.[17]

More persuasive perhaps, but still incomplete, is the bureaucratic explanation with the proposition that a fleet of battleships was brought about by the professional naval officers' desire for a "dream navy" that emulated the British fleet. It suggests that the New Navy was less the product of professional concern over future imperialistic clashes than a symptom of puberty — the wish to match, better yet outmatch, the fleet of the nation that had given birth to the United States.[18]

Clearly, historians and political scientists have seen the emergence of the U.S. Navy as a European-style battle force as the result of multiplicity of external systemic and domestic influences; all are part of the truth. This chapter proposes a further variable that has received comparatively little attention, at least in the way it is treated here. It proposes that the creation of the New Navy was the response, in part, to an American perception of technological insecurity. It argues that American naval planners in the 1880s and 1890s were reacting to a new, technology-induced "system" of insecurity that had little or nothing to do with the politics of interstate relations per se. To paraphrase Glenn H. Snyder, the U.S. decision to pursue major power status at sea had much less to do with a reassessment of the "balance of power" than a new "balance of terror" that contemporaries believed had been created by the technological revolution at sea.[19]

The notion that technology can be an independent source of national insecurity and military planning is not a new one. It is central to much of the arms race literature, and it is the cornerstone of Barry Buzan's distinction between the study of international relations and national security studies.[20] This chapter subscribes to Buzan's thesis that, "The development of military means follows a technological logic which is separate from the pattern of amity and enmity among states."[21]

Technological change in the means of warfare is as old as war itself. However, it was not until the industrial revolution of the nineteenth century that this became a determinant of interstate relations and part of a nation's calculation of the possibility of war. Rapid and unpredictable naval-technological change during the fifty years or so that led up to World War I was at the bottom of the tendency of military planners to estimate the threat of "capabilities" as opposed to "intentions." The fear that an international competitor might use a fleeting technological advantage to spring a surprise attack was at the heart of the "permanent insecurity" that dominated the condition of the great powers before World War I.

There is a contemporary policy-relevant reason as well for paying attention to the influence of technological insecurity on American strategic decisions one century ago. Specifically, if any of the host of variables that arguably shaped the New Navy then is to offer "lessons" for students of U.S. force planning now, technological insecurity is the variable-of-choice. The point may be put in the form of this general proposition: as the war-making intentions of potential opponents become more ambiguous, technological "threats" will tend to become the focus of military force planning.

"The Spirit of the Age"

Between 1850 and 1890, fleets changed beyond all recognition. The technology of ship-of-the-line in 1850 was little different from the sailing man o' war that fought the sea battles of the seventeenth century. The ironclads at the end of the nineteenth century already embodied most of the technologies that would be found on the dreadnoughts of World War I and even the battleships of World War II. The only thing the navies of 1850 and 1890 still had in common was that their power rested with large surface ships and cannon fire.

Students of naval history have long been fascinated with this period, mostly so with an eye on the naval strategic and tactical changes it wrought. The writers of the "golden age" of navalism—Mahan, Corbett, Colomb, and others—were concerned with the material implications of the revolution at sea to the extent that they reaffirmed or falsified the "principles" of warfare under sail. I propose that the era's technological revolution had a much more profound impact: rapid technological change in the means of war at sea introduced a wholly new and destabilizing factor into the relations of nation-states. In the first place, the very notion of technological change, or at least change that seemed to occur almost on a daily basis, was unprecedented. In the second place, and most disturbing from the perspective of military planners, technology appeared to have upset the old calculation of the balance of forces based on numbers; for the first time, the *quality* of material had become a potentially decisive factor in the outbreak and outcome of war at sea. And thirdly, the rapidity of change, combined with the planner's uncertainty how well his new weapons would perform, yet the certainty that they would soon be obsolete, introduced a novel, technology-inspired, sense of insecurity into the relations of the major powers.

In his book *The Anatomy of British Sea Power* Arthur J. Marder commented on the "spirit of the age" during the last two decades before World War I. He cited in particular the prevailing belief that, unlike an earlier era, the next war would be sudden, without a formal declaration, and probably begun with a surprise attack.[22] Volatile naval war-making technology was the material basis for this "spirit." The central characteristic of this technology was the ability to inflict an unprecedented level of destruction.

"The Great Race"

The New Navy was a latecomer to what was then called the "Great Race" between gun and armor manufacturers. In one sense, the American timing was fortunate; by 1890, some thirty years of expensive experimentation in

Europe with "one off" types had finally concluded with a standard design battleship, the British *Magnificent* class.

The competition had opened in 1858 when the French built the *Gloire*. She was the world's first seagoing ironclad, and was armed with explosive shell-firing guns. The British reluctantly followed suit and completed their first ironclad, the *Warrior*, three years later. British reluctance was motivated by two concerns. First, it had long been Whitehall's golden rule that it was better "to follow and overtake than to initiate."[23] This had been an eminently sensible policy while technological innovation was slow, its impact on battle performance marginal, and, most important, as long as foreign navies modeled themselves after the British. However, a few shell-firing ironclads had the power to literally sink the Royal Navy's numerical superiority in wooden ships armed with solid cannon balls. In the second place, those responsible for the design of warships were particularly unhappy with the French for forcing a race between guns and protective armor, when it became evident soon enough that this could not be won by the latter. The Royal Navy's chief constructor thus lamented that the French decision to protect their warships with iron plating was made, "Unhappily for England . . . and unhappily for herself."[24]

The *Gloire* and *Warrior* were the starting point for history's first technological arms race. The competitors came in different hues and colors. They included Europe's principal powers and their navies (mainly Britain, France, and Italy), the gun manufacturers vs. the producers of armor, gun makers vs. gun makers, armorers against armorers, and the "push" of technology versus the "pull" of the naval professionals. This last phenomenon was obvious to one contemporary participant: "There was not . . . any real pressure on the part of the foreign navies to force the hands of our own, and it is by no means certain that any decided course followed by the British Navy would not have been generally adopted by others. The real pressure came from the inventor acting on powers that were outside the Navy, forcing it to change its mind in spite of itself."[25]

The *Gloire* and *Warrior* were the first and last ironclads in which designers sought to preserve the balance of offensive gunfire capabilities and defensive hull protection that characterized the sailing ship of the line. Even as the two ships were being completed, it was obvious that heavier guns already being tested demanded more protection than the 4.5 inches of wrought iron wrapped around the *Warrior*. By 1865, British and French ships were covered with 6 to 7 inches of iron. Five years later, 9 inches were the norm, and 14 inches or more were common by 1870. The use of iron for protection reached its peak when the *Inflexible* was launched in 1881. The ship's central "citadel" area that housed the guns was surrounded by iron plating two feet thick.

The citadel ship was the culmination of a design philosophy which held that offensive gunfire was the ship's best protection, and that therefore all protective efforts should concentrate on making certain that a single enemy blow could not knock out its guns. Gun makers promptly exploited the ship's vulnerability elsewhere, and invented the quick-firing gun. Defensive countermeasures were made possible by the newly developed ability to mass-produce steel and the invention of lighter weight compound armor: designers reverted to full or near-full belt armor. Nevertheless, the best efforts of the metallurgical industry could not reverse the obvious trend: the penetrative power of the gun had beaten the resisting power of armor. A report by the British Admiralty in 1871 had already drawn the inescapable conclusion. So far, it said, "the powers of offence, represented by artillery, and of defence, by armour, have advanced *pari passu*, sometimes one, sometimes the other, slightly in advance." Now, however, "we appear . . . to be closely approaching a period when the gun will assert a final and definitive superiority."[26] The best to be said for providing armor protection was that it was better than no protection at all.[27]

The point of no return had already been reached in 1865. In that year, the standard British 9-inch heavy gun was capable of penetrating 10 inches of iron plating at a range of 1,000 yards. Ships were then protected by up to 6 inches of armor. Six years later, when the heaviest armor afloat measured 12 inches, the standard 12-inch gun penetrated 15 inches of iron at 1,000 yards. By the late 1880s, ships were protected by up to 18 inches of so-called "compound armor," but the 16.25 inch gun at the time was capable of penetrating 19 inches at 2,000 yards.[28] In short, from 1865 on, the destructive power of shipboard artillery consistently outperformed the heaviest armor afloat. Put in another way, every capital ship launched after the *Gloire* and *Warrior* was sinkable by its own guns: warships had become offensive *ship killers!* This itself was a revolutionary development, for despite all its guns, the sailing ship of war had always been a *defensive* platform first; thanks to its thick oaken hull, it was much better at resisting gunfire than at sinking its like.[29]

The rapidity of technological change and the uncertainty which direction it would take made the Victorian naval planner's job much more difficult than his predecessor's. The slow, evolutionary change of ships and their armaments during the preceding centuries meant that rivals fought with similar fleets and weapons that changed little from one war to the next. Both sides knew the quality of the other's materiel, if for no other reason than captured ships were commonly recommissioned into one's own navy.[30] It followed that the balance of power at sea, and therefore the prospect of victory in a next war, were mostly a matter of calculable numbers. Slow and predictable change also meant there were few naval "secrets" to keep or ferret out. Since warships were impossible to hide, it took few specialized intelligence-gathering activities for all sides to be reasonably confident about each other's strengths and weaknesses.

The technologization of naval war changed this: *qualitative* asymmetry became a potentially decisive factor in war planning. The fear that a few ships with new-and-improved weapons might get the best of a larger but "obsolete" fleet prompted the systematization of intelligence collection and analysis as a continuous peacetime activity. The British navy created a Naval Intelligence Department (NID) in 1870, and the U.S. Navy formalized its technical intelligence-gathering activities with the establishment of the Office of Naval Intelligence (ONI) in 1881.[31] By the late 1880s, all the major naval powers maintained permanent naval attachés abroad. London and the Royal Navy were the focal point of their attention, for it was here, wrote the U.S. Navy's Chief Engineer, James W. King, in the 1870s that "may be found naval attachés of nearly every important nation, watching and studying with endless vigilance the principles and science of naval architecture and engineering."[32]

The industrial revolution at sea confronted naval planners with the problem of technological obsolescence for the first time in history. Fred T. Jane (of *Jane's Fighting Ships*) thought that "a different ideal every year" was a "blessed thing" that arrested "naval decay;"[33] the *strategic* consequences were profoundly disturbing, however. The slow pace of technological change in the past had allowed ships that were only partially completed at the end of one war to be left on the "stocks" and wait for a new threat of war. It could be years before the ship was finished, but that rarely affected the state-of-the-art of its fighting capacity.[34] A reserve of stocked ships also meant that last year's loser in battle could oftentimes make a quick comeback. Rapid technological change signified that fleets were now built to fight a come-as-you-are war in which only the latest "reply ships" counted. With no reserves to draw on, battle would therefore be a single roll of the dice with no chance of recovery for the loser. An "initial naval disaster," Admiral "Jackie" Fisher warned Royal Navy officers in the 1890s, will be "irretrievable, irreparable, eternal."[35]

The rapid pace of "block obsolescence" had systemic consequences that went beyond balance of power calculations between traditional rivals, such as Britain and France. For the British in particular, it triggered the equivalent of the modern nuclear "Nth country problem." With the genie of technology out of the bottle and readily for sale, it became possible for second- and even third-rank nations to leapfrog the Royal Navy's hard-won advantage in numbers and experience, and acquire the latest trappings of great-power status overnight. The most prominent newcomers were the United States, Germany, Italy, and Japan.[36] Unable to keep up a modern fleet large enough to offset the global proliferation of "emerging threats," the British were compelled to give up "splendid isolation," and conclude regional *partnerships* of power and influence instead.[37] Technology had reshaped the international system.

A "Bolt from the Blue"

The *Warrior*'s main armament in 1862 boasted 48 68-pounder guns. Each gun fired projectiles weighing 64 pounds that were delivered with a "muzzle energy" of 570 foot/tons.[38] The ship's total deliverable destructive energy therefore amounted to 27,360 foot/tons. Twenty-eight years later, the *Benbow* carried two 16.25-inch plus ten 6-inch guns with a combined muzzle energy of 141,472 foot/tons, i.e. more than a fivefold increase. By way of comparison, the brute firepower of Nelson's *Victory* was about one-fifth of the *Warrior*'s, or one-twenty-fifth of the *Benbow*. Parenthetically, the *Dreadnought* of 1906 delivered 438,160 foot/tons of muzzle energy, i.e., the equivalent of about 80 *Victories*.

Considering that this enormous increase in firepower took place during a single generation of naval officers, it is no wonder that the battleship was seen by contemporaries as a weapon of mass destruction. Although written a few years later (1916), Rear Admiral Fiske's portrayal of the battleship's destructive power is eerily prescient of a nuclear scenario. He wrote how one battleship had enough firepower, to "whip an army of a million men just as quickly as it could get hold of its component parts . . . , knock down all the buildings in New York afterward, smash all the cars, break down all the bridges, and sink all the shipping."[39]

The analogy between the battleship and nuclear weapons carries further than this specter of destruction: improvements in weapons design brought "nuclear plenty" in the early 1950s; improvements in guns, shell design, and propellants made the ability to destroy at sea progressively cheaper. It is quite true that warships became increasingly expensive (due largely to their heavy armor)—the *Warrior* cost £252,000, and the *Benbow* £764,000. But the unit cost of hitting power went down. The *Warrior's* cost of 1,000 foot/ton of muzzle energy was £9,211, whereas the *Benbow's* was £5,400. The trend continued through the development of the dreadnoughts and super-dreadnoughts of World War I. The *Dreadnought* could deliver 1,000 foot/tons at a cost of £4,071; the *Orion* could do the same for £3,264.[40]

While guns offered increasingly more bang-for-the-buck, the cost of ship protection went up. The *Warrior's* iron cladding was responsible for 6.2 percent of her total displacement. By the 1890s, the ship's main armor accounted for some 25 percent. The upshot was that it made economic sense for fleets to stress the offensive. The choice was not much different from the dilemma that was central to the ballistic missile defense debate of the late 1960s and again in the 1980s: each improvement in defensive strength could quickly be offset by a cheaper increment in offensive strength.

The superiority of gunfire over protection made truly annihilating sea battles possible for the first time in history. True, "decisive" battles had been fought before, but sailing fleets had rarely lost a battle because of catastrophic losses due to gunfire. Sailing fleets had also been "annihilated" before, but the term did not then have its modern destructive connotation. In fact, the sinking of an enemy ship was, as one writer put it, "a matter of regret."[41] A much better way of "annihilating" the enemy was to "nullify" him by capturing his ships. This not only diminished his strength, but it also added to one's own.[42] The ship-killing capacity of modern guns had effectively eliminated this option.[43]

The prospect of utter destruction turned the thoughts of naval planners to ways of avoiding "irretrievable, irreparable, eternal" destruction. One "solution" was to avoid the enemy's first blow by striking first. Survival, wrote Fisher, dictates an "instant offensive," preferably "five minutes before war breaks out." The whole affair would be over in less than one-half hour.[44] The British press aired the theme of preventive attack in 1897–98 with the suggestion that upstart European navies be destroyed à la Copenhagen.[45] It re-surfaced a few years later, apparently at Fisher's instigation, and this time was more specific about the "target"— Germany's emerging High Sea

Fleet.[46] On the British side too, the specter of a bolt-from-the-blue began to preoccupy naval planners. In *The World Crisis*, Winston Churchill writes extensively about his concern as First Lord of the Admiralty over the "extraordinary rapidity and suddenness the Prussian nation was accustomed to fall upon its enemy."[47] He thought that the chances and consequences of a naval attack without warning were much more serious than a German invasion of France. Armies took time to mobilize, thereby giving the victim time to prepare his defense. In any case, divisions lost in battle could easily be replaced; not so battleships.[48] The latter were always mobilized—itself another break with the past.[49] Their constant readiness meant, to repeat Churchill, that the British "must not assume that if it made the difference between victory and defeat, Germany would stop short of an attack on the Fleet in full peace without warning or pretext."[50] He and his adversaries across the North Sea had discovered the "reciprocal fear of surprise attack" long before Schelling made it part of the vocabulary of strategic studies.[51]

There was another way that the era's security managers sought to manage the devastating power of the new weapons—a way also familiar to modern strategic studies: exploit the specter of devastation to *deter* others from using their destructive capacity. Deterrence, not war-fighting, was at the heart of Admiral Tirpitz's "risk theory," and, though unspoken, the Royal Navy's two-power standard as well. The problem was the "solution's" credibility. The efficacy of the threat to use overwhelming destruction hinged on the threatener's willingness to risk his own instruments of destruction. The superior battlefleet might "win" in the sense that it sank more ships than it lost, but the losses might be unacceptable. One British commentator in 1875 put his finger on the dilemma when he warned against concentrating the fleet's firepower in a few expensive ships: "In the numerous fleets of the olden times, the fate of an individual ship was a less momentous question. But if you concentrate the whole power of the Navy in a few ships . . . you throw upon the officers in command an intolerable weight of responsibility. You will restrain and chill that gallant and almost reckless ardour with which the great battles of the past were fought and won."[52]

The commentator, Sir Thomas Brassey, had discovered the problem of "self-deterrence." Nearly forty years later, the leaders of the British and German fleets fully expected that their opposite numbers would quickly seek the North Sea Armageddon that fifty years of technological upheaval had made possible. But instead of expanding the naval planner's range of strategic choices, technology had actually conspired to limit his freedom of action.

Both sides turned their engines of destruction into "fleets in being," hoping that the other would be the first to make a mistake.[53] The creator of the High Sea Fleet at least thought that, in the end, not technology but "the old traditional English naval prestige" decided the outcome.[54]

Conclusion

Technological innovation during the Victorian years revolutionized more than war at sea: it introduced a radically new variable into interstate relations. Clausewitz had summarized the "old," pre-industrial calculus of war and peace with the dictum that war is an extension of politics—a deliberate choice by statesmen in the furtherance of specific political goals. The political nature of war meant that statesmen could reasonably anticipate its possibility. There would probably be some kind of dispute in progress, notes and protests would be exchanged, preliminary military movements would be observed next, and there would be, as Churchill put it, "financial perturbations in the Exchanges of the world indicating a rise of temperature."[55] If war did break out, its tools and the tactics would be familiar to both sides.

"Runaway technological revolution," especially at sea, overturned these certainties.[56] As naval planners sought to come to grips with the new technologies in their strategies and tactics, they were of two minds. On the one hand, they welcomed the "decisive edge" of bigger guns and thicker armor. On the other, they felt out of control: *technology*, not professional judgment, produced weapons. Most naval officers in the 1870s preferred "handy ships" with medium-caliber guns over the behemoths that were being produced. But since they could not prove that bigger might not turn out better, and while other nations retained the capacity to build big gun ships, there was "no choice in the matter." Technological hedging ("friendly rivalry" in the era's words), not fear of impending war, dictated that other powers be met "on equal terms."[57]

History's first technological arms race set the stage for a new set of expectations about war and the circumstances that could trigger its eruption. The alarming words of one young U.S. Navy officer in 1883 were symptomatic. The United States, he warned, was totally unprepared to defend against Italy's new monster ironclad, the *Dandalo*. With her 100-ton guns, the world's biggest, the ship could lie off Coney Island and bombard New York at will.[58] The United States and Italy had no political cause for war; even if they had, the *Dandalo*'s 3,700 nautical miles range would have kept her far away from America's eastern seaboard. But what mattered was the existence of a technical capability to hurt that the United States could neither offset with similar weapons nor defend against. The New Navy was the country's "accommodation with technology."[59]

Notes

1. Harold Sprout and Margaret Sprout, *The Rise of American Naval Power 1776– 1918* (Princeton: Princeton University Press, 1944), 222.
2. Ibid., 210.
3. *Report of the Secretary of the Navy, 1889.* Cited in Sprout and Sprout, *Rise of American Naval Power*, 207.
4. Ibid., 213.
5. James D. Richardson, ed., *A Compilation of the Messages and Papers of the Presidents, 1789–1897*, vol. 9 (Washington, D.C.: 1900), 200–1. Cited in Walter LaFeber, *The New American Empire: An Interpretation of American Expansion 1860–1898* (Ithaca: Cornell University Press, 1963), 127.
6. See George W. Baer, *One Hundred Years of Sea Power: The U.S. Navy, 1890– 1990* (Stanford: Stanford University Press, 1994), 11.
7. The author is indebted to George Baer for the observation that the purpose of U.S. naval power shifted from commerce protection to national security. See Ibid., 11.
8. Ibid.
9. Kenneth Hagan, *The People's Navy: The Making of American Sea Power* (New York: the Free Press, 1991), 185.
10. See, for example, Robert Seager II, "The Years Before Mahan: The Unofficial Case for the New Navy, 1880–1890," in *The Shaping of American Diplomacy, Vol. I: 1750–1900*, ed., William Appleman Williams (Chicago: Rand Mc- Nally, 1956), 338–43.
11. Baer, *One Hundred Years of Sea Power*, 10.
12. Hagan, *People's Navy*, 193.
13. For the diplomatic history of America's Samoan entanglement, see Samuel Flagg Bemis, *A Diplomatic History of the United States*, 5th ed. (New York: Holt, 1967), 453–59.
14. Cited in Holger H. Herwig, *Politics of Frustration: The United States in Ger- man Naval Planning, 1889–1941* (Boston: Little, Brown, 1976), 15.
15. George H. Quester, *Offense and Defense in the International System* (New York: Wiley, 1977), 87.
16. The U.S. Congress decreed in 1886 that U.S. Navy ships only use domesti- cally produced materials. This was done largely to foster an indigenous steel

industry. The Sprouts have observed that this gave the steel industry a vested interests in a "continuous and progressive development of the Navy," thus becoming "active lobbyists and propagandists for naval expansion." Sprout and Sprout, *Rise of American Naval Power,* 194

17. Although these are British costs, there is no reason to believe that the differential would have been much greater for U.S.-built ships. The British *Inflexible* battleship of 1881, with a displacement of 11,880 tons, cost £68 per ton of displacement, compared with £64 per ton for the 9,150-ton *Colossus* coastal defense ship of 1879.

18. This argument is implicit in, for example, Warner Schilling's claim that the Navy's building proposals from 1890 to 1917 were keyed to the size of various other navies, and not navy war plans against those navies. "Admirals and Foreign Policy, 1913–1919," (Ph.D. dissertation, Yale University, 1953). Cited in Vincent Davis, *The Admirals Lobby* (Chapel Hill: the University of North Carolina Press, 1967), 123–24. Rear Admiral Bradley A. Fiske was even more explicit in 1916, when he argued that the growth of American economic power to match Great Britain's meant that the country should have a fleet "exactly equal to the British navy." See his *The Navy as a Fighting Machine* (New York: Scribner's, 1916).

19. Glenn H. Snyder, "The Balance of Power and the Balance of Terror," *The Balance of Power,* ed. Paul Seabury (San Francisco: Chandler, 1965), 184–201.

20. Barry Buzan, *People, States and Fear,* 2d ed. (Boulder, Colo.: Lynne Rienner, 1991) and *An Introduction to Strategic Studies: Military Technology and International Relations* (New York: St. Martin's Press, 1987).

21. Buzan, *People, States and Fear,* 2d ed., 271.

22. Arthur J. Marder, *The Anatomy of British Sea Power: A History of British Naval Policy in the Pre-Dreadnought Era, 1880–1905* (New York: Alfred Knopf, 1940), 21–22.

23. Oscar Parkes, *British Battleships: "Warrior" 1860 to "Vanguard" 1950: A History of Design, Construction and Armament* (Hamden, Conn.: Archon Books, 1970), 420.

24. Nathaniel Barnaby, *Naval Developments in the Century* (Toronto: Linscott, 1904), 62.

25. Vice Adm. P.H. Colomb, *Memoirs of Admiral The Right Honorable Sir Ashley Cooper Key* (London: Methuen, 1898), 340. Cooper Key was captain of the Royal Navy's gunnery training ships HMS *Excellent* from 1863 to 1866. In this role, he was responsible for the test and evaluation of the navy's guns. He was First Sea Lord from 1879 to 1886.

26. Cited in ibid., 521.

27. Captain Philip Colomb offered this interesting piece of "operations analysis"

in support of armor in 1873: "I have always looked at it in this way—that the value of armour is simply this—'to compel your adversary to fire so many fewer shots at you in any given time,' and I am satisfied that every inch of armour you put on the ship effects that purpose. You compel him to carry heavier guns, and by compelling him to carry heavier guns, you compel him to fire fewer shots per minute . . ." Cited in Sir Thomas Brassey, *The British Navy: Its Strength, Resources, and Administration*, vol. 3. (London: Longmans, Green, 1883), 346–47.

28. Data are derived from various sources and are available from the author. They are contemporary estimates, based on results obtained at the time at land-based firing ranges. The Spanish-American War proved that improvements in accuracy had fallen far behind improvements in smashing power. In the Battle of Manila, only 142 out of 5,895 shells fired at virtually point-blank range hit the Spanish ships, Two months later at Santiago Bay, the Americans scored 129 hits out of 8,000 rounds fired against stationary targets between one-half and three miles away. Peter Padfield, *Aim Straight: A Biography of Sir Percy Scott, the Father of Modern Naval Gunnery* (London: Hodder and Stoughton, 1966), 85, 87–88.

29. Empirical evidence of the sailing ship's "unsinkability" is readily found in the very few ships that were actually sunk by gunfire. For instance, of the 137 warships the French lost to the British during eighteenth century War of the Austrian Succession and Seven Years War, only three appear to have been due to gunfire. Date based on William Laird Clowes, *The Royal Navy: A History from the Earliest Times to the Present*, Vol. 3 (London: Sampson Low, Marston, 1903), 312–14.

30. More than 200 captured enemy ships were recommissioned into the British fleet during the French Revolutionary and Napoleonic wars. See Otto von Pivka, *Navies of the Napoleonic Era* (London: Newton Abbot, 1980), 221–38. As late as 1850, one-third of the 150 ships on the Royal Navy's "Navy List" were reportedly "foreign models." Capt. S. Eardley-Wilmot, RN, *The Development of Navies During the Last Half-Century* (New York: Scribner's, 1892), 2.

31. For the origins of the NID and ONI, see Thomas G. Fergusson, *British Intelligence, 1870–1914: The Development of a Modern Intelligence Organization* (London: Arms and Armour Press, 1984), and Jeffrey M. Dorwart, *The Office of Naval Intelligence: The Birth of America's First Intelligence Agency, 1865–1918* (Annapolis, Md.: Naval Institute Press, 1979).

32. Cited in Dorwart, *Office of Naval Intelligence* 7–8. King made three trips to Europe between 1869 and 1876 to report on progress in naval technology. He later published his findings in an influential book, *The War-Ships and Navies of the World* (Boston: A. Williams, 1880 and 1881).

33. Fred T. Jane, *Heresies of Sea Power* (London: Longmans, Green, 1906), 294–95.

34. Few ships remained on the stocks as long as the nine 74-gun ships that were authorized by the U.S. Congress in 1816. The act empowered the President to keep the vessels "on the stocks, and kept in the best state of preservation" until a "public exigency" required their activation. The first two ships were laid down in 1817 and launched in 1820. The next four were started in 1818, two of which were completed between 1845 and 1864. The third ship, the *New York*, was still on the stocks when she burnt in 1861, and the fourth, the *Virginia*, was broken up on the stocks in 1874. See, Sprout and Sprout, *The Rise of American Naval Power*, 88–89, and Stephen Howarth, *To Shining Sea: A History of the United States Navy, 1775–1991* (New York: Random House, 1991), 129.

35. Admiral of the Fleet Lord Fisher, *Records* (London: Hodder & Stoughton, 1919), 94–95.

36. See also Bernard and Fawn M. Brodie's *From Crossbow to H-Bomb* (Bloomington: Indiana University Press, 1973), 162 for this observation.

37. By the early twentieth century, "the Western hemisphere was left to the United States; Japan assumed the task of protecting British interests in the Far East; even the Mediterranean, the 'windpipe' of the Empire, became a French naval responsibility after 1912." Paul Kennedy, *Strategy and Diplomacy 1870–1945* (London: Fontana, 1989), 56.

38. "Muzzle energy" measures the amount of working energy that is released at the point of a gun barrel. It is a function of initial shell velocity and shell weight—the greater the velocity and/or shell weight, the more muzzle velocity and therefore hitting power is produced. The term made its appearance in ordnance manuals in the 1870s, and became the common reference in contemporary estimates of comparative gun power.

39. Fiske, *The Navy As a Fighting Machine*, 60.

40. Calculations based on multiple sources. They are available from the author.

41. Eardley-Wilmot, *Development of Navies*, 61.

42. When, a few hours before Trafalgar, Nelson and one of his captains discussed what would constitute a "glorious victory," they spoke of captures. In his final instructions, Nelson made it clear that the enemy's ships were only to be destroyed as a last resort if they evaded capture. Alfred Thayer Mahan, *The Life of Nelson: The Embodiment of the Sea Power of Great Britain*, vol. 2 (Boston: Little, Brown, 1897), 373.

43. Curiously, one late-century author, who should have known better, still thought that battlefleet action would conclude with boarding and capture. In a little-known book of his, Fred T. Jane gave a fictional account of an Anglo-French battle which ends with both sides ramming each other, and the vic-

torious British crews boarding the French ships to take them home as prizes. *Blake of the "Rattlesnake" or the Man Who Saved England* (London: Tower, 1895), 44–52.

44. *Records*, 90–92.

45. Ruddock F. Mackay, *Fisher of Kilverston* (Oxford: Clarendon Press, 1973), 319. "Copenhagen" referred to the British seizure of the neutral Danish fleet in 1807 in order to prevent it from joining Napoleonic France.

46. Ibid., 319–20. Scholars are divided on whether Fisher was serious about a preventive strike against the German fleet at Kiel. Marder writes that he was "convinced" Fisher was never serious [*From the Dreadnought to Scapa Flow: The Royal Navy in the Fisher Era, 1904–1919, Vol. 1: The Road to War, 1904–1914* (London: Oxford University Press, 1961), 113]. Mackay, on the other hand, believes that Fisher "was almost certainly serious," and he cites the comment of Lord Selborne, the admiral's political master at the Admiralty, that, "He meant it." Mackay, *Fisher of Kilverston*, 319, 320. In any event, German naval planners took Fisher's threat seriously enough to declare the next ten years the Navy's "danger zone." Afterward, the fleet would presumably be too strong for the British to risk attack.

47. Winston S. Churchill, *The World Crisis 1911–1918*, vol. 1 (London: Odhams Press, 1938), 116.

48. The French naval attaché in Berlin wrote in 1906: "If the fleet is lost it is irreparable. Army corps can be replaced in a week; ships cannot." Cited in P.K. Kemp, *The Papers of Admiral Sir John Fisher*, Vol. 2 (London: Navy Records Society, 1964), 297.

49. As late as the 1830s, it reportedly took the British navy three to six months to collect a crew for a large frigate or ship-of-the-line, and another six months to "bring order and discipline." Sir Henry Briggs, *Naval Administrations 1827–1892* (London: Sampson Low, Marston, 1897), 58.

50. Churchill, *World Crisis*, vol. 1, 118.

51. Thomas C. Schelling, *The Strategy of Conflict* (Cambridge: Harvard University Press, 1960), 208–29.

52. Thomas Brassey, *The British Navy: Its Strength, Resources, and Administration*, vol. 3, (London: Longmans, Green & Co., 1882), 203.

53. See Jan Breemer "The Burden of Trafalgar: Decisive Battle and Naval Strategic Expectations on the Eve of the First World War," *The Newport Papers* (October 1993), especially 33–37.

54. Grand Admiral Von Tirpitz, *My Memoirs*, vol. 2 (New York: Dodd, Mead, 1919), 31.

55. Churchill, *World Crisis*, Vol. 2, 117.

56. The term "runaway technological revolution" is borrowed from William H.

McNeill, *The Pursuit of Power: Technology, Armed Force, and Society Since AD 1000* (Chicago: University of Chicago Press, 1982), 277.

57. Brassey, *British Navy*, 21. This is a good source for professional naval opinion on big vs. small ships in the 1870s.

58. Cited in Dorwart, *Office of Naval Intelligence*, 17. Senior U.S. military planners, including Navy Secretary Tracy, employed similar scenarios to justify American naval preparedness. For Tracy's call for a fleet to "prevent a fleet of ironclads from shelling our cities," see Sprout and Sprout, *Rise of American Naval Power*, 207.

59. Robert L. O'Connell, *Sacred Vessels: The Cult of the Battleship and the Rise of the U.S. Navy* (Boulder, Colo.: Westview Press, 1991), 71.

8 Mission Possible: Organizational Learning in Peacetime

Emily O. Goldman

Do military organizations adjust to changes in their strategic and technological environments in peacetime, particularly when their main enemies have been vanquished or disappeared? If they do so, how and why? The dominant view of military organizations is that they resist change—that, like other entrenched bureaucracies, they seek first and foremost to preserve organizational health.[1]

In peacetime, threats to the organization are more likely to come from within the state, from other bureaucratic actors or from budget cuts, than from enemies abroad. Responding to bureaucratic incentives, the services will stick to current routines,[2] altering them incrementally at most, even at the expense of performing their missions. Only civilian intervention can overcome these obstacles to change.

Several works challenge this pessimistic prognosis.[3] One approach that has not been explored sufficiently in the literature is the organizational learning perspective.[4] It provides an interpretation of strategic adjustment[5] as a process of encoding inferences from experience into organizational routines to achieve targets.[6] My use of the term innovation does not imply that the change is necessarily good. A learning perspective demonstrates how military organizations can adjust to their strategic environment in peacetime without being forced to by civilians.

I examine three instances of U.S. strategic adjustment—mechanization, amphibious warfare, and carrier aviation[7]—between the two world wars, a period when the international environment was, like today, similarly under-determining.[8] The 1920s and 1930s are particularly interesting because the U.S. military is credited with having made important strategic strides in this period. The Navy came to appreciate the centrality of air power in the achievement of naval objectives. The Marine Corps dramatically revised its understanding of the organization's role in providing security and adopted as its new core task the amphibious assault mission.[9] Contemporary policy-makers are trying to replicate the processes associated with these "innova-tions."[10] So it is important to engage in a systematic analysis to understand more fully how adjustment unfolded. Examining the Army's approach to-ward mechanization is instructive as a negative case because adjustment was minimal. If the factors identified by the learning perspective as stimulants to adjustment are fewer or absent in the case of mechanization, we can have greater confidence in our conclusions about how adjustment occurs, what triggers and impedes it at the organizational level, and in the policy pre-scriptions derived from the analysis.

The findings support the claim that military organizations can innovate in response to a dynamic peacetime environment, provided they have the right sorts of pressures and resources to reduce the level of ambiguity that confronts them in peacetime. Three factors are key to reducing ambiguity: domestic political inducements; international vulnerability; and credible knowledge that supports the proposed innovation.[11] Pressure or support from civilians or other military actors can reduce ambiguity by increasing the political incentives and opportunities (or desirability) for reevaluating service tasks. Although civilian intervention can play a role, it is a far more modest one than the bureaucratic approach requires and it is not necessary for in-novation. Strategic vulnerabilities (or urgency) refer to the pressures created by specific geopolitical circumstances and that reduce ambiguity by per-mitting military professionals to focus their planning and simulation activi-ties. Finally, credible knowledge about the proposed innovation (or possi-bility) reduces ambiguity by providing optimism about the prospects for change. The credibility of the knowledge base depends on the limits and capabilities of technologies, and the opportunities for bringing experience to bear to expand the knowledge base over time. These findings challenge the dominant bureaucratic explanation that characterizes the military in peacetime as unresponsive to external threats to national security and pre-occupied with internal threats to organizational interest.

Organizational Perspectives on Innovation

The most popular paradigm of organizational behavior is the organizational process model, which lies at the heart of bureaucratic interpretations of military behavior.[12] The organizational process model views government action as the outputs of organizational processes. The model makes three key assumptions. First, organizations define goals in terms of constraints, or imperatives to avoid falling beneath certain performance levels. The central goal is health, defined as maximizing resources and autonomy, and preserving the organization's essence, or self-concept. Second, organizational activity has a programmed character that constrains the ability of the organization to change.[13] Behavior is an enactment of preestablished routines built on standard operating procedures (SOPs).[14] SOPs are not the enemy of the organization but its essence. They help the organization do what it was designed to do: "replace the uncertain expectations and haphazard activities of voluntary endeavors with the stability and routine of organized relationships."[15] In nonstandard situations, organizations search for new options but search is constrained by existing routines, training, and experience. Changes that do occur reflect adaptation of existing procedures in the face of threats to organizational equilibrium, or the addition of new tasks without sacrificing core tasks.[16] Third, organizational behavior is driven by the quest to avoid uncertainty by solving problems of immediate urgency in response to short-run feedback from the environment.[17]

Several hypotheses flow from these assumptions.[18] First, organizations will be risk averse and develop alternatives that support existing goals, defined in terms of protecting resources, autonomy (jurisdiction and independence), and organizational essence (the views of the dominant group in the organization on what missions and capabilities should be).[19] Second, when these goals conflict, organizations privilege autonomy because monopoly jurisdiction (few or no bureaucratic rivals) means fewer competitors for resources, while independence enhances the organization's control over how it spends its resources.[20] Third, because action is determined by routines and SOPs, change will produce incremental adjustments to programs that are consistent with existing tasks.[21]

From the perspective of the organizational process model, we would expect that in peacetime the U.S. services will be risk averse, sticking to current routines or marginally adapting them in support of existing roles and missions; to search for ways to protect and maintain existing roles and missions; to resist adoption of dramatically new roles and missions; and to seek to increase resources and autonomy by adding new missions to repertoires while not jeopardizing the central position of existing missions. Overall, we would expect organizational inertia to be high.

Under the conditions that prevailed during the interwar period, we would expect the Army to be interested in mechanization as a way to augment resources but determined to fit armor doctrine into traditional infantry and cavalry SOPs. We would expect naval leaders to have developed air power but to fit it into standard doctrine and practice by using air power for spotting and scouting to support the battleship, not for independent strikes. Finally, we would expect the Marines to cling to their traditional peacetime missions, which afforded them a great deal of autonomy, perhaps gradually adding new missions but not totally displacing traditional ones. The organizational process model will be falsified if we see the displacement of core missions rather than the expansion of repertoires; the adoption of strategies or doctrines that threaten resources, autonomy, or essence in important ways, particularly autonomy; and support of change by members of sub-branches when it undermines the organization's self-concept.

An alternative model of organizational behavior—the organizational learning model[22]—posits different types of obstacles to adjustment in peacetime. It makes three key assumptions. First, the basic motivating goal of an organization is to achieve an optimal result in the outside world.[23] Second, to achieve this goal, organizations will reevaluate beliefs about causation that define their tasks, and redefine tasks, skills, and procedures accordingly. Third, organizations redefine tasks based on observations and interpretations of experience.[24] This is the context in which organizations "learn."[25] The conditions most likely to promote learning emanate from the organization's external environment. They are "the *desirability* of finding new cause-effect chains, the *possibility* of finding them, and the *urgency* for finding them."[26]

Desirability refers to the domestic political incentives motivating bureaucratic actors to engage in soul-searching. Pressure from civilians can trigger learning, as George Breslauer notes, "by providing the impetus, political incentive, and political opportunity for a significant reevaluation of assumptions."[27] Lack of civilian support can restrict opportunities for such reevaluation.[28] Pressures from other military actors can also stimulate learning. If one organization in the process of addressing an international vulnerability needs another organization to fulfill its military mission, political pressures will rise, thus heightening the desirability for reevaluating organizational tasks.

Haas notes, however, that "the existence of political incentives may not be enough to trigger learning."[29] The possibility must also exist, and this is a function of the state of knowledge or available pool of experience that the organization can draw upon. The pool of experience, in turn, is affected by the capabilities and limitations of technology and by the opportunities for gathering necessary data to develop a credible knowledge base in peacetime. Possibility is less a question of resources than of credible knowledge that supports the proposed innovation.[30]

Finally, learning is stimulated by urgency, which is the result of pressures in the international environment. In peacetime, short of crisis, urgency is greatest where interests are most vulnerable. Even during periods of low external threat, geostrategic vulnerabilities created by geography, international agreements, and technological developments influence strategic adjustment. Urgency reduces ambiguity in two ways. First, it aids the identification of the problem by making it clear which vulnerabilities need to be addressed. Second, it increases actors' motivations to pay attention to certain problems and arrive at solutions.[31] By enhancing strategic focus in these ways, urgency helps clarify the organization's strategic priorities so experience can be brought to bear.

Urgency is tied to the scope of a nation's international responsibilities and the vulnerability of its interests. If the nation is a global power, responsibilities will be broad and diffuse, reducing opportunities for leaders to focus on particular problems and bring experience to bear. Problem identification will be more difficult.[32] Moreover, if vulnerability is low, there will be less incentive and motivation to reevaluate the tasks of the organization and to produce new knowledge. Between the wars, an insular United States could easily withdraw militarily from continental Europe. However, the vulnerability of regional interests heightened strategic sensitivity in the Pacific and motivated actors to direct their attention there to devise ways to reduce vulnerabilities. Geopolitical circumstances presented focal points around which learning could take place.

A favorable conjunction of desirability, possibility, and urgency enhances opportunities for learning in two key ways: by increasing the pressure on the organization to focus its strategic priorities and bring experience to bear on the strategic problem in question; by increasing the organization's ability to examine past experience, augment it with new information, and reevaluate programs and tasks accordingly.

Several hypotheses flow from this model. First, organizations accept risk in order to achieve the most desirable result in the outside world. They do so even when they understand that by doing so they may lose some autonomy and resources. Second, organizations can overcome inertia provided there is a favorable conjunction of desirability, possibility, and urgency.

From the organizational learning model, we would expect U.S. service leaders to respond to the external security environment rather than to bureaucratic interests, to adopt new missions to enhance military effectiveness in the future, and to relinquish missions no longer deemed relevant. Nonincremental change should be tied to learning and the acquisition of new knowledge, and there should be a strong correlation between the credibility of the experiential base that supports the innovation and learning. Finally, adjustment should be greatest for the services that face the most favorable conjunction of desirability, possibility, and urgency. Overall, we would expect organizational inertia to be low.

In the interwar period, advances in mechanization, amphibious warfare, and carrier strike forces should be linked to a credible experiential base and a growth in consensual knowledge. The constraints on adjustment should be higher for the Army than for the Navy and Marine Corps, because the North American continent was nearly invulnerable while the U.S. insular Pacific possessions were very vulnerable. Urgency was higher for the Navy and Marine Corps than for the Army. The organizational learning model would be confirmed if we see nonincremental changes in organizational process; far-reaching changes in training and education, which would indicate reevaluation of the theory of causation that defines the organization's tasks; changes in core tasks; the voluntary relinquishing of missions, even if it jeopardized autonomy and resources; and changes in organizational routines in the face of experience, despite a negative impact on bureaucratic interests.[33] Alterations in tasks that jeopardize autonomy yield the strongest evidence for the organizational learning model.

Mechanization

Following World War I, the War Department adhered to the conviction that man remains the fundamental instrument in combat. Mechanized forces should operate in close support of the infantry, more efficiently performing the scouting role. To the extent that armor development proceeded, it was tailored to existing infantry doctrine. Adjustment was adaptive, a change consistent with existing roles and missions.

The organizational process model asserts that organizational health is the foremost concern of military organizations, even more so when the probability of war is remote. But only by protecting the turf of one sub-branch — the infantry—was the Army's mechanization strategy one that preserved organizational health. Mechanization was tied to the continental defense mission and this defensive frame of mind only justified the budget reductions Congress was imposing.[34] Continental defense undercut any strategic rationale for an aggressive mechanization policy which would have given the Army an offensive potential and a legitimate claim to more resources.

Were Army leaders simply following standard operating procedures? Did Army leadership identify with the parochial sub-branch concerns of the infantry for protection of its turf? Marginally perhaps, but the evidence is not conclusive. There was broad support among the Army leadership for mechanization. In 1928, Secretary of War Dwight Davis ordered the organization of the first experimental mechanized force to serve as a technical and tactical laboratory.[35] Davis also organized a board of General Staff officers to begin planning for long-range mechanization. The board recommended the creation of a follow-on experimental mechanized force since the first was disbanded in September 1928 after completing its mission. With the exception of Chief of Infantry, Major General Stephen Fuqua, who perceived a threat to the infantry's control over tanks, the board members supported the reconstitution of a mechanized force and they prevailed over narrow branch rivalries.[36] This point is important for assessing self-concept-related claims made by the organizational process model because the infantry was firmly entrenched as the dominant fighting arm in the Army.[37] The chiefs were acting against the Army's organizational essence. They did not identify with the narrow views of the infantry.[38]

Obstacles to armor development are better explained by the absence of factors deemed important by the organizational learning model. How urgent was learning? Were there strategic pressures encouraging the Army to mechanize? General John Pershing articulated the Army's primary mission in 1919: defense of the American continent against invasion.[39] As an insular nation with no great powers contiguous to its borders and no imperial commitments, this defensive mission made perfect sense. Operating on the

North American continent made mobility necessary.[40] Yet since tank doctrine had evolved in a static warfare situation, tanks were viewed as siege
weapons. Pershing endorsed the view that tanks had no role to play in continental defense.

How desirable was learning? Were there domestic pressures on the organization to reevaluate core tasks as they related to mechanization? Pershing's testimony went beyond simply articulating the Army's core mission.
It was instrumental in Congress's decision under the National Defense Act
of 1920 to disband the tank corps as an independent organization and place
it under the Chief of Infantry.[41] Pershing's recommendation dovetailed with
Congressional concerns over the affordability of a separate tank service.[42]
With reduced military budgets, the consensus was that the United States
could not afford an independent tank organization. The reorganization constrained tank development severely. It was not the result of bureaucratic
inertia but Congress's decision did make it easier for the infantry to pursue
its parochial interests of ensuring that tanks conformed to infantry tactics.
Furthermore, once the infantry was designated as the using arm, all design
work on heavy tank models was canceled.[43] Fiscal stringency influenced the
development of equipment and organization, making it difficult to augment
the experiential base. This situation reinforced the opinions of the tank skep-
tics over the tank enthusiasts.

Mechanization development met further fiscal obstacles in the 1920s.
The existence of surplus wartime equipment gave Congress an excuse for
limiting appropriations for equipment. Wartime equipment was obsolete
and suitable tanks were crucial to organization of a mechanized force. The
Great Depression sealed further the fate of armor development. Tank modernization and reequipment of a mechanized force were not high on the
priority list of War Department leaders searching for ways to maintain the
Army with ever more limited funds.[44] And mechanization was very expensive.[45] When the second mechanized force was finally constituted in 1930,
it was forced to use obsolete equipment. At a variety of crucial turning points,
fiscal stringency squelched armor development. It shaped decisions about
organization and equipment appropriations, constraining the experiential
base and reinforcing traditional Army task definitions. Up to this point, the
evidence can be interpreted to support the organizational process model.
Civilian support seems a key factor. But the logic of the organizational process model falters when we examine what shaped civilian decisions and

when we see how Army leaders responded when incentives from civilians changed in the 1930s.

How possible was learning? What was the nature of the experiential base for armor development at the close of World War I? There were competing views on how to incorporate mechanization into Army doctrine, which reflected differing experiences among units during World War I. Divisions that had an opportunity to train and fight with tanks were enthusiastic supporters while those with no experience were unenthusiastic.[46] In the end, two aspects of wartime experience overwhelmed the tank enthusiasts: the limited nature of that experience; and the static warfare situation which framed that limited experience. U.S. ground forces were in the war too short a time to conduct extensive tests and accumulate sufficient combat data. So the Army accepted British and French concepts of tank use, which linked the tank to trench warfare as a close support weapon for the infantry.[47] That role for the tank was judged to be largely irrelevant to what the Army perceived as its postwar mission: continental defense.[48] The course of American armor development was affected considerably by subsequent domestic political decisions but the lessons of the war provided the initial set of experiences that framed decisions about armor.[49] From the organizational learning perspective, the World War I experience created the interpretive frame through which subsequent tank experience was viewed. Most Army officers saw the role of the tank through a static rather than a mobile warfare frame. This accounts for obstacles to adjustment better than the bureaucratic model because there was not sufficient experience to overturn the dominant frame, while bureaucratic incentives for change (e.g., Congressional appropriations) did exist. This point is key to mediating between the two models of organizational behavior because the World War I experience informed Pershing's 1919 testimony to Congress, and that testimony was instrumental in Congress's decision to disband the tank corps. Possibility preceded desirability at the outset; subsequently the two fed on each other, stunting opportunities for learning.

The possibility for armor development was curtailed further by the limited mechanical capabilities of tanks in the 1920s. Slow moving tanks could support infantry assaults, though with difficulty; yet they were incapable of performing the mobile independent missions tank enthusiasts envisioned for them. The adaptive approach to armor development was reinforced by the capabilities of the tanks that were available at any particular time for maneuvers. Limited capabilities limited experimentation, and, as the Chief Ordnance Department historians point out, "Doctrine depended upon what tests proved tanks could do."[50]

One final decision ensured that mechanization would be grafted onto existing service missions. In 1931, Chief of Staff General Douglas MacArthur disbanded the second mechanized force. The practical effect was to further delimit the experiential base for armor development. The first experimental mechanized force had been disbanded after two months. Now, the second mechanized force, organized in November 1930, was disbanded in June 1931. MacArthur's decision governed Army mechanization policy for the rest of the decade. The General wanted to promote mechanization while also assuaging the infantry and the cavalry.[51] While he recognized the importance of mechanization and sought to promote it, his funding priorities were conditioned by the tank's technical limitations and the limited experiential base it had produced.[52] MacArthur remained convinced that mechanized combat was inherently limited by weather, terrain, and availability of fuel.

In a vicious cycle, MacArthur's priorities angered Congressional supporters of mechanization who feared the General would spend additional appropriations on men rather than modernization. In 1932, they opposed any increase in War Department appropriations.[53] This point is critical for assessing resource-related claims made by the organizational process model. It is difficult to account for the failure of Army leaders to respond to resource incentives, particularly at the height of the depression. At this juncture, mechanization was the only way to increase War Department appropriations.[54] Political incentives for bureaucratic actors to reevaluate core tasks existed, but they were not enough because the possibility for reevaluation, which was a function of the state of knowledge, barely existed.

Strategic adjustment in mechanization was adaptive. But by only the most narrow definition, protecting infantry turf, was it a strategy that preserved organizational health. More telling are the insights provided by the organizational learning model, which direct attention to the absence of any of the factors that might have stimulated a reevaluation of existing missions. Insularity, the absence of great power competitors, and continental security negated urgency. Desirability did not begin to rise until the early 1930s in the guise of Congressional pressure for mechanization. By then, possibility was minimal. Fiscal and technological constraints had already converged to limit an already limited experiential base from which learning could proceed.

The static warfare frame persisted. While the parochial interests of the infantry were served, these were not the sole, nor even dominant, factors behind the Army's adaptive approach to tank warfare. Budgetary limitations, which severely constrained the experiential base, played a far more significant role in shaping roles and missions than did vested organizational interests and standard operating procedures. The organizational process model underestimates leadership support for mechanization. It also elevates a secondary level factor (infantry parochialism) to a primary level cause by overlooking the process by which wartime experience shaped Pershing's views on the tank and his subsequent testimony, which in turn influenced Congressional decisions that only then resulted in increased infantry control over mechanization.

Amphibious Warfare

In 1933, the Marine Corps created the Fleet Marine Force and adopted the amphibious assault mission as the service's new core task. Strategic adjustment was innovative, something the organizational process model has difficulty explaining. The result was not, however, entirely antithetical to the goals of organizational health as defined by that model. The amphibious assault mission is frequently characterized as an institutional panacea: it gave the Corps a much needed and desired raison-d'être, a singular identity; it restored marine pride and confidence after an onslaught of negative press over the barbarous conduct of some Marines serving in Hispaniola;[55] it gave the service a prominent military role, one essential to national defense and obviously distinct from the Army's and Navy's, particularly since the Army periodically threatened to absorb the Corps.[56] Moreover, amphibious assault was a role the Corps did not hold in contempt like it did colonial duty; and it required the Corps to maintain a permanent force in readiness. The Marines finally found a solution to their historic problem of bureaucratic survival by staking out a mission unique to that service. The amphibious assault mission would ensure bureaucratic survival and escape from legislative parsimony.

On the other hand, the Marines engaged in a very risky strategy, choosing ultimately to displace their traditional missions with a new mission rather than simply expanding their repertoire.[57] Moreover, the amphibious assault mission sacrificed autonomy to the Navy and at a time when Congress was unwilling to devote resources to the Fleet Marine Force because of its interventionist and overly provocative character. The Marine Corps, though ostensibly a fully autonomous service within the Department of the Navy, had always depended on the Navy for missions. Amphibious assault did not change that; on the contrary, it sacrificed autonomy. By contrast, the Corps's traditional missions were important sources of autonomy and particularly relevant to peacetime. Moreover, expeditionary duty, a mainstay of the Corps between the wars, was not under serious threat from the Army.[58]

How urgent was learning? Following World War I, political developments raised the nation's geostrategic vulnerabilities, heightened urgency, and brought the advanced base mission to the forefront of American military planning in the Pacific.[59] The Treaty of Versailles gave the Japanese possession of former German Pacific islands that lay astride U.S. supply routes to the Philippines. The Washington naval treaties restricted the number and size of U.S. battleships and the fortification of certain bases in the Pacific while placing no limits on mobile forces that could seize and defend advanced bases. In the Navy's revised War Plan Orange, the Marines' wartime role of accompanying the fleet became essential.

How desirable was learning? The desirability of reassessing service missions dated back to 1900 when the Navy's General Board began pushing the Marines to accept the advanced base role.[60] The General Board continued applying pressure, despite the reluctance of Headquarters Marine Corps (HQMC) to provide men if it meant detracting from other duties, and the failure of Congress to provide necessary appropriations.[61] The advanced base mission gained a temporary boost when U.S.-Japanese diplomatic relations soured in 1906–1907 and again in 1913, and the Corps prospered by relating its manpower requests to the advanced base mission.[62] But Corps leaders refused to sacrifice traditional duties, even while accepting the advanced base mission as the service's principal *war* mission. When one-third of Corps strength was tasked to serve as infantry in Europe during World War I, the advanced base force was maintained at full strength, but the mission remained one of many tasks Corps leaders sought to preserve.[63] Moreover, expeditionary duty in Haiti (1915) and in the Dominican Republic (1916) prevented designation of any permanent advanced base units.[64]

After World War I, many senior officers continued to believe the Corps flourished in direct relation to its distance from the Navy.[65] Colonial infantry duties provided important peacetime missions that were more likely to enhance the Corps's claim to scarce resources.[66] There were also those who argued that preparing for large-scale ground maneuvers like in World War I was the Corps's main duty in peacetime.[67] So the Corps initially embraced the advanced base mission as an expansion of its repertoire, a behavior consistent with the expectations of the organizational process model.

By 1931, however, the Corps had committed itself to serving the fleet in wartime by seizing bases for naval operations and preparing in peacetime for the successful execution of that wartime function. How do we account for this shift? Following World War I, heightened urgency had reduced ambiguity in the Corps's strategic environment while political incentives to engage in a reevaluation of service missions also climbed. Chief of Naval Operations (CNO) Robert E. Coontz pressed CMC Barnett in January 1920 to provide a West Coast expeditionary force built around the advanced base force concept.[68] Plan Orange called for the capture of bases in the Caroline and Marshall Islands which the Japanese now occupied.[69] The mission was not only to defend advanced bases but also to seize them from the enemy. Naval leaders needed the Marines to create the units and develop the doctrine to conduct amphibious landings against defended shores. The most recent experience with amphibious landings was the unsuccessful British assault on Turkish defenses in 1915. The disastrous Gallipoli campaign convinced naval planners the world over that amphibious landings in the face of heavy opposition could not succeed. This was hardly a doctrine upon which to stake an organization's identity. But the Navy's War Plans Division could see no way to prosecute Plan Orange other than by amphibious assault.

Civilian support, however, was uneven throughout the 1920s and amphibious warfare doctrine developed slowly. The onset of the Great Depression tightened resources further. But CMC Ben Fuller (1930–1934) steadfastly held that the Corps's primary duty was the wartime role of seizing and defending bases. In 1931 he persuaded the CNO to establish the Fleet Marine Force (FMF), a permanent unit composed of base defense and amphibious assault units. In Holland Smith's estimation, the FMF "firmly established the Marine Corps as part of the organization of the U.S. Fleet, available for operations with the Fleet ashore or afloat."[70]

How possible was learning between the wars? When Corps Headquarters officially embraced the base seizure mission as part of its repertoire in 1920,[71] CMC John A. Lejeune (1920–1929) began the process of redirecting the Corps's role from colonial infantry to amphibious assault in support of the fleet.[72] Broadening the experiential base was one important component.[73]

In Marine Corps schools, Lejeune increased the time spent studying amphibious warfare and the British landings at Gallipoli.[74] In-depth studies
revealed that flaws in the Gallipoli operation could be corrected, a critical
step in building credible knowledge around the feasibility of amphibious
assault. Training exercises in 1923–24 and 1925 demonstrated that seizing
advanced bases from an enemy was possible. By 1931, theoretical instruction
at Marine Corps schools was overhauled and three years later, a detailed
manual entitled "Tentative Manual for Landing Operations" was adopted as
official doctrine. From this point forward until the outbreak of war, a series
of Fleet Landing Exercises (FLEXes) provided continuous practical training
for the Marines to test their doctrine and make improvements. The FLEXes
were critical to the progress made in developing amphibious warfare doctrine. Through trial and error, they provided a body of knowledge and experience that further reduced ambiguity about the possibility of adjustment.
Experience proved the main principles of the doctrine sound.[75]

Adopting the amphibious assault mission would be consistent with the
organizational process model if the Marines had embraced it as an additional
mission. But instead of seeing amphibious assault as an additional mission,
as an incremental growth in responsibilities, they saw it as a *replacement* for
traditional core missions. Moreover, this shift is not consistent with the interpretation of organizational goals that the model advances. It was not clear
that resources would rise given prevailing views in the White House and
Congress. By the early 1930s, the Depression was well underway and despite
the Manchurian incident of 1931, President Hoover did not regard Japan
as a threat and remained committed to nonintervention and hemispheric
defense. Although the election of Franklin Roosevelt in 1933 gave the Corps
an ally for the amphibious assault mission in the White House,[76] by that
time, isolationism in Congress had grown and, with it, the perception of the
FMF as provocative and interventionist. Moreover, Congress and the Navy
remained unsympathetic to Marine Corps pleas for more landing craft to
facilitate peacetime training.

Most critically, the strategy sacrificed autonomy to the Navy, autonomy
the Corps had derived from its traditional peacetime missions. The Navy
was not seriously interested in addressing the naval gunfire problem to support the base seizure mission.[77] Moreover, the admirals who controlled naval
aviation were more interested in building the Navy's carrier force then in
developing close air support techniques for the "less crucial" amphibious

assault mission. After all, amphibious assault was distinctly secondary to the problems of fleet action on the high seas.

There was little consensus among Corps leaders at the time about how or even whether the Corps should adjust given its repertoire of peacetime responsibilities. Yet amphibious assault ultimately prevailed because it was linked to a pressing geostrategic challenge that confronted the United States at the close of the First World War. Steady growth of the experiential base revealed that success was possible, and a new more optimistic consensus emerged from careful analysis of Gallipoli. A favorable conjunction of desirability, possibility, and urgency reduced ambiguity in the Corps's environment and stimulated a fundamental rethinking of its core tasks. Even if one allows that the adoption of amphibious assault was an institutional panacea for the Marine Corps, the organizational process model cannot explain the decision to sacrifice autonomy, particularly when civilian and Navy support were waning. Moreover, Corps leaders pursued a very risky strategy by pinning the service's future on a mission that experts worldwide had deemed hopeless.

Carrier Aviation

Carrier aviation represents a hybrid form of strategic adjustment. The foundations of aerial victory were laid in the 1920s and 1930s, easing the way for the U.S. Navy to substitute the carrier task force for the battle line. But the aircraft carrier did not come into its own as the "main striking force of the fleet until well into World War II." Up until then, naval aviation "remained a distinctly auxiliary service, charged with scouting, long-range patrol, raiding, and protection of the battle line."[78] Unlike the Marines, who embraced amphibious assault in peacetime and refocused their education, training, and doctrine around it, the Navy did not place the carrier strike force at the center of its doctrine and operations until the destruction of the U.S. battle line at Pearl Harbor by a Japanese carrier strike. The key questions are how to account for the extent of adjustment that did occur, and what factors hindered further adjustment.

In his analysis of the U.S. Navy between the wars, Waldo Heinrichs claims that bureaucratic inertia was the culprit.[79] Arguing from the organizational process model perspective, Heinrichs writes that in peacetime, precedent and routine take hold. The Navy is conservative and incrementally adaptive; it is in its organizational interest to be so because the most pressing engagement is the battle of the budget. Here intraorganizational compromise and consensus is the name of the game. Adjustment occurs in piecemeal fashion and only extreme financial pressure or the imminent threat of war will produce innovation.

Heinrichs contends that the Navy failed to innovate; that this failure stemmed from organizational inertia; and that Navy planning served a bureaucratic rather than a strategic function. His interpretation contrasts sharply with Stephen Rosen's.[80] Rosen argues that Rear Admiral William Moffett, the battleship commander who became the first Chief of the Bureau of Aeronautics, transformed the place of aviation in the Navy between the wars.[81] Moffett redefined the role of carriers as independent strike forces, and won a power struggle within the organization to create a career path for aviators, keeping them in the organization where they could develop strategy, tactics, and doctrine for the effective use of air power.[82]

Both Rosen's and Heinrichs's versions contain elements of truth. The U.S. Navy did make significant strides in carrier aviation between the wars but did not fully adopt the carrier strike force concept. Heinrichs, however, mischaracterizes the obstacles as bureaucratic. It was not the presence of bureaucratic inertia deemed critical by the organizational process model but rather the weakness of key stimulants deemed crucial by the organizational learning model that produced the hybrid result.

How urgent was learning? By restricting the fortification of insular possessions in the western Pacific, the Washington Five Power treaty heightened urgency. It denied the U.S. Navy the advanced fleet bases necessary to operate land-based aircraft in the western Pacific, producing the paradox of defending Far Eastern commitments with inadequate power projection capabilities.[83] Fleet aviation, centered on the carrier concept, offered a way for the U.S. Navy to remedy this deficiency within treaty constraints. Despite the pro-battleship biases that existed, the changing security and technological environments created new pressures and possibilities for U.S. naval planners to adjust.

How desirable was learning? What were the domestic and bureaucratic incentives and obstacles? As early as 1919, there was support for aviation among the Navy leadership, particularly the General Board, to develop aviation to the fullest.[84] There was significant gun-club opposition, but battleship commanders appreciated the value of carrier aircraft for spotting and

scouting. Moreover, the moving force within the Navy behind a more independent role for the carrier—Moffett—was a successful battleship admiral. Some of his biggest allies were other battleship admirals like Joseph
Reeves and then-President of the Naval War College William Sims.

How possible was learning? The answer to this question provides the
greatest insight into the development of carrier strike forces between the
wars. A main hindrance to learning was technological uncertainty about
aircraft capabilities and the effectiveness of different types of carriers.[85] These
hindered the development of new consensual knowledge, raised ambiguity,
and limited prospects for learning. The limitations of carrier aircraft continued to reinforce the pro-battleship sentiment of many admirals until after
the battles of the Coral Sea and Midway.[86] Moreover, while the value of the
large fast fleet carrier as a separate offensive striking force was demonstrated
in Fleet Problem IX of 1929,[87] it was still not clear how to make the most
effective use of the carrier, nor how to achieve an optimal number within
the limits imposed by international treaties.

Exercises with the *Lexington* and *Saratoga* in 1929 demonstrated the
advantages of large carriers. But they were far larger than needed to accom-
modate the small air groups anticipated for the future. Proponents of small
carriers argued for a large number of platforms to fight a war that might not
be decided in a decisive fleet engagement but over the course of a lengthy
war of attrition.[88] Given treaty limits on total carrier displacement, building
as many carriers as possible meant building small ones. Given the treaty
restrictions on tonnage then in effect, it was not self-evident that large carriers
represented the best possible investment.

There were lively disputes over the relative merits of small and large
carriers, yet no way to resolve those arguments short of actual testing and
operational experience. Hone and Mandeles conclude that "the 'delay' in
obtaining the *Essex* type was not the result of bureaucratic conservatism or
lethargy. It was instead the result of a lack of sufficient experience."[89] Those
who challenged Moffett's claim that the primary function of the main body
of carriers to increase the attack power of the fleet did so in the course
of realistic exercises;[90] there was simply insufficient evidence that carriers
had become the dominant type of ship. They were vulnerable to attack, had
greater difficulty operating at night and in bad weather, and were particularly
susceptible to dive bomb attacks. Doubts about carrier potential were
grounded in reasonable assessments of technological uncertainties raised in
the course of experience. From the organizational learning perspective, the

results of exercises were too ambiguous to entirely overturn the dominant interpretive frame that saw the carrier as supporting the battleship rather than displacing it as the organizations' core offensive weapon system.

The learning that did occur stemmed from Navy efforts to war-game Plan Orange. Between the wars, a body of knowledge grew up around planning exercises conducted at the Naval War College.[91] The perplexing problems of a Pacific campaign provided grist for simulation exercises which took on a greater air of strategic reality by the late 1920s as a direct consequence of brutally realistic gaming. Previously, a Pacific campaign was envisioned as swift, offensive, and decisive; after 1928, a vision of a protracted war of attrition predominated in which numerical inferiority in battleships was compensated for by air superiority.[92] The assumptions underlying the Navy's view of strategy and warfare were challenged and transformed. From a mere transit itinerary, the Navy produced a doctrine of progressive transoceanic offensive operations.[93]

These intellectual breakthroughs highlighted the importance of the carrier as an independent offensive striking force and the need to mass aircraft for strikes rather than assigning aircraft to each battleship to act as its eyes.[94] As Hone and Mandeles point out, "continuing advocacy is insufficient in itself for successful innovation. The organization must also be able to gain experience with the innovation and alter its methods on the basis of that experience."[95] It needs a means of testing new ideas that provides evidence to show what works and what does not.

The Navy's experiential base also received a boost, paradoxically, from the Washington naval treaties.[96] Two battle cruiser hulls were converted into large carriers and the results of fleet exercises with them opened up new operational possibilities for naval planners. Moreover, by restricting carrier displacement, the treaties made it impossible for designers to provide sufficient flight-deck armor to repel dive-bomb attacks. Major fleet exercises revealed the ease of spotting the battle fleet from the air and destroying any carrier operating with the battle fleet. This was an important consideration in the decision to detach the carrier from the battle fleet and let carriers operate independently.

In the final analysis, Navy planning did respond to heightened urgency. U.S. leaders had made extensive political commitments in the Far East. Should they decide to make good on those promises, the Navy would have to execute a strategic offensive against Japan. Revisionists maintain the Philippines were really not important and that naval leaders called for their

defense because it justified a large battle fleet and the Mahanian-type engagement they hoped to fight.[97] But it was civilians who defined the national
interest as defense of the Philippines and the Open Door in China. The
fact remained that Japan could not menace the continental United States
nor the western hemisphere. It could, however, close the Open Door.

Learning did occur but the Navy did not fully develop the doctrine of
multicarrier task forces. Full-fledged innovation was hindered less by bureaucratic inertia than by experiential obstacles. The organizational process
model underestimates the support of battleship admirals for aviation, over-
looks the progress made through simulation at the Naval War College, and
does not pay sufficient attention to the debates over carrier development
which hinged on questions of technical feasibility. The experiential base was
constrained by treaty restrictions and technological uncertainties, each
of which introduced considerable ambiguity into the organization's
environment.

Conclusions

Strategic adjustment is a process that is shaped by organizational constraints. Organizations can adjust provided the appropriate stimulants are
present. Moreover, service organizations can be the originators of innovative
approaches to providing security. They are neither mere passive recipients
of new ideas nor necessarily conservative obstructionists. This does not mean
that learning and innovation occur easily. But when they do *not* occur, we
would be hasty to attribute the cause to bureaucratic inertia. In fact, the
organizational process model does not get one very far at all. It asserts that
innovation in peacetime is rare and when it does occur, it is to serve some
bureaucratic interest. The empirical findings demonstrate that the claims
made by the organizational process model do not square with the historical
record. Adjustment responded to strategic needs and to the quality of the
knowledge base. By some estimates, bureaucratic interests were served; by
others they were harmed. But in no sense were they singularly decisive. This
is an important finding because recent historiography champions the organizational process model's interpretation and most scholars continue to pay
lip service to it.[98]

The organizational learning model fares better. A favorable confluence
of stimulants for learning accounts for the process of task reorientation in

the Marine Corps. The absence of these stimulants provides a better explanation for the Army's adaptive approach to mechanization and the Navy's embryonic development of the carrier strike force than does the organizational process model's hypotheses about organizational health. Table 8.1 lays out the stimulants and summarizes the findings of the case studies about how the confluence of these stimulants affected strategic adjustment.

What do these general theoretical findings suggest for the United States today? The U.S. military today is being asked to do more with less. One strategy to accomplish this is to capitalize on new technologies, or novel combinations of existing technologies, as force multipliers. Existing or nascent technologies promise a dramatic revision in the way security and military planners will think about and plan for future hostilities. But will the

TABLE 8.1 Adjustment Stimulants

	Desirability	Possibility	Urgency	Adjustment
Mechanization	low(a)	low(b)	low(c)	adaptive
Amphibious Warfare	moderate(d)	high(e)	high(f)	innovative
Carrier Aviation	moderate(g)	moderate(h)	high(i)	hybrid

Key

(a)Infantry opposition; funding cuts and mechanization expensive; Congressional pressure rises only in 1932.

(b)Limited mechanical capabilities of tanks; limited WWI experience; Experimental Mechanized Forces short-lived.

(c)Insular; no great power adversaries; continental defense priority.

(d)Congressional isolationism and view of Fleet Marine Force as interventionist and provocative; Hoover pro-continental defense; *but* declining civilian interest in colonial intervention; CNO desire for advanced base mission.

(e)FLEXes; though inadequate landing craft and amphibious troop carrier; learning from Gallipoli.

(f)War Plan Orange; geopolitical vulnerabilities; Washington treaty limits; Japanese retention of mandates.

(g)Gun club opposition; few funds because battleship modernization expensive; General Board support.

(h)FLEXes; Naval War College simulations; availability of large carriers; *but* technical limits of carrier aircraft; battleship improvements proceeding.

(i)Geopolitical vulnerabilities; regional orientation; Washington treaty limits; Japanese retention of mandates.

military be able to take advantage of that promise? Doing so will involve accepting some risk in changing the way the services execute their tasks and in the determination of what tasks they should plan to execute. The ability to capitalize upon the potential promise of new technologies will greatly depend upon the ability of military organizations to adjust.

Urgency is important for reducing ambiguity, focusing strategic priorities so experience can be brought to bear, and fostering innovation. But overall, urgency is now low. The nation's interests are broad, diffuse, and reasonably secure; ambiguity is high so setting strategic priorities will be difficult. A weak hierarchy of strategic priorities means adaptation will be the likely pattern of adjustment.

There are, however, those who would opt for innovation and press the U.S. military to make a revolutionary leap in the way it provides security because, they argue, U.S. defense requirements have changed. The security environment of today differs fundamentally from that of the Cold War when there was a clear military threat to plan against. The number of traditional interstate wars is declining while the number of irregular factional conflicts is rising. Given that the United States is more likely to face situations that call for neutral applications of force, policing duties, and other military operations short of war, it must design its military forces more specifically in terms of their political purposes. It is no longer sufficient to think in terms simply of countering a defined military threat, particularly since there is evidence that other states and non-state actors are changing their notions of war. Intrastate and nonconventional wars employing low-intensity conflict, guerrilla, and terrorist operations are far more in evidence than middle range conflicts pitting Clausewitzian armies against each other.[99] In sum, as advocates of the revolution in military affairs (RMA) argue, the United States can no longer depend solely on attrition-based models of conflict.

For proponents of the RMA, important insights from this analysis hinge on the nature of possibility. The possibility of learning is critically important for innovation and the high level of interest in supporting simulation and testing raises optimism about innovation at present. The cases together demonstrate that only sustained augmentation of the experiential base can build credible knowledge, a crucial stimulant to innovative adjustment. New ideas may readily be generated but unless they are rigorously tested and proven sound, they have little chance of prevailing. This is precisely the logic underlaying the Joint Staff's proposal to establish a "Vanguard Force" in the U.S. military today. This joint standing task force, comprised of one-fifth of the active force structure, would be charged with working out in detail the organizations and doctrine to meet the new organizational concepts outlined in *Joint Vision 2010*. The Vanguard Force would serve as a development base for the American revolution in military affairs, based on the notion, born out by these interwar cases, that innovative adjustment requires experimentation so that military forces can work out how to do things differently.[100]

Acknowledgments

I would like to thank the following people for helpful comments on this and earlier drafts: Jan Breemer, Michael Desch, Lynn Eden, Colin Elman, Theo Farrell, Ted Hopf, Chaim Kaufman, Miko Nincic, Edward Rhodes, Mark Shulman, Bartholomew Sparrow, and Peter Trubowitz. An earlier version of this chapter appeared as "Organizations, Ambiguity, and Strategic Adjustment," *Journal of Strategic Studies* 20 (June 1997), 41–74. I am grateful to the *Journal of Strategic Studies* for permission to publish this version of that article.

Notes

1. See Barry R. Posen, *The Sources of Military Doctrine: France, Britain, and Germany Between the World Wars* (Ithaca: Cornell University Press, 1984). Other works in this tradition include Richard Betts, *Soldiers, Statesmen, and Cold War Crises* (Cambridge: Harvard University Press, 1977) and Timothy David Moy, "Hitting the Beaches and Bombing the Cities: Doctrine and Technology for Two New Militaries, 1920–1940," PhD Dissertation, University of California at Berkeley, 1987. Despite some provocative recent scholarship that casts serious doubt on bureaucratic and organizational interpretations of the military [see in particular Edward Rhodes, "Do Bureaucratic Politics Matter? Some Disconfirming Findings From the Case of the U.S. Navy," *World Politics* 47 (October 1994), 1–41], this model continues to hold tremendous sway in the academic and policy communities. A survey of recent writings on military behavior reveals that scholars always feel the need to engage the bureaucratic interpretation, regardless of what particular perspective they are championing. Rhodes discusses some of the reasons why this may be so.

2. Routines guide the behavior of organizations. They include "the forms, rules, procedures, conventions, strategies, and technologies around which organi-

zations are constructed and through which they operate." Barbara Levitt and James G. March, "Organizational Learning," *Annual Review of Sociology* 14 (1988), 320.

3.   The classic statement of the professional military is Samuel P. Huntington, *The Soldier and the State* (Cambridge: Harvard University Press, 1957). The military is a profession that strives to achieve efficiency in attaining its goals. For the military, this means maximizing its ability to secure the state. Military organizations respond to the dictates of strategic geography, technological developments, and enemy behavior in rational pursuit of their goals. Rosen builds on this perspective and argues that military organizations do not need to be pressured by civilians to innovate. Visionary officers can lead campaigns to innovate in peacetime. See Stephen Peter Rosen, "New Ways of War: Understanding Military Innovation," *International Security* 13 (Summer 1988), 134–68; Stephen Peter Rosen, *Winning the Next War: Innovation and the Modern Military* (Ithaca: Cornell University Press, 1991). Kimberly Marten Zisk, *Engaging the Enemy: Organization Theory and Soviet Military Innovation, 1955–1991* (Princeton: Princeton University Press, 1993) also denies that military organizations have to be forced to innovate. She attempts to construct a model that combines the bureaucratic and professional approaches, arguing that while officers react to domestic threats to their organization before foreign military threats, they can innovate in reaction to shifts in enemy doctrine. critiques of the bureaucratic approach from a cultural perspective include Jeffrey W. Legro, *Cooperation Under Fire: Anglo-German Restraint During World War II* (Ithaca: Cornell University Press, 1995), and Elizabeth Kier, "Culture and Military Doctrine: France Between the Wars," *International Security* 19 (Spring 1995), 65–93.

4.   The literature on organizational learning is extensive. For an overview, see Levitt and March, "Organizational Learning," 319–40.

5.   Adjustment is operationalized as alterations in the combat tasks—or "roles and missions"—of service organizations. Roles and missions define how the military services provide security and reflect the organizations' estimates of present and future threats and challenges. By identifying the tasks the services will train for and prepare to execute, roles and missions reflect service priorities about how to fight. It is also useful to think in terms of different *patterns* of strategic adjustment. Adjustment may be innovative (adoption of new goals, or new strategies and structures in pursuit of existing goals); or it may be adaptive (minor changes consistent with existing goals, strategies, and/or structures). I adopted these definitions from Theo Farrell, "Innovation in Military Organizations Without Enemies," paper presented at the International Studies Association Annual Convention, San Diego, April 16–20, 1996, 1–2. While the tendency has been to view innovation as positive and forward-

looking, and adaptation as a negative attachment to outmoded ideas or procedures, neither is inherently good nor bad. James Q. Wilson notes that there
are as many bad innovations as good ones, that executives are particularly
prone to adopt innovations that enhance their own control and power, and
that the military is rich in such examples. James Q. Wilson, *Bureaucracy:
What Government Agencies Do and Why They Do It* (New York: Basic Books,
1989), 227–28. My use of the term innovation does not imply that the change
is necessarily good. For an excellent discussion of why doctrine is not a useful
way to operationalize innovation in military organizations see Theo Farrell,
"Figuring Out Fighting Organizations: The New Organizational Analysis in
Strategic Studies," *Journal of Strategic Studies* 19 (March 1996), 122–35.

6. Following the lead of Levitt and March, my interpretation of organizational
learning builds on some classical observations about organizations: organizational behavior is routine-based, history-dependent, and target-oriented.
Levitt and March, "Organizational Learning, 320.

7. By selecting cases of adjustment in the United States between the wars, we
can control for systemic factors like relative power position of the state, the
domestic environment of financial stringency, national attributes that encouraged military disengagement, and the nature of civil-military relations.
Future research should examine different countries, to explore the impact of
different political systems and different civil-military relations. In addition, a
longitudinal study of the United States would be useful because as Farrell
hypothesizes, "as organizations and their environments change, so change
occurs in the way organizations innovate." Farrell, "Figuring Out Fighting
Organizations," 127.

  The cases have also been selected to provide variance on the dependent
variable to explore the factors associated with different patterns of adjustment.
The adoption of amphibious warfare by the Marine Corps represents an innovation, a change in the service's core task. This is indisputably the consensus among historians. See Allan R. Millett, *Semper Fidelis: The History of the
United States Marine Corps* (New York: Macmillan, 1980); Jeter A. Isely and
Philip A. Crowl, *The U.S. Marines and Amphibious War* (Princeton: Princeton University Press, 1951); Craig M. Cameron, *American Samurai: Myth,
Imagination, and the Conduct of Battle in the First Marine Division, 1941–
1951* (Cambridge: Cambridge University Press, 1994). There is also scholarly
consensus that the Army adopted mechanization in a way consistent with
traditional task definitions, to support the infantry and cavalry rather than as
an independent offensive force in its own right. See Russell F. Weigley, *The
American Way of War: A History of United States Military Strategy and Policy*
(New York: Macmillan, 1973); Constance McLaughlin Green, Harry C.
Thomson, and Peter C. Roots, *The Ordnance Department: Planning Muni-*

tions for War, U.S. Army in World War II: The Technical Services, 6, part 3 (Washington, D.C.: Office of the Chief of Military History, 1955). This provides an opportunity to investigate an undisputed case of adaptation. Carrier aviation represents a hybrid case of adjustment. There is dispute among scholars about whether Navy policy is best characterized as innovative (e.g., the adoption of a new mission for carriers as an offensive striking arm of the fleet) or as adaptive (e.g., aviation developments grafted onto existing doctrine to support the battleship by spotting and scouting). Rosen (1988 and 1991) emphasizes the progress made in developing the carrier into an independent strike force between the wars, while Waldo H. Heinrichs, Jr., "The Role of the United States Navy," in Dorothy Borg and Shumpei Okamoto, ed., *Pearl Harbor as History: Japanese-American Relations, 1931–1941* (New York: Columbia University Press, 1973), 197–223, argues that naval aviation remained distinctly subordinate to the battleship until Pearl Harbor. These three cases span the adaptation-innovation continuum. In principle, coding the dependent variable along this continuum implies that there should also be a "do nothing" coding. The case of mechanization comes closest to this end of the continuum, but even the Army adapted to the tank.

8. See Emily O. Goldman, "Thinking About Strategy Absent the Enemy," *Security Studies* 4 (Autumn 1994), 40–85 for an analysis of British strategic adjustment between the wars.

9. The Army also came to recognize that industrialization was as important to military success as tactics and strategy. For a detailed discussion of the mobilization planning case, see Emily O. Goldman, "The U.S. Military in Uncertain Times: Organizations, Ambiguity, and Strategic Adjustment," *The Journal of Strategic Studies* 20 (June 1997), 41–74, especially pp. 59–63. This case allows us to examine competing claims about how organizations approach long-range planning and how they adjust when planning requires changing standard procedures.

10. The CNO Executive Panel's Naval Warfare Innovations Task Force Briefing to Admiral Boorda identifies three past naval warfare innovations, two of which come from this period, carrier air and amphibious warfare, and seeks to replicate the process that produced those innovations. (June 16, 1995), 11 (author's copy).

11. See James G. March and Johan P. Olsen, "The Uncertainty of the Past: Organizational Learning under Ambiguity," in James G. March, ed., *Decisions and Organizations* (New York: Basil Blackwell, 1988), 335–58. The factors I focus on correspond roughly to what March and Olsen call learning incentives and information exposure.

12. Graham T. Allison, *Essence of Decision: Explaining the Cuban Missile Crisis* (Boston: Little, Brown, 1971), 78–94. See also Richard Cyert and James

March, A *Behavioral Theory of the Firm* (Englewood Cliffs, N.J.: Prentice-Hall, 1963). For a discussion of Allison's models, see David Welch, "The Organizational Process and Bureaucratic Politics Paradigms: Retrospect and Prospect," *International Security*, 17 (Fall 1992), 122–46; Jonathan Bendor and Thomas H. Hammond, "Rethinking Allison's Models," *American Political Science Review*, 86 (June 1992), 301–22.

13. Herbert Kaufman, *The Limits of Organizational Change* (University, Ala.: University of Alabama Press, 1971).

14. The classic case study is Edward L. Katzenbach, Jr., "The Horse Cavalry in the Twentieth Century: A Study in Policy Response," in *The Use of Force: International Politics and Foreign Policy*, eds. Robert J. Art and Kenneth N. Waltz, 2d ed. (Latham, N.Y.: University Press of America, 1983), 203–22.

15. Wilson, *Bureaucracy*, 221.

16. Richard H. Hall, *Organizations: Structure and Process*, 2d ed. (Englewood Cliffs, N.J.: Prentice-Hall, 1977), 56.

17. A strategy of insulating or hedging against uncertainty by planning for all possible events is one that Kurt Lang contends military organizations are predisposed to pursue. Kurt Lang, "Military Organizations," in *Handbook of Organizations*, ed. James G. March (Chicago: Rand McNally, 1965), 856. Such an approach may be the preferred one but it is immensely costly. A cheaper strategy is to monitor external sources of uncertainty and react after the event. James D. Thompson, *Organizations in Action* (New York: McGraw-Hill, 1967), 67; Chris C. Demchak, *Military Organizations, Complex Machines* (Ithaca: Cornell University Press, 1991), 32–33.

18. A big conceptual problem plagues the organizational process model. Many hypotheses can be derived from it and it is possible to deduce contradictory values on the dependent variable so that the theory is nearly unfalsifiable. For example, preserving self-concept or essence by protecting vested interests may jeopardize resources, while grabbing additional missions may increase resources but sacrifice autonomy and identity. If any change serves some interpretation of parochial interests, the theory would be validated. The question then becomes what type of change does *not* support the theory. To address the falsifiability issue, I examine a series of hypotheses, each of which is separately falsifiable since they do not always point to the same value on the dependent variable.

19. Morton H. Halperin, *Bureaucratic Politics and Foreign Policy* (Washington, D.C.: Brookings Institution, 1974), 28.

20. Wilson, *Bureaucracy*, 195. Halperin also notes that bureaucracies "are often prepared to accept less money with greater control than more money with less control" because of the high priority attached to turf. Halperin, *Bureaucratic Politics and Foreign Policy*, 51.

21. For military organizations, this hypothesis is an unusually strong one because the armed forces in peacetime are the quintessential "procedural organization." Outcomes cannot be observed short of war, so activities in peacetime become means oriented. As Wilson writes, "*How* the operators go about their jobs is more important than whether doing those jobs produces the desired outcomes." In procedural organizations, SOPs are pervasive. Wilson, *Bureaucracy*, 163–64. This attribute makes the case of innovation in *military* organizations a most likely case for the organizational process model and a least likely case for alternative models that hypothesize a greater propensity for innovation.

22. There is no agreed upon definition of learning. See Philip E. Tetlock, "Learning in U.S. and Soviet Foreign Policy: In Search of an Elusive Concept," in *Learning in U.S. and Soviet Foreign Policy*, eds. George W. Breslauer and Philip E. Tetlock (Boulder, Colo.: Westview, 1991). I adopt Jack Levy's minimalist definition of learning as a "change of beliefs, skills, or procedures based on the observation and interpretation of experience." The pool of ideas drawn upon can include simulated as well as historic experiences. This definition of learning as experience-induced belief change does not require that actors make the correct inferences from experience. Jack S. Levy, "Learning and Foreign Policy: Sweeping a Conceptual Minefield," *International Organization* 48 (Spring 1994), 291, 296.

23. Ernst B. Haas, "Collective Learning: Some Theoretical Speculations," in *Learning in U.S. and Soviet Foreign Policy* ed. Breslauer and Tetlock, 81–82; John D. Steinbruner, *The Cybernetic Theory of Decision* (Princeton: Princeton University Press, 1974), 64.

24. Learning is an individual cognitive exercise. Organizations learn "only through the individuals who serve in those organizations, by encoding individually learned inferences from experience into organizational routines." Levy, "Learning and Foreign Policy," 287–88. Individual interpretations of experience depend upon the frames through which events are comprehended. An organization's interpretive frameworks tend to be resistant to experience. Levitt and March, "Organizational Learning," 324.

25. Learning and strategic adjustment are not synonymous. Strategic adjustment may occur as adaptation or learning. Adaptation involves developing better ways to do the same task without reevaluating one's entire program, often by taking advantage of new technology. The conversion of battleships from coal to oil and modification of their guns for substantial increase in firepower are examples of adaptation. Learning involves questioning the theory of causation that defines the organization's tasks, and shifting means or ends based on new knowledge derived from observations and interpretations of experience. See Haas, "Collective Learning," 72–74.

26. Ibid., 84–86.
27. George Breslauer, "Ideology and Learning in Soviet Third World Policy," *World Politics* 39 (April 1987), 443.
28. The inclusion of civilian pressures and incentives in the organizational learning model as part of desirability does not count against the learning model and concede the argument to the organizational process model. The key point is how civilian pressure operates, namely whether it is *necessary* for surmounting organizational inertia as the organizational process model stipulates, or whether it provides modest incentives and creates modest obstacles. Desirability is neither a necessary nor a sufficient condition for learning.
29. Haas, "Collective Learning," 85.
30. If possibility referred only to resources, it might be considered a bureaucratic variable, and thus count against the learning model (i.e., organizations adjust in response to resource incentives in order to enhance organizational health). But possibility hinges on the state of credible knowledge, to which resources contribute but are not determinative.
31. Colin Elman pointed out these distinct arguments to me.
32. This is a similar argument to that made by Andrew Krepinevich in his explanation for why certain military organizations are better able to exploit the advantages of military revolutions than others: because of their ability to focus more precisely on specific contingencies and competitors. See Andrew F. Krepinevich, "Cavalry to Computer: The Pattern of Military Revolutions," *The National Interest* 37 (Fall 1994), 39.
33. The learning model assumes the causal importance of inferences from experience. Research shows that individuals make systematic errors in interpreting experience. See Daniel Kahneman, Paul Slovic, and Amos Tversky, eds., *Judgement under Uncertainty: Heuristics and Biases* (Cambridge: Cambridge University Press, 1982). Individuals, however, may also use history and experience instrumentally, interpreting it in a way that reinforces existing beliefs or serves their interests. Levy, "Learning and Foreign Policy," 306–07.
34. Robert K. Griffith, Jr., *Men Wanted for the U.S. Army: America's Experience With An All-Volunteer Army Between the World Wars* (Westport, Conn.: Greenwood Press, 1982), 53–58; Mark Skinner Watson, *United States Army in World War II, Chief of Staff: Prewar Plans and Preparations* (Washington, D.C.: Historical Division Department of the Army, 1950), 26.
35. Timothy K. Nenninger, "The Development of American Armor 1917–1940, Part III, The Experimental Mechanized Forces," *Armor* 78 (May–June 1969), 33–39.
36. Ibid, 35.
37. George F. Hofmann, "The Demise of the U.S. Tanks Corps And Medium Tank Development Program," *Military Affairs* 37 (February 1973), 24.

38. In another example, Timothy K. Nenninger, "The Development of American Armor 1917–1940, Part IV, A Revised Mechanization Policy," *Armor* 78 (September–October 1969), 45, describes how Fuqua also disagreed with War Department mechanization policy in 1931, which authorized all branches to mechanize, because this challenged the designation of tanks as infantry weapons. Nevertheless, Chief of Staff Douglas MacArthur's 1931 directive governed Army mechanization policy through the decade.

39. Hofmann, "The Demise of the U.S. Tanks Corps," 21, 23.

40. Ibid., 23; Timothy K. Nenninger, "The Development of American Armor 1917–1940, Part I, The World War I Experience," *Armor* 78 (January–February 1969), 49.

41. Pershing's testimony was highly valued at the time. According to an *Army and Navy Journal* report, as quoted in Hofmann, "no one officer in the Army has wider knowledge or more complete grasp of the military lessons learned through the war." Hofmann, "The Demise of the U.S. Tanks Corps," 23.

42. Timothy K. Nenninger, " The Development of American Armor 1917–1940, Part II, The Tank Corps Reorganized," *Armor* 78 (March–April 1969), 35.

43. Green et al., *The Ordnance Department*, 195–96.

44. That manpower was privileged over tank modernization does not mean that the Army leadership identified with the parochial priorities of the infantry. It takes years to train an officer. It is always easier to reopen production lines than it is to restore deactivated forces. This is true even today for the high tech U.S. armed forces.

45. Between 1925 and 1939, the average allotted to tank development was approximately $60,000 per year. In 1931, the cost of a single Christie tank, without armor, engines, guns, or radios was $34,500, and seven years later, the Ordnance Department estimated the cost of a medium tank to be $50,000. As a result, only one experimental model could be built in any one year. Green, et al., *The Ordnance Department*, 195.

46. In 1920, the Chief of the Tank Corps noted that differences of opinion about the advantages of tanks ran "from enthusiastic support of the two divisions with whom we had an opportunity to train and to fight, to damning by those who did not get us (tanks)." Quoted in Hofmann, "The Demise of the U.S. Tanks Corps," 23.

47. Nenninger, "The Development of American Armor," Part I, 46–51.

48. The infantry and cavalry were also expected to develop greater mobility to support the Army's defensive mission. Hofmann, "The Demise of the U.S. Tanks Corps," 23.

49. Weigley finds the experiential argument convincing. He writes, "Perhaps part of the explanation for the absence of an American Fuller, Liddell Hart, or Guderian after the World War is that, despite some worrying about the futility

of warfare on the Western Front, the brief American participation in the war, with no Verdun or Passchendaele, did not provide so much inducement to American soldiers as to British or German to look for ways to avoid repetition of the deadlock in the trenches." Weigley, *The American Way of War*, 219.

50. Green, et al., *The Ordnance Department*, 192. Ordnance Department engineers did have access to a great deal of technical intelligence about foreign tank developments and experimentation. Green, et al. discuss the role of technical intelligence and conclude that "utilization of technical intelligence was at times both prompt and intelligent, at other times laggardly and unimaginative" (214). They attribute limitations on research and development to the small size of the staff in the Office, Chief of Ordnance, which meant each person was overburdened and so could not devote any extensive amount of time to any one problem; lack of funds; dictates from above that specified characteristics of any new item which curtailed experimentation; and the temper of the American people which made involvement in war so unthinkable that vigorous pursuit of new munitions developments hardly seemed urgent. Lack of funds, in particular, prevented the testing of new devices, which might have challenged existing doctrine for the tactical use of tanks. Green, et al. (205) describe how research funds were spread very thinly because the Ordnance Department had to serve all the branches of the Army and no branch would acquiesce to the needs of another. So existing doctrine persisted which further obstructed tank design.

51. Nenninger, "The Development of American Armor," Part IV, 45–49.

52. Weigley notes that MacArthur's impact on mechanization was mixed. He did not accept Fuller's and Liddell Hart's ideas, but he did encourage the use of the internal combustion engine, releasing the cavalry from the constraints that infantry speed had placed on tank motion. Weigley, *The American Way of War*, 218.

53. Nenninger "The Development of American Armor," Part IV, 47.

54. Not all members of Congress supported mechanization, but the Chairman of the Subcommittee on Military Affairs of the House Appropriations Committee, Ross Collins, Democrat from Mississippi, was an aggressive advocate and his committee championed an independent mechanized organization. Collins was sensitive to the need to keep mechanization costs down, yet was willing to appropriate more funds for it. However, the War Department determined priorities and during the early 1930s mechanization received only a small share of military appropriations. Ibid., 46–47.

55. Cameron, *American Samurai*, 31–33; Merrill L. Bartlett, *Lejeune: A Marine's Life, 1867–1942* (Columbia: University of South Carolina Press, 1991), 149–51.

56. Under the constraints of postwar demobilization and drastic budget cuts, the

Army relinquished any role in amphibious warfare. Cameron, *American Samurai*, 37.

57. The Marine Corps historically assumed multiple responsibilities: guarding ships, shore installations, consulates, and embassies; serving as shore parties, boarding parties, and gun crews; as hemispheric policemen, colonial light infantry, and as regular infantry during World War I. Millett, *Semper Fidelis*, 147–263, 318; Moy, *Hitting the Beaches*, 20. With America's acquisition of an insular empire after the Spanish-American War, the Marines also adopted the advanced base mission to defend the Navy's coaling stations and bases. Jack Shulimson, *The Marine Corps's Search for a Mission, 1880–1898* (Lawrence: University Press of Kansas, 1993), 207.

58. Particularly after the Philippine Insurrection of 1899, the Army was not eager to participate in other military occupations. Millett, *Semper Fidelis*, 164. After World War I, the War Department focused on preparing to fight another conflict pitting mass armies against each other.

59. Moy, *Hitting the Beaches*, 25.

60. Millett, *Semper Fidelis*, 270–79; Moy, *Hitting the Beaches*, 23.

62. Millett, *Semper Fidelis*, 275.

62. Ibid., 282.

63. Ibid., 307.

64. Ibid., 285–286.

65. Ibid., 325; Bartlett, *Lejeune*, 123, 199.

66. The impact of the colonial infantry phase (1898–1941) on the Corps, according to Millett, is "elusive." Interventions helped recruiting, kept the Corps in the popular press, increased Corps effectiveness as infantry in small units, and provided a mission more important than sea duty. It also increased the Corps's reputation for "peacetime" utility and strengthened its claims for more manpower. On the negative side, growing Congressional distaste for reform occupations threatened fiscal requests, though by the early 1930s, when the Hoover and Roosevelt administrations renounced military occupation as a tool of U.S. foreign policy, the Corps had already embraced the amphibious assault role. Millett, *Semper Fidelis*, xvi, 263.

67. Isely and Crowl, *U.S. Marine and Amphibious War*, 29.

68. Millett, *Semper Fidelis*, 320.

69. Quoted in ibid., 29.

70. Holland Smith and Percy Finch, *Coral and Brass* (New York: Scribner's 1949), 60.

71. Amphibious assault, up to this point, had not superseded traditional peacetime functions *in practice*. Millett, *Semper Fidelis*, 321–22.

72. See ibid., 322–26; Moy, *Hitting the Beaches*, 32–37.

73. A counter-argument might be made that amphibious warfare was very old,

and the new technologies developed between the wars were minor application level changes. Hence, the emergence of a new core task, and the ideas
that underlay it, cannot be attributed to technology and experience. However,
Isely and Crowl dissent. They write, "Although the germs of later amphibious
training may be found in this early [1901] advance-base activity, it is clear
that the great weight of the emphasis was not on offensive landing operations.
In fact there is little resemblance between this early concept of the main
function of the marine corps and its subsequent role as a military organization
specially trained for amphibious assault against enemy shores. Although in
theory the advance-base force was supposed to be prepared to seize as well as
to defend bases, in practice all of the training concentrated on the defense.
. . . Some spade work had been done in the field of advance-base work, but
it is clear that this did not imply landings against defended shores. . . . The
advance-base force was in actuality little more than an embryo coastal artillery
unit." Isley and Crowl, *U.S. Marine and Amphibious War,* 23–24.

74. Moy, *Hitting the Beaches,* 44.

75. Isely and Crowl, *U.S. Marine and Amphibious War,* 14–71; Millett, *Semper Fidelis,* 337–41.

76. Moy, *Hitting the Beaches,* 49–50.

77. Millett, *Semper Fidelis,* 332–33.

78. Heinrichs, "The Role of the United States Navy," 205–6.

79. Ibid., 197–223.

80. Rosen is best known in both policy and social science circles for articulating some of the organizational requirements for peacetime innovation. "New Ways of War" and *Winning the Next War.*

81. See Thomas C. Hone and Mark D. Mandeles, "Interwar Innovation in Three Navies: U.S. Navy, Royal Navy, Imperial Japanese Navy," *Naval War College Review* 40 (Spring 1987), 73–74.

82. Rosen, *Winning the Next War,* 69–71; Hone and Mandeles, "Interwar Innovation in Three Navies," 73–75.

83. The Japanese Navy, unlike its western counterparts, could make extensive use of long-range land-based bombers which were subject to no arms control limits by operating them from the island chains mandated to Japan at the end of the war.

84. Thomas C. Hone and Mark David Mandeles, "Managerial Style in the Interwar Navy: A Reappraisal," *Naval War College Review* 32 (September–October 1980), 97–98; Thomas C. Hone, "Navy Air Leadership: Rear Admiral William A. Moffett as Chief of the Bureau of Aeronautics," in *USAF Warrior Studies—Air Leadership: Proceedings of a Conference at Bolling Air Force Base April 13–14* (Washington, D.C.: GPO, 1984), 89–90.

85. From the organizational process perspective, one might argue that carrier

limitations were due to decisions by the battleship-dominated Navy leadership not to invest in carrier development. The evidence does not support the claim. First, the low proportion of the Navy's property investment in carriers (10% from 1919 to 1941) largely owed to the Washington treaty limits on aircraft carrier tonnage. From this, we cannot impute Navy desires. Second, there was clearly a movement of resources toward naval aviation during the same period as evidenced by the growth in the percentage expended on naval air strength. Finally, money for modernization was spent primarily on battleships but advances in battleship design introduced the possibility that the battleship could retain its armor and endurance levels while increasing its speed; not incidentally, the speed of destroyers and cruisers to screen the battle line would have to rise. Given treaty limits on individual displacement, the only way to build faster warships was to increase the efficiency of engineering designs to meet rising technical demands. This was more costly. Nor does the argument hold up that the Navy was responding to civilian incentives. The Navy submitted appropriation requests based on functional category (operating expenses, equipment, alterations, etc.), not on individual unit needs, and could shift funds from one program or vessel to another without a special congressional appropriation. In sum, obstacles to learning cannot be traced to a Navy leadership that did not support carrier development; nor can it be blamed on civilian constraints. See Thomas C. Hone, "Spending Patterns of the United States Navy, 1921–1941," *Armed Forces and Society* 8 (Spring 1982), 443–62.

86. Emily O. Goldman, *Sunken Treaties: Naval Arms Control Between the Wars* (University Park, Pa.: Pennsylvania State University Press, 1994), 96–102.

87. The fleet problems were developed in the 1920s as a means of testing scenarios and throughout the 1920s and 1930s, they were a valuable testing ground for aviation concepts. In Fleet Problem IX in 1929, which included participation of the converted battle cruisers *Lexington* and *Saratoga*, Admiral Pratt's carrier task force achieved a devastating surprise attack on the Panama Canal. Archibald Turnbull and Clifford Lord, *History of United States Naval Aviation* (New Haven: Yale University Press, 1949), 271–73; Hone and Mandeles, "Interwar Innovation in Three Navies," 75–76.

88. George W. Baer, *One Hundred Years of Sea Power: The U.S. Navy, 1890–1990* (Stanford: Stanford University Press, 1994), 142–43.

89. Hone and Mandeles, "Managerial Style in the Interwar Navy," 91.

90. Ibid., 95.

91. Michael Vlahos, *The Blue Sword: The Naval War College and the American Mission, 1919–1941* (Newport, R.I.: Naval War College Press, 1980) remains the authority on the subject.

92. Michael Vlahos, "Wargaming, an Enforcer of Strategic Realism: 1919–1942," *Naval War College Review* 39 (March–April 1986), 10–12.

93. Ibid., 17–19.

94. Rosen, *Winning the Next War*, 69–71.

95. Hone and Mandeles, "Interwar Innovation in Three Navies," 78; Hone and Mandeles, "Managerial Style in the Interwar Navy," 98.

96. Goldman, *Sunken Treaties*, 158–62.

97. See, for example, Heinrichs,"The Role of the United States Navy," 201–2.

98. In particular see Moy, Shulimson, and Cameron on the Marine Corps. For a popular contemporary rendition, see Michael Klare, *Rogue States and Nuclear Outlaws: America's Search For A New Foreign Policy* (New York: Hill and Wang, 1995).

99. Mark R. Shulman, "Project 2015: Reconstituting for the New World Disorder," draft (February 24, 1995), 9.

100. For a discussion of the Vanguard Force concept, see James R. Blaker, "A Vanguard Force: Accelerating the American Revolution in Military Affairs," Progressive Policy Institute, forthcoming.

9 . . . *From the Sea:* The Process of Defining a New Role for Naval Forces in the post-Cold War World

Edward A. Smith, Jr.

In September 1992, the United States Navy and Marine Corps published the white paper *From the Sea.* The paper represented the fruits of the Naval Service's efforts to deal with the changes in the national security environment wrought by the end of the Cold War and to redefine itself in terms of twenty-first century roles and missions. Although intended for general publication, the paper's primary focus was internal: to engender a fundamental shift in naval thinking—away from the open ocean confrontation with the Soviet Navy, and toward a much more subtle and more flexible use of naval forces commensurate with a more uncertain strategic environment. The final and much abbreviated white paper outlined this "new" strategic concept for the Naval Service and heralded a broad transformation of the Cold War Navy.

The following chapter addresses the thought process behind *From the Sea* and how the Navy created its own internal consensus. It differs somewhat from those preceding in that it is a first-hand account of the internal Navy debates which led to that seminal white paper. In this sense, it is a natural continuation of Emily Goldman's work in the immediately preceding chapter. Indeed, it focuses on many of the "how" questions she raises. How did a large, well-established institution such as the Navy stimulate—or impede—strategic adjustment? What assessment of the potential problems and requirements of a new age drove that institution to conclude that a shift in focus from blue-water to littoral operations was necessary or even possible?

How much did the changed requirements reflect the collapse of the Soviet Union? How much was the new concept a response to the external pressures of public opinion, Congress, and the budget described by Rhodes, Shulman, Tubowitz, Nincic et al., and Sparrow? And, how much did they reflect a successful institutional adaptation of the kind Emily Goldman describes?

At its heart, this history outlines a process of strategic adjustment that was begun and sustained from within the institution itself. The development of the ideas contained in *From the Sea* and later amplified in *Forward . . . From the Sea*, and their institutionalization within the U.S. Navy and Marine Corps illustrate a dynamic interaction between military institutions and the set of ideas and assumptions that define their purpose and shape their planning and behavior. The examination of "how" the Naval Service reinvented itself in the early 1990s thus highlights both the central role of institutions in the generation and weighing of new ideas, and the critical impact of ideas in reshaping the institutions that generated them. The picture which emerges from this history of that process is that, while the end of the Cold War dictated a change in strategic direction for the Naval Service, the determination of what that direction would be was the product of self-conscious, self-examination by that service. Today, as the Naval Service strives to implement the concepts of *From the Sea* and *Forward . . . From the Sea*, and to relate them to a still larger incipient "Revolution in Military Affairs," it is useful to put the white paper process and debates into the context of a far-reaching strategic adjustment parallel to those undertaken by the Naval Service in the 1890s and the interwar years.

Getting Started

The detailed discussions that led to *From the Sea* occurred over a six month period from October 1991 through April 1992, in a forum with the uninspiring name, the "Naval Forces Capabilities Planning Effort." The NFCPE began in response to a directive from Secretary of the Navy H. L. Garrett to the Chief of Naval Operations and the Commandant of the Marine Corps: they were to assess the naval capabilities the United States would need as it entered the next century.[2] The timing was significant inasmuch as the directive was drafted and the initial phase of the study took place amid the death throes of the Soviet Union, in the months after hardliners attempted but failed to overthrow the government of Mikhail Gorbachev. It was obvious to all NFCPE participants from the start that the old world order was dying and that the United States Naval Service would have to change. However, the Secretary's instructions were to go beyond simply reacting to the immediate effects of the Soviet collapse and to create "a new zero-based plan for naval forces spanning the next fifteen to twenty years," in effect, to provide an entirely new strategic concept for the naval forces of the United States.[3]

The NFCPE was carried out in three phases. During the first phase, from October through December 1991, a working group consisting of eighteen captains/colonels and commanders/lieutenant colonels drawn from the Navy and Marine Corps staffs and from the Marine Corps Combat Development Center (MCCDC) was set up. The working group reported twice a week to a six-member flag steering group headed by Rear Admiral Ted Baker and Major General Matt Caulfield which provided immediate supervision and feedback. Finally, the overall effort was chaired jointly by then Vice Admiral L. W. Smith and Lieutenant General H. C. Stackpole, the Navy and Marine Corps staffs' respective directors for operations and planning, who were responsible for reporting back to the two service chiefs and the Secretary. The working group was asked to assess:

- what had or had not changed in the national security environment; and
- what implications these changes held for the roles and missions of forces.

The group was to postulate planning assumptions about the future environment for use in later deliberations and was to produce a clear vision of the future role of naval forces. The implicit starting point for the first phase was an emphatic "zero": What was it, analysts were to ask—*if anything*—that naval forces did for the national good that justified the money taxpayers were spending to build and maintain them?

During the second phase, from January through April 1992, the working group was revised and expanded to twenty-five members in order to include a full spectrum of operational expertise and representatives from the fleets and Navy theater commanders and to ensure that all segments of the Naval Service participated actively in the final product. This group and the flag oversight group was directed to build upon the assessments of what had or had not changed in order to develop a new strategic concept, to define the capabilities required to pursue such a concept in a new maritime strategy, and, then, to complete the first draft of a white paper explaining the new concept.

To this end, the group was required to tackle a long list of touchy questions directly affecting the services' internal constituencies. How could future national security needs in the maritime arena be met at the least possible cost? How could the Naval Service use its forces more flexibly and better integrate Navy and Marine Corps capabilities? Could the Naval Service relinquish some of its historical roles? Could the infrastructure at home and abroad be slashed? Finally, and given the declining Soviet threat, what kinds of forces would the United States need for the future? Providing answers to these questions involved wrestling with complex issues of future Navy roles in presence, crisis response, and deterrence, and of the size and character of the forces that would be required to fulfill these roles. Yet, it was clear that the final white paper needed to be simple, direct, and concise if it were to have any value either inside or outside the Navy.[4] Therefore, the final paper could not incorporate in any detail the extensive underlying debate on the issues and, it had to limit itself to describing the new strategic concept and the capabilities it demanded.

During both phases, the effort was formally blessed as the Department of the Navy's "highest priority." The working group was given a "blank check" to requisition whatever support it required and was encouraged to conduct a series of very frank and not-for-attribution exchanges with experts of its own choosing both inside and outside the Naval Service. Over the course of the study, visitors included the Secretary and Undersecretary of the Navy, the Chief of Naval Operations, Commandant of the Marine Corps, directors of air, surface, subsurface and amphibious warfare, intelligence personnel, civilian and military planners including those from the Air Force and Army, senior Congressional staff members, and defense thinkers from industry, academia, and research corporations. The group was also invited to task the Center for Naval Analyses for statistical and analytical support and did so extensively throughout its deliberations. Finally, the group took advantage of a rapidly growing body of published material that included President Bush's Aspen Address and a variety of speeches and articles by Congressional thinkers such as Senators Nunn and McCain and then-Representative Aspin and others. To encourage free, "out-of-the-box" thinking unconstrained by bureaucratic interests, all the group's internal debates were conducted on a strictly enforced not-for-attribution basis. Representatives from the different warfare communities—the principal internal constituencies—and from the fleet and theater commanders were encouraged to keep their respective chiefs informed of the direction the proceedings were taking, but under the same strict not-for-attribution guidelines. Finally, to further insulate the group, participants were detached from their parent commands for the duration of the study and were offered separate performance evaluations covering the period of the study.

The process of building consensus within the Naval Service began midway through the second phase when, in late February 1992, the working group briefed its preliminary findings to what was reported to be the largest convocation of Navy and Marine Corps flag and general officers ever assembled—by one reckoning 80 percent of the three and four star officers in both services and some 50 additional flag officers. The participants were given thick dossiers of "read ahead" materials including outlines of the working group findings and a selection of the published material the group had considered. During a three-day session at the Quantico Marine Corps Base—isolated from Washington and away from most telephones—all participants were encouraged to speak freely both in plenary meetings and in smaller seminar groups which considered geographic and functional issues such as command and control. By the session's conclusion, there was a general agreement as to the basic premises of the working group's analysis and as to the direction the final study would take. Nonetheless, a lively debate over the white paper's specifics continued throughout the final drafting and review process right up to its publication in September 1992. At that point, the debate ended. Thereafter, the sentiment was, as one senior flag officer succinctly and forcefully put it, "This ('. . . *From the Sea*') is now our future. Let's get on with it. Get aboard, or get out."

The final phase, that of fleshing out the operational dimensions of "littoral warfare" and of defining the force structure required to provide effective naval capabilities for the new age, began even before the publication of *From the Sea*. When first submitted for review and comment by the Navy and Marine Corps leadership in April 1992, the draft white paper had been accompanied by a voluminous "Capabilities Package" that outlined the NFCPE's estimate of what would be necessary to implement *From the Sea* in coming decades. That in turn sparked a Navy staff reassessment of Navy roles and missions and a special wargame was sponsored by the Secretary of the Navy to test both these expansions and the *From the Sea* concept—all before the paper's actual publication. These efforts subsequently continued on the Navy and Marine Corps staffs and in the activities of groups such as the Navy Staff's Resources Requirements Review Board and the Chief of Naval Operations Executive Panel. Although a subsequent amplification of *From the Sea* entitled *Forward . . . from the Sea* was issued two years after the initial publication, it pointedly did not change the original work but largely confined itself to expanding that paper's explanation of forward presence. More recently, both the Navy and Marine Corps have published "Operational Concepts" spelling out in more detail how they implement *From the Sea*, and how its concepts are fully congruent both the 1994 National Military Strategy and the joint operations foreseen in *Joint Vision 2010*. Indeed, the years since the original white paper's publication have been marked by a growing appreciation among naval officers of just how radical a change *From the Sea* really was. In effect, the Navy "reinvented" itself and began its own "Revolution in Military Affairs" well before similar adjustments were even considered by the other armed services.

What Changed?

The decision of the Department of the Navy's leadership to undertake the NFCPE was a clearly a reaction to a myriad of changes in the country and the world. However, from beginning to end, it remained an internal Navy Department reaction to those changes and not one directed or pressured from outside. As might be expected, both the Navy leadership and the group began with a visceral feeling that naval power would remain a vital part of dealing with these changes. However, the "zero-based" starting point for the effort forced participants to start by questioning this deep-seated assumption, that is, by questioning the very existence of the institution in light of the changes in the world around them. The first problem confronting the NFCPE, therefore, was to identify *which* world and domestic changes would be decisive for the future of U.S. naval forces—that is, which would have the heaviest impact on future naval force requirements or, indeed, remove the requirement for naval power entirely. The working group proceeded from two very basic assumptions: first, that, given a continued if diminished threat to lives, territory and interests, the American people would accept the need to maintain some form of military forces; and second, that the American people would be unwilling to abandon entirely their leadership role in the world, necessitating something more than military forces for a simple continental defense. To the degree that naval forces met these requirements for military force efficiently and effectively, the public would be willing to support some form of navy. The group did not immediately address the *specific* requirements, or the way in which that navy would plan to meet them, thus letting budget and resource questions as to the size or nature of the future navy follow from the ensuing detailed analysis.

Even with these assumptions, the candidates for consideration as definitive change were many and varied: they ranged from domestic and global demographic shifts through ecological and environmental concerns, to problems of budget and prospects for the domestic and world economies. Almost all would certainly affect either the nature of the Naval Service or the frequency and types of crises it would be called upon to handle. As each candidate was considered, the list gradually narrowed to a small number of broad transformations that were judged to be the most far-reaching and the most salient for assessing naval roles and missions in the next century.[5] What emerged was a set of three fundamental "sea changes" in the world environment:

- the collapse of the Soviet Union and with it the Cold War national security order;
- the rise of a global economic interdependence; and
- the accelerating pace of technological change.

These headings were never intended to encompass entirely the way that the world of the twenty-first century was likely to be different from that of the twentieth. Rather, these phenomena were deemed essential elements bearing on the core question of why and how naval forces would be called upon to do things differently in the future.

Collapse of the Soviet Union

The disintegration of the Soviet Union was an obvious starting point; it had, after all, invalidated the Forward Maritime Strategy upon which Navy forces and operations had been based since the early 1980s, and had been the impetus for the entire effort. Nonetheless, its importance for the NFCPE stemmed not so much from the loss of a defining naval adversary as from the fact that the collapse had signaled a fundamental shift in the nature of the world system within which navies would be used. Here was a transformation that evoked parallels to 1815 and the end of the protracted Anglo-French and Napoleonic Wars of the eighteenth and early nineteenth centuries. These historical parallels, in fact, gave rise to discussions of how the Royal Navy had dealt with its changing roles and missions in the first half of the nineteenth century. The focus of the NFCPE discussion, however, was on two specific aspects of the overall Soviet collapse that had altered fundamental aspects of the worldwide national security system:

- the change in the nature of deterrence, and
- the shift from alliance to coalition as the basis for international security cooperation.

The change in deterrence seemed to affect the future requirements for naval forces on several planes. "Deterrence" in its Cold War-Soviet context had always carried an understood if not stated prefix—"strategic nuclear." The collapse of the USSR had removed the "strategic nuclear" and "Soviet" connotations and revealed a much more complex problem in which deterrence was no longer exclusively nuclear—or even nuclear, biological and chemical—in character, but was and would remain a core element of military strategy at all levels.

To begin with, the massive nuclear arsenal created by the Soviets continued to exist. Even the most optimistic of assessments estimated that the successor states would take years to dismantle it—if they did so at all. Therefore, as during the Cold War, there would continue to be other states able to destroy this nation and, thus, that some form of strategic nuclear deterrent would be required. To be sure, the nature of post-Cold War strategic nuclear deterrence had changed. The deterrence problem had been characterized then by the doctrine of "mutually assured destruction" by which tens of thousands of nuclear warheads on each side were tightly controlled by a single hair trigger, but with little likelihood that either side's trigger would actually be pulled. The problem posed by Soviet disintegration was one of multiple but possibly less reluctant nuclear triggers—that is, an increased likelihood that a smaller number of warheads might be loosed. This continuing, if altered, threat demanded that some form of strategic nuclear forces remain an operative part of the national security equation even as a draw-down in such forces was undertaken by all sides.

However, this relic of Cold War deterrence was overshadowed by new deterrence problems. Far more pressing was that of the proliferation of weapons of mass destruction. Intelligence estimates indicated that a growing number of countries would come to possess some form of nuclear, biological, or chemical capability over the next two decades. That prospect seemed to make it dramatically more likely that some regime or non-state actor would actually use a weapon or device either against their neighbors or against the U.S.—a problem very different from that of Cold War strategic nuclear deterrence. Here again, the collapse of the Soviet Union and the Cold War system of client state relationships was a factor. The Russians were no longer in a position to discourage acquisition of weapons of mass destruction by former Soviet clients or to offer credible security guarantees against neighbors who did acquire them. Further, the Persian/Arabian Gulf wars had underlined the utility of such weapons for threatening neighbors or deterring outside intervention.

Such a spreading nuclear, biological, and chemical threat posed two additional questions for naval planners. How could naval forces arrest or at least discourage the proliferation of such capabilities? What constituted an effective deterrent to their use? The latter, in particular, provoked vigorous debate over the usefulness of a massive nuclear deterrent in dealing with regional states that had only a small arsenal of weapons of mass destruction. The NFCPE concluded that potential opponents presumed that any such attack on United States territory would provoke a strategic nuclear response, so that a massive U.S. counterattack under those circumstances was still credible. Similarly, nuclear or biological attacks on U.S. forces, wherever located, would make a nuclear response almost mandatory and therefore believable as a deterrent.

In other situations—attacks on allies or on non-nuclear states in general or threats to use or acquire nuclear and biological weapons—the likelihood (actual or perceived) of the United States using its nuclear arsenal to respond became more and more tenuous. The debate concluded that, if Americans themselves were questioned whether they would actually use their strategic arsenal to retaliate against anything less than a direct attack with weapons of mass destruction on U.S. territory or forces, then, almost by definition, that arsenal's credibility as a deterrent was uncomfortably open to question by others. Further, as the working group deduced, precision guided munitions, which the United States had already demonstrated that it would use, were probably a far more credible and, thus, effective deterrent for these "lesser" threats.

The proliferation of weapons of mass destruction pointed to yet another aspect of how deterrence had changed, for the focus of twenty-first century deterrence was likely to be second and third tier states rather than the former Soviet Union. This shift implied a considerable broadening in the scope of deterrence, from highly specific task of deterring global thermonuclear war to the far more extensive one of deterring regional crisis and conflict. To make matters worse, projected demographic changes in second and third tier states, a widening gap between haves and have-nots, and an already evident resurgence of religious, ethnic, and tribal hatreds promised no lack of strife for the future.

During the Cold War bipolarity, deterrence of such regional conflict had been part of both sides' overall strategy, in the framework of preventing a superpower confrontation that could escalate to global war. The same bipolarity had permitted regional actors to balance off one superpower against the other, making possible actions—such as Egypt's attack on Israel in 1973—that might otherwise have provoked superpower intervention. In the absence of an exploitable superpower bipolarity, but with the continued potential for U.S., UN or coalition intervention, these local powers now were left to their own devices in deterring extra-regional intervention. In practice, they had to obtain some means of deterring the United States, without whose participation extra-regional intervention would generally be impossible. As even major regional powers lacked the military forces to defeat the United States militarily, they would have to threaten political rather than military defeat—that is, losses that were politically unacceptable within the United States. Not only was this prospect a clear departure from the parameters of Cold War deterrence, but it implied, with equal clarity, a major change in what naval forces would be called upon to do and how they would do it.

The second major impact of the Soviet collapse was on the system of formal long term alliances that had become a constant of international security cooperation. The NFCPE took as a given that alliances last only as long as the threat that led to their creation. The question posed by the Soviet collapse was, therefore, how security cooperation would function in the absence of any overarching threat at all. It was problematic whether NATO, the core alliance, would find a new raison d'être. In fact, the Gulf War had made it apparent that even a rejuvenated NATO would operate in new modes of cooperation; it would be much more like a coalition—that is, an informal temporary alignment of powers to meet a single transitory threat. For NATO members at least, the alliance structure did evoke habits of co-operation and a base of communication, credibility, and interoperability. However, future operations were likely to be outside the NATO area and would be defined in terms of coalition warfare transcending the historic alliance relationships. The problems of setting up and operating a multi-national effort to undertake effective military or other national security action would have to be solved on an ad hoc basis. In effect, each coalition contingency would require the establishment of a NATO-like cooperation, communication, credibility and interoperability without the benefit of the alliance's forty plus years of experience. The successes of Desert Storm, however, invited the false assumption that a coalition could readily be put together and, despite some difficulties, confidently be expected to function well in combat.[6]

Again, these discussions led the NFCPE to more questions. What difficulties would the United States face in coalition operations not drawing on the legacy of Cold War cooperation? What actions would the United States have to take to ensure that future coalitions could be formed and then operate successfully? These questions were particularly relevant as the trends wrought by the demise of the Soviet threat all militated against the fundamentals of cooperation that had brought success in Desert Storm. NATO military forces themselves were declining precipitately in size and capability. U.S. bases and forces overseas were in steep decline, as were the level and frequency of exercises. These problems and the altered world security structure implied not simply that the old naval mission of "presence" needed updating but rather that it would gain a critical new dimension, that of laying the groundwork for potential multinational efforts. The Desert Storm experience indicated that essential elements had to be in place *before* the coalition became necessary. Long-term (if not necessarily continuous) interaction with potential partners was called for by whatever U.S. or other NATO forces could be brought to bear. However, as overseas bases declined in number, this kind of long-term, preparatory presence and interaction would fall increasingly to naval forces deployed to critical areas.

For the United States Naval Service, therefore, a twofold effect of the Soviet collapse was seen: it would expand the requirements for effective deterrence from a strategic nuclear context to one far wider in its nature, scope, and scale; and it would place a renewed emphasis on the traditional roles of presence and crisis response—albeit without the earlier requirement to guard against uncontrolled escalation of local crises into confrontations.

Global Economic Interdependence

The second major "sea change," the rise of a global economic interdependence, was less obvious than the Soviet collapse, but figured prominently in the discussions of non-defense visitors to the group, especially those from Capitol Hill. The NFCPE group was left with little doubt that it would profoundly alter the world. The choice of this issue as a critical one had a major influence on the direction of NFCPE discussions in that it led directly to the core of the question of what, if anything, the Naval Service did that made it worth the money taxpayers spent on it. Equally important, the choice was also an implicit recognition that the post-Cold War world would be defined in economic terms far more than in political or military ones. Hence, the initial focus of deliberations became the role naval forces would play in protecting the economic security of the United States during the twenty-first century. As the discussion of the nature of economic interdependence proceeded, however, two questions became central. What were the national security interests, economic and otherwise, that naval forces would be called upon to defend overseas? How might naval forces be expected to support the application of U.S. and Allied *economic* power?

The idea of global economic interdependence implied an expanding network of interests and trade that would constitute an increasingly important element of American national economic strength. The military or naval connection to national economic security, however, was not made clear in contemporary policy or academic writings. That interdependence meant an inextricable linking of the U.S. economy to a widening circle of other economies had gone largely unstated. Also unstated was that the preservation of the stable global environment conducive to peaceful economic growth had in turn become essential to the long-term welfare of the United States itself. Thus, "global economic interdependence" was really a set of interlocking *dependencies* that would make even a continental-scale economy like the American one vulnerable to crisis and conflict abroad. This linkage between economic interests and a stabilizing national security strategy indicated that the traditional missions of crisis deterrence and response would take on a new economic significance, but it also pointed to other "economic" roles—some familiar, some not—that military forces might be expected to play in the future.

The traditional Cold War concern with maintaining access to overseas resources and markets remained, but in a globally interdependent world, it had changed in emphasis. Economic interdependence meant that the Navy would still be concerned with ensuring access to resources and markets, but not, as previously, with doing so specifically in time of war. Therein, however, lay a problem, for while the military requirements for wartime access were relatively clear, securing peacetime access carried unsavory connotations of gunboat diplomacy of the nineteenth century, something that would have no place in the twenty-first. What was called for was recognition that a subtler "presence" could help ensure American interests, economic and otherwise, were taken into account abroad. Similarly, the long-standing task of protecting American lives overseas took on a new economic meaning in connection with the dispersion of commercial and technological talent that enabled the United States to compete in the global economy. The picture that began to emerge was one of a complex network of interests on which naval forces would have perhaps an indirect, but nonetheless important, impact.

The working group attempted to collect American economic interests around the world in a manageable and straightforward list suitable for contingency planning. This effort was unsuccessful, because it demonstrated the opposite—that there was *no* limited set of economic interests or, accordingly, of countries or contingencies in which the United States would be compelled to act. Further, as operations in Liberia, Haiti, and Somalia underlined, no list of economic interests and related contingencies could by any means define all possibilities. Indeed, the message of economic interdependence seemed to be that despite an occasional wistful yearning toward isolationism on the part of some Americans, the future would be one not simply of global economic interdependence but rather of global interdependence pure and simple. In that future, political and economic national security would be increasingly entwined and, from the standpoint of naval planning, indistinguishable.

Perhaps more important than the attempt to define individual economic interests and related naval missions was the NFCPE's recognition that *potential* American interests in an interdependent world were truly global and that, therefore, the range of regional instabilities which could affect U.S.

national security interests was very broad indeed. This universality did not suggest that American naval forces would be called upon to play the role of global policeman—they had neither the resources nor the willingness to assume any such role. It did suggest, given the inability to forecast future crises accurately, that the Naval Service could not hope to plan forces or capabilities on the basis of any limited geographic list of concerns either now or, especially, over the long term. Inevitably, it was noted, the crisis that arose to confront us would be number 21 on a list of 20—if it made the list at all. This problem was particularly acute for naval forces as they historically have become involved in smaller and less predictable crises. Overall, it meant that the planned forces and capabilities had to be able to deal with a broad range of generic problems all over the world rather than concentrating on a geographically limited list of likely contingencies.

While the idea of global economic interdependence did little to delimit or identify the objectives of naval operations in the future, it did point to an increasing reliance on economic pressures to deter or contain conflict and crisis. That is, the greater the economic interdependence, the more numerous the external trade dependencies and, at least theoretically, the more acute the susceptibility to outside economic pressures.[7] Present and future sanctions-enforcement operations themselves might differ very little from those of the nineteenth century, but, as the very idea of global economic interdependence suggested, the trade they now sought to interdict was substantially different in scope and complexity from that of the earlier age. That consideration suggested a reason for the limited success of recent efforts to enforce sanctions—that naval forces could no longer act independently in this role but required close interaction with other agencies of national and international economic power. In effect, it appeared that naval forces could effectively enforce sanctions only when specific and targetable vulnerabilities were identified and the trade to be interdicted was reliably tracked. A corollary to this inference was that whereas sanctions enforcement could be highly resource intensive, the better the focus and direction, the fewer the ships needed.

The lessons the NFCPE drew from its assessment of the impact of global economic interdependence upon the Naval Service were, then, two: that naval forces could not usefully plan to meet only a limited list of contingencies but would have to prepare to react anywhere on the face of the globe; and that operations in support of economic sanctions would need to be taken into account and would require an unprecedented degree of intra- and inter-governmental cooperation.

Accelerating Technological Change

The problems posed by the accelerating pace of technological change were the subject of much discussion within the NFCPE—not as to what changes and technology might confront the United States but on how we would have to deal with a constant and relatively unpredictable state of technological change. Two aspects of this permanent state of change were of concern in planning for future naval capabilities. The first had to do with the technologies the military would face or to which it would have access; the second was the role an increasingly instantaneous mass media would play in the conduct of future naval operations.

For most of the Cold War, military and civilian technologies had been largely separate, with the military technologies more heavily funded and generally more advanced than those of the civilian sector. The situation was now for the most part reversed. Constant technological change was likely to mean that the civilian sector, especially in areas such as information technologies, would be better funded and would grow at geometric rates. For their part, military technologies tended to be subsumed into large highly complex systems, and they were tied to a lengthy and often cumbersome acquisition process—a combination that condemned them to, at best, arithmetical rates of growth. As sophistication of military technologies increased, so too did the time required to develop and field new weapons. The drawdown in defense budgets in the United States and elsewhere only compounded the problem by lengthening lead times and reducing the margin for error. Finally, technological change in the future might be so far-reaching as to make any naval forces planned now obsolescent even before they entered service. Short of wartime, it was assessed, the gap between military and civilian technology would not be closed, and the challenge for military planners would be to exploit quickly and efficiently the technological advances of the civilian sector. From this perspective, then, a permanent state of accelerating technological change confronted military planners with the dual problem of how to maintain sufficient flexibility in both hardware and in the acquisition process to take advantage of new "commercial off the shelf

(COTS)" civilian technology as it became available, and of how to deal with opponents who could do likewise.

The former was a formidable but tractable problem. The latter, however—essentially a question of dual use technology proliferation—posed a more difficult challenge, one whose scope could not be sufficiently bounded for rational long-term planning. If a system could be bought on the open market without the expense of military research and development normally required, then any state, or even non-state, might obtain and use it. The threat of technological surprise took on a wider meaning in such circumstances, and military technological superiority became a matter of scale and operational adaptability rather than of aggregate system capabilities. Indeed, given an opponent who only needed to inflict damage on a force, not defeat it, a high-technology arms race became possible in which small critical acquisitions by a potential opponent could compel substantial efforts to produce an effective deterrent.

The core problem of the accelerating pace of civilian and military technological change was that of adaptation, whether to the opportunities or to the threats presented by new advances. The corollary was a mounting need to monitor technological change, to understand its military potential, and to track its proliferation—a new urgent aspect to the old problem of technological surprise.

The second major impact of technological change was seen in the development of instantaneous mass media—in the NFCPE's shorthand, "the CNN factor." It was apparent that the success of future military operations, particularly in crisis responses, would be defined in political as well as military terms, and that political success in turn was heavily dependent on media response. The implications were that the media could no longer be excluded from operations and that planning needed to consider how results would be reported in the press. Desert Storm coverage had underlined a whole range of relevant factors: casualties and damage to one's own forces, immediacy of response, proportionality of means, and the extent of collateral damage, to name a few. The Iraq experience also highlighted the degree to which *both* parties to the conflict were "served" by the reportage; Central Command planners had to consider not only how actions would be portrayed to the American public, whose continued support was needed for success, but also, what problems and opportunities the same coverage would present to Saddam Hussein.

The direction of technological change here was clearly toward further increase in the simultaneity of media coverage and, more interestingly, toward its ever more rapid global dissemination in the future. This development seemed likely to have only a limited impact in the information saturated West, but it stood to play a major role in countries of the second and third tier, where control of the media was tantamount to control of the state.

Assessing the Threat

An undercurrent throughout the discussion of the three "sea changes" was uncertainty as to exactly how the changes would affect the size and nature of the threats naval forces would face. Indeed, the 1992 National Military Strategy, with which the NFCPE group worked, had defined the threat itself in terms of uncertainty and the risk of being caught unprepared. NFCPE planners and intelligence analysts were confronted with a threefold problem:

- for the short term, of assessing how rapidly the old Cold War military threats were declining so as to be able to draw down forces rationally;
- for the middle to longer term, of determining what the residual military threat would be, so as to be able to plan the right force structure for the Naval Service; and,
- for beyond the foreseeable future, of defining what manner of military threat might force the United States to reconstitute all or part of the military-industrial base the nation was now planning to dismantle.

With respect to the third issue, the NFCPE working group was careful to note that the narrow margins of security assumed in planning for the middle-to-long term rested on the superiority of American military technology in a number of critical areas. Thus, a hypothetical threat that could compel reconstitution had to be envisioned in terms not only of some new global adversary that would cause a general, massive rearmament, but also—and perhaps more importantly—of lesser opponents with access to new systems that undercut a technological advantage underpinning the margin of security. An example would be a potential enemy's acquisition of an effective counter to stealth or cruise missiles.

To make matters worse, the ambiguities of the military threats that forces were to face would be compounded over time. The further into the future the NFCPE attempted to project, the more uncertain became the supporting threat assessments provided to it and the greater were the risks of wagering the scarce resources on the wrong programs. Yet, there was no way to avoid crucial decisions on programs that might take ten to fifteen years to enter service and might remain the core of our naval capabilities for thirty or forty years beyond that. In effect, the NFCPE was being asked to map out, for the first half of the next century, strategy and structure to address a series of unknowns. To gauge those unknowns, to discern something of the size and nature of the military threat therefore became critical, with respect to both what navies could do to deal with the new world and what they would need to do it.

In these deliberations, the working group accepted from the start that it was not possible to predict any specific crisis, threat or weapon system that U.S. naval forces might face in the decades to come. At the same time, the group recognized that a purely "generic" threat was insufficient even for planning much less for convincing a reluctant public to pay for what one hoped would be "adequate" forces. Fortunately, intelligence analysts supporting the NFCPE were able to be specific enough to provide some indication of the scale and sophistication of forces that might be encountered. It was vital therefore to distinguish carefully between what intelligence could and could not know.

Intelligence *could not* predict future intentions. Thus, one could not know how much specific countries would spend on defense or which weapons and systems they would be buy over the next decades. By extension, therefore, it also could not be known what the orders of battle would be in 2010 and beyond or what specific weapons and military capabilities U.S. naval forces would face.

On the other hand, intelligence *could* know, with an acceptable margin of error, what a given country's probable population and general economic situation would be from 2010 to 2020 as well as, again in general terms, its economic and educational infrastructure and its technological and industrial base. From these relatively reliable outlines, analysts then could extrapolate what a nation's military potential might be, should it decide to exercise a military option.

One result was a rough measure of the *scale* of military forces that the country might generate and sustain; the measure used as an index the maximum number of men who could be sustained under arms and postulated Iraq as the standard for a major regional power. Similarly, the maturity of a state's domestic technological and industrial base and its ability to buy expensive military technology in the international arms market (which was assumed to be fairly open) provided an index of the likely level of *sophistication* of its military forces.

Using these parameters, very rough indices of scale and sophistication of military forces were established. Countries were assessed simply as able to generate either small, medium, or large-scale forces and of being able to produce (or procure and then maintain) either low, medium, or high-technology systems in suitable quantities. Nations were then grouped by region. In most regions, all countries clearly fell into the small-to-medium category as to scale and the low-to-medium one for technology. However (the vestigial but still formidable Russia aside), two regions—Northeast Asia and the Middle East—contained countries with both the demographic and economic wherewithal to raise and maintain large-scale forces and to equip them with modern, if not state-of-the-art technology. Likewise, both areas not only encompassed economic and security interests of the United States but also would be affected by direct products of the "sea changes": access to weapons of mass destruction, insusceptibility to deterrence, released ethnic hatreds, and proliferation of technology. Implicit was that even in the absence of a Soviet threat there remained the potential for regional challenges supported by formidable arrays of military force.

Since the naval armaments that would be operational through at least 2010, if not 2020, were for the most part already in existence or being built, planned, or developed, the NFCPE team could also project what kinds of technologies might be available on the international arms market. That analysis, in turn, would characterize the systems that would be on the market, or at least the levels of sophistication represented, as well as when they might be offered and in what numbers. A "trickle down" effect was assumed that in turn implied a hierarchy of sophistication. That is, "high-technology" militaries might be expected to have at least a substantial quantity of the most modern equipment available; "medium-technology" forces would possess hardware one to two generations old; and "low-tech" militaries would be limited to weapons more than two generations removed from the "state of the market."

This analysis gave a concrete enough idea of who and what might pose a military threat to allow the group usefully to ask what kinds of military threat future U.S. naval forces might have to deal with and how widespread each kind might be. The latter provided an important clue for U.S. force planning; it suggested that relatively small numbers of older, less sophisticated naval units would suffice to operate in most parts of the world but that in two or three regions large high-technology forces would still be required.

Taken together, the process of bounding of the future threat "picture" and isolating the three fundamental "sea changes" delineated some radical changes in the operational environment of naval forces. It seemed to the NFCPE, nevertheless, that much in the roles and missions of the future would resemble historical, traditional models more than they did those of the past fifty years. The next step, therefore, was to examine something that appeared not to have changed fundamentally: what navies did.

What Had Not Changed

Because the mandated starting point for both the first and second phases of the NFCPE was "zero," its members were forced to grapple with a number of basic questions about what navies in general, and the U.S. Naval Service in particular, did. How did naval forces contribute to the national good? How had they done so in the past? Would those functions differ in the future given the end of the Cold War and the presumed absence of a blue-water threat? If so, how? What roles might naval forces be expected to play in the unfolding world scene? This analysis involved an attempt, using universal or legislatively mandated functions for the armed forces as well as a broad historical perspective, to reduce what naval forces did to a set of "constants." These constants could then be considered in light of changes in the world environment to see how the new core missions would differ from the Cold War paradigms.

Why Does a Nation Need Naval Force?

The answer boiled down to two quintessential functions: keeping peace and waging war. These two functions were not seen as entirely distinct but rather as broad, overlapping spheres of activity. Further, they were envisioned as lying on both sides of a threshold of violence, with, for example, peacekeeping sometimes involving the violent application of force and warfighting sometimes stopping short of it. Taken together, these possibilities formed a continuum, with routine peacetime operations at one end, global war at the other, and contingency operations and various levels of regional conflict between.

Within this schema, the wartime function of naval forces, whether in regional or global conflict, was by far the easiest to define and understand: "prompt and sustained combat incident to operations at sea."[8] Indeed, the whole focus of those parts of the U.S. Code and Defense Department Directives outlining military responsibilities was on war. Disagreements aside as to the scale and nature of the forces required for them, the roles themselves were well understood and accepted by both the naval officers in the NFCPE study group and by the public at large.

Such ready understanding was emphatically *not* the case with regard to "peace operations" either in the aggregate or in the particular. First, the concept itself was unclear. It implied peacemaking and peacekeeping—that is, producing or enforcing a cessation of hostilities—but it might equally extend to vaguer notions of "nation building." Routine peacetime naval operations in and near potential crisis areas were obviously involved, as matters of forward presence or deterrence, but there was little agreement as to how they entered the equation or as on what scale. Indeed, there was a strong tendency, even among NFCPE participants, to focus solely on the familiar aspects of "warfighting" and to treat all other peacetime functions as lesser included cases, operations any force equipped for war would surely be able to undertake.[9]

Second, while within the Navy there seemed to be at least a visceral understanding of forward peacetime operations and overseas presence, there was less appreciation of such operations outside the service—as a succession of visitors to the NFCPE made abundantly plain. Indeed, most non-service visitors seemed to view peacetime operations as a matter solely of training or of being in position to react to crisis—a function, they assumed, that U.S. based air forces would be as well or better placed to fill. There was no broad understanding even inside the Naval Service of the peculiar capabilities maritime forces brought to an unfolding crisis or, indeed, of why they seemed to be the instrument of choice for political leaders dealing with overseas crises. Finally, and again even within the Navy, the appreciation of the deterrent role of naval forces was hobbled by the habitual association of "deterrence" with the phrase "strategic nuclear." Any broader sense of the word that encompassed the idea of "conventional deterrence" or "crisis deterrence" was ill-defined and lacked concrete connection to peacetime operations or forward presence. Indeed, there was a vigorous debate even among the naval officers in the group over how, if at all, "presence" contributed to deterring crises and conflict.

The naval role in peace operations that seemed clearest both to NFCPE analysts and outside visitors was in the area of crisis response—where, it was generally conceded, navies had historically played a leading, if not predominant, role. However, there was considerable ambiguity both as to how that role had changed in the absence of superpower competition and how it was defined in the context of peace operations. To appreciate the overall concepts of peace operations and warfighting, and to identify the "constants" in these traditional naval missions, the NFCPE reviewed the roles naval forces had played in crises over the past forty years.

Role of Naval Forces in Crises

It was evident that many analysts outside the Navy were assuming that "navies fight navies" and that absent a blue-water Soviet threat, the necessity for U.S. naval involvement in crises would decrease. The working group nevertheless found that the history of U.S. military responses to crises throughout the post–World War II period indicated otherwise.

At the request of the NFCPE, the Center for Naval Analyses (CNA) updated a 1978 study, *Force without War* by Barry Blechman and Stephen Kaplan.[10] This update found that, from 1946 to 1991, there had been 325 instances in which U.S. military forces of some description had responded to a crisis—more than seven per year. Of these, only about 12 percent involved *any* Soviet military reaction and, for the previous ten years, none at all. Of course it could have been argued that U.S. military actions were motivated by the potential for Soviet involvement, but there have been about five military responses per year *since* the effective end of that possibility. Apparently there was some "normal" frequency of crises, not related to the Cold War, that—barring a decisive shift in national strategy—the United States would continue to meet with military force in the future. What, then, were the parameters of naval involvement in those "normal" crises?

It was immediately apparent that most of the crisis responses by the United States military were *not* of the scale of Desert Storm. Most, indeed, were rather minor incidents, involving a wide variety of security problems and falling far short of a violence, much less of organized conflict. Since the late 1970s, the most frequent reason for military reactions had been threats to American citizens, followed closely by internal wars and revolts, and then by invasions or cross border threats. The majority of crises, 63 percent, occurred in the Middle East. Most responses had been on a very limited scale and had used only forces available in the immediate area—at least in part because there had often been little or no intelligence warning. Reactions tended to be brief, more than half lasting thirty-five days or less, and one in five less than ten days. Time had been a factor in the small scale of responses, as it effectively limited the ability of the United States and its allies to bring more forces to bear.

Throughout the Cold War and up to the year of the NFCPE, maritime forces had most frequently responded. About 83 percent of all U.S. military responses from 1946–1991 had included naval forces, with about half being solely naval forces. Since the 1986 Goldwater-Nichols Act, with its emphasis on joint operations, fewer operations have been exclusively naval in character, but a far greater proportion, 95 percent, had at least involved naval units. Of the naval responses since 1977, around 70 percent had involved carriers, around 59 percent had involved Marines and 17 percent surface combatants only.

Two underlying constants accordingly suggested themselves. First, in crisis response, sea-based forces are chosen to counter a wide variety of local *land*-based forces; the focus is littoral *not* "blue water." That is, naval forces are used not simply to counter other naval forces; very few of the countries who instigate U.S. reaction have any real maritime capability of their own. Second, it is an intrinsic quality of naval units, whether in combination with other armed forces or without them, that makes them an instrument of choice. Their repeated use over forty-five years reflects more than simply a predilection of individual decisionmakers toward the Navy.

These points were significant not because of any inclination in the NFCPE to believe that "naval forces can do it alone"—they plainly could not—but because they emphasized that any future joint strategy had to take into account the inherent usefulness of sea-based forces in responding to crises.

The history of Cold War crises indicated that most of the unique qualities of maritime forces arise from their operating in and from an environment of almost universally accepted international character—the high seas; further, the importance of this linked to the politics and timing of crisis responses. This political context and the requirement for precise orchestration in turn helped the group define some important distinctions between the military requirements for peacetime operations and those for wartime operations. It observed that the use of military forces in peace and crisis is far more constrained by politico-diplomatic considerations—and thus timing—than is true in open combat. In slightly different terms, the peacetime operational requirements stress tight control over the visibility of military action, particularly in the sensitive early stages. Thus, the potential utility of military forces as an instrument of policy tends to vary according not only to what the forces can do but also to the degree to which the conspicuousness and timeliness of their actions can be managed.

In crisis reactions, the timeliness of a military option was seen to be a function both of how quickly a force can be brought to bear and of how long it can be sustained in that use. Both are factors in how avoidable and credible a potential response is perceived to be—that is, how valuable as a deterrent it is. For example, a threatened action that all know cannot unfold within the probable timeframe of the crisis or that might be forestalled by diplomatic or political action will probably not be very credible. Likewise, a single action that demonstrably cannot be sustained or repeated invites the opponent to "ride it out"—again limiting its utility as a deterrent.

The NFCPE saw a similar situation with respect to the question of visibility. If United States policymakers seek to calm a situation or avoid a crisis, military actions are likely to be kept low key; anything requiring permission of third countries and, thus, high profile diplomatic action tantamount to coalition formation, or involving significant publicity, is unlikely to be of much use. Further, the NFCPE observed, as a contingency develops and a political decision is made either deliberately to raise military visibility or simply to accept the consequences of it, a tradeoff arises between visibility and timeliness: the greater the profile of the military reaction required, the greater the likelihood of delay in obtaining any required foreign approval. In practical terms, therefore, forces that take longer to get to the crisis area but that require no diplomatic preliminaries and can therefore be positioned at lower levels of visibility early on, might actually be the first units on scene once the political decision is made to take decisive action.

This visibility-timeliness tradeoff indicated to the working group that forward seaborne forces might well remain the core of the U.S. military reaction far into the crisis. In terms of both crisis and transition to war, there appeared a strong likelihood of a heavy reliance on sea-based elements of joint forces to provide initial capability on the scene and to secure initial entry into the area, such as in seizing the ports and airfields needed to disembark and sustain (usually heavier) follow-on forces.

Finally, the NFCPE perceived that as a crisis winds down, visibility again becomes a political consideration. It noted that as the political objective shifts in the post-crisis period from resolving the problem to enforcing the measures by which it had been resolved, so too would the set of military force options. Supporting such political objectives may mean retaining substantial forces on station—but out of sight—throughout the denouement, however protracted. A further complication is the strong likelihood that foreign or coalition support would diminish more quickly than the residual threat, leaving on-scene U.S. forces exposed and with a declining base of local support.

The questions of timing and visibility suggested to the NFCPE group one intrinsic quality that made maritime forces the centerpiece of crisis reactions: the ability to operate *from* the sea. The implications of this ability became more apparent as the roles of these forces for presence, surge, and deterrence were traced across the spectrum of conflict: from peacetime operations (including presence) to low-intensity conflict (including law enforcement, anti-terrorism, peacekeeping, contingency operations, and peacemaking) to regional conflicts and, finally, even to global war (with its attendant requirements for reconstitution).

The Spectrum of Conflict

For the NFCPE, peacetime operations were characterized by a duality of objectives and effects. Activities in themselves routine, such as training and maintenance, the analysts perceived, clearly can fulfill another operational purpose as well, depending on where and how they were conducted. Thus, "upkeep," that is, maintenance, in a foreign port, might equally exercise U.S. access to those facilities, ensuring their continued availability on a low-profile, apparently routine basis in incipient crisis. Similarly, training with the forces of other nations quickly becomes a military-to-military tie, establishing the credibility of U.S. forces, and enhancing interoperability with potential coalition partners. This point suggested to the NFCPE that such ordinary activities are in fact a fundamental aspect of peacetime operations and that they have a place in the "peacetime presence" part of the spectrum of conflict.

For naval forces, such peacetime operations were seen as essentially global in scope, limited only by the extent of the high seas and the time-honored diplomatic regime for navies. They seemed to embody an "enabling" function applicable to a number of different strategic objectives. Diplomatically, a highly visible presence like a pattern of port visits helps to develop links with local leaders and citizenry, shows continued U.S. interest and commitment, and indirectly ensures that U.S. interests were taken into account. From the standpoint of national security, operations and exercises with local forces demonstrate U.S. capability and lay the groundwork for meaningful cooperation as coalition partners, should that later be necessary. These activities and objectives—which do not differ in substance from those of navies for the past two centuries—had been an underlying, if unstated, aspect of the Cold War, but it was clear that they met the requirements of a changed world order as well.

Indeed, future peacetime operations were deemed likely to differ from those of the Cold War in only three respects: the increased necessity to seek out opportunities for local overseas interaction, the increased reliance on routine overseas naval presence as the most acceptable and least intrusive means of maintaining contacts, and a new ability to arrange U.S. naval operations strictly with regard to local requirements and not having potentially to deal with Soviet forces in the area. The NFCPE group was quick to note two significant effects of the last point on forces and capabilities. First, it was also no longer necessary to be everywhere all the time, but simply to be *able* to be anywhere at the right time with the forces needed. Second, the carrier battle group no longer needed to be the denominator. These two points were thought particularly significant because they suggested that considerable economies of force might be obtained by precisely tailoring the forces to the situations.

The operative aspect of peacetime operations, then, was regarded as the ability of naval forces to take advantage of the international character of the high seas to remain nonintrusive and nonthreatening while operating in a given region. Nonetheless, participants readily recognized that "presence" went well beyond the essentially diplomatic and coalition building functions of peacetime operations, extending to "low intensity conflict." The nature of these activities had much influence on the capabilities required for effective presence. The NFCPE analysts divided low-intensity conflict into two general realms: law enforcement and conflict deterrence.

Law enforcement operations were distinguished by their being aimed at individuals and groups rather than state actors. They would include the traditional naval function of deterring piracy, but extend as well to anti-terrorist operations such as the reaction to the *Achille Lauro* incident, and to counternarcotics. In each case the forces required—at least for individual operations—would be small, but the standing presence required would be more or less continuous and might in the aggregate involve substantial numbers, as in the case of counternarcotics patrols. Conflict deterrence, on the other hand, was a broad category that encompassed counterinsurgency, peacekeeping, peacemaking and contingency operations. In contrast to law enforcement operations, it would be directed against actual or would-be state entities, and the forces required would be larger, potentially requiring a surge capability. However, continuous presence would not be required (with the caveat that limited time might be available to respond to some events, such as threats to U.S. citizens).

Contingency operations, in which there was a particular need for large forces close at hand, was further broken down into shows of force, noncombatant evacuation operations (NEO), and raids or reprisals. The first and second were largely self-explanatory and (with such exceptions as an opposed NEO) seemed unlikely to cross the threshold of violence. The raid, however, was a limited war proposition; as such, it evoked a special set of requirements and became the subject of particular investigation and discussion in the NFCPE.

The concept of a "raid" or contingency strike, in the NFCPE construct, illustrated in many ways the overlap between peacetime and warfighting functions. Unlike peacetime "presence" operations, the geographic scope of a raid would be very narrow, generally limited to specific identified targets. Also, it would be of extremely short duration; for the most part, raids would involve action "across the beach" followed by a rapid withdrawal once objectives were achieved. Second, a raid would emphatically *not* be a "campaign." It would be preemptive and either retaliatory or demonstrative in nature and sharply circumscribed as to timeframe and area, though it might be very intense. Also, the success of a raid would hinge on detailed planning. In practice, the upshot was that a given raid might have to be single service effort, depending on what forces were immediately available. Whatever joint capabilities could be usefully brought to bear would be used, especially the national intelligence support on which targeting would heavily rely. Finally, and to a degree not matched by other forms of wartime or peacetime operations, the success of the raid would be judged in political and media-reaction terms. Planning would therefore tend to focus on avoiding losses, producing visible results but only "acceptable" (that is, limited in type and amount) collateral damage, and minimizing the time delay between provocation and response. These latter considerations, particularly the speed of response, also implied that a raid would probably be a unilateral American action.

In the realm of warfighting—that is, lesser regional conflict, major regional conflict, and global war—interesting relationships with other parts of the spectrum emerged. The term "lesser regional conflict" had been discounted in most Defense Department discussions (in favor of acknowledging a range of regional conflicts) but it offered the NFCPE group some distinctions useful for "the gray area" between the raid and the major regional conflict. For example, like a raid, a lesser regional conflict would be limited geographically, usually to a single country or border area, but its military operations would no longer take place "across the beach" but rather both off and on shore. Also, unlike the raid, the lesser regional conflict *would be* a campaign and, therefore, of indeterminate duration—a factor that would drastically affect the issues of visibility and timeliness. In a further contrast to the raid, a lesser regional conflict could not be handled solely by forward deployed "presence" forces, but clearly required reinforcement and sustainment. Nonetheless, unlike major regional or global conflicts, it required little or no mobilization of reserves. In another distinction from low-intensity raid operations, some damage and losses was expected and, within limits would be accepted by the public and media; the criterion here would be to minimize losses while winning the campaign. Finally, this form of conflict could not be unilateral, but must involve at least one local ally—the aggrieved party—or, where possible and perhaps after a period, a coalition.

The NFCPE envisioned the next point on the spectrum, major regional conflict, as retaining many aspects of lesser regional conflict, but again the group noted important differences. First, the geographic scope of a major regional conflict might be expected to be larger, potentially extending to the entire region and the contiguous seas. Therefore, there might be a blue-water naval component; at a minimum, however, the conflict would stretch beyond the immediate off shore areas and would involve substantial ground and air elements, which would in turn require sustainment from the sea and therefore uninhibited control of the sea lines of communication. Also, unlike lower levels, major regional conflicts would be increasingly likely to involve at least the presence of nuclear, biological, or chemical weapons of mass destruction in the arsenals of regional aggressors, and even in their absence, there might be conventionally armed tactical ballistic missiles. On the other hand, like a lesser regional conflict, any major regional conflagration would be not a single operation but a campaign, perhaps more than one. It might, however, be of longer duration than a lesser regional conflict, its military operations probably far larger, more intense, and more complex. Therefore, it would require a range of capabilities necessitating a large-scale mobilization of reserves and at least a partial mobilization of the economy to obtain material and convey it to the theater.

While public and media support would remain crucial to the long-term success of the conflict, the emphasis in the major regional conflict would be on sustaining that support and winning the conflict. The implication for the NFCPE was that while campaign planners would have to avoid *major or protracted* losses, moderate losses had to be expected and more or less accepted. Further, large-scale reinforcement and sustainment would be critical to the success of any major regional conflict, limited only by hedges against a second major conflict. Finally, this level of regional conflict would be likely to require not only the full range of American military capabilities but also significant coalition support, potentially to the degree that unilateral U.S. action without it would be risky or even, over the short term, impossible.

With regard to global war, the NFCPE saw that while the likelihood of a "bolt from the blue" nuclear holocaust was greatly diminished, there was a potential for "multiple major regional conflicts" short of nuclear annihilation. (One participant observed that World War II had been, in essence, "just" two simultaneous major regional conflicts.) The idea of such a limited global war offered some interesting nuances with respect to other levels of conflict (some of which may reinforce its improbability). To begin with, concern in such a global conflict would necessarily focus on the use of weapons of mass destruction, whether directly against the United States, as in a missile or terrorist attack, or in regional contexts. As in the earlier concept of global thermonuclear war, the duration of the conflict would in effect equal the rate of escalation: if the rate of escalation could be controlled, the conflict could devolve into a World War II-style war of attrition; if not, then it could escalate into the classic holocaust nightmare. In the latter case, though mass destruction might be limited to a single region, the ecological impact would be global. If uncontrolled escalation did not occur, the conflict would entail a series of campaigns probably on a continental scale, possibly involving significant action on the oceans. Finally, in view of the potential scale of these operations, full military and industrial mobilization would be required. Unlike the case of major regional conflict, however, the focus here would be on allocating forces and material, as they became available, among a variety of fronts.

The short and mid-term probability of such a war seemed to the NFCPE remote, to say the least. It was thought worth noting, however, that there were gradations of "global" conflict and that its characteristics could be seen at a level far below the total nuclear holocaust to which the Cold War had conditioned thinking. In fact, it required only a sharp diminution of U.S. and Western forces, and a sharp increase in the capability of, and access to, weapons of mass destruction by two or more regional powers or coalitions. Global conflict, in essence, could be engendered by little more than the simultaneous outbreak of two Desert Storms.

Conclusions and Retrospective

Was the NFCPE an innately self-serving search for a new justification for an old organization or did it reform that organization to deal with a new reality? Were the participants able to pull free of their institutional biases and Cold War formation sufficiently to address that new reality clearly and dispassionately? Was *From the Sea* evidence of significant and meaningful adaptation to a new world or a failure to get beyond an old vision rooted in a century-old U.S. maritime strategy? It is certain that no group of professionals from *any* discipline will entirely escape the prevailing predilections of their profession or of particular subgroups within it. That fact was recognized and accepted from the start in the work of the NFCPE, but it was balanced by two factors. First, the participants were all military officers who pursued their profession as a vocation not a business, and who saw their task in terms of their country's ability to respond to future threats and in terms of lives that might be lost if their judgments proved false—a shared sense of responsibility which, like Samuel Johnson's aphorism about how being hanged in the morning "concentrates one's mind" focused the debates on something higher than the immediate bureaucratic goals. Second, within this context, there was a concerted effort to balance differing community viewpoints and to seek out rather than exclude vocal proponents to represent those viewpoints in the working group and in the Quantico discussions.

Overall, there was a conviction that the answers sought needed to spring from those most familiar with the capabilities and limitations of naval power—experienced naval officers—and that a failure to deal adequately with the challenge sooner or later would result in a far less satisfactory solution imposed from outside the Navy. As one participant noted, "We can do this and get it right now, or have it forced upon us by others later—and probably get it wrong." When the issue of the credibility of the effort arose, it was answered with the observation that the logic of the debate rather than the credentials of the debaters was the key and that the final white paper would stand or fall on its own merits.

Unfortunately the full force and logic of the debates was only indirectly reflected in the final white paper. Nonetheless, the basic structure was clear. The NFCPE's review of crisis response and the use of military force across the spectrum of conflict indicated that the central functions of naval force had *not* altered substantially as a result of the "sea changes" at the end of the Cold War, a fact that eased acceptance by the Naval Service as a whole. What was different, rather, was the effort needed to exert effective military force at various levels of conflict. It was obvious that considerably less military force would be required to avoid a global thermonuclear war.[11] Less obvious, and much debated, was the rise in the magnitude of effort required to deal with major regional opponents, either to provide credible presence and reaction forces or to act decisively in conflicts, particularly in the two or three regions where long-term, large-scale, and well equipped opposition was likely. That shift in relative scale of effort was the result of a narrowing of the margin of superiority over regional powers that the United States and its allies had enjoyed during the Cold War. That convergence, in turn, reflected both the deep cutbacks in Western defense spending and the continued or expanded outlays of some regional powers. The NFCPE observed that much of the current American margin of superiority had been built on the technological fruits of Cold War and was, therefore, vulnerable not only to post-Cold War budget cuts but also to the sale of critical dual-use technologies on the world market. Compounding the effect of this problem was that, in adopting a littoral strategy, the U.S. Naval Service was committing itself "to go in harm's way" where regional powers would be strongest—and that, in the wake of Desert Storm successes, it would be expected to do so with few or no losses. In each case, the NFCPE analysis tended to be much broader than the later *"Bottom-Up-Review"* and, therefore, more enduring.

It was clearly in littoral warfare that the NFCPE had made its most revolutionary change. The Navy had been put in the position of a man whose fondest wish has been granted. Since the days of Mahan, it had sought "sea control." The end of the Cold War had granted this wish, and the Navy was confronted with the question: "Now that we have sea control, what can we do with it?" The NFCPE began to respond to that question by recognizing that sea control was no longer an end in itself, but a means to an end and declared that that "end" was the projection of power and influence ashore . . . from the sea. Indeed, the final *From the Sea* white paper carefully noted that continued control of the sea was the prerequisite to such power projection. Nonetheless, the notion of a landward focus for naval power represented a sharp departure both from the U.S. Navy's Mahanian tradition and from the historic role of navies in general. Instead of indirectly influencing "history" through the use of seapower *at* sea, as Mahan had proposed, the NFCPE implied that, with sea control won, naval forces could now project sufficient power *from* the sea—short of the use of nuclear weapons—to have a decisive direct strategic impact on events ashore. But, such a capacity had never before existed in any navy. Historically, the ability of a fleet to directly influence events ashore had been limited to the range of its guns—about 2 miles in Napoleonic times and about 10 miles by the end of World War I. The U.S. Naval Service had pioneered the use of carrier aircraft and amphibious forces in a power projection role in World War II and the advent of ballistic missile submarines had permitted navies an extensive use of naval forces in a strategic nuclear role. But the direction taken by *From the Sea* was to suggest naval forces could play a decisive role in something more than an island campaign and without resort to nuclear weapons. Such a role depended on capabilities and an approach to warfare that neither the U.S. Naval Service nor any other navy had developed at the time of the NFCPE deliberations. What was discernible in 1992 was rather a promise that precision munitions in general and Tomahawk cruise missiles in particular could be used to strike very specific targets from well off shore and that light unit tactics could transform amphibious operations.

Some of the most revolutionary naval thinking which grew from the white paper has centered on the questions of how the impact of off shore strike forces might be sustained and sufficiently multiplied to have the decisive impact sought. It is this thinking which is at the core of Navy's current deliberation over how a revolution in military affairs might be implemented. That "revolution" and *From the Sea*, imply a fleet that could ultimately be very different from the one we have known for the last seventy-five years. But, however different the thought or revolutionary the technology, the change in the nature of the fleet is necessarily evolutionary; ships last a long time—thirty to fifty years—and whole new fleets are far too expensive to build quickly. What can change quickly, and has, is the way in which naval forces are used. Here, the Tomahawk strikes in Bosnia and Iraq provide an indication of the different direction taken and a precursor of things to come.

In *From the Sea*, the Naval Forces Capabilities Planning Effort provided a new *strategic concept*—not a force plan, a new maritime strategy, or a new naval doctrine. It defined the post-Cold War need for a flexible littoral strategy, outlined the types of capabilities naval forces would require to implement it in a joint context, and called for development of appropriate naval strategies and tactics. The fact that, in so doing, the NFCPE appears to have accurately defined the parameters of a *naval* revolution in military affairs and the first steps needed to carry it out, underlines the freedom, logic, and scope of its discussions—and the willingness of Navy's leadership to risk a leap into the unknown by implementing it. Indeed, the entire process is a testimony to the institutional capacity of military organizations to undertake nonevolutionary and truly innovative strategic adjustment. In contrast to many of the preceding chapters, the Navy's move to adopt a littoral focus occurred despite the absence of strong domestic political inducements, much less civilian intervention, and despite the absence of an immediate or highly visible strategic vulnerability—indeed, in reaction to changes in the international environment that retained considerable ambiguity. Rather, the development of a new strategic concept reflected a successful effort to employ the resources and expertise within the Navy and Marine Corps to develop a clearer appreciation of the changing challenges to American interests, a common consensual understanding of the tasks the Naval Service was likely to be called upon to undertake, and an optimal approach for dealing with the anticipated roles and missions of the twenty-first century.

Notes

1. Originally published in *U.S. Naval War College Review*, 43 (Winter 1994–1995).

2. The initial draft of this directive was actually provided to the Secretary by the NFCPE and was approved and amended by him. The first meetings of the group, therefore, were focused on questions of how much change might be required and, thus, how broad the Secretary's charter would need to be. The group's recommendation was for a very far-reaching review and the Secretary strongly concurred.

3. Secretary of the Navy H. L. Garrett III, memorandum for the Chief of Naval Operations/Commandant of the Marine Corps, November 20, 1991. The senior leadership of the Navy Department fully appreciated just how open-ended this guidance was and, when queried by participants, underlined repeatedly that *nothing* in either forces or doctrine should be considered "sacred" or beyond question.

4. One visitor familiar with Congress admonished the group that anything over ten pages had no hope of being read on Capitol Hill, much less in wardrooms around the fleet.

5. It was acknowledged that social and demographic changes in the United States itself could have a substantial impact on the composition of the Navy and Marine Corps and on public and Congressional support for the Service. After considerable debate throughout much of the NFCPE, these concerns were set aside as not having an overriding impact on the fundamental character of what the Naval Service did or how it did it.

6. That assumption ignored the fact (clear to the working group) that the basis for the success of the Desert Storm coalition had been built during and because of the Cold War. Cooperation and communication were possible because, in most cases, the partners either were NATO members and continued to use NATO procedures or had established Cold War ties to NATO members. The credibility that made regional states willing to join the coalition had been established by forty years of Cold War operations in the area—such as by the U.S. Middle East Force, which had demonstrated both the nation's capability to fulfill its promises and the constancy of its commitment. Finally, the basic compatibility of coalition military forces derived from repeated exercises together, the use of NATO doctrine, and the incorporation of alliance standards in the Western military equipment with which most of the forces were armed. Even then, the process of forming and operating the coalition was time-consuming, arduous, and imperfect.

7. This principle seems to be borne out by the repeated use of sanctions, embargoes, and quarantines in post-Cold War international security efforts—not that they had any striking, immediate success. These measures have involved

both unilateral and multilateral naval operations, often over protracted periods of time, a portent of future requirements upon the U.S. Navy.

8. Title 10 U.S. Code, Section 5062.

9. The group tended to divide itself into two factions throughout these discussion: the "operators" (Navy) and "warriors" (Marine Corps) on the one hand, and the "Washington political-military 'wonks' " on the other. The latter attempted to expand the treatment of subjects such as "influence" and "deterrence," while the former insisted any extensive treatment of such roles would jeopardize the white paper's acceptance in the Fleet. Accordingly, many of the issues raised about peacetime use of naval forces were not revisited until the drafting and publication of *Forward . . . From the Sea* in 1994—after . . . *From the Sea* had already been accepted thoroughly within the Naval Service.

10. Barry M. Blechman and Stephen S. Kaplan, *Force Without War: U.S. Armed Forces as a Political Instrument* (Washington, D.C.: Brookings Institution, 1978).

11. However, it should be noted that the potential future Russian threat and the spread of nuclear, biological, and chemical weapons were by far the greatest points of unease for the working group.

Part V

Theory and Practice

10 Structure, Agency, and Choice: Toward a Theory and Practice of Grand Strategy

Emily O. Goldman and John Arquilla

One of the most important foreign policy and national security choices confronting U.S. political and military leaders today, with profound long-term implications for the nation and world, is how to adjust America's strategic orientation in the absence of a compelling external imperative. Not since the close of World War I have U.S. leaders had to face such ambiguous external threats, such an ill-defined global distribution of power, and fluid alignment patterns. In the absence of a clear threat to anchor U.S. strategy, political and military leaders struggle to redefine the nation's diplomatic, military, and economic postures to preserve a capacity to respond to future unforeseen dangers and challenges abroad, while meeting more immediate demands at home.

With this contemporary strategic dilemma in mind, the contributors to this volume have examined strategic adjustment at several critical historical junctures in U.S. history: the nation's awakening as a great power in the 1890s, its ambivalence toward accepting the mantle of world leadership after the First World War, and its new found primacy, bestowed upon it by the dissolution of the Soviet empire. Few scholars have systematically studied strategy in peacetime. The work that exists tends to focus on periods immediately preceding conflict, when significant threats coalesce. This volume examines strategic adjustment during lengthier periods of peace when no major wars seem likely for the foreseeable future, and when external pressures are weak relative to those that emanate from internal political, social and cultural forces. By so doing, the volume develops a deeper understanding of strategy in both peace and war.

Military historians Williamson Murray and Mark Grimsley observe that while "the main lines of a state's strategy are frequently easy to discern. . . . the process by which that strategy has evolved is often extremely complex, and the Mahanian notion that sound strategy might spring forth by the discovery and application of eternal principles falls short of reality. Strategic thinking does not occur in a vacuum . . . ." [1] This volume unpacks the domestic side of grand strategy, the facet traditionally black-boxed by realist interpretations. It develops the notion of strategy as "process" rather than only outcome. Strategy can be understood as a flow through time of the choices agents make given structural constraints and opportunities they perceive. Any analysis of process thus consists of assumptions about structure, agency, and choice. Structure has social, political, organizational, bureaucratic, ideational, and technological dimensions. Agents include political elites, bureaucratic actors, the media, and a whole host of societal actors. Choice can be a process of maneuvering within social constraints or among competing political and organizational interests. It often means forging consensus and building coalitions. Frequently it involves innovation and institutionalization. Collectively, the contributions to this volume have developed a rich interpretation of strategy which challenges its dominant portrayal as a process of aligning means with ends to cause security for the state, attuned above all to the external balance of power, and carried out by agents of the state in pursuit of the national interest. The multidimensionality of strategy can be seen by examining how contributors characterize structure, agency, and choice.

The Structural Context for Strategy

At the height of the Cold War, Samuel Huntington characterized military policy as both domestic and foreign:

> Major changes in military policy reflect changes in the relations of the government to its domestic and foreign environment. If the external balance of power changes and the government sees opportunities to expand its territory and power abroad, these changes in its external environment will be reflected in its military policy. The changes in

military policy, in turn, may require changes in aspects of domestic policy. Similarly, changes in the domestic environment—such as rapid industrialization of the country, or a change in its form of government—may lead to alterations in its military policy and its foreign policy . . .

At any given time, military policy thus reflects the interactions between the external environment and goals of the government and its domestic environment and goals.[2]

The interconnectedness of internal and external factors in strategy remains underexplored. Scholars only recently have taken up the challenge of developing strategy's internal foundations.[3] Grand strategy is usually cast as a response to the outside world. Paul Kennedy subscribes to the very broadest definition of grand strategy as an endeavor by national leaders "to bring together all of the elements, both military and non-military, for the preservation and enhancement of the nation's long-term (that is, in wartime *and* peacetime) best interests,"[4] yet describes the task more specifically as "structur[ing] the armed forces, and the economy and society upon which they rest, to be in a good position to meet contingencies."[5] Even in peacetime, strategic planning will focus on the external world, on future contingencies and adversaries that may threaten the nation's security.

This volume has problematized the structure agents of strategymaking attend to, challenging its external systemic characterization. For Nincic, Rose, and Gorski, the constellation of social forces and preferences provides the critical structure within which strategy is made, particularly in democratic states where policy legitimacy rests ultimately on popular support or at least acquiescence. In peacetime, popular opinion defines the limits of defense spending, the burden of international military operations the nation will choose to carry, and the conditions under which force can be legitimately employed as a method of statecraft. Leaders attend first to cues from the public. With no consistent cues from the outside world, politicians look inside by default, even if those cues provide little consistent concrete guidance. Electoral considerations are never too far in the background. The authors place public opinion in its broader domestic context, noting other forms of social identity, such as lobbies, political parties, and economic classes. Collectively, these form the social setting to which the agents of strategy attend. Rhodes makes an even more forceful case for the preeminent position of societal factors, but of a different sort. He stresses the importance of social consensus for binding the nation together. The agents of strategy-making must consider cultural and social foundations of national identity, which structure a society's role and purpose in the world.

Sparrow also highlights the critical role of the public for structuring strategy when he observes ways public attitudes in the 1890s provoked a national outcry over Cuba, which political leaders could not ignore, and produced a broad and popular crusade for imperialism. Sparrow, like Nincic, Rose, and Gorski, concedes the power exerted by social context depends upon the public's political attentiveness and level of information. In the 1890s, there was a nearly 90 percent literacy rate in the country and Americans read and granted credibility to their newspapers. Nincic, Rose, and Gorski add that politically aware citizenry are likely to adopt elite and media views if the elites are united in their position. In the 1890s, the federal government was ill-equipped to assemble basic information on government policy and transmit it to the public so the press became the conduit for elite opinion to the public on matters of foreign policy. In 1898, the "yellow press" was united in its position that the sinking of the *Maine* meant war. Nincic, Rose, and Gorski, however, qualify that the poorly informed and politically inattentive majority are not easily molded from above. As literacy rates have declined in the United States, the societal structure the agents of strategymaking confront has become more unwieldy.

For Trubowitz, the structural context for strategymakers is more directly political. Agents of strategy must operate against a backdrop of regional and party competition. Political leaders seeking electoral advantage respond to the interests of geographically defined constituencies. The international interests of constituents reflect differential rates of economic development and integration into the world economy. In Trubowitz's account, regional economic differentiation structures strategic adjustment by producing territorial identities that shape, constrain, and influence behavior of politicians at the national level.

In Smith's account, organizational context shapes strategymaking. His chronicle of the Navy's process of drafting its white paper, " . . . From the Sea," charts the service's efforts to balance community viewpoints and build consensus around tasks it was likely to be called upon to undertake. His analysis resonates with Nincic, Rose, and Gorski's by demonstrating how in peacetime, when threats are low, consensus is crucial to developing vision as a basis for action. For Smith, however, an organizational consensus must be forged. His analysis logically suggests the dynamics of intraorganizational consensus-building apply also to the challenge of interorganization consensus-building. In the post-World War II era, interservice controversy replaced traditional service-civilian conflict as a matter of emphasis. There had been earlier opportunistic efforts by the services to pursue their own agenda (e.g., Pacific War strategy), but it was during the Cold War when interservice rivalry came to the fore. Though development of new weapons and a new role for the United States in world affairs altered the functions and activities of the services, the unity and complexity of modern warfare, built into the very structure of the Defense Department, has made interservice rivalry a mainstay of the strategic adjustment process. With passage of the Defense Reorganization Act of 1986 (the Goldwater-Nichols law), jointness became the watchword, but has hardly eliminated the impact of interservice rivalry on peacetime policy.

Smith implicitly adopts Stephen Rosen's view of military organizations as complex political communities. Rosen writes, "the central concerns [of the military] are those of any political community: who should rule, and how the 'citizens' should live."[6] Services are not monolithic but rather composed of subunits with their own interests and subcultures. At any one time, but particularly in peacetime, competing theories about strategic priorities exist. Strategic adjustment is played out against a political backdrop of intraorganizational competition. Smith's account parallels Trubowitz's political coalition-building perspective. Both conceive the structural context to which agents of strategymaking must attend as intensely political.

Goldman's interpretation of strategy formation highlights the structure created by bureaucratic rivalry and budgetary constraints. She, however, emphasizes the context of knowledge and experience. Her accounts of strategic adjustment in the interwar Army, Navy, and Marine Corps show how agents of strategymaking are influenced by the experiential base available to them, weighing the feasibility of strategic options against the limits and capabilities of technologies. Experiences of the past and growth of knowledge over time structure the way strategy unfolds.

The structural context created by technology is explored extensively by Breemer. In his account of U.S. strategic adjustment in the 1880s and 1890s, the agents of strategy were responding to a technologically induced system of insecurity. Rapid technological change created an environment of tremendous uncertainty for military planners. Weapons of mass destruction—

battleships—portended annihilating sea battles, while rapidity of technological change threatened block obsolescence for first-rank sea powers and
chances that second-and third-rank powers might leap-frog ahead.

Breemer's analysis directs attention to changes in technology and warfare
that stimulate strategic adjustment. His thesis resonates loudly with contemporary military planners striving to adapt U.S. military strategy and foreign
policy to warfare in the information age. In the century covered by this
volume, the technological context of warfare has shifted several times. By
one account, there have existed three war forms in the twentieth century:
an early modern pre-Cold War form dating from the mid-eighteenth century
to the mid-twentieth century; a late-modern Cold War form dating from the
mid-twentieth century to the early 1990s; and a post-modern post-Cold War
form which is presently emerging.[7] With the transition from one to the other,
perception of the threat has shifted from enemy invasion, to nuclear war, to
subnational and nonmilitary threats. In concert, force structure emphasis
has shifted from the mass army, to the large professional army, to the smaller
professional army with reserves sharing missions. Each war form has also
affected public attitudes toward the military, from support, to ambivalence,
to apathy or skepticism.

Yet military revolutions, be it the current information revolution or the
industrial revolution to which Breemer refers, are not mere artifacts of technology. Changes in military organization, strategy, and ways of making war
typically reflect large-scale changes in social organization. As the Tofflers
argue, the way a society makes war reflects how it makes wealth.[8] The information warfare revolution is a logical outgrowth of the knowledge-based
economies upon which modern society rests, just as the industrial warfare
revolution depended upon not only industrial weaponry, steam transport,
and the dreadnought, but also the full mobilization of societies for war and
the rise of nationalistic and often popular states. Political and social innovations like seventeenth-century statism and eighteenth-nineteenth–century
democratic revolutions have been critical to transformation in modes of
warfare as much as developments in metallurgy, cavalry, gunpowder, transport, and communications.[9] By focusing on the technological dimensions
of military change, however, Breemer's analysis complements the social,
cultural, and political foundations of strategic adjustment emphasized by
other contributors.

The structure to which the agents of strategymaking attend is multidi-
mensional. It is not simply a question of responding to or anticipating ex-

ternal threats and challenges. Diverse and potentially competing pressures emanate from social, political, and organizational environments. This interpretation resonates with the contemporary environment for U.S. strategy characterized by an independent and resourceful mass media with more avenues to influence public perceptions, increasing party competition, widespread public skepticism about U.S. activism abroad, and continuing rivalry among and within service organizations that interpret jointness as a way to protect service turf and budget share.

Agents of Strategy-Making

Interpretations of strategy in this volume engage a broad cast of actors inside and outside government. If strategic adjustment is viewed as a question of choice, who does the choosing and what are their incentives? For Trubowitz and Nincic, Rose, and Gorski, the agents are political leaders interested in garnering public support, electoral advantage, and votes. Trubowitz's strongest case for strategic adjustment is linked to politicians driven by narrow political self-interest. His analysis is predicated on the assumption that politicians are entrepreneurs striving to benefit their constituents in order to assure reelection.

Not addressing agency directly, Rhodes's strategymakers seem guided by a public interest to bind the nation together so that cultural, ethnic, and economic divisions do not undermine the ability of the state to act decisively when required. Rhodes raises the importance of national cohesiveness for strategic action, an enduring theme throughout history. Even the ancient Israelites, a loose confederation of twelve tribes, recognized they lacked the central leadership and unity to prevail over their Philistine and Amorite enemies, who consistently defeated them in battle — to the point of capturing the sacred Ark of the Covenant. Seeing this, tribal elders went to the prophet Samuel and asked him to "make us like other nations." Samuel created a monarchy to optimize Hebrew power, and the enemies of Israel were soon put on the run.[10] In peacetime, Israel's devotion to centralized power and political cohesiveness waned and the country split in two. Thereafter, one kingdom lost its independence to outside invaders, followed not long after by the other.

Social dislocation and ethnic diversity are not likely to threaten U.S. national survival today, though they are having such an impact in ethnically

ruptured states in Eastern Europe facing the twin challenges of marketiza-
tion and democratization. The assault on national identity and cohesiveness
by a multicultural society, however, weakens the ability of the United States
to act with assuredness and purpose in the world. The United States has
never been an ethnically homogeneous society, but in the past, large influxes
of immigrants were accompanied by what James Kurth describes as a "massive and systematic program of Americanization."[11] Today, a coalition comprised of African Americans, Latino Americans, Asian Americans, and femi-
nists subscribe to an ideology that champions America as a multicultural
society rather than a leader, or even member, of Western civilization. This
multicultural ideology threatens the ability of the United States to operate
as a national state, to defend the values of liberalism, consitutionalism, rule
of law, and free markets the nation fought for in two bloody hot wars and
one long cold war in the twentieth century.[12] In the 1890s, American leaders
had to struggle with the question of what gave the American nation purpose
and identity, and what made the nation a nation. American leaders confront
that daunting challenge again today, but this time accompanied by an increasingly powerful political and intellectual elite, new agents of strategymaking, bent on deconstructing America and Western civilization.

Shulman and Sparrow direct our attention to the influence specific societal actors wield in directing strategic change. In Shulman's account, the
agents of consequence were a cohesive political group that reflected an
intellectual movement dedicated to promoting a particular vision of national
mission. In his words, "navalists" were "effective agents of the dramatic shift"
in U.S. strategy in the 1890s. They were individuals with diverse backgrounds, from disparate parts of the country, civilian and military, both inside
and outside government. They were united in a belief that America must
take its leading role among nations. They were the decisive actors who institutionalized the ideas that undergirded the new navalist strategy at the end
of the nineteenth century. Cohesive special interests continue to play a role
in directing U.S. strategic adjustment. Ethnic voting groups have encouraged foreign involvement, i.e., the Congressional Black Caucus lobbied for
firm coercive diplomatic efforts in Haiti; American Poles have voiced vigorous support for Poland's inclusion in NATO.

Sparrow focuses on the media as a decisive agent in strategic adjustment.
Newspaper publishers of the day transformed their medium to popular entertainment in order to transcend gender, class, and ethnic divisions, appeal

to the widest possible audience, and boost sales. He details how through sensationalist accounts, journalists, not politicians, set the political agenda for U.S. policy toward Cuba. They were able to do so because the press dominated communication with the public and could give its "spin" on political issues. In Sparrow's words, it was "the press, rather than the President, the Republican party, or the State Department, [that] incited the United States to go to war" with Spain. It was this war that accelerated and consolidated the emergence of the United States as a world power. He shows how government spending actually followed the reports of the "yellow press."

Sparrow's account of the agents of consequence resonates with contemporary concerns about how the press can drive policy in the absence of clear threats to anchor strategy. We know, for example, U.S. intervention in Somalia was impelled by televised graphic pictures of starving children; that pictures of dead and splayed U.S. Army Rangers not only prompted U.S. withdrawal, but also transformed the administration's orientation toward the use of force in general. Nor is "foreign policy by CNN"[13] unique to Somalia. Policy toward Bosnia has in many instances been a response to televised crises of the day, whether of the April 1993 siege of Srebrenica that brought ethnic cleansing home and heralded the new policy of lift and strike, or of the siege of Sarajevo three months later, which reopened the question of deploying U.S. ground troops. Sparrow's account traces the impact of the press on public perceptions and the subsequent indirect impact on elite perceptions. Photographers waiting to film an amphibious assault on the beaches of Somalia cause one to ponder the power of the press to directly influence elite perceptions.

Goldman, Smith, and Breemer direct our focus to the military organization as an agent of consequence, based on the implicit assumption that in the rational state, bureaucracies can wield immense influence. Breemer traces how military planners struggled to come to grips with new technologies. U.S. strategic adjustment flowed directly from their attempts to manage the devastating power of new weapons. Smith documents how the Secretary of the Navy directed the organization to develop an entirely new strategic concept to guide U.S. naval forces into the twenty-first century. It was the Navy itself that declared its primary business to be projection of power ashore, a landward focus that represented sharp departure from Mahanian tradition and from the historic role of navies in general. Strategic adjustment was begun and sustained from within the institution, a product of self-conscious self-examination. Smith summarizes, "the entire process is a testimony to the institutional capacity of military organizations to undertake non-evolutionary and truly innovative strategic adjustment. . . . the Navy's move to adopt a littoral focus occurred despite the absence of strong domestic political inducements, much less civilian intervention, and despite the absence of an immediate or highly visible strategic vulnerability. . . ."

Smith's contemporary case validates insights from Goldman's historic reading of military organizations as originators of innovative approaches to providing security, rather than as passive recipients of new ideas or reactionary obstructionists. In the most compelling interwar case, she shows how the Marine Corps of the 1920s and 1930s, like the Navy of the 1990s, transformed its core mission to one of amphibious assault, despite Presidential ambivalence, Congressional distaste, Navy neglect, and expert consensus worldwide that assault against defended shores was impossible.

Smith's, Goldman's, and Breemer's analyses confirm the characterization of service organizations as guided by narrow institutional self-interest to be misleading. The military can be guided by motives higher than immediate bureaucratic goals, by the public interest. As a participant in that process, Smith asserts military officers saw their task as one of ensuring the country's ability to respond to future threats and challenges. The prospect of lives that might be lost weighed heavily in their deliberations.

Contributors to this volume, each in their own way, cast doubt on the statist characterization of agency. The actors involved are diverse, their motives variegated. Over time, agents of consequence have evolved, transformed, gained and lost resources and influence. The "yellow press" disappeared entirely. Ethnic interest groups have emerged on the scene in new and influential ways. Powerful economic interests, many the legacy of the "military-industrial complex" that grew out of the economic mobilization planning for World War I, continue to have large stakes in the military establishment and constrain strategic adjustment.

The services' abilities to influence public perceptions and play in the public as well as bureaucratic arena have risen since the end of World War II along with the military's importance in American society. The services expanded public relations activities, developed public information offices and legislative liaisons, and increased the number of and membership in backstop organizations like the Navy League and Air Force Association. They have been increasingly active at the grassroots level in order to reach public opinion, for example using the reserve structure to build support among local constituencies.[14]

The evolving structure of the American state has influenced strategy in peacetime by introducing new actors and shifting the power among existing institutions. A new agent, the National Security Council, was created in 1947 to promote political-military consultation and bridge the gap between civilian policymakers and military strategists. Since its inception, an elaborate system for coordinating the views of the various agencies involved in policy formulation has developed.[15] Greater institutional coordination between military and civilian elites means more strategic coherence, even though in peacetime, civilian politicians will always be prone to respond more directly to societal pressures, and military elites to bureaucratic incentives.

The continual evolution in the balance of interbureaucratic power in the American state has altered the share of resources among bureaucracies and changed the locus of strategic decisionmaking. The Departments of Commerce, Labor, Agriculture, and Interior were privileged in the pre-World War II American state. In the immediate post-World War II years, State and Treasury dominated a government organized around the economic agenda of promoting international trade and investment. By 1949, the U.S. government took on a wartime complexion as military-security concerns moved to the forefront. The military establishment became transcendent, the intelligence communities mushroomed, and NSC shouldered aside State.

Reflecting this continual evolution, the Clinton administration created a National Economic Council, a cluster of economic agencies co-equal collectively to the NSC, designed to open up strategymaking to a broader array of actors, particularly economic ones. The move to include economic players in what have been traditionally considered military affairs reflects the importance of economic, trade, and competitiveness considerations in the current U.S. strategic outlook. Creation of the National Economic Council, along with the proposed reorganization of the Department of Defense to address new national security problems like the environment, counter-narcotics, peacekeeping, and humanitarian assistance, resulted from a belief that the Cold War bureaucratic balance was ill-suited for the current international environment.

Over time, the balance of influence among the services has also changed, spurred as much by technological change as by resources. The Navy, until the 1940s traditionally the first line of defense, now had to share resources and influence with an independent Air Force that claimed to be purveyor of strategic offense. Nor has Congress's role been static. Congress as an agent of consequence in military and strategic policy has grown over time. Congress always had the power of the purse and responsibility for raising an Army and equipping the Navy. In the post-Vietnam era, it took a far more active role, micromanaging defense and using the purse strings to influence debates on military strategy.

Structure is dynamic, and so is agency. The formation, implementation, and evolution of strategy has been shaped by shifting sets of actors and institutions, whose influence wax and wane with resource capacities, the ability to communicate with the public and shape popular conceptions of strategic needs, and power vis-à-vis other state institutions. As state institutions, state-society relations, civil-military relations, and the balance of power among political institutions evolve, so too does the strategic adjustment process. Each individual chapter in this volume has examined the United States at one historical turning point. There are drawbacks to adopting the single-country longitudinal approach, but the virtues are greater and they cannot be gleaned from analyses of strategic adjustment that look at multiple states at a single point in time,[16] or multiple states at different points in time.[17] Collectively, by examining strategic adjustment in one state over time, this volume permits us to explore how agency, structure, and process evolve.

Strategic Choice

This volume has also advanced multiple interpretations of strategic choice. Some contributors cast strategic adjustment as a process of responding to or mediating among competing interests. Nincic, Rose, and Gorski characterize strategic choice as a process of maneuvering within constraints created by societal interests. They recognize that ultimately the public must foot the bill, and so must be convinced of the appropriateness and desirability of any strategic endeavor. Adjustment means framing policies to mobilize support, and rallying segments of the political establishment together, all the time recognizing the limits societal preferences impose on the ability of leaders to impose consistency. Even nondemocracies pay dearly for failing to generate support for strategic endeavors in peacetime. The early Romans, achieving only a limited victory in a bitter twenty-year war against Carthage, shifted their continental strategic outlook to a balanced mix of land and naval forces. Their resolute pursuit of naval power over the twenty-year interwar period enabled Rome to enter the Second Punic War with an unchallengeable navy, giving it a war-winning edge. But this strategic adjustment succeeded only because Carthage failed to compete in the naval arms race with Rome, in part because of the disinclination to bear the costs of such a competition.[18]

For Trubowitz, strategic choice is a politicized process of coalition-building, logrolling, and vote-trading. Strategymaking involves mediating among competing political and commercial interests. Similarly, Smith characterizes the process as mediating among organizational constituencies and balancing differing community viewpoints. He details how in the second phase of the Naval Forces Capabilities Planning effort process, the initial core working group was expanded to include a full spectrum of operational expertise from every warfare community, with representatives from the fleets and Navy theater commanders. They were tasked to deal directly with questions that affected the services' internal constituencies—questions at the heart of the roles and missions controversy that has exacerbated interservice rivalry since the end of World War II and led to unnecessary duplication in U.S. force structure.

The Royal Navy's response, a century ago, to the need for political support to sustain budgetary levels in a low-threat era can be understood with reference to Trubowitz's and Smith's coalition-building models. Initially, the Admiralty simply reported its internal debates about the future of sea power to Parliament, which resulted in "politicians of both parties keep[ing] naval budgets low." The Royal Navy remedied this negative situation by fostering a navalist school of thought from both within and outside its ranks, apotheosized through the work of Admiral Sir Herbert Richmond. In Germany, Britain's emerging rival for naval mastery, a similar institutional response to the need for political coalition-building arose in the form of Admiral Tirpitz's sponsorship of the *Flottenverein* ("Fleet Professors") whose job was to expound the virtues of a German strategic shift toward greater sea power.[19]

Goldman's account shares Smith's focus on consensus-building and his view of strategic adjustment as a process of articulating new roles and missions, of a service reinventing itself. Building on a rich body of learning theory, she models strategic choice as military innovation, emphasizing the role of simulation and testing as a conduit for evaluating new ideas and reducing uncertainty. Strategic adjustment involves developing new options based on observations and interpretations of experience.

Rhodes also views choice as creating new options and developing new paths that heretofore did not exist. Strategic adjustment means forging a new myth of national identity to consolidate society in the face of social and cultural dislocation. This need resonates today in contemporary Russia. Evolving social and economic experiments with democracy and capitalism have produced social, cultural, and economic dislocation, tearing society to its core. Russia's identity as the vanguard of communism, bulwark against the capitalist West, and strategic superpower in a global bipolar competition has disintegrated. No new identity has been forged. A redefinition of national identity, however, need not be a response to societal need. It may stem from the goals of a particular leader and it may ultimately undermine social cohesion. Russian strategic adjustment, when viewed through the prism of the last 400 years, reflects a shift from a principally north-south axis, featuring Swedes and Turks as key opponents, to an east-west axis, featuring competition with continental European great powers in the west, and a long cold (and sometimes hot) war in the east, against, variously, China, Britain (the Great Game) and Japan. This shift in Russian strategic identity was begun by Peter the Great, who was driven by the idea of Russia becoming a great military power and a modern European state. Victory in the Great Northern War over Sweden (1700–1720) and a continuing rollback of the Turks from the Ukraine made the shift practicable. But it was Peter's ideas about "Europeanization" and his overall view of Russia's status in the world that impelled him to reorient his nation to the West.[20] Paradoxically, the Petrine reforms undermined national cohesion, deepening the gulf between the Russian masses and elites that had heretofore been bridged by shared religious beliefs and cultural assumptions.[21]

Other contributors conceive strategic adjustment as a process of institutionalization. For Shulman, strategic adjustment in the 1890s succeeded because the navalists institutionalized their ideas through intellectual, institutional, and political means. Navalists altered popular discourse by reinterpreting history to lay the intellectual framework for a new navy. They reformed and modernized the Navy, improving its image as a more efficient service. They galvanized the financial and institutional support necessary to fund a blue-water naval establishment. Navalists also reorganized the service's educational system, creating a way to transmit and sustain the vitality of the battleship philosophy. The navalists were so successful in institution-alizing new ideas, according to Shulman, that the nation has paid the price ever since in the form of an institution—the Mahanian navy—that is the single most expensive organization ever.

For Sparrow, the legitimation of existing naval institutions and creation of new ones was indispensable for the momentous shift in U.S. strategy witnessed in the 1890s. He shows how a lasting shift in committed govern-ment funding, in essence institutionalizing a new balance in the allocation of state resources, was requisite for great-power status. Relatedly, Breemer describes how the rapidity of technological change in the Victorian age made the systematic collection and analysis of intelligence a vital activity in peacetime military planning. The United States, as did other naval powers, formalized its intelligence-gathering activities by establishing an Office of Naval Intelligence and maintaining permanent naval attaches abroad.

Goldman and Smith further develop the argument of strategic adjust-ment as institutionalization. For Smith, broad transformation of the Cold War Navy requires that the new ideas contained in . . . *From the Sea*, and later *Forward . . . From the Sea*, be institutionalized within the Navy and Marine Corps. Goldman's account suggests how that might be achieved. Crucial to redirecting the Marine Corps's roles from colonial infantry and afloat security to amphibious assault was theoretical overhaul of instruction at Marine Corps schools. Similarly important to the emergence of carrier doctrine was the institutionalization of realistic war gaming at the Naval War College which continues to this day. Finally, the establishment of the Army Industrial College, which delivered instruction on logistics and mobilization planning, was crucial to the transition of Army thinking about modern war. The notion of strategic choice as one of maximizing national interests, or as a process of aligning means with ends to cause security is only one of many ways to characterize the strategymaking process.

Conclusion

The interpretations put forth in this volume reveal it is not axiomatic who the agents of strategy are, what environment they are attending to, or what the process of choice looks like. As we consider the issue of American strategic adjustment in the coming years, we should look closely at the various frames of reference suggested by the contributors to this volume. For example, the U.S. military, both a complex organization and a powerful bureaucratic actor—whose subcomponents pursue interests that are competitive as often as they are complementary—clearly needs to craft a set of ideas about the future of military power that will help to build and sustain political support for defense spending, and will provide it with the possibility for renewed freedom of action. Seen from this perspective, thinking about the current revolution in military affairs (RMA) may be a 1990s counterpart to 1890s navalism.

The RMA may also play neatly to the need both to shape and to react to public opinion, as some views of the future of armed conflict suggest the possibility that wars may be fought more cheaply and less bloodily—both factors having great inherent appeal to the American mass public and the increasingly powerful media. In this respect, the drive for "information dominance" echoes closely Mahan's call for naval mastery a century ago. Indeed, the fact that the U.S. military has sponsored much of the research into the RMA deepens the similarity to nineteenth-century navalism.

In closing this volume, we urge that any doubts about the greater explanatory power of the levels of analysis developed in preceding chapters—vis-à-vis the rationalist systemic frame of reference—should be dispelled when the near-term future is considered. For the United States faces a world system that poses much less threat than it did ten years ago. Russia has clearly ended its global competition with the United States, focusing inwardly on its own retrenchment and need for strategic adjustment. Its efforts at social and economic renewal, the foundations of any military resurgence, have been halting, riotous, and chaotic—and may ultimately fail. China, a popular source of speculation and concern, remains many decades away from wielding military influence beyond its local environs—and even near to home it is surrounded by smaller states with robust capabilities for balancing against the PRC (e.g., Vietnam, Indonesia, Taiwan, Japan, and South Korea). How can system level theory, in the face of such diminished threat, explain the continued American expenditure of approximately a quarter trillion dollars annually on defense? Quite simply, it can not. To understand the continued high levels of spending on defense, and the frenetic efforts at institutional redesign and doctrinal and strategic adjustment, one must look to the role of ideas, the play of domestic and bureaucratic politics, and the many other indicators of the fundamentally internal sources of strategic adjustment.

Notes

1. Williamson Murray and Mark Grimsley, "Introduction: On Strategy," in *The Making of Strategy: Rulers, States, and War*, eds., Williamson Murray, MacGregor Knox, and Alvin Bernstein (Cambridge: Cambridge University Press, 1994), 3.

2. Samuel P. Huntington, *The Common Defense* (New York: Columbia University Press, 1961), 482.

3. Richard Rosecrance and Arthur A. Stein, eds., *The Domestic Bases of Grand Strategy* (Ithaca: Cornell University Press, 1993).

4. Paul Kennedy, "Grand Strategy in War and Peace: Toward a Broader Definition," in *Grand Strategies in War and Peace*, ed. Paul Kennedy (New Haven: Yale University Press, 1991), 5.

5. Paul Kennedy, "American Grand Strategy, Today and Tomorrow: Learning from the European Experience," in *Grand Strategy*, ed. Kennedy, 184.

6. Stephen Peter Rosen, *Winning the Next War* (Ithaca: Cornell University Press, 1991), 19.

7. Charles C. Moskos and James Burk, "The Post-modern Military," in James Burk, ed., *The Military in New Times: Adapting Armed Forces to a Turbulent World* (Boulder, Colo.: Westview Press, 1994), 141–62.

8. Alvin and Heidi Toffler, *War and Anti-War: Survival at the Dawn of the 21st Century* (Boston: Little, Brown, 1993), 34.

9. Brian R. Sullivan, "What Distinguishes a Revolution in Military Affairs from a Military Technical Revolution?," Paper prepared for The Revolution in Military Affairs Conference, sponsored by the Joint Center for International and Security Studies and *Security Studies*, Monterey, California, August 26–29, 1996, 3.

10. This story is nicely exposited in *1 Samuel*, Chapters 6–9.

11. James Kurth, "The *Real* Clash," *The National Interest* 37 (Fall 1994), 13.

12. Ibid., 12–14.

13. "This Time We Mean It," *Time* (February 21, 1994).

14. Samuel P. Huntington, "Inter-service Competition and the Political Role of the Armed Services," in *Total War and Cold War: Problems in Civilian Control of the Military*, ed., Harry L. Cole (Columbus: Ohio State University Press, 1962), 178–210.

15. Mahan first began to preach the idea of closer civil-military coordination in the late nineteenth century. Changes began to appear, however, only after the war with Spain. Each service established separate bodies for planning and coordination. The Navy created the General Board, the Army created the General Staff, and in 1903 the Joint Army-Navy Board was formed. Additional reforms in the post-World War I years included the Rogers Act of 1924, which established a professional staff of foreign service officers in the State Depart-

ment, the reorganization of the Army General Staff, and the gradual evolution of the Office of Naval Operations. Finally, a new and stronger Joint Board of the Army and Navy, the logical precursor to the Joint Staff, was created to promote interservice cooperation. In the last year of World War II, the need for military government directives and surrender terms led to the creation of the State-War-Navy Coordinating Committee, the immediate predecessor to the NSC. See Ernest R. May, "The Development of Political-Military Consultation in the United States," *Political Science Quarterly* 70 (June 1995), 161–80 and Louis Morton "Interservice Co-operation and Political-Military Collaboration," in *Total War and Cold War*, ed., Coles, 131–60.

16. Allan R. Millett and Williamson Murray, eds., *Military Effectiveness*, vol. 2, *The Interwar Period* (Boston: Allen and Unwin, 1988).

17. Kennedy, ed. *Grand Strategy* and Rosecrance and Stein, eds., *Domestic Bases*.

18. The most comprehensive scholarship on the origins and conduct of the First Punic War is J. F. Lazenby, *The First Punic War* (Stanford: Stanford University Press, 1996). Also, see Hans Delbrueck, *Warfare in Antiquity* (Lincoln: University of Nebraska Press [1920]1990), 301–7.

19. On this point, see D. M. Schurman, *The Education of a Navy* (Chicago: University of Chicago Press, 1965), 2–5. While the organizational response to the need to create political support brought such theorists as the Colomb brothers and Julian Corbett to the fore, the Royal Navy's own analysts did first-rate work. See, for example, H. Richmond, *The Navy in the War of 1739–48* (Cambridge: Cambridge University Press, 1920).

20. On the power of Peter's ideas over policy, see Robert K. Massie, *Peter the Great* (New York: Ballantine, 1984), the principal theme of which is that his visit to Western Europe in the late seventeenth century shaped his overall view of Russia's place in the world. Pares, *A History of Russia* (New York: Alfred Knopf, 1948), 183–215, makes a similar argument, noting especially the importance of the expatriate Swiss Lefort, who lobbied the young czar to travel to Europe in order to "bring back to Russia teachers of all those arts of which his country was most in need" (p. 187).

21. David B. Ralston, *Importing the European Army* (Chicago: University of Chicago Press, 1990), 39–40.

Index

Note: References to figures or tables are indicated by an "f" following the page number. References to notes are indicated by an "n" following the page number.

Index compiled by Fred Leise.